William N. White, J Van Buren, James Camak

Gardening for the South

How to grow vegetables and fruits

William N. White, J Van Buren, James Camak

Gardening for the South
How to grow vegetables and fruits

ISBN/EAN: 9783337374624

Printed in Europe, USA, Canada, Australia, Japan

Cover: Foto ©Lupo / pixelio.de

More available books at **www.hansebooks.com**

GARDENING FOR THE SOUTH,

OR HOW TO GROW

VEGETABLES AND FRUITS.

BY THE LATE

WILLIAM N. WHITE,
OF ATHENS, GA.

WITH ADDITIONS BY MR. J. VAN BUREN, AND DR. JAS. CAMAK.

REVISED AND NEWLY STEREOTYPED.

ILLUSTRATED.

NEW YORK:
ORANGE JUDD AND COMPANY,
245 BROADWAY.

Entered according to Act of Congress, in the year 1868, by

ORANGE JUDD & CO.,

In the Clerk's Office of the District Court of the United States for the Southern District of New-York.

Lovejoy, Son & Co.,
Electrotypers & Stereotypers,
15 Vandewater Street, N. Y.

CONTENTS.

Publishers' Preface.. 5
Preface to the Revised Edition...................................... 7
From the Preface to the First Edition............................. 8

CHAPTER I.
Formation and Management of Gardens in General.............. 11

CHAPTER II.
Soils—Their Characteristics... 20

CHAPTER III.
The Improvement of the Soil.. 25

CHAPTER IV.
Manures.. 30

CHAPTER V.
Manures—Their Sources and Preparation........................ 42

CHAPTER VI.
Rotation of Crops.. 60

CHAPTER VII.
Hot-beds, Cold Frames, and Pits.................................. 67

CHAPTER VIII.
Garden Implements.. 73

CHAPTER IX.
Propagation of Plants... 87

CHAPTER X.
Budding and Grafting..112

CHAPTER XI.
Pruning and Training..122

CHAPTER XII.
Transplanting...134

CHAPTER XIII.
Mulching, Shading, and Watering..................................140

CHAPTER XIV.
Protection from Frost... 152

CHAPTER XV.
Insects and Vermin.. 156

CHAPTER XVI.
Vegetables—Description and Culture..............................161

CHAPTER XVII.
Fruits—Varieties and Culture......................................334

PUBLISHERS' PREFACE.

GARDENING FOR THE SOUTH had long been out of print, and in 1865 its distinguished author made an arrangement with the publishers to produce a new and enlarged edition. A number of the engravings were made at once, with a view to the immediate publication of the work. Its author wished to make it especially full, as regarded Southern fruits, and delayed completing his manuscript until the American Pomological Society should have met in 1866, in order that he might compare notes with his pomological friends. This meeting was postponed until 1867, and before this took place the author was removed by death. The incomplete manuscript of the work was placed in the hands of Mr. J. Van Buren, of Clarksville, Ga., an eminent pomologist and friend of the author, who, as a labor of love, compiled and mainly wrote out that portion relating to fruit culture. The publishers would, on behalf of Southern fruit-growers, express their thanks to Mr. Van Buren for the kind office he has performed, as well as to Dr. Jas. Camak, who revised the other portions of the work. The manuscript of Mr. White contained tables of chemical analyses of most of the plants described, but as they were not from the most recent authorities, and would increase the size of the work more than they would add to its value, they have been omitted. The original plan of Mr. White included a treatise on ornamental gardening for the South, but this could not be properly included in the present volume. It is believed that the work will be more valued by his many friends, as well as by pomologists generally, for the portrait which is given of its lamented author.

PREFACE TO THE REVISED EDITION.

The revised edition of Gardening for the South was mainly prepared by our lamented friend, W. N. White, the author of the first edition, whose sudden death left the work in an incomplete state. At his special request, made while on his death-bed, we have undertaken to finish the work begun by him, to the best of our ability, and while we do so, we ask the indulgence of the reader to pass over and forgive any imperfections he may detect, for we feel conscious of our inability to present to the public as perfect and interesting a work as would have been done had the author been permitted to have finished it.

The necessity for a new and revised edition must be apparent to every reader, as the former edition was published in 1856; since which time the discoveries, improvements, and progress in Agriculture and Horticulture have been very great.

Ten years' additional experience in Agriculture and Horticulture, by the talented author of the first edition, is our warrant for recommending the present work to the favor of the public, as few men were more ardently devoted to the culture of the soil than he was.

Should opinions and facts be found stated in the present work at variance with those in the former edition, it will be attributed to the experience alluded to above, for with him it was always a pleasure to acknowledge an error when it was found to be such. Many and valuable additions have been made to all the departments, and more particularly to the lists of varieties, both of vegetables and fruits, together with the improved methods of cultivation, as the object of the author was to present to the public a practical work adapted to the soil and climate of the Southern States.

J. Van Buren,
Dr. Jas. Camak.

FROM THE PREFACE TO THE FIRST EDITION.

I have thought that, upon a subject so accordant with my tastes as is horticulture, I might prepare a work adapted to our climate and useful to the public. The repeated inquiries made of me, as a bookseller, for a practical treatise on the subject, and these inquiries growing more frequent with the manifest growth of the gardening spirit among us, led to the undertaking. Yet written as it has been, in the intervals of trade and subjected to its constant interruptions—now advancing but a line at once, again a page, or an article—suspended totally for nearly two years, then hastily finished, looked over, and printed under circumstances that rendered the author's revision of the proof impossible—many defects of style, and errors of the press, are manifest. These, if the work contain the information sought, practical men will readily excuse in a first edition.

To claim much originality in a modern work on gardening, would display in its author great ignorance or great presumption. If it did not contain much that is found in other horticultural works, it would be very defective. Gardening is as old as Adam, and what we know to-day of its principles and operations have been accumulated, little by little—the result of thousands of experiments and centuries of observation and practice. Hence, from the gardening literature of our language, have been selected, for this work, those modes of culture which considerable experience and observation has proved adapted to our climate. The species and varieties of plants found here most desirable for use or ornament, have been selected and described. This mass of material has been modified and increased by pretty copious garden-notes of my own. Still, it has been my object, to make a useful and reliable, rather than an original work. Where an author's language suited my purpose, it was at once incorporated into the text. If the expression is sometimes changed, it is generally to make it more concise. * * * *

The necessity of a Southern work on gardening is felt by every horticulturist in our midst. Our seasons differ from those of the Northern States in heat and dryness, as much as the latter do from those of England. Treatises perfectly adapted to their climate we are obliged to follow very cautiously. English works require the exercise of a still greater degree of judgment in the reader, the climate of England being still more cool and humid. Again, our mild winters admit of garden work nearly every day of the year. All the heavy operations of trenching, manuring, laying out, pruning, and planting trees, shrubs, and hardy ornamental plants, are at that season most conveniently performed. In this particular aspect, our climate is much like that of the south of England. Hence, while the calendars of operations, in works prepared for the Northern States, seldom agree with our practice, those in English works are often found to coincide with it. But even where the time of performing certain operations is the same in both countries, the long, dry summers, and still milder winters of this climate, often render necessary a peculiar mode of performing the same.

We need then works upon gardening specially adapted to our latitude and wants. But with the exception of the valuable matter scattered through our agricultural and horticultural periodicals, Holmes' "Southern Farmer and Market Gardener," written some years since, and briefly treating of the kitchen garden department merely, is the only work containing anything reliable on the subject.

1*

The chief original features then, of this work, are, that it endeavors to give more or less information upon the whole subject of gardening; and information, too, that is practically adapted to our climate, habits, and requirements. In the fruit garden department, especially, a good deal of new matter is to be found. Throughout the entire work, processes are frequently described, and methods of culture given, which are suited only to climates and seasons like our own. Those varieties of plants and trees are pointed out which experience has proved are best adapted to our orchards and gardens. * * * *

Unusual prominence is also given to the general subject of manures, as they are the foundation, not only of successful gardening, but of profitable husbandry. Besides the various works consulted, the experience of horticultural friends has been freely communicated. Valuable hints have been derived from Rev. Mr. Johnson and Mr. Thurmond, of Atlanta, Prof. J. P. Waddel, Dr. M. A. Ward, and Dr. James Camak, of Athens, Right Rev. Bishop Elliott, of Savannah, Dr. J. C. Jenkyns and Mr. Affleck, of Miss.; and especially from J. Van Buren, of Clarksville, Ga., whose successful efforts to make known and diffuse native Southern varieties of the apple, rendered him a public benefactor. It is hoped we shall yet see a work on fruit trees from his pen.

If this treatise, with all its imperfections, shall in any degree increase the love of gardening among us; if it shall cause orchards to flourish, shade trees to embower, and flowers to spring up around any Southern home, the author's purpose is accomplished.

GARDENING FOR THE SOUTH.

CHAPTER I.

FORMATION AND MANAGEMENT OF GARDENS IN GENERAL.

Situation.—The situation of the flower-garden and lawn should be immediately adjacent to the dwelling, in order to yield the highest degree of pleasure. The most satisfactory arrangement is to form the lawn directly in front, and the flower-garden on the side, sufficiently near to be overlooked by the drawing-room windows, while the sides of the dwelling, in part, and its entire rear, including the kitchen and servants' yard, are sheltered and concealed by trees. A dwelling thus embayed in well-grown trees is always regarded with pleasure. As neither the fruit or kitchen garden, especially the latter, can be considered ornamental, they should not, though near the dwelling, be placed obtrusively in view. Near they should be, for if either is distant, time is lost in watching its progress; it is in danger of being neglected; and even if this is not the case, its choicest products may gratify the palate of any one besides its owner. A good arrangement is to place them in immediate connection with the pleasure-ground, proceeding from the shrubbery to the fruit department, and thence to the kitchen garden. The latter should also have an independent approach. It should be near the stables, in order that it may be copiously replenished with manure without too much labor.

Much, however, depends upon the soil. The best at command, in the vicinity of the dwelling, should be chosen. Proximity to water is also highly important, especially if it can be readily employed for irrigation. Low situations are more liable to late and early frosts, but their abundant moisture renders them desirable for summer crops. A diversity of soils and exposures in the same inclosure is desirable.

Care should be taken that the productiveness of the kitchen garden be not diminished by the proximity of large trees, which are injurious by their drip to all plants beneath them, and by their shade and extended roots to those more remote. The small, fibrous roots of trees extend far beyond their branches, and one is not safe from these devourers much short of the length of the stem which they nourish. If trees exist too valuable to be removed, dig a deep trench near them, and cut off all roots that extend into it. This will probably relieve the adjacent crops from their injurious effects.

Aspect and Inclination.—A light exposure to the south is generally to be recommended. Gardeners take pride in having early crops, and this compensates in some measure for their shorter duration in such an exposure. A northeastern aspect is to be avoided, as our worst storms are from that direction. A north-western exposure, though cold and late, is less liable to injury from late and early frosts, as vegetation in such situations is sheltered somewhat from the rising sun, and does not suffer so much if it becomes slightly frozen. It is not the frost that injures plants so much as the direct heat of the sun falling upon the frozen leaves and blossoms. Hence an easterly aspect is generally objectionable for tender plants.

Cabbage, cauliflower, strawberries, spinach, lettuce, and other salads, are much more easily brought to perfection in a northern aspect. Many of these run up to seed immediately if exposed to the full sun. Of fruit trees the apple succeeds well on a northern slope. The soil, too, is usually richer, and will retain its fertility longer, other things being equal, in such an exposure. It is a great advantage, if the garden slope at all, to have it slope in more than one direction, thus giving a choice of exposure, and generally also of soil, as it is thereby adapted to both late and early crops. But when the drainage is good, a level is to be preferred, as by the aid of the fences any desired exposure can be obtained for particular plants. Indeed, in southern climates nothing after quality is more to be regarded than the inclination of the soil.

Whatever be the situation or aspect, a garden must be as level as possible. Any considerable inclination in a southern latitude subjects the richest portion of the soil to the danger of being washed away by its violent storms. In the rich, mellow soil of a garden cultivated as it should be, if there be much perceptible slope, a single storm will often cause a loss of manure and labor that will require considerable expense to repair. If the ground is not level at first, it is necessary to resort to hillside ditching or to throw it at once into terraces of convenient breadth. To do this the eye cannot be trusted; a leveling instrument is required. The steeps of these can be clothed with blue grass, or strawberry plants, to prevent them from washing.

Each terrace must be so raised just at its edge, that it will retain all the water which falls upon it, permitting none to flow over even in the heaviest storms. Any excess of water should be carried off by proper underdrains, if needed, and not suffered to run off the surface. Surface ditches are a poor substitute. Terracing is not very expensive. The horizontal line is first determined with a level and staked off. A few turns of the plow are made on the hillside just below the stakes, and the earth thrown up with a shovel to the staked line. If more earth is required, the plowing and shovelling must be repeated until a sufficient bank is formed to retain the water. During the first year, occasional breaks in the bank may happen from violent storms, but if well repaired, after the banks become settled, they will rarely be broken over by the accumulation of water, particularly if proper underdrains or surface ditches are provided.

Size.—A garden should be proportioned to the size of the family, and their partiality for its different products. A small garden with a suitable rotation of crops, and well manured and cultivated, will yield more pleasure and profit than an ordinary one of three times its size. An active, industrious hand can take care of an acre, provided with necessary hot-beds, cold frames, etc., keeping it in perfect neatness and condition; or if the plow and cultivator be brought into requisition, as they should be in large gardens, four times that amount can be under his care, provided there is not much under glass. In market gardens Henderson allows seven men to ten acres.

If but little room can be allowed near the house, cabbages, carrots, turnips, potatoes, and the common crops, can be grown in the field, if *well enriched*, and be cultivated mainly with the plow. The fruit garden should be in a separate compartment, as the shade of the trees is very injurious, and the exhaustion of the soil by their roots still more so. Dwarf pears upon the quince stock are the least hurtful, and may be admitted into the vegetable department along the walks.

Form.—The form will often depend upon the situation of the garden or the inclination of the ground. When a matter of choice, a square or parallelogram is most convenient for laying out the walks and beds. A parallelogram extending from east to west gives a long south wall for shading plants in summer, and a long sheltered border for forwarding early crops. An oblong shape has the further advantage of giving longer rows for the plow or cultivator.

Laying out.—A convenient plan is given in figure 1, showing the hedge enclosing the whole; and the adjacent border, *b b*, which should be about twelve feet wide. The remainder of the space is taken up with walks and the plots, *a a a a*. The walk next the boundaries should not be less than four and a half feet in width. The long central walk should be at least five or six feet wide, and in large gardens still wider, so as readily to admit a cart. In this case the main walk should proceed as in the figure, from the entrance until near the farther border, where a larger portion than in the plan should be taken off the adjacent plots, to form a circular turning place, around an arbor or tool-house.

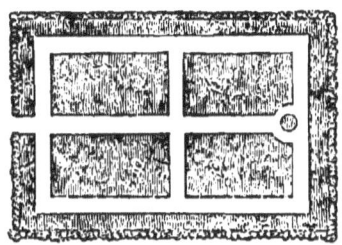

Fig. 1.—GARDEN PLAN.

If the ground is to be cultivated with the plow, the central cross-walk should be omitted, making two instead of four oblong plots. In this case the borders should be made of sufficient width to give room enough for all those vegetables that will not admit cultivation with this implement.

The other vegetables may be successfully cultivated in these two plots in long rows. Where only the spade and hoe are used, these plots may be further subdivided into smaller ones by walks three to four and a half feet wide, extending from the borders to the main walk; and a portion of these should be laid out each year by very narrow alleys into beds four feet wide, for onions, beets, carrots, etc. The earth should be dug out of the main walks, four inches deep, and spread evenly on each side over the adjacent ground. The walks may be filled with gravel, so as to be dry and comfortable, or fresh tan, if accessible, will answer very well, and will keep out the weeds for two years, when it should be used as a dressing for the strawberry beds, and its place filled with a fresh supply. No more walks or alleys should be made than are required for convenience in gardening operations.

Box is the best edging wherever it succeeds, which it does admirably throughout most of the South. All main walks should be wide enough for two persons to walk abreast, for which not less than four and a half feet are required.

Fencing.—The objects of fencing are to procure shelter for delicate plants from cold winds, also shade for those that require it, and, above all, to keep out of the garden intruders of all kinds, that the owner may enjoy its fruits without molestation. A high, close board fence, or a stone or brick wall, answers a tolerable purpose; but the only thing to be relied on is a living hedge. The Osage Orange, the Pyracanth, the Cherokee and single White Macartney roses, thrive in the South, and are all good for this purpose. Osage Orange plants may be raised from seed, or bought at the nurseries for five or six dollars per thousand. The Pyracanth, or Evergreen Thorn, (*Cratægus pyracantha*), will make a hedge as effectual as the Osage Orange, and, as it is an evergreen, is much the more desirable. The blossoms in spring are very showy, and it is covered in winter with bright scarlet berries, and hence it is often called the Burning-bush. It grows freely from cuttings in sandy soil, but these cuttings should remain in the nursery-bed a year, to become well rooted before use. Mr. Nelson gives the following directions for planting and trimming a hedge, which apply equally well to Osage Orange and Pyracanth:

"**Planting.**—First dig a trench where the hedge is intended to be grown, two spades deep, throwing the surface to one, and the subsoil to the other side; then throw the surface soil down on the bottom of the trench, and if it is very poor, add a little manure, or good surface earth. Autumn is by far the best time for transplanting, and it can safely be done as soon as the leaves are dropped. Cut down the plants to within four inches above the roots before planting. Several authors recommend planting in double rows, but I decidedly prefer a single one. Assort the plants in two parcels, those of large and those of small size, and lay the smaller ones aside for the richest ground. Stretch the line firmly, and place the plants in as straight a line as possible, one foot apart; fill up the trench with earth, leaving about two inches above ground; press the earth not too firmly, but water plentifully, and after that, level the whole nicely."

"**Trimming.**—It is perfectly useless to plant a hedge and leave it to be killed by weeds, or grow without trimming. A young hedge will require the same amount of labor as a row of Indian corn. The plants having been cut down so much, will, of course, start vigorously the ensuing spring. A good hedge ought never to be trimmed in any other than in a conical shape, as in figure 2.

Fig. 2.—SECTION OF HEDGE.

When trimmed in a conical shape, *every shoot will enjoy the full benefit of air, light, and moisture*, and by this simple and natural method, a hedge can be shorn into *a strong wall of verdure, so green and close from bottom to top, that even a sparrow cannot, without difficulty, pass through it.* In order to make a hedge so thick and impervious as above mentioned, it is necessary to go to work even in the first summer, with a pair of hedge shears, pruning the young growth, when about three months old, at the same time laying down some of the most vigorous shoots to fill up any vacant places found near the ground; these shoots may be fastened to the ground with hooked pegs. They may be considered as layers, will soon send up a number of sprouts, making the hedge impenetrable for pigs, and nearly for rabbits. The young twigs may be trimmed in a wedge shape, not more than one foot high, and at the base, six inches broad. The next season the hedge may be allowed to grow one foot higher, and three or four inches wider at the base. This pruning is most readily given with a reaping hook, (a sharp sickle without teeth), making the cut with an upward stroke. Thus the management must be continued until the hedge has attained the intended height, allowing an addition of four inches broader at the bottom for every foot more in height. A hedge, regularly trimmed twice a year, in June and November, with the exception of the first years, when it requires a little more care than afterward, will continue impenetrable for fifty or even one hundred years."

The Cherokee rose, (*Rosa lævigata*), by planting the cuttings by the side of a plank or wire fence, two feet apart, will grow up and cover it in a short time, and effectually repel man and beast; but it grows so rampant that it requires constant shortening-in. It is also apt to die out at the bottom, and become unsightly, and is in all respects much inferior to the single white Macartney, (*Rosa bracteata*), an evergreen, and very easily grown from cuttings. It is very thorny, and of beautiful foliage. It never dies out at the bottom, whether pruned or not, and south of Virginia, is very hardy, and of luxuriant growth. A satisfactory fence can be made with this, by setting good chestnut or cedar posts, eight feet apart, planted about two and a half feet in the ground. Bank up the soil to form some twenty inches high along the line of the fence, then form the usual paling fence, or nail a good wide bottom board, and finish the fence with heart pine six inch planks, or with stout wire, strained through holes in the posts. The wire fence may be four feet high. The roses should be rooted cuttings, and may be planted at first, even eight feet apart, and by layering and training the bottom shoots, if the ground is kept in good order, in three years they will repel every intruder. It is better, where plants are abundant, to set them out four feet apart. This hedge requires less pruning than any other to keep it impenetrable. After the posts and slats have decayed, the bank itself, grown over with roses, will repel all intrusion. The roses should be set at about the original level of the ground, and not at the top of the bank. My own hedge of Macartney rose, when three years old, trained on a common fence of rails and paling, formed a barrier perfectly secure, and very ornamental. I see but one objection to it. It is in summer always in blossom, and therefore attracts all the bees in the neighborhood. In my fruit-garden I have thought that the injury done to peaches and grapes by wasps and bees has been much greater since the hedge has grown up than before. It is a fine bee plant. In a more northern climate the sweetbrier might answer as a tolerable substitute.

The American Holly makes an efficient and beautiful hedge, but is slow of growth and very hard to transplant. It can, however, be safely planted by selecting a mild, cloudy day the last of February, or early in March, *cutting off the top* as directed above by Mr. Nelson for the Osage Orange, and exposing the roots meanwhile to the air as little as possible. Thousands of yards can be thus planted with little loss.

For an ornamental hedge about a cemetery lot or elsewhere, the Irish Yew and the Tree Box are decidedly the best plants that can be used. The narrow-leaved variety of Tree Box grows naturally, just the right shape, and needs very little trimming after two or three years. The Yew likes shade.

The Japan Quince planted by the side of a common

picket or plank fence will, in a few years, make a good enclosure for a fruit or vegetable garden, and in flower is very ornamental.

After hedges are established, a trench should be cut on the garden side, two and a half or three feet from their base, sufficiently deep to keep their roots from extending into the beds and injuring the crops.

CHAPTER II.

SOILS—THEIR CHARACTERISTICS.

Soils.—In all climates the character of the soil is of as much importance as situation or aspect. Soils are of two classes. They may be composed of matter derived directly from the decay of rock, like clay, loam, sand, lime, and other earthy and alkaline matters. Such a soil is classed as inorganic. Soils may likewise originate from the action and decay of plants and animals (organized beings,) as for example, peat, mould, and shell-marl. Such a soil is classed as organic. A good soil is the result of the proper union of both these classes.

The mechanical texture of a soil is likewise especially to be regarded, as on this depends the proper retention of manure and moisture. There are two grand divisions of soils, the *heavy and light*, which pass into each other by imperceptible gradations.

The best classification of soils is that of Schübler, a German, and is founded entirely upon the relative proportions of the chief constituents of all soils, viz., clay, sand, lime, and humus. He classes them as follows:

Argillaceous Soils.—These contain over fifty per cent of clay, and are readily known by their tenacity and greasiness to the feel, caused by the predominance of the clay in them. They are difficult to work, and in dry weather bake like brick and are not permeable to light dews and rains. In drying, they crack, exposing, in summer, the large roots of plants to the air and sun, and breaking the smaller ones. After heavy rains they become so saturated that they are for a long time unfit to work, and the plants therein die from excess of moisture. In short, they are very cold when they are wet, and very hard when they are dry. The crops are full ten days later in coming to maturity, than in a good, sandy loam. Ordinary clays contain about twenty-five per cent of sand. If less than fifteen per cent, they are only fit for brick-making and pottery.

Clays are rich in alkalies, and have the property of retaining potash, phosphoric and silicic acids, and all salts necessary to the growth of plants; also of condensing ammonia and other gaseous matters. Hence they retain the virtues of manure better than most other soils. Where there is present lime and organic matters in sufficient quantity, clays, not too stiff, are excellent for wheat.

A *Sandy Soil* is in texture the opposite of the preceding and the lightest of all soils. It contains not over ten per cent of clay. Such soils are harsh to the feel, lack cohesion, permit the water that falls upon them to pass instantly through them, and, as they heat up quickly, the crops raised in them soon suffer from drought. In them vegetation is early, but less vigorous and sustained. They do not readily combine with manures, the soluble parts of which are leached into the subsoil, or are washed out by the rains; so that, if manure be not constantly applied, they will yield but a moderate crop. Gravels are, in this respect, from the coarseness of their particles, still worse than sands, and are very properly called "hungry soils." Indeed, the fertility of a soil depends in a very great degree upon the fineness of its particles. Sand is sparingly soluble in water containing alkaline matter in solution, and in this state forms a portion, and sometimes an important portion, of the food of plants. It is soluble silica, in other words, dissolved sand, which the plant of wheat or maize has extracted from the soil and deposited upon the exterior of its stem, that gives the stalk or straw its stiffness, and the lack of which in sufficient quantity subjects it to the attacks of rust. Silica usually forms a small proportion, too, of grains, legumes, and succulent roots.

For garden purposes, the only kind of sand suitable is that which is fine and has been rounded by moving water. The angular particles of road sand form hard, impermeable masses, and it should never be employed. (*Lindley.*)

A *loamy sand* is a better soil than the preceding, and contains from ten to twenty per cent of clay. These light soils are best adapted to tap-roots and bulbs and for striking cuttings, while those heavier are better fitted for plants with fibrous roots.

A *sandy loam* contains between twenty and thirty per cent of clay, while all soils containing from thirty to fifty per cent of clay are classed as ordinary *loams*.

In a garden designed for the cultivation of a variety of plants, both a light and a moderately heavy soil are desirable. But the best soil for general purposes is a loam of medium texture, rather light than otherwise, arising from a suitable admixture of the two, as they reciprocally correct the defects of each other. Where the other essentials are present naturally, or added by man, such a soil is suitable for the production of nearly all garden crops. Any soil, by judicious culture, draining, and ameliorators, or amendments, can be converted into such a loam.

Lime in greater or less proportions is generally present in soils, commonly as a carbonate. It is sparingly soluble in water, and is especially, when combined with acids, as in the sulphate (gypsum,) or the phosphate of lime (bone earth,) an important portion of the food of our most useful plants. There are some plants, however, as the Kalmia, to which its presence, to any appreciable extent in soils, is injurious. Any one of the foregoing soils that contains from five to twenty per cent of lime is classed as *marly*, (as a marly clay, a marly loam, etc.) When it contains over twenty per cent, it is classed as *calcareous*. A small percentage only of lime is required for the successful growth of plants. Marly soils, other things being equal, are the best adapted to fruit trees and wheat. They are also classed as argillaceous, loamy, sandy-loamy, and loamy-sandy marls, etc., according to the relative amounts in them of clay and sand; while if they contain above five per cent of humus (vegetable matter in a state of decay,) they are classed as humus marls, which may be also argillaceous, if containing fifty per cent of clay; loamy, if from thirty to fifty per cent; and sandy, if less than thirty per cent of clay.

Calcareous Soils (which contain more than twenty per cent of carbonate of lime) also are classed in the same manner with marly soils, according to the relative amounts of clay, sand, and humus they contain—as argillaceous, or loamy calcareous, etc.

Organic Soils.—Shell marls, though of organic origin, are naturally classed with the calcareous soils. The other organic soils are mainly of vegetable origin, resulting from the decay of plants, and are named humus soils. This last class is of three orders: 1st. Soluble mild humus, that is, vegetable mould in a fit condition for the nourishment of the plants which grow in it, such as thoroughly rotted peat, black or leaf-mould. 2d. Acid humus, which contains a free acid, injurious, if not destructive, to most plants. 3d. Peat or other fibrous vegetable matter, which, though free from acidity, is not yet in a proper condition to impart nourishment to plants. Humus soils may be argillaceous, loamy and sandy, and also contain, or be destitute of, calcareous matter.

Humus has the property of producing a constant supply of carbonic acid by slow combination with oxygen. It aids greatly in keeping a soil in an open state, so as to allow water and air to pass freely through it, and by virtue of its porosity it condenses and retains gaseous matter within, and it absorbs saline substances. Though such a soil freely parts with a superabundance of water, yet in dry weather it imbibes from the atmosphere large supplies of moisture. Schübler found that 100 pounds of dry humus would hold 190 pounds of water without losing a drop. In dry weather 1,000 grains of it spread upon a surface of fifty inches absorbed from the atmosphere in three days 120 grains of moisture. Of silicious sand the same amount absorbed nothing; sandy clay, 28 grains; loamy clay, 35; stiff clay, 35; garden mould, 52. Hence the best defence we have against drought is an abundant supply of decayed organic matter in a loamy soil. Clay, sand, humus, and lime, will neither of them, if pure, sustain a healthy vegetation; but properly mixed, constitute the main ingredients of the richest soils in the world. As good loam contains sufficient lime, therefore loam, peat, and sand, in varying proportions, are constantly employed by gardeners as the essentials for proper development of the plants they wish to grow therein.

Where true peat cannot be obtained, leaf-mould from the woods, black muck from the swamps, well decomposed and sweetened by exposure, or thoroughly rotted turf mixed with powdered charcoal, are the best substitutes.*

The *depth of a soil* is quite as important as its texture. If not naturally deep, it must be made so by trenching. Deep soils retain a constant supply of moisture in dry weather, so that the plants do not suffer; they do not become too wet in rainy seasons, as the earth drinks in and retains the rain below the surface; hence they are not so

---

* (Rural Cyclopedia, Dr. Lindley.)

liable to wash away. If equally rich, they furnish plants with a more abundant supply of food than shallow soils. Especially for all tap-rooted plants, a deep soil is indispensable. In the preparation of your garden, then, see that the ground is dry, deep, and rich. Good vegetables will not grow in a wet soil; a shallow soil will not furnish them with a regular supply of moisture; and the crops growing upon a poor soil never repay the labor bestowed upon it.

CHAPTER III.

THE IMPROVEMENT OF THE SOIL.

A soil may be improved in texture, in depth, and by the addition of such constituents necessary for the growth of plants as may be wanting.

The *texture* of a *clayey soil* can be rendered more pervious by *thorough draining*, deep trenching, and by the application of sand, ashes, lime, and unfermented manure. Any clayey, retentive subsoil will be greatly benefited by good underdrains. A wet soil is always cold, as water has a much greater capacity for heat than has earth. The same quantity of heat that will warm the earth four degrees will warm water but one. Water, also, is a bad conductor of heat *downwards*. Boiling water can be gently poured over cold water without heating the latter, except a very little at the surface. Now, if the soil in spring be saturated with water colder than the summer rains, unless it be removed by drainage, they cannot descend to carry warmth into the ground; neither will the wet soil conduct the atmospheric heat downwards with much rapidity. But draw off the cold water by proper drains, and the warmer water can percolate through and raise the temperature of the soil. As the warmer water settles, the porous space it occupies will admit warm air. (*Thompson*.) Drainage, also, by admitting the atmosphere, renders the soil much more friable. Soils well drained have likewise been found to suffer far less from summer droughts than before. Underdrains should be not less than three feet below the surface, and four feet is much to be preferred.

Trenching renders the upper stratum of soil more light and friable, acting as drainage, but imperfectly. Its great utility is in increasing the quantity of soil to which the roots of plants find access.

Ashes and lime each have the property of rendering heavy soils lighter, and light soils more tenacious, and both more productive, especially for potatoes, turnips, beets, and peas, which delight in calcareous soils. In cold climates, plowing clay lands deeply in the fall, and exposing them to the action of the winter's frost, is very beneficial, but in sections where there is little frost and abundant and heavy washing rains, it is worse than useless. Turning under coarse vegetable or carbonaceous matter, as straw, leaves, pine straw, corn-stalks, a crop of cowpeas, clover, or any other green crop, bog or leaf-mould, decomposed peat, and even tan-bark itself, so deeply beneath the surface as not to interfere with cultivation, will by the slow decomposition of these materials much increase the fertility of a clay soil by improving its texture. It is most improved by drainage if needed.

The frequent working of the soil with the hoe and spade, thereby admitting the ammonia and fertilizing gases of the atmosphere, is itself very beneficial to clay soils, if done when the earth is dry. A clay soil is exceedingly injured if worked while wet. It is so difficult to work, and so liable to bake into a hard crust after every rain, that it will well repay, where materials for the purpose are at all convenient, to lay out a good deal of time and labor in improving its mechanical texture.

The *texture* of a *sandy soil* is much more easily improved than a clay, as the percentage of clay required to convert any sand into a loam is not very large and can easily be added. Fortunately, too, in sandy soils, clay is generally near at hand, often lying but a few inches beneath the surface. A few loads of stiff clay, scattered thinly over the surface in autumn, are worth more applied to such a soil than any manure, for the clay will render manures permanent in their effect, which else would leach through without benefit to the crops. The effect of the clay itself is lasting. Lime, as before observed, stiffens the texture of a sandy soil, and gypsum has the same effect. Ashes, leached or unleached, are also an excellent and profitable dressing to such a soil, but the best of all applications is a good clay marl. Peat, vegetable manure, and carbonaceous matters of all kinds, such as refuse charcoal, are good applications to these sandy soils, as they enable them better to retain the fertilizing properties of the manure applied, though they do not much affect the texture of the soil. Sandy soils very often rest upon a clay bottom, so that the thorough trenching which a garden should receive will often greatly improve its texture. Working such a soil while wet, and the continual use of the roller, will also render it more tenacious. But clay is the great improver, and it is astonishing how small a quantity of fine clay will cement a loose sand into a good loam.

To conclude, in regard to the texture of soils, choose or make for your garden a loam of medium texture a little inclined to sand, and the finer its particles the better. Clays and sands both become objectionable as they depart from this friable, loamy texture, and the first step in their improvement is to bring them to this condition. A medium consistency best agrees with vegetation.

The *depth of soil* in the garden is as likely to need improvement as its texture. A deep soil is necessary that the roots may penetrate it freely in search of food, and be able to endure our summer droughts. The roots of a strawberry have been traced five feet down in a deep, rich soil. The difference in the freshness and growth of plants raised upon trenched soils, and those growing upon soils prepared in the common manner, is remarkable. In lawns, the color of the grass will indicate very exactly the greater or less depth of the soil. The depth of soils may be increased by subsoil plowing, or trenching.

Trenching is the mode of improving the depth of the soil in smaller gardens, and is usually performed in this manner: At one end of the plot to be trenched, you dig with the spade a trench three feet wide, and two feet deep; you throw the earth out on the side away from the plot to be trenched. Shovel the bottom clean, and make the sides perpendicular, leaving a clear open trench across the plot. Open another trench the same width, and put the surface spadefull of that into the bottom of the former trench, and the next spadefull upon that, until opened to the same depth as the *first* one, adding meanwhile the necessary manures and amendments. When the plot is entirely trenched in this way, the last trench will remain open, which must be filled with the earth thrown out from the first one, which finishes the work.

Most subsoils are, however, so poor that this mode of trenching will do more harm than good, except in worn-out soils or in old, overrich gardens. It is, in general, a better plan to remove from the first trench opened all the rich surface mould, and place it on one side; then trench the subsoil to the required depth, throwing out enough earth at one end of the trench to give room to operate, leaving it still at the bottom. If the subsoil is stiff, it will be greatly improved by intermixing with it while trenching, as "amendments," leaves, straw, tan-bark, saw-dust, or any other vegetable refuse, putting the coarsest materials at the bottom. Now cover the loosened subsoil with surface mould from the adjacent strip, which is next to be trenched, and loosen the bottom of this strip also to the required depth, adding amendments as before. Proceed thus until the plot is finished, covering the subsoil of the last strip with the surface mould taken from the first one opened. If the soil is too light, clay should be added to it while being trenched. If it needs drainage, the drains should be laid at the same time. Drain tile forms the most perfect mode of drainage where they can be obtained at a reasonable rate. They should be laid *deep*, below the bottom of the trenches.

Trenching is an expensive operation, but "nothing," says Mr. Barry, "is so expensive and troublesome, as an ill-prepared soil." This process is found to be of great advantage in England, where there is no lack of moisture, and still more so by the market gardeners of the North; while in our own dry, warm climate, it is, as I know by trial, absolutely indispensable. Ground thus prepared is not so liable to wash away, as it will readily soak up the heaviest rain, if properly terraced. There is no point of greater importance than this. Poor ground deeply moved sometimes yields better than rich with shallow tillage, and when the ground has been prepared once in this manner, it will feel the benefit forever after. Increasing the depth of the soil in this mode is to all intents and purposes increasing the size of your garden; for one-fourth of an acre thus prepared will yield in a dry season as much as an acre will with shallow tillage; and the growth of the plants in a good season will be fully doubled. Trees, especially, feel the benefit of this preparation, and all fruit-gardens should be thus prepared. No matter how deep you may work the soil for trees or plants, their fibers will penetrate it, and feel the good effect.

Trenching should be performed in the fall—the coarse

manure dug in at that time. At the top it should be well manured with well-rotted dung, charcoal dust, ashes, or other good manure, dug in shallow, taking care to level the ground while trenching, so as to prevent washing. Another good coat of compost should be added just before planting in the spring.

Subsoil plowing is much cheaper and answers a very good purpose when the spot to be prepared is large. A common turning plow goes first, and plows as deep a furrow as practicable. It is followed by the subsoil plow in the same furrow, which should loosen the soil, without turning it up, to the depth of eighteen or twenty inches, unless it is a stiff clay or gravel.

CHAPTER IV.

MANURES.

Anything which, by being added to the soil directly or indirectly, promotes the growth of plants, may be considered a manure. Strictly speaking, manures are the artificial food supplied to plants. Those substances, that, when added to the soil, promote plant-growth more by changing its texture, correcting its acidity, and otherwise modifying its condition than by the nourishment they directly afford to plants, we shall, borrowing a French term, call amendments. Such are sand, coal ashes, lime, clay, marl, old plaster, etc., when applied to soils that need them. Many of these substances, like marl, lime, rubbish, rotten chips, broken charcoal, etc., act both as manures and amendments.

Manures may be classified into organic, inorganic, and

mixed; into nitrogenous, carbonaceous, earthy, and saline; and into general and special. Organic manures include those both of animal and vegetable origin; inorganic manures are derived from minerals.

Manures may have a two-fold action—*directly* assisting vegetable growth by entering into the composition of plants, and by supplying them with moisture and nutritive gases which they absorb from the atmosphere. Manures may also *indirectly* assist the growth of plants either by destroying vermin or weeds; by decomposing in the soil, and rendering available any stubborn organic remains therein; by protecting plants from sudden changes of temperature; or they may act as amendments by improving the texture and physical condition of the soil. All the above properties probably never are combined in any one manure, each being characterized by superiority in some one of the above qualities.

The manures most generally applicable are those composed of substances which *directly enter into* and *are essential* to the *growth* of plants. What are these substances?

"Plants," says Liebig, "contain combustible and incombustible ingredients. The latter, which compose the ash left by all parts of plants on combustion, consist, in the case of our cultivated plants, essentially of phosphoric acid, potash, silicic and sulphuric acids, lime, iron, magnesia, and chloride of sodium." It is now fully established "that the constituents of the ash are elements of food, and hence indispensable to the structure of the different parts of the plant."

The few ashes that remain after burning a plant are all that it got necessarily from the soil. From eighty-eight to ninety-nine per cent of the weight of the plant has escaped into the air, from which, and from water, the plant has derived it immediately or remotely. The composition of their ashes varies in different parts of the same plant and slightly in the same species when grown on different soils; but they are always a valuable manure for the species from which obtained, and, slowly dissolving in the soil, they furnish the roots with just the salts required to nourish the growing plant.

But, in general, over nine pounds in every ten have disappeared under the action of fire. The combustible portions which have been expelled are carbon, hydrogen, oxygen, and a little nitrogen, which have been derived from carbonic acid, water, and ammonia, which are, as elements of food, equally indispensable as the substances of which the ashes of plants are composed.

The incombustible constituents of the plant come from the soil alone, and are taken up by the roots.

After the gaseous constituents of plants are driven off by combustion, the small percentage of ashes remaining, we have stated, consists of *silicic and phosphoric acids, potash, sulphur, lime, magnesia, iron, chlorine and soda*, (the two latter generally unite as chloride of sodium), all of which, in greater or less proportions, enter into the composition of our field and garden crops. These earthy or saline constituents are found within the cells of plants, or deposited as a lining to the cell-walls, or entering into their substance. They are useful to the plant itself, and useful in the plant's products as affording food to man. Some of them are always present in the azotized substances formed by plants. Thus sulphur and the phosphates are, with ammonia, necessary for the formation of albumen, fibrin, and caseine, which are essential constituents of our blood.

Of these substances *Lime, Potash, Soda, Phosphoric Acid, Sulphur, and Chlorine*, are all the gardener will have occasion to supply, the others being always present in sufficient quantity in all cultivated soils.

Lime generally occurs as a carbonate. Partially soluble in water, it is an important portion of food to most of our cultivated plants. It is indispensable to such plants as beets, potatoes, peas, beans, fruit trees, and vines, but to Kalmias and coniferous trees it is injurious. It is of special value when combined with phosphoric acid, as in bone earths, or with the sulphuric, as in gypsum. Lime in the soil enables it better to absorb and retain heat. It is of great value as an application to cold, tenacious soils, rendering them of more open texture, and making the organic matters therein available to plants. It, on the other hand, makes light soils more adhesive, acting as an amendment. It decomposes organic matters, whether vegetable or animal, and forms with them a partially soluble compound peculiarly fitted for the food of plants. But as it has the property of setting free ammonia, *it should never be applied in connection with fresh animal manures.* Mixed with *stable manure or guano*, it would speedily free them from nearly all their ammonia, that indispensable and most costly constituent of the food of plants.

This will not happen to any great extent, and there will be little loss, if the mixture takes place in, and both the lime and manure are entirely covered with the soil, which will at once absorb whatever ammonia the lime sets free.

The great value of lime, aside from the small quantity directly available to plants, is in hastening, as above stated, the decomposition of decaying matters in the soil, and rendering them assimilable by plants. The old black mould of kitchen gardens and other soils rich in humus, it will suddenly render wonderfully productive, and they will consequently speedily become exhausted, unless new supplies of organic manures are added. Lime alone, added to a soil, will speedily exhaust it if the crops are removed and no return of manure is made.

Potash is another alkaline substance indispensable to healthy vegetation. It occurs in all plants, and this, and lime and soda, are regarded by Liebig as specially destined to serve as bases for the organic acids of vegetation.

Caustic potash acts upon decaying matters like lime. As a manure, it is always used in the form of a salt, generally as a carbonate, but also as a chloride and a nitrate. As a carbonate, it is found in wood ashes, which are everywhere considered as a most valuable manure, and which add great efficacy to all composts to which they are applied. The abundant potash from burning the brush and timber is one cause of the great fertility of freshly cleared lands. Chloride of potassium exists in soapboilers' refuse, which is a good manure, chiefly from the presence of this salt therein. Nitrate of potash (saltpetre) is the most useful of the salts of potash, promoting the vigor of plants and rendering their tissues solid. Potash, like lime, should not be combined with animal manures, but in composts of vegetable refuse will be found very useful, particularly as an application to vines and fruit trees. Upon turnips, cabbages, and other members of the cabbage tribe, it has, when applied in the form of soapsuds, an immediate good effect. (*Lindley.*)

Soapsuds is also most excellent as a manure for roses. Potash has the same effect as lime upon the texture of soils, in rendering adhesive-ones more friable, and light ones more adhesive. Soils, in cultivation, if not manured, soon part with so much of their soluble potash, that rest and fallowing are required to render available that which exists naturally in all clayey soils, but not in a soluble form to the extent required by growing plants. After ammonia and phosphoric acid, potash is the most likely to be of benefit to the soil.

Soda is present in the structure of plants, but in smaller quantities than potash, for which it is regarded by Liebig as a natural equivalent. Some plants which naturally grow in a soil containing a salt of soda will grow equally well if a salt of potash is present, while, if both are absent from the soil, they will not thrive. Hence if a soil contain enough alkaline matter for many plants, it does not much matter whether it be potash or soda; but in general it will be more productive if both these alkalies are present. For plants which naturally inhabit the sea-shore, such as asparagus and sea kale, its presence in the form of common salt (Chloride of sodium) is indispensable. (*Lindley.*) The nitrate of soda is similar in its beneficial action upon plants to the nitrate of potash, but it is not yet settled whether the good effects of these salts are owing to their nitrogen, or in part to their alkali.

Phosphoric Acid.—Next to ammonia, this is usually the most necessary application to soils, because the first element exhausted. Where not present in sufficient quantity, its supply, artificially, is even of more urgent necessity. A supply of ammonia may, in some measure, be derived from the atmosphere, but the phosphates must be restored by man. The presence of the phosphates in the soil is required that ammonia may have its full effect.

"In wild plants, the phosphates are less abundant than in cultivated crops. The latter produce a large quantity of blood, forming food in a short space of time; hence more phosphates are required. All plants that are useful for animal food have great power of taking up the phosphates, and cultivation increases this power. Evergreen and perennial plants extend their vegetating processes over many years, and do not in a given period require so large a quantity of the phosphates as the ordinary cultivated plants, and their falling leaves restore much of the inorganic matter to the soil. But cultivated plants are mostly annual and herbaceous, grow rapidly, and require an abundance of phosphates, which are annually removed with the crop. If the crop, like that of wild plants, was left upon the soil, the plants in their decay would restore all they had taken. Phosphoric acid is present in the blood, is a constituent of the brain and nerves, and enters largely into the bones of the animals that consume these plants or their seeds and roots. Providence never permits food-plants to grow, unless all the elements are within their reach that are necessary to nourish and develope the bodies of the beings that are to feed upon them. Those manures are most valuable which furnish the materials necessary for forming the azotized compounds required for the food of man and animals. Hence the great value of manures containing ammonia and the phosphates which do not exist abundantly and are annually required and taken away by the crops." (*Balfour, Liebig.*)

"Alkaline and earthy phosphates form," says Liebig, "invariable constituents of the seeds of all kinds of grasses, of beans, peas, and lentils." It is said, in the ash of tea-leaves, they amount to 17 per cent.

Bones, certain mineral substances, and the phosphatic guanos, contribute to furnish the necessary supply. The apparent effect of phosphates applied to the soil is to stimulate vegetation and to promote the formation of roots. If used for the drainage of pots in the form of broken bones, or at the bottom of vine borders, the roots soon find their way down to, and extract nutriment from them.

The phosphates, like all other plant food, to be of service, must be within the reach of the roots of plants. Fertility is not to be measured by the quantity of plant food a soil contains, but only by that portion which exists in a finely divided state, as it is only with such portions that the rootlets of plants can come in close contact. An ounce of bone in a cubic foot of soil produces no marked effect upon its fertility if unbroken. Dissolve it and let it be distributed through the soil, and it will suffice for the food of 120 wheat plants. The most abundant application of earthy phosphates in coarse powder can, in its effects, bear no comparison with a much less quantity, which, in a state of minute subdivision, is dispersed through every part of the soil. A rootlet requires, where it touches the soil, a most minute portion of food, but it is necessary for its very existence that this minute supply should be at that precise spot. (*Liebig.*)

Phosphates, then, to produce their best effect, must be made soluble, as it is only in this state that they can penetrate every portion of the soil. Broken bones dissolve and part with their phosphoric acid very slowly in the soil, but what good effect they produce continues a long time. If finely ground, the present good effect is much more evident. By mixing them in this state with sulphuric acid, it combines with a portion of the lime, converting it into gypsum or sulphate of lime; while the rest remains in combination with the phosphoric acid as a biphosphate (superphosphate) of lime. This is soluble in water, and when applied to the soil is diffused through it, and can be readily, and if not in excess, soon totally absorbed, by the rootlets of growing plants, and consequently its good effects upon the soil will soon disappear. One peck of bones, thus prepared, will have as much present effect as 16 bushels of ground bones undissolved. (*Lindley.*)

The soluble phosphates, in estimating the values of manures, are now regarded as the most important ingredient, next to ammoniacal salts, and, as before stated, are often, indeed, more necessary to supply.

Sulphur.—Plants contain, either deposited in their roots or seeds, or dissolved in their juices, variable quantities of compounds containing sulphur. In these, nitrogen is an invariable constituent. These are always accompanied by alkaline phosphates and alkaline earths, and for both, in each seed there exists a fixed and unchangeable relation; whenever the percentage of phosphoric acid increases or diminishes in any seed, there is the like increase or diminution in the compounds of sulphur. In the seeds of cereals and in those of leguminous plants, two of these compounds exist, and a third in the juices of all plants, but in the greatest abundance in the juices of those plants we use for the table. (*Liebig.*)

This sulphur is obtained from the sulphates naturally contained in or applied to the soil, especially from gypsum, or sulphate of lime. Gypsum, it is believed, acts in two ways, being sparingly soluble in water; it acts directly as food for plants, supplying them with sulphur and lime, and indirectly, by its action on the volatile carbonate of ammonia which it unites with and fixes. When they meet in solution, a double action takes place; both substances are decomposed, and their elements unite in the forms of carbonate of lime and sulphate of ammonia. The latter salt is not volatile, and the ammonia is thus retained in the soil for the use of the crops. Gypsum is very beneficial to green crops, as the cabbage, potato, also to maize, and especially to clover, peas, and other leguminous crops. (*Lindley.*) A bushel of it has been known to yield an extra ton of clover hay to the acre when applied broadcast. Gypsum is very useful to sprinkle on manure heaps and upon the contents of privies, to fix the ammonia contained therein.

Sulphur alone may sometimes be used to advantage as a manure. It is not soluble in water, but when finely divided, it will slowly unite with the oxygen of the air.

Sulphur is destructive to most insects, and found very serviceable to sprinkle about green-houses and vineries for the prevention of mildew.

Chlorine.—In districts remote from the sea, the chlorides of sodium, calcium, and magnesia, when applied to the soil, are useful to vegetation. These compounds are frequently found in the sap of plants. As nearly all soils contain more or less of common salt, the application of any chloride is seldom absolutely essential, but is frequently very serviceable, especially to certain crops.

Chemistry has endeavored to ascertain by analyzing the ashes of plants which of these substances is most important to a given plant. As a result of these inquiries, plants have been divided into four classes, according as one or another inorganic element is found to predominate in their ashes.

1. *Silex Plants.*—Those that abound in silica, as the grasses, equisetums, etc.

2. *Alkali Plants.*—Those that contain alkaline salts in large proportions, as beets, potatoes, and the vine. Potash salts are necessary to all land plants, especially to conifers and other trees, while soda salts, particularly its chloride, to all marine plants.

3. *Lime Plants.*—Those that contain the earths, especially lime and magnesia, as clover, peas, beans, etc.

4. *Phosphorus Plants.*—Those that contain the phosphates, as the cereals, wheat, corn, rye, oats, fruits. All food-bearing plants contain more or less of the phosphates in their ashes, as cabbages, turnips, onions, etc.

Phosphates of lime and potash are the inorganic substances most likely to be needed in soils, as they are soonest exhausted. The salts of lime, as the carbonate and sulphate, after these, are generally next valuable. Lime, however, is injurious to heaths. Nitrogenous manures, so generally serviceable, are injurious to conifers and stone fruits. (*Lindley.*)

An analysis of stable manure shows it to contain all the elements required for the food of plants; every part of it has been formed of vegetable products, and is ready when rendered soluble to enter into and minister again to their growth.

The decayed parts of any plant rendered soluble, and likewise its ashes, are among the best manures for plants of its own species. Vineyards have been kept fertile by digging into the soil the fresh prunings of the vines, and indeed are said to have increased in richness from the slight manuring their own leaves afford. So forests, we know, are enriched by the falling leaves.

It is by putrefaction that all animal and vegetable remains are rendered available to plants, but if they are allowed to decompose without care, the loss is immense; the soluble parts are washed away, the gases pass off into the air, and a large proportion of the manure is dissipated.

The Indirect Action of Manures.—Some manures ameliorate the soil by *absorbing and retaining moisture* from the atmosphere. This property is as beneficial to a clay as to a sandy soil during drought, as at such times clays are often baked so as to be impervious to the dew, and suffer nearly or quite as much as more sandy soils. The best absorbents of moisture are stable manure, thoroughly decomposed tan-bark, and the manure of the cow and pig, in the order named. After these come sheep and fowl manure, salt, soot, and even burnt clay is not without its virtue. All these absorbents are much more effectual when finely divided, and the soil itself is a good absorbent in proportion to its *richness*, fineness, and the friability produced by frequent culture. In the power of retaining moisture absorbed, pig manure stands preëminent; next that of the horse, then common salt and soot.

Some manures are beneficial in absorbing not only moisture, but nutritious gases from the atmosphere, which they yield to the roots in a concentrated form. All animal and vegetable manures have the power of attracting oxygen from the air during decomposition. Charcoal and all carbonaceous matters have the power of absorbing carbonic acid gas in large quantities, supplying constantly to the roots of plants an atmosphere of carbonic acid, which is renewed as quickly as it is abstracted. The same substances are especially valuable for their power of absorbing ammonia. Charcoal will absorb ninety times its volume of ammoniacal gas, which can be separated by simply moistening it with water.

Decayed wood absorbs seventy times its volume, while

leaf-mould, perfectly rotted tan-bark, and in fact all vegetable manures, are exceedingly valuable in this respect.

Manures *indirectly assist the growth of plants by destroying weeds and predatory vermin.* This is not a property of animal and vegetable manures, (except that guano repels most insects). They foster these enemies of the crop, but salt, lime, and ashes, applied to the surface of the soil, are very destructive to nearly all insects, while the roots of weeds and grasses, if composted with ashes or lime, are completely destroyed and converted into an excellent manure.

Another indirect action of manure in assisting the growth of plants is in *decomposing and rendering available* any stubborn organic substances in the soil. Stable manure, and all decomposing animal and vegetable substances, have a tendency to promote the decay of any organic remains in the soil. All putrescent substances hasten the process of putrefaction in other organic bodies with which they come in contact. Even peat and tan-bark, *mingled with stable dung and kept moist,* are converted into good manure; common salt in small proportions has a similar septic property, and the efficacy of lime in this respect is well known.

Ashes are of equal value, but not so easy to obtain in sufficient quantity. Neither ashes or lime should ever be mixed with manures that are rich in ammonia, such as cotton seed or animal manures, as they would cause great waste of ammonia by setting it free and permitting it to be lost in the atmosphere.

Inorganic substances are sometimes released from their combinations, and rendered soluble by the application of carbonaceous manures. Ashes from which the soluble potash has been leached, if composted with swamp muck, are enabled to furnish plants with a further supply. By composting the two, the value of both is greatly increased. Such a compost may be mixed with ammoniacal manures, not only without loss, but with decided benefit, and the ammonia will be retained.

Another indirect agency of manures is in protecting plants from sudden changes of temperature. There is no doubt that rich soils and those abounding in animal and vegetable remains, are less liable to change their temperature with the incumbent atmosphere than those of poorer constituents, for the decomposition of manures gives warmth to the soil. Corn can be grown in high latitudes upon rich land only; upon a poor soil it would perish.

The last indirect effect of manures upon plants is by improving the texture of the soils in which they grow. Decomposing in the ground, they leave interstices as they become less in bulk, making it more light and porous. The effect of manure in rendering a stiff soil light and friable is very well known. It is equally true that vegetable manures give to sandy soils greater tenacity, enabling them better to retain moisture and ammonia.

Manures, then, should be adapted to soils and circumstances. Cohesive and binding manures are most suitable for open sands; those of open texture, for stiff clays; those that readily attract and retain moisture, for dry soils; heating, dry, strawy, and turfy manures, for wet or clayey soils; and those of slow decomposition for hungry gravels.

CHAPTER V.

MANURES.—THEIR SOURCES AND PREPARATION.

Having considered the modes in which manures act upon the growth of plants, a still more important inquiry remains, viz.: What manures can we obtain and render available? The scarcity of manures with us is a great difficulty in gardening. But a small amount of live stock is kept in proportion to the number of acres in cultivation. What is thus obtainable is not well husbanded, and is needed for corn and cotton. Still, on most country places, enough is wasted to supply not only the garden, but to leave a surplus for the field crops. In town, wherever a horse and cow can be kept, enough can be made for a large garden, while even a pig, if kept at work in his pen, with the aid of soapsuds from the house, will convert some fifteen loads of weeds, yard sweepings, chips, tan-bark, and leaves, into a valuable manure.

Of Saline and Earthy Manures the most available are ashes, leached and unleached, which should be most carefully saved, as potash is one of the elements drawn most largely from the soil, and this ashes supply most cheaply. They contain besides potash, phosphoric and sulphuric acids, manganese, chlorine, soda, magnesia, carbonate of lime, and soluble silica. They may be applied directly to any crops, and especially to fruit trees. Composted with swamp earth and other vegetable matter, they correct its acidity, and form an excellent manure for all crops, and in connection with lime form the best compost for orchards.

Lime may be applied in this compost for trees and for all garden crops. Shell lime is the best to employ, as it contains some phosphate of lime, which is still more valuable. If lime is used alone, mix it intimately with the surface soil, but do not plow or spade it in. Its effect in improving the texture of soils, we have already considered. In soils of but moderate fertility and free from carbonaceous matters, it is often more injurious than useful.

Lime rubbish from old brick walls, and the plastering of old houses, contains nitrate of lime. This salt furnishes nitrogen abundantly to plants. This rubbish also contains a portion of hair and silicate of lime, and is a very powerful manure. One ton is sufficient for an acre.

Common salt, on lands so distant from the sea that the

spray does not reach them, is a very beneficial manure. It is the cheapest mode of supplying plants with soda and chlorine, and of course is beneficial to apply to asparagus and other marine plants. The refuse salt which has been used for bacon is the most valuable, as it contains in addition the blood and juices of the meat, which greatly increase its virtues. It may be directly applied to asparagus without injury, and at the rate of six or eight bushels per acre applied in autumn, it benefits all garden crops, keeping the soil moist and free from insects and worms. It is well to supply it at the same time with lime, in the lime and salt mixture hereafter described.

Gypsum.—Of this a very small quantity will suffice. One bushel per acre yearly is all that is needed. In absorbing ammonia from the manure heap, charcoal dust and leaf-mould are much cheaper. It is the cheapest way of supplying the soil with what sulphur is required.

Marl, where it can be obtained, may be applied with advantage, especially to sandy soils. It is generally beneficial in proportion to the quantity of lime it contains.

Some marls contain both phosphate of lime and potash in considerable quantities, and hence are of increased value. Before largely applying it, experiments should be made on a small scale, as some marls, upon trial, are found to be injurious.

Soot is rich in ammonia; very little of this can be procured, but it should be carefully preserved and applied in small quantities to cabbage and other plants infested with insects. It drives these off, and its ammonia also promotes the growth of the plants.

The Nitrates of Potash and Soda are applied in a finely powdered state during wet weather by English cultivators, and are found useful upon clays and loams, but of no benefit on light, sandy soils.

Burnt Clay has been found to possess considerable value

as a manure. By burning, it loses its adhesiveness, which in its natural state prevented air from permeating it, and water from passing off. Its saline constituents, and those also of the roots of the plants it contains, are set free, while it is rendered permeable to the air and freely admits the advancing roots of plants. The burnt particles absorb ammonia from the air, and hold it in their pores until washed out by showers into the soil to act as nourishment for the crops. It may be prepared in connection with charcoal, as hereafter shown. There is some loss of organizable matter which is more than made up by chemical changes produced.

Organic Manures, beginning with those of vegetable origin. The very best is cotton seed cake, where it can be obtained. Properly prepared, it is scarcely inferior in strength to guano itself. It may be applied with advantage to any crop.

Charcoal renders the soil light and friable, gives it a dark color, and additional warmth for early crops. The bed whereon charcoal has been burnt is always marked by a most vigorous growth of plants when it becomes sufficiently mixed with earth. It contains also small quantities of salts of potash and other fertilizing salts.

It absorbs both carbonic acid and ammonia from the air, and yields them to the roots of plants. It is most marked in its effects on plants which require abundant nitrogen. As it is indestructible, its beneficial effects last as long as it remains in the soil, supplying the rootlets of plants with carbonic acid, which is renewed as fast as abstracted. Its good effects begin to be seen when the dust is applied at the rate of forty bushels per acre. Charcoal is invaluable for destroying the odor of decaying animal matter, retaining all the gases in its own substance ready to yield them up for the use of plants. Hence, the best application of this substance is not directly to the soil, but to compost it with putrescent animal matters, urine or night soil, of which it will absorb all the odor and fertilizing gases given off during their decomposition. Composted with the last named substance, it becomes *poudrette*, and is second only to guano as a fertilizer.

In striking cuttings or potting plants, fine charcoal is a valuable substitute for sand, plants rooting in it with great certainty. Plants will flourish in powdered charcoal alone with considerable vigor, and, added to the other materials used in potting, it is found greatly to promote healthy growth in most plants.

Fine charcoal can be obtained in considerable quantities from the old hearths where it has been burned; also from the refuse of smith's shops, founderies, and machine shops. All the refuse of the garden that will not decay, pea-brush, trimmings of trees, cabbage and corn stalks, together with tan-bark, saw-dust, and fresh shavings, may be collected, the coarser materials placed at the bottom and set on fire when the heap is building; then covered with the finer, beating all well together, cover it well with short, moist rubbish, weeds and clods. Bermuda grass turf is the best material for this purpose if you are troubled with it, and it is better if it has been obtained from a clayey loam. After the heap is well on fire, clayey turf, together with the clay of the soil, may be added to the top, and a large quantity of the charcoal mixed with burnt clay is thus prepared. At first there is great difficulty to keep the piles on fire, and strict attention is required. Thrust a stake in different places, that the fire may run through the entire heap, and if it breaks out in any of these, stop them anew with rubbish and brush, cover with earth, and make holes in a new place. When the smoke subsides, the heap is charred enough. When finished and the fire put out, store it up for use. The mixture thus prepared has been found beneficial in every instance, and is a most valuable manure, especially for roses, producing invariably an abundance of fibrous roots, clean, healthy, vigorous growth, and luxuriant blooms. (*Paul.*)

Beside charcoal, there are many other vegetable substances of great value as absorbents of the fertilizing salts and gases that would otherwise escape from animal manures. Carbonaceous matter of every sort should be provided for this purpose. Gather the leaves of trees of all kinds, including pine straw. They contain many substances necessary for the growth of the plants from which they fall, or available to other plants. Throw them into the stables and yards, moisten them and sprinkle them with the lime and salt mixture, and if kept in a damp state and turned over once or twice, they form the best manure known for all kinds of trees and shrubs, and indeed afford all the necessary constituents, organic and inorganic, of all cultivated plants.

Swamp Muck is another valuable absorbent. Gather the black earth of swamps, place in piles and let it dry out the superfluous moisture, and haul it to the compost heap or yard. Swamp muck, by its elasticity, keeps the soil light and open, and is excellent both for absorbing and retaining moisture therein. It may be reduced with ashes or lime, either of which will destroy all its naturally acid properties. The salt and lime mixture is the best and usually the cheapest for this purpose, but leached ashes mixed with carbonaceous matter have an additional part of their potash rendered soluble and available for plants, and should be used thus where obtainable.

The Lime and Salt Mixture is thus prepared. Take three bushels of unslaked lime, dissolve a bushel of salt in as little water as possible, and slake the lime therewith. If the lime will not take up all the brine at once, (which it will if good and fresh burned), add a little more of the brine daily, turning and adding until all is taken up. Keep it under cover until wanted for use. Of itself it supplies plants with chlorine, lime and soda, and acts like lime or ashes in reducing stubborn vegetable matters and correcting their acid properties.

With a load of swamp earth, mix a bushel and a half of the lime and salt mixture intimately while it is in a moderately moist state, and in thirty days it will be decomposed. Upon a layer of this earth six inches thick, spread a coat of fresh stable manure, each day covering it with ten times its quantity of prepared muck, which will absorb all the gases and salts. Let the pile accumulate until four feet high, and then turn it all over, mix it again, and cover the whole with a thick coat of prepared muck. If too dry to ferment, add water, and in three weeks it will be fit for use, and will be found equal to common stable manure, and is entirely free from insects of all kinds. In reducing composts of all kinds, the heap must be kept moist or no fermentation will be produced. Keeping it "always moist but never leached" is the way to produce a strong compost.

A thick layer of the muck should be kept also in the hog-pens and stables to absorb the urine, removing the solid manure from the latter daily, and the muck at the end of each week. Upon this muck also the house slops of all kinds should be poured, and where charcoal is not employed, a bushel every three days should be thrown into the privy to destroy the offensive gases produced. The muck, whether prepared with the above mixture, with ashes or lime, will retain all the virtues of the animal manure. Neither lime nor ashes, unless in excess, when thus combined with vegetable matters, will drive off the ammonia.

Leaf-mould, or the black surface soil of the woods, is of still more value. This is free from the acid properties of swamp muck, and may be supplied directly to most plants in the flower-garden, many of which will not flourish unless this material is present in the soil. It is of still more importance for potting plants in the green-house. For the kitchen and fruit garden it is best composted like swamp muck with fresh animal manure. It is indispensable in garden culture.

Tan-bark is another material abounding in carbon, which may, to some extent, be used as an absorbent of animal manure. It may be beneficially applied directly to strawberries, to which it answers the double purpose of mulching and manure. But the crowns of the plants must not be covered; and for all purposes it should be obtained as much decomposed as possible. Tan may be applied directly to Irish potatoes when ready to cover in the furrow. After they are dropped and the manure applied, a coat of old tan, composted with ashes or the lime and salt mixture, may be given, and finish planting by covering this with earth. It improves the yield materially and the quality also, as all carbonaceous matters do. Where swamp muck or leaf-mould can be obtained, it is hardly worth while to use tan as an absorbent of animal manures.

It is not of sufficient value to be worth hauling far. In trenching, it may, with other coarse matters, be mixed with the *bottom* soil to lighten its texture and act as a reservoir of moisture. For corn it may, after composting with ashes, be mixed with the surface soil, when, if not in excess, it will be of some service to the crop.

It is very difficult to reduce, but if kept moist, the lime and salt mixture will do it. It may be strewed in the stock-yard six or eight inches thick, and sprinkled pretty thickly with the mixture. The treading of the stock will mix it. Let the whole be turned over in a moist state once or twice, and in the course of the winter it will become a valuable application to the plants that do well with fresh manure. There are abundant elements of fertility in tan, but it is more difficult to render them available than with any other vegetable substance; and it is, upon the whole, quite a dangerous article to experiment with. Reduced thoroughly by composting it with stable manure, using in this case no lime, and then mixed with decayed leaves and plenty of sharp sand, it makes a tolerable compost for growing those plants which require peat, such as Azaleas and Rhododendrons. Tan, properly composted, will prove of most use in light soils deficient in vegetable matter, and when less decomposed, for opening the texture of close, heavy clays.

Decayed chips, saw-dust, shavings, etc., are best applied to Irish potatoes, as directed in the case of tan-bark. They should be covered with soil to promote a more speedy decay. They have much the nature of tan-bark without its acidity, and may be likewise, when somewhat decayed, composted with stable manure and used as peat. All these substances are valuable for burning clay or for charring, and then to be incorporated with urine, night soil, or superphosphate of lime. In the case of tan-bark, this is undoubtedly the safest and most profitable way to use it.

Green Manures are various crops, raised to turn into the ground in a fresh state for fertilizing it. For this purpose all the weeds of the garden should be employed while green, unless they are thrown to the pigs. Over any vacant spots in the garden not wished to be used in autumn, rye or barley can be sown, which will keep the soil from washing, and when large enough may be either cut for feed, or turned into the soil as the plots are wanted for use. Spinach should be sown in considerable quantities, as it grows all winter, and, spaded into the soil in spring, adds a good deal to its fertility. The seed can be saved in any quantity with little trouble.

But the most fertilizing plants for this purpose are leguminous plants, like the Cow-pea, as they draw nourishment largely from the atmosphere, and afford a great amount of foliage for turning under as manure. This class of plants is also quite rich in ammonia. This mode of manuring was practised by the ancient Romans, and is specially adapted to warm climates where vegetation is rapid and luxuriant. A good vetch that would make its growth in the winter months to be turned into the soil in the spring would be a most desirable addition to our cultivated plants. The spotted Lucerne, (Californian clover), is the best plant for this purpose on soils already pretty good.

Animal Manures.—This is the most important class, and the greatest attention should be paid to collecting, preserving, and economizing them. All animal manures, when compared with the preceding class, are more rich in nitrogen, and more easily decomposed and rendered soluble; but though the effect of this class of substances is much more obvious, it is not so lasting.

Its value consists in part of certain volatile and soluble substances, which, in the common mode of preserving manure, are dissipated in the air or washed away by heavy rains. In this climate it is necessary to shelter manure from the sun and rain. All animal matter is either directly or indirectly derived from vegetable substances; hence, every portion of the same that can be rendered soluble is a valuable food for plants. Among the most important animal substances employed as manures are urine, and dung of all kinds. The first of these is almost invariably wasted, though in the case of the cow, it is of more value than the solid excrements. It should be carefully saved by bedding the yard and stables with swamp muck, wood earth, or some other absorbent. Urine is particularly rich in ammonia. This may be absorbed by the muck or by sprinkling the floor of stables and the manure heap frequently with fine charcoal or gypsum; this substance, sprinkled upon the floors of stables, forms a compound like the urate of commerce, so powerful that 500 pounds will amply manure an acre. If you can obtain no other absorbent, tan-bark is not without its value, but the weeds, sweepings of walks, and other refuse of the garden, particularly leaf-mould and the dark top-soil of pastures, are to be preferred. Urine may be diluted with three times its bulk of water and permitted to grow stale, and be applied at night or in moist weather directly to the growing crops.

The principal animal manures are those of the horse, the hog, the cow, and the sheep. Of these horse manure is most valuable in its fresh state. That of the hog comes next, then that of the ox, while the cow is at the bottom of the list, because most of the enriching substances in her food go to the formation of milk, leaving the manure comparatively weakened. The richer the food given to animals, the more powerful is the manure. If animal manures are employed in a fresh state, they should be mixed intimately with the soil, and given to such coarse feeding crops as corn and the garden pea. But nearly all plants do better if the manure is composted and fully fermented before use. Pig manure, used alone, is considered pernicious to the growth of the cabbage and turnip tribe, and gives an unpleasant taste to many other vegetables, but composted with muck or mould, it is much more beneficial as well as more durable.

In managing animal manures, decomposition must be promoted—the volatile parts must be preserved from dissipation in the air, and the soluble portions from being washed out by rains. That it may ferment, it must be kept in a body, that heat may be generated and its natural moisture retained, while beneath it a layer of some absorbent substance should be placed, to receive and retain its soluble parts, and as fast as it is thrown from the stables, it should be covered with layers of muck to retain the ammonia. Horse manure, especially, should not be exposed at all; it begins to heat and lose ammonia almost immediately, as may be perceived by the smell. Mix it with other manures and cover it with absorbents as soon as possible. Keep the stable bedded with muck, and over this a good bed of leaves.

The Manure of Birds is richer than that of any other animals; as the solid and liquid excrements are mixed together, it is particularly rich in nitrogen and the phosphates. Three or four hundred weight of the manure of pigeons, fowls, turkeys, etc., is of equal value with from fourteen to eighteen loads of animal manure.

Peruvian Guano is a manure of this class. It is the manure of sea-birds, which has accumulated in tropical latitudes where it seldom or never rains. These birds feed upon fish entirely; hence, the manure is remarkably rich in nitrogen. Guano is this substance with the water evaporated, and contains from 7 to 18 per cent of ammonia. When it can be bought pure and the freight is not over 25 per cent on its cost, it is for many crops one of the cheapest manures to be obtained, as it is so easily applied—the labor of applying other manures often approaching the price of guano. It is well to apply about two hundred weight per acre with one-half the usual quantity of other manure. Guano should never, in a fresh state, come in contact with seeds or the roots of plants, as it is sure to destroy their vitality.

The great value of guano is in forming liquid manure; one pound of guano to five gallons of water applied once a week will add wonderfully to the growth of any plants watered with this mixture. For very delicate plants twice the above quantity of water should be given. If guano is not to be had, the manure of fowls is a good substitute. This liquid is especially valuable in the flower-garden. It must be poured upon the roots, and not upon the leaves or collars of the plants. On lawns, a pound sprinkled upon each square rod will restore their verdure. A great advantage of supplying guano, is that no seeds of weeds are scattered in the soil.

The Peruvian is the only guano rich in ammonia. There are other guanos which contain little ammonia, but are rich in phosphates, some of them as much so as bone phosphate of lime. Among the best of these are the Columbian and Sombrero varieties. If these are finely ground and mixed in equal proportions with pulverized Peruvian guano, the mixture is really more valuable as a manure for most plants and soils than the same amount of pure Peruvian, for ammonia, to be useful, requires the phosphates to be present, and the cost is much less. The mixture contains a sufficient proportion of ammonia for its phosphates, and its effect is more lasting. If the phosphatic guano is by the addition of sulphuric acid converted into a superphosphate, its value is greatly increased. This mixture is better than the Peruvian guano for maintaining the beauty of lawns, and for the whole cabbage tribe it is greatly superior.

Bones are, when properly prepared, still more useful than most of the phosphatic guanos. They contain sixty-six parts of earthy matter, mostly phosphate of lime; and thirty-four parts of gelatine. Gelatine is rich in nitrogen, so that in bones are united the most desirable organic and inorganic manures. Applied whole, bones decompose too slowly to be of much value, and would be greatly in the way of tillage. They may be broken small with a sledge-hammer or crowbar, in a large wooden mortar, lined at the bottom with a thick iron plate. When beaten small, the fine dust can be sifted out, and the remainder moistened and thrown up in heaps, to ferment a few months. Bones can be dissolved by boiling them in strong lye, or, better, by mixing them with wet, unleached ashes, and when dissolved and dried by mixing with woods earth, burnt clay, ashes, or sand, can be applied broadcast or in the drills. The best way to treat bones is to dissolve them in sulphuric acid, forming superphosphate of lime. A carboy of sulphuric acid, costing about four dollars, at wholesale, in the cities, and containing one hundred and sixty pounds, will dissolve three hundred to four hundred and eighty pounds of bones. The bones should be previously ground or finely broken. Put about sixty pounds of bone-dust or phosphatic guano in a tub, and add water enough to wet the mass, say about 40 lbs. See that it is well moistened. Add 20 lbs. of sulphuric acid, which is usually enough, and briskly stir the mass. If, after standing a day or two the bones are not sufficiently dissolved, add more acid and water, pouring it on gradually, and after a little the bones will entirely dissolve and form a pasty mass with the acid and water. When the mass is dried, it will assume the appearance of a granulated powder, and it is then fit for use. It may also be used diluted with thirty times its bulk of water as a liquid manure, but it is more convenient to mix it with saw-dust, woods earth, or fine charcoal, and apply it dry. Never mix a superphosphate with lime, ashes, or any alkali, for by so doing it is converted again into a phosphate, and your labor and sulphuric acid are lost. One cwt. of bones with, say half the amount of sulphuric acid, will be enough for an acre.

The acid has converted the bones into a superphosphate of lime, which is very soluble, and is readily taken up by the plant. This is the most valuable of all manures for the turnip, and the quantity needed for the acre is so little that the expense is less than that of almost any other application.

The addition of guano renders it still more valuable. It may be used three days after its preparation, but improves if kept longer. Fifteen bushels of compost may be prepared from 1¾ bushels of bones and the absorbents required; and two bushels of this applied to an acre will, for the present, equal in effect 16 bushels of half-inch bones. (*Lindley.*) If bones are coarsely broken and mixed with hot stable dung in the formation of a hot-bed, they will generally be found perfectly fine when the material of the bed is removed. They can also, at any time, be further broken up by composting with hot stable manure, covering the mass with absorbents to retain the ammonia of the gelatine and manure.

Night Soil and chamber slops should be composted as before directed with charcoal, or the black mould from woods. Gypsum may be added to the mixture; all smell is thus destroyed, and an offensive nuisance is converted into a valuable application to any crop. Where charcoal is freely used, this substance becomes perfectly inodorous. Guano and poudrette are the best possible manures for the cabbage tribe and other plants that need phosphates and nitrogen. Both these manures are exceedingly powerful, but their effects do not last beyond one season. The fertilizing properties exist in the right proportions to be taken up at once by the plants, and nearly all their nutritive properties are exhausted the season they are applied. If in a hole or dry ditch are deposited all the leaves or vegetable refuse that can be collected, and over this is poured daily the house slops, and all smell prevented by the timely application of charcoal or woods earth, a compost is formed exactly similar in its constituents to farm-yard manure, and containing all the eight substances by which plants are artificially fed. (*Lindley*.)

Liquid Manure.—Almost any manure may be applied to the soil with benefit in a liquid state. It generally implies urine or the drainings of dung heaps and stables, chiefly consisting of urine and the dissolved excrements of animals. Diluted more or less as required, it can be applied about once a week to plants in any stage of *growth*, and is particularly useful to those grown in pots. The soil should not be oversaturated with it, and it should be used alternately with pure water. Do not give it to plants in a state of rest.

There are several other substances which, when they can be obtained, should be carefully applied. Among these, the most available are the offal of slaughtered animals, their carcasses, hair, and bristles, leather, refuse from the tanners and shoemakers, woollen rags, fish, blood, etc. All these contain the elements required by growing plants in a very concentrated state. The hair, bristles, etc., may be applied directly to any crop. These matters are very powerful, and a small quantity will suffice. Slaughter-house offal, and the carcasses of any animals that may have died, should be buried deeply in a pit, with absorbents beneath, and covered with muck or loam. In a year it will become a most valuable manure.

The following table from Boussingault gives a comprehensive view of the proportion of nitrogen contained in the most common manures, and of their quality and equivalents, referred to farm-yard dung as the standard. Thus ten lbs. of fresh cotton-seed cake is equal in value to one hundred lbs. of fresh or wet farm-yard dung, as far as the nitrogen in each is concerned. To form a perfect table of equivalents, the phosphates, potash, etc., must be also taken into consideration. The ammonia merely indexes the value. As a manure it is worth in the markets of the world about 14 cents a pound, according to Prof. S. W. Johnson. Insoluble phosphoric acid is valued by him at $4\frac{1}{3}$ cts., and soluble phosphoric acid about $10\frac{1}{2}$ cents per pound for application to ordinary crops. Potash is not generally so deficient in soils as to be worth its market price to be used as a manure, unless in the form of wood ashes. Phosphoric acid in a soluble state is the only substance that approaches ammonia in money value for use as a manure.

	Water per 100.	Azote in 100.		Quality according to state.		Equivalent according to state.	
		Dry.	Wet.	Dry.	Wet.	Dry.	Wet.
Farm-yard dung	79.3	1.95	0.41	100	100	100	100
Dung from an Inn yard	60.6	2.08	0.79	107	107	94	51
Dung water	99.6	1.54	0.06	78	2	127	68
Withered leaves of carrots	70.9	2.94	0.85	150	212.5	66	47
do. do. do. oak	25.0	1.57	1.18	80	293	125	34
Oyster shells	17.9	0.40	0.32	20	80	488	125
Oak saw-dust	26.0	0.72	0.54	36	135	256	74
Oil cake of cotton seed	11.0	4.52	4.02	231	1000	32	10
Solid cow dung	85.9	2.30	0.32	117	80	84	125
Urine of cows	88.3	3.80	0.44	194	110	51	91
Mixed cow dung	84.3	2.59	0.41	132	102.5	75	98
Solid horse dung	75.3	2.21	0.55	113	137.5	88	73
Horse urine	79.1	12.50	2.61	641	652.5	15½	14½
Mixed (horse dung)	75.4	3.02	2.71	154	185	66	54
Pig dung	81.4	3.37	0.63	172	157.5	58	63
Sheep dung	63.0	2.99	1.11	153	277.5	65	36
Poudrette of Belloni	12.5	4.40	3.85	225	962	44	10½
Pigeon's dung	9.6	9.02	8.30	462	2075	21½	5
Guano from England	19.6	6.20	5.00	323	1247	31½	80
Idem	23.4	7.05	5.40	361	1349	28	74
do. imported from France	11.3	15.73	13.95	807	3487	12½	28½
Dried muscular flesh	8.5	14.25	13.04	730	3260	13½	3
Liquid blood	81.0		2.95	795	3045	12½	3¼
Fresh bones	30.0		5.31		1426		7½
Feathers	12.9	17.61	15.34	903	3835	11	2½
Cow hair flock	8.9	15.12	13.78	775	3445	13	3
Woollen rags	11.3	20.26	17.98	1029	4495	9½	2¼
Horn shavings	9.0	15.78	14.26	809	2590	12½	3
Wood soot	5.6	1.31	1.15	67	287.5	149	35
Vegetable mould		1.03		53		189	33

Composts.—The composting of manure should take place, as a general thing, as fast as it is made. In the garden, out of sight, there should be a compost heap for receiving all kinds of rubbish that can have the least value as fertilizers. Make a shallow excavation of a square or oblong form, with the bottom sloping to one end. Into this collect the litter and sweepings of the yards, decayed vegetables of all kinds, brine, soapsuds, and slops from the house, woollen rags, leaves, green weeds, and garden refuse. After it has accumulated a little, turn it over, adding a little of the salt and lime mixture, and keep the whole inodorous, by covering it with rich mould or black earth from the woods. If the heap is formed entirely of vegetable materials, ashes or lime should be added; but if it contain animal matter, they would do harm by setting free the ammonia. The heap should not be deep, but, like all other manure heaps, should be kept "always moist, but never leached," by the addition of liquids from the house and kitchen. If this compost be for a sandy soil, the addition of clay would be very beneficial.

Composting is the best way of rendering available all sorts of refuse organic matter, but do not introduce those antagonistic in their effects. For instance, never compost lime with animal matters which, in their decomposition, form ammonia.

Special Composts are prepared for different species of plants, and they are of great utility in floriculture. Composts for plants in pots are made up of loam, leaf-mould, sand, peat, and manure. The loam is the decomposed turf from a rich, old pasture, which should not rest upon clay, and the upper three inches only are taken. It should lie one year before using. Leaf-mould is the dark surface soil of the woods, formed from decayed leaves. Sand should not be from roads, but fine surface or river sand. The manure is unfit to use if less than a year old, and improves by frequent turning, and lying two years. Peat is the black soil from swamps, mingled with very fine sand. It should be exposed a year and frequently turned before using. Black woods earth, mingled with one-third pure sand, is the best substitute. The proportions of the most common composts are given in the following table:

Number of Compost.	Loam.	Leaf-mould.	Sand.	Peat.	Manure.
1	1			3	
2	3	2	1		1
3	3	1	1		1
4	1			2	
5	4	4	1		
6	4		1		1
7	3	2	1		
8	4	2	1		
9	1	1		1	
10	1	1	1		1

CHAPTER VI.

ROTATION OF CROPS.

The same crops cannot be grown from year to year upon the same soil without decreasing in productiveness. All plants more or less exhaust the soil, but not in the same degree, nor in the same manner; hence, as different plants appropriate different substances, the rotation of crops has considerable influence in retaining the fertility of a soil. If the same kind of plants is continued upon the same soil, only a portion of the constituents of the manure applied is used; while by a judicious rotation everything, in the soil or in the manure, suitable for vegetable food, is taken up and appropriated by the crop. However plentiful manure may be, a succession of exhausting crops should not be grown upon the same bed, not only because abundance is no excuse for want of economy, but because manure freshly applied is not so immediately beneficial as those remains of organized matter which by long continuance in the soil have become impalpably divided and diffused through its texture, and of which each succeeding crop consumes a portion.

Some crops are so favorable to weeds, that if continued long upon the same bed, the labor of cultivating them is much increased, while if raised but once in a place and followed by a cleaning crop, the weeds are easily kept under. Besides, many crops planted continually in the same soil are more liable to be attacked by the insects and parasites which are the peculiar enemies of those plants.

Many insects injurious to plants deposit their eggs in the soil which produced the plants they have infested, ready to commit their depredations upon the succeeding crop; but if this is changed to a distant locality, they often perish for want of their proper food. So, many parasites leave their seeds or spores in the soil, to the increased injury of the succeeding crop, if of the same species.

Again, different plants derive their principal nourishment from different depths of soil. The roots of plants exhaust only the portions of soil with which they come in contact. Perpendicular rooted plants throw out few side roots, and derive most of their nourishment from a considerable depth, while fibrous-rooted plants seek their food near the surface. Plants of the same species extend their roots in a similar direction, and occupy and exhaust the same strata of earth.

Different plants by means of their roots act differently upon the physical nature of the soil. Surface roots spread abroad their tufted fibers, which in their decay break up and lighten the surface soil, while the roots of clover have a somewhat similar effect upon the deeper strata.

The most exhausting crops are, in general, those which are allowed to perfect their seeds, as they extract from the soil all the essentials of the plant, from the root to the seed. The seeds of many species draw from the soil more largely its ammonia, phosphates, etc., than the total amount extracted in the formation of all other parts of the plant. Root crops are generally less exhausting, and plants cultivated for their leaves are usually still less so.

A rotation was formerly thought necessary from an idea that each plant throws off from its roots into the soil certain matters which are injurious to others of the same species afterward grown upon the soil. It was also thought that there were some tribes of plants, the fig for instance, of which the acrid juices from the root injured the soil and the plants grown near them, while of others, as legumes, the sweet juices were beneficial to the soil and the adjacent or succeeding crops. These views are not now considered tenable.

Enough has been stated to show the necessity of a change of crops, and the following are found the best rules to observe in practice:

1st.—Crops of the same species, and even of the same natural order, should not succeed each other.

2d.—Plants with perpendicular roots should succeed those with spreading and superficial roots, and *vice versa*.

3d.—Crops which occupy the soil for several years, like asparagus, rhubarb, etc., should be followed by those of short duration.

4th.—Two crops alike favorable to the growth of weeds should not occupy the soil in succession.

5th.—Crops abstracting largely from the soil the sulphates, phosphates, and nitrogenous principles, should not follow each other immediately, but be succeeded by those which draw less from the soil and more from the atmosphere. These exhausting crops should follow and be followed by those which bear and will profit by heavy manuring.

6th.—Plants grown for their roots or bulbs should not follow those grown for the same purpose, and still less should plants grown for their seeds follow each other directly in succession.

The following are found in practice to be convenient crops to succeed each other in rotation, beginning after an application of manure, viz.: Onions, lettuce, cabbage, carrots, manure; or, turnips, celery, peas, potatoes, manure.

The following is also a very good rotation:

1. The cabbage tribe to be followed by

2. Alliaceous plants, as onions, leeks, etc., to be followed by legumes, as beans or peas. Peas may be followed the same year with celery.

3. Tap-rooted plants, as carrots, beets, parsnips.

4. Surface roots, as onions, potatoes, turnips.

5. Celery, endive, lettuce, spinach, etc.

Celery is excellent to precede asparagus, onions, cauliflowers, or turnips; old asparagus beds for carrots, potatoes, etc.; strawberries and raspberries for the cabbage tribe; cabbage for the tap-rooted plants; potatoes for the cabbage tribe.

In these rotations it is not necessary to apply manure to every crop. For the bulbous roots, as the onion, and for plants cultivated for their leaves, as spinach and asparagus, the ground can scarcely be too rich; and the bulk of the manures may be applied to them and the cabbage and turnip crops, while for plants raised for seed it is best that the foliage should not be stimulated into too great luxuriance by fresh manuring.

In practice these rules should as far as possible be followed, but it is often necessary to vary from them or let a part of the soil lie, for a time, idle. Rotations in gardening become less necessary if the ground is trenched deeply and manured highly. Vacant ground thus treated may be filled at once with any crop ready for planting.

To get the highest possible results from a garden, there must be not only a general rotation of crops year by year, but a number of sub-successions each year, as fast as the crops are removed. One-fourth of an acre thoroughly manured and kept perfectly free from weeds, upon which a constant succession of crops is kept up, will yield more than an acre managed in the common way. It is not, however, always necessary to wait until the crop occupying the soil is removed before another is put in. Simultaneous cropping, that is, making two crops occupy the ground at the same time, as in field culture the cowpea in corn-fields, can often be resorted to in the kitchen garden. In the fruit garden, De Candolle says the vine and the peach can with advantage be grown together, the light shade of the peach not injuring the vines.

Directions to meet all circumstances cannot be given, still the following hints may be suggestive of the best methods to secure in the kitchen garden satisfactory results.

For instance, in the fall a portion of the garden may be occupied with spinach; this should be heavily manured, and may keep the ground until time to plant melons and other vines, when just enough of the ground may be deeply dug to form the melon hills, and the crop will be ready to remove before the melons begin to run. The melon crop may be followed by one of turnips. All such plants as radish, lettuce, and other small salads, need take up no room; they can, any of them, be raised between the potato beds or drills, or between melon hills, rows of corn, etc., and they will come to perfection before the potato or other crops require the ground. Radishes can be raised between the rows in the beds of all kinds of plants that are slow in coming up, as carrots, parsnips, etc., and will be ready to remove by the time the others come up.

Any vacant spot that occurs early in summer should be occupied with plantings of extra early or sweet corn, potatoes, beets, kidney beans, for preserving for winter use, and cucumbers for pickling. Those coming later in the season may be occupied by sweet potatoes until July, then corn, cow-peas, or rutabaga turnips. Where the early onions grow, both in the alleys and in the centre of the bed, before much of the crop is removed, may be planted with late cabbages or Siberian kale. Cabbages will head if the winter sorts be planted as late as the early part of August, and Early Yorks put out in September, if in rich, moist ground, and well cultivated. Sweet corn may be planted until August. Still later, every unoccupied corner should be covered with turnips and winter radishes, which may cover nearly the whole garden, being sown in drills between the rows of plants not yet quite ready to be removed. After the frost has come, any vacant spaces should be immediately sown with spinach, onions, and other crops for early spring use, or with barley or rye for the cow. The secret of successful cultivation, says Downing, is an abundant supply of manure. A small extent of ground well manured and trenched deeply, by these sub-successions, will produce an enormous amount of vegetables, while only the same surface needs to be hoed, manured, and kept free from weeds, as if it produced but one crop. To be sure, more manure and more labor are needed, but nothing like the amount which would be required to produce the same crops without these sub-successions. Many other sub-successions will occur to a thoughtful gardener, but to derive the full benefit of them the grounds should be trenched at least thirty inches deep when the garden is formed.

Profits of Gardening.—The results of the above mode of procedure, in the case of the garden of the Retreat for the Insane, at Utica, New York, were published by Dr. Brigham. The land was good and yearly manured. The product was as follows on one and one-fourth acres of land:—1100 heads lettuce, large; 1400 heads cabbage, large; 700 bunches radishes; 250 bunches asparagus; 300 bunches rhubarb; 14 bushels pods marrowfat peas; 40 bushels beans; sweet corn, 3 plantings, 419 dozen; summer squash, 715 dozen; squash peppers, 45 dozen; cucumbers, 756 dozen; cucumber pickles, 7 barrels; beets, 147 bushels; carrots, 29 bushels; parsnips, 26 bushels; onions, 120 bushels; turnips, 80 bushels; early potatoes, 35 bushels; tomatoes, 40 bushels; winter squash, 7 wagon loads; celery, 500 heads—all worth 621 dollars in Utica market, but supplied one hundred and thirty persons with all they could consume. Only one man was required to do all the necessary labor.

The supply of Northern markets with early fruits and vegetables is becoming yearly more and more profitable to all points which have direct steam communication with their great cities. Charleston, Savannah, and Norfolk, now ship very largely asparagus, peas, snap beans, cucumbers,

Lima beans, squashes, okra, and of fruits the apple and peach. The pear and the Delaware grape will be still more profitable in time. Chicago, Cincinnati, St. Louis, etc., will soon largely receive similar supplies by railroad from Southern points.

Forwarding Early Crops.—Early crops in the open air should be planted in a sheltered situation, on a dark-colored, silicious soil. It may be brought to a proper state by the admixture of sand and charcoal. Crops, on the contrary, may be retarded by planting in a border sheltered from the sun, and of a lighter color and more aluminous. There are many plants which do much better if sown in the fall. Rhubarb, parsley, etc., come up more freely if suffered to be in the ground all winter. Potatoes, too, may be early planted, and if they come up, should be sheltered by a covering of straw or litter, added from time to time to keep them from frost. Cabbage, cauliflower, broccoli, etc., sown in autumn and transplanted, may be kept out all winter in boxes made by nailing four pieces of boards together, eight inches wide. Cut the pieces 12 inches long at the bottom, and 10 at the top; nail them together at the corners. After the frosts begin to be severe, throw in a handful of loose straw, which will prevent the sudden freezing and thawing of the plants. Great care should be taken to produce early crops, as they are less liable to be injured by insects or weeds, and very much increase the satisfaction of gardening. Early plants may be obtained by sowing them in a box set in a warm window, or may be raised in autumn and protected in winter in a cold frame or pit, or grown any time during winter in a hot-bed for those more delicate, or in a cold frame under glass for the hardier kinds. Such plants, when set out in the spring, need to be gradually hardened, and then require shading a few days until established. Radishes sown under glass without heat early in January are generally fit for use early in March. But to forward plants with any success requires suitable structures for the purpose.

CHAPTER VII.

HOT-BEDS, COLD-FRAMES, AND PITS.

Frames or Hot-Beds are most usually employed for forwarding plants. The frame for general use has from three to five sashes, (see fig. 3), and is made for convenience about four and a half or five feet wide, and the

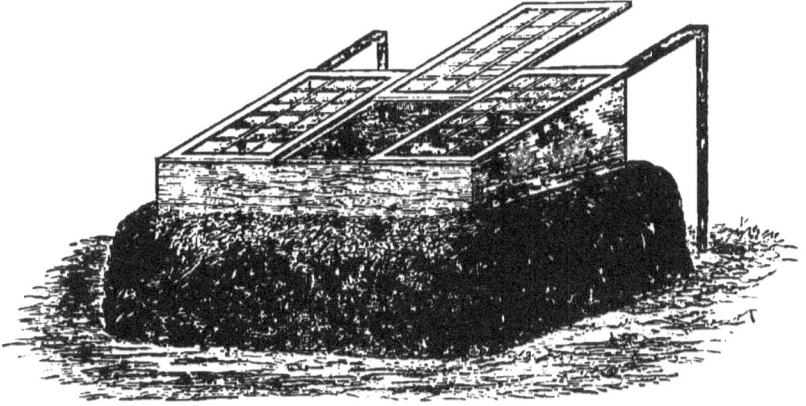

Fig. 3.—HOT-BED AND FRAME.

length depends on the number of sashes, which are usually about forty inches wide. Use the smallest glass you can obtain, certainly not over seven by nine; a smaller size is preferable, as it is not so liable to be broken, and can be more readily repaired. These sashes are made without cross-bars, the glass overlapping like the shingles of a house, and resting on bars extending lengthwise of the sash. The lap of each pane of glass need not be over half an inch, and if the glass is set in the sash when freshly painted with two coats of paint, no puttying is necessary, if the sash is well made. The frame should be made of inch and a half plank as high again in the back as in the front, to give the sashes the proper slope to the sun, and sufficient inclination to carry off the wet. The front, of course, is towards the south. Let the back and front be nailed to corner posts, so as to admit the ends to fit in neatly, which ends are to be made fast to the posts by common carriage bolts, in order that the frame may be taken asunder to store when not in use. All joints in the sides and ends should be tongued and grooved to prevent the admission of cold air or the loss of warm air from the bed. Each end should be made an inch and a half higher than the back and front, and grooved out one-half its thickness, to permit the sash to slide and leave the other half to support the outside. At the corner, also, of each sash, let another piece of scantling be placed, and on the top of these, narrow strips the length of the sash are to be nailed, for the sash to slide upon. Between the sashes, nail an inch strip a little thicker than the sash to the narrow plank on which they slide, and put on the sash; and upon this strip, in cold weather, lay another narrow strip, projecting over the sash a little, to cover the joint and keep out the cold. Provide for the bed a full supply of good horse manure from the stable, mixed with moist litter, preferring that which is fresh, moist, and full of heat. If there is not sufficient litter in the mass the heat will not be lasting; so as a substitute add oak-leaves or tan-bark. There should be at least one-third litter in the heap. Shake it up and mix it well together, sprinkling with water if dry, and throw it into a compact heap to ferment. In two or three days if warm, or if cold in a week, turn it over, and if dry and musty in any part, water again. Let it be two or three days longer, and then work it over thoroughly, as before, and water if necessary. In a dry, sheltered situation opening to the south, mark out the dimensions of the bed, making it fully a foot longer and wider than the frame each way. Throw out the earth about ten or twelve inches deep. Then begin to form the bed by spreading a thin layer of the prepared manure upon the ground, mixing the long and short well together. Upon this spread other layers mixed in the same manner, beating each layer with the back of the fork, but not too heavily, to keep it level, and equally firm throughout. Stakes should be placed at the corners to work to. The edges should be kept true and the corners firm, to do which the outside of each layer must be first laid down, and to make the manure keep in place a proper admixture of long litter is required. Continue until the bed is three feet above the surface, then spread the fine manure that is left, evenly over the top, and water freely. As soon as finished let the frame and glass be put on with care, and keep them close until the heat rises and a steam appears upon the glass. As soon as the heat rises, give air at noon each day, but keep closed in the evening and at night, unless the heat is very violent, when a little air should be given. In three days, if the manure was sufficiently moist, the bed will be ready for use. If it has settled unequally, raise the frame and level the surface. Place in the frame six inches of fine, dark-colored, sandy garden-soil, spread it evenly, and put on the sash. When warmed through, sow in pots plunged in the mould, or in small drills from one-eighth of an inch to an inch deep, varying in depth with the size of the seeds, and cover by sifting fine earth on the surface. Water gently by sprinkling with tepid water through the fine rose of a watering pot. When the plants appear, they should have air every day freely (unless absolutely freezing) which will bring them up strong, and prevent their dropping off by excess of confined moisture. There are very few days which will not permit opening the bed, not by sliding down the sashes, but by raising them at the back, holding them open by a triangular block to slip in so that they can be opened from two to five inches. Open the bed in the middle of the day, as above, but close early that the plants may not become chilled. During warm, gentle rains, the sash should be opened, but closed very carefully during cold or heavy washing storms. About 60° is the proper temperature; it should not rise above 75°. Such a bed as this is invaluable for striking cuttings of all kinds, in which case there should be an inch of clear river sand or charcoal spread over the surface. Annuals of all kinds for the flower garden, tomatoes, peppers, cabbage and lettuce plants, etc., will be ready, if the bed is made in January, for transplanting quite as soon as they can be removed with safety. Make the bed six or eight weeks before the plants will be required. The quantity of manure required to form a hot-bed varies with the season and external temperature, a larger bulk being needed in January than at a later season. Even a small bed should have the mass not less than five feet long by four feet wide, to maintain the proper heat. If the soil whereon it stands is clayey the whole bed should be made above ground, as the water settling in the trench would check the heat of the entire bed. If the bed is made early in the season it will require the application of fresh materials at the sides or " linings " to keep it at the proper temperature.

The best substitute for stable manure in forming a hot-bed is spent tan, but to keep it in its position a plank bin or a brick pit is required. It takes more time for the heat to rise, but it is longer continued, milder and more manageable than stable manure, and is quite sufficient for a seed bed. A little slightly fermented stable manure is needed to be added to the center of the bed, as it will start fermentation sooner.

In sowing the bed let the more tender plants, as egg-plants, peppers, etc., be sown under the same sash, and separated by a thin plank partition under the cross-bar from the rest of the frame. The finer and more delicate seeds will require the sash above them to be shaded until the plants appear, or each pot may be separately covered until the seeds are up. At night, if cold, cover the bed with plank shutters, old carpets, or mats. Gradually, as the plants grow strong, accustom them to the air as the season grows mild. This can be done by opening the frames entirely during the day, and leaving them exposed during mild nights, or by transferring them to the cold frame.

Cold Frames are made just like those for the hot-bed, only the box need not be over 15 inches high at the back, and are excellent for wintering nearly hardy plants of all kinds, and also for forwarding the more hardy plants, as hardy annuals, cabbage, lettuce, etc. Indeed, they are quite as indispensable as the hot-bed, and less expensive, as they require no manure, but rest directly on the soil. They are also of great service in hardening off hot-bed stock, which should be transferred to them before it is set out in the open ground. In very severe weather, the heat may be kept in by earthing up the sides and covering the sash with mats during the night. Air should always be given when the weather will admit, or the plants will grow up yellow and spindling. In managing frames, the secret of success is to give plenty of air. Plants raised in cold frames are generally more hardy and desirable than those from a hot-bed, unless the latter are repotted early, and when reëstablished, transferred to the cold frame, to harden them. A cold frame or pit covered with tiffany (a prepared thin cotton cloth) is even better than one covered with glass, for the purpose of hardening off young stock.

Frames of all kinds should be painted of a light color, every year, both for the preservation of the wood and for the destruction of insects and their eggs, that are concealed in their crevices and angles. A frame for raising seedlings or striking cuttings need not be over 18 inches deep at the back, to 9 inches in front, as it is important to keep the seedlings near the glass.

Pits.—Fig. 4 shows a section of a lean-to pit, in which tall plants may be set upon the bottom, while a stage may be put in to bring small plants near the glass. All pits should be built of brick, and those with the walls built hollow above the surface are preferable. In a pit 6 feet wide the back should be about 15 to 18 inches higher than the front. Pits are also useful in protecting delicate plants in summer, from heavy rains and scorching suns, and for bringing up many seedlings in the spring that do not require artificial heat. In all cases ample provision must be made for drainage, as plants will not flourish in damp, confined air. When a pit is desired merely to *preserve* plants during the winter, it is better that the glass should face rather to the north, that is from north-east to north-west, in order that growth may not be excited, and the plants thus kept perfectly at rest during the winter. If the pit faces any other quarter the air within gets heated and the plants keep on growing late in the autumn, are stimulated into temporary growth too early in the spring, and are much more in danger of destruction by frost. The pit should be kept as dry as possible and ventilated daily when the frost is not too severe, and to protect the roots of plants from frost and to prevent the necessity of frequent waterings, the pots should be plunged in some dry material, as sand or tan-bark. Very little water should be given to plants in their dormant state, for they cannot assimilate it. Many plants, as geraniums, etc., in such a pit will require but one or two waterings during an entire winter. Plants thus managed will endure a very low temperature, and start into more vigorous growth in spring.

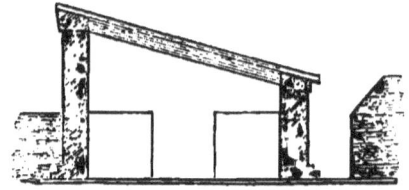
Fig. 4.—SECTION OF PIT.

At night, if cold, and during severe weather by day, it will be necessary to cover the glass with mats or shutters, to prevent the frost from penetrating and the heat from being lost by radiation.

CHAPTER VIII.

GARDEN IMPLEMENTS.

The principal implements employed in gardening are the following:

1. Implements for Preparing and Operating upon the Soil.

SUBSOIL PLOW.—This is of great service in large gardens; it answers as a tolerable substitute for the spade in trench-

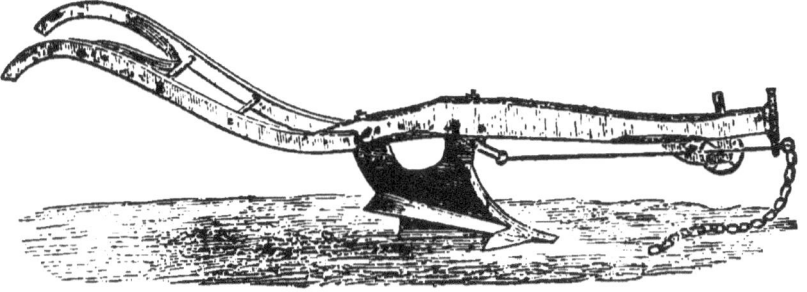

Fig. 5.—SUBSOIL PLOW.

ing for orchards and market gardens, doing the work more cheaply and expeditiously, but not so well. It requires a powerful team to manage it. One form is shown in fig. 5.

THE ONE-HORSE TURNING PLOW is very efficient in deeply stirring the soil among plantations of trees and the larger garden crops. The whiffletrees should be short that the trees and plants may not be injured. A strong animal is required, and the plow must not come too near the trees and plants. The common plantation plows are also quite useful in garden culture.

The Cultivator supersedes in a great degree the necessity of hand-hoeing among the main crops in market gardens. By passing it over once a week between the rows, all the hoeing required is a narrow strip of a few inches in the row. The first working of the season should be with a narrow plow, to stir the soil deeply; then keep it light with the cultivator. The teeth are made of various shapes. That given in figure 6 has harrow teeth.

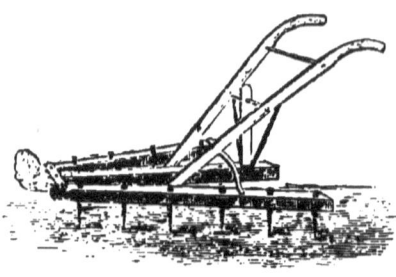

Fig. 6.—HARROW-TOOTHED CULTIVATOR.

The Wheelbarrow is indispensable in the smallest garden. In carrying manures, applying composts, moving soils, and gathering crops, it is of constant service. The handles and frame should be of tough wood, but the sides and bottom may be of poplar or any light material.

The Garden Roller. (Fig. 7.)—This consists of two cast iron sections one foot in width and twenty inches in diameter, with an iron handle. Weights can be attached to the inside to make it heavier. Being made in two sections, the earth is not scraped up while turning around. It is very useful in keeping grass lawns smooth and velvety, and is valuable to follow the putting in of all seeds in sandy soils. Lawns should be rolled when the ground is moderately soft with rain, after each mowing. A tolerable substitute, for a small plot of grass, is a

Fig. 7.—GARDEN ROLLER.

Turf Beetle, made of plank three inches thick, eighteen inches long, and ten wide, with a handle inserted in the centre, (fig. 8). With this the lawn should be beaten, when the turf is set, to a perfect level. If the handle is slightly inclined towards the operator, it is easier to bring down the sole perpendicularly. This is quite as effectual a mode of smoothing a lawn as by the use of the roller, but much more time and labor are required.

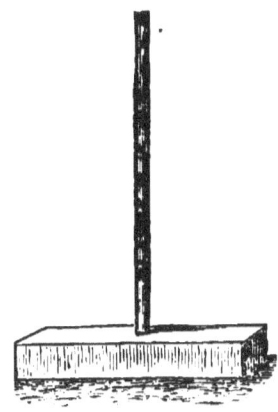

Fig. 8.—TURF BEETLE.

THE PICK.—This is indispensable in trenching hard clay subsoils which the spade cannot penetrate. It consists of a wooden handle inserted in a head composed of two iron levers both pointed with steel, one of which should come to a point and the other be made about two inches wide for cutting roots or any obstructions.

THE SPADE.—The best are Lyndon's, made of cast steel. A large one is required for lifting trees, trenching, etc. A light six-inch spade (figure 9) is very convenient for removing small shrubs and plants, which are a little too large to be lifted with a trowel. The long-handled shovels and spades are perhaps best, except for the small sizes.

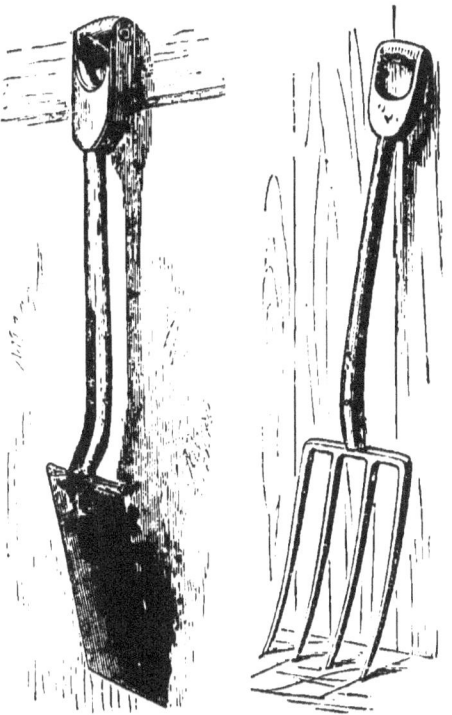

Fig. 9.—SPADE. Fig. 10.—MANURE FORK.

SHOVELS are necessary for loading and spreading composts and manures. The round-pointed one is most convenient for garden purposes. Let it be of steel.

MANURE FORKS (figure 10), with from four to eight tines, are indispensable for moving fresh, long manures with celerity and ease.

SPADE FORK.—A four-tined or asparagus fork, also called a spade fork, made of cast steel with wide tines cut out of a solid plate, as in figure 11, is one of the most desirable of garden tools. With this implement, in a stony or stiff soil, spading can be done more rapidly, with greater ease to the workman, and quite as effectually. It is also used to loosen the earth, and for digging manure into asparagus beds, or about trees, without injury to or cutting the roots.

Fig. 11.—SPADE FORK.

THE CROWBAR is used in the garden, mostly for setting poles for climbers, pea brush, or other fixtures for training plants, and for removing rocks and other obstructions.

HOES.—These are of constant use in gardening. They are of two kinds, the draw-hoe and thrust-hoe, but the draw-hoe is the most convenient. The most useful are the round and square draw-hoes, etc.; made of a cast steel plate six inches long and four wide; the common cotton hoe for ordinary use; the triangular draw-hoe (fig. 12) for digging furrows and sowing seeds; and the narrow semi-circular or narrow square turnip hoes with sharp edges for

Fig. 12.—TRIANGULAR HOE.

scraping the surface and killing weeds. For breaking up the crust which forms after a rain, the scuffle hoe, fig. 13, is of great use. This hoe, the six-inch spade, and the trowel, are the favorite tools for the personal use of amateurs, being all light and in constant requisition. The handles of all hoes should be smooth and light, and there should be no extra weight about the implement.

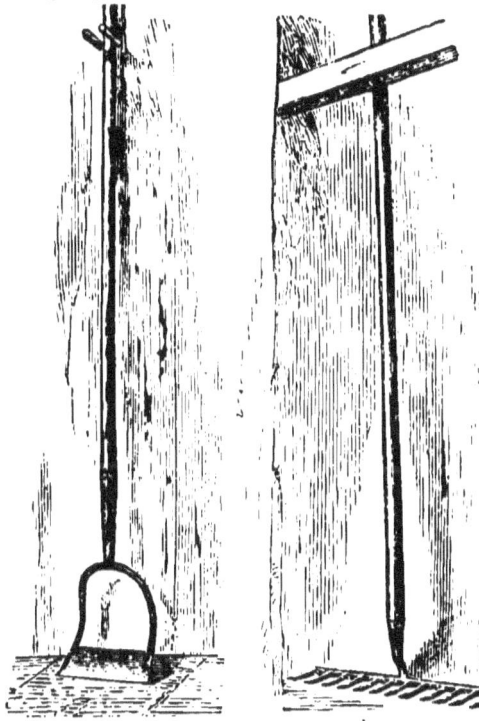

Fig. 13.—SCUFFLE HOE. Fig. 14.—STEEL RAKE.

The Garden Rake (figure 14) is indispensable for levelling and finely pulverizing the ground preparatory to sowing small seeds after it has been spaded or hoed. The best are those hammered out of a solid bar of steel, as they never lose their teeth or get out of order.

The Potato Hook is useful for many of the purposes of both hoe and rake, as for loosening the earth among young plants, for covering seeds in drills, and also for digging out Irish and sweet potatoes without cutting them. This is also called the hoe-fork; one form is shown in fig. 15.

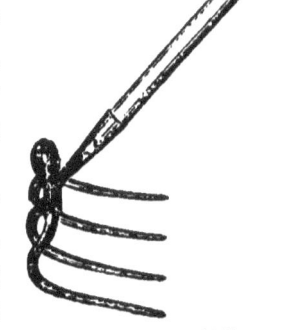

Fig. 15.—HOE-FORK.

DRILL RAKES OR MARKERS are made of wood, and the teeth placed at a greater or less distance for sowing different seeds. In using, the first drill is guided by stretching a line, and afterwards the first tooth is kept in the drill last made to guide, and thus all the rows in a long bed can be made perfectly parallel. Several different sizes are required. That represented in figure 16 has a set of teeth on each side, at nine and twelve inches apart. By using every mark, or every other one, four different distances may be marked with this.

Fig. 16.—DOUBLE MARKER.

THE DIBBLE is very convenient in transplanting cabbages and all those plants that readily succeed when moved. It is usually made of a stick of hard wood about fifteen inches long; the point should be a little blunt. The hole is made with the implement, the plant is put in, and set by again inserting the dibble so as to press the earth against the roots. Figure 17 shows two forms.

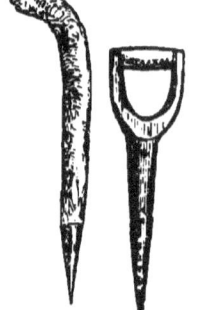

Fig. 17.—DIBBLES.

THE TROWEL is an indispensable implement for removing flowers and other tender plants, as they can be taken up with a ball of earth attached, without injury or mutilation to the roots. It should always be of polished steel. The blade is shaped like the curved portion of the section of a cone, as in figure 18.

Fig. 18.—TROWEL.

THE TRANSPLANTER consists of the two parts, *a* and *b*, fig. 19, hinged together on one side at *c*. When a plant is to be taken up, the transplanter is sunk into the ground with the foot to the required depth. The handles are then pressed apart, which compresses the earth closely about the root of the plant operated upon, which with the ball of earth enclosed, can be readily removed bodily and with no more disturbance than if planted out from a pot. The hole in which it is set must be previously prepared for receiving it.

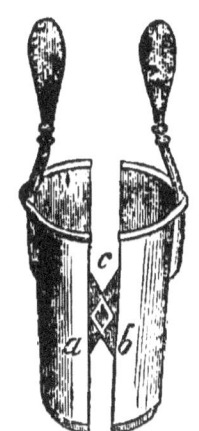

Fig. 19.—TRANSPLANTER.

THE GARDEN REEL AND LINE.—The line should be a good hemp cord ¼ of an inch in diameter. The axis of the reel is fastened in the earth. It is indispensable where neatness and regularity are desired in the rows and plats. It can be easily and quickly wound up when not in use. Figure 20 gives the form usually sold by the implement dealers; a wooden one can be easily made.

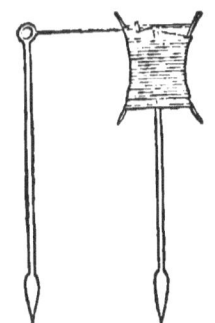

Fig. 20.—REEL & LINE.

THE LEVEL is necessary in laying off terraces and drains. A frame shaped like the letter A may be used with a plumb line attached at the point, and long enough to reach below the cross-bar. Make a mark upon the cross-bar, at the place where the line hangs when both legs are upon a level surface. A spirit level, which may be screwed on to the cross bar, is more convenient.

SCREENS for sifting earth, for filling flower-pots or covering small seeds, are best made with rather stout wires, and the meshes should be of two or three sizes, varying from ⅜ of an inch to an inch in diameter; the frames may be square or round.

2. Cutting Implements, for Operating on Plants.

THE PRUNING-SAW (fig. 21) is from fourteen to eighteen inches long, has fine teeth, and a hooked handle, for hanging upon a limb, while in the tree.

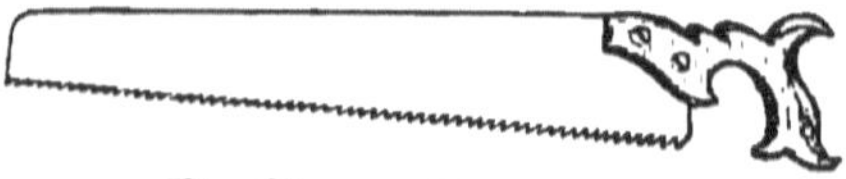

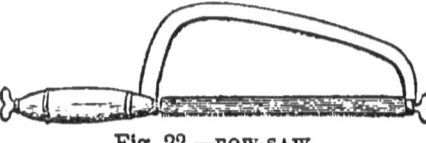

Fig. 21.—PRUNING SAW.

It is also used in cutting off large stocks for grafting. One with a blade tapering nearly to a point will be found convenient.

THE BOW-SAW (figure 22) has a narrow blade, stiffened with an arched back, the blade of which can be made more or less stiff, by tightening the screw on which the back turns, is the best for gardening purposes, and indispensable for sawing off stocks horizontally, near the ground. A small tenon saw is very convenient.

Fig. 22.—BOW-SAW.

HAND PRUNING-SHEARS.—Various patterns are made, one of the latest of which is given in figure 23. They are useful in clipping hedges, shortening in peach trees,

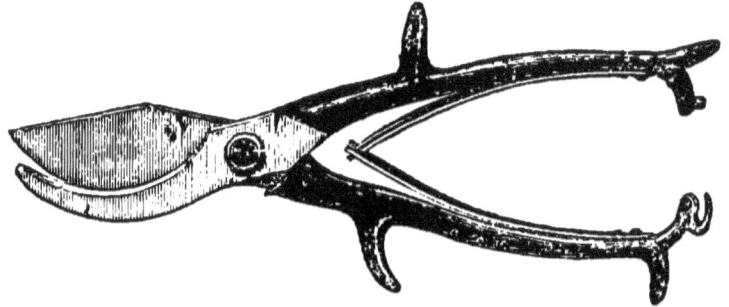

Fig. 23.—PRUNING SHEARS.

and cutting out small, dead branches. One man, with them, can do as much as four with a pruning-knife. Small sizes are made for ladies, and are very highly finished.

POLE PRUNING-SHEARS are fastened to a long handle, and worked with a cord passing over a pulley. They are used for removing dead branches, or those infested with insects, from high trees. Branches an inch in diameter can be cut off with this instrument. They are best with a sliding centre. Figure 24 shows one of the several forms.

Fig. 24.—POLE PRUNING-SHEARS.

HEDGE SHEARS (figure 25) are needed for giving an even face to a hedge in pruning it, and also for trimming box edgings.

PRUNING-SCISSORS are also made with a sliding centre and spring. They cut as smoothly as a pruning-knife, and are very convenient for ladies to use when pruning rose-bushes.

VINE-SCISSORS are used in thinning grapes, when they are too much crowded in the bunches.

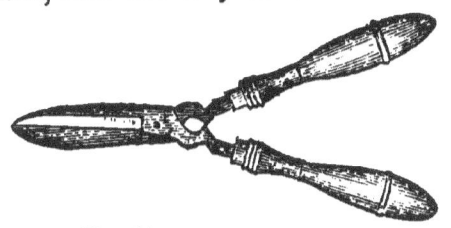
Fig. 25.—HEDGE SHEARS.

PRUNING-KNIVES.—Those of English make (Saynor's) are the best. One of moderate size, about four inches long, is most convenient for the pocket. Another, of larger size, for heavy work, is desirable. For some uses those with a blade more curved than in figure 26 will be found convenient.

Fig. 26.—PRUNING KNIFE.

THE BUDDING-KNIFE has a broad, flat blade, the edge of which is rounded outwards, to make the incision in the bark more readily. It has an ivory haft, thin and smooth

4*

at the end, for raising the bark. Figure 27 shows the most common form.

Fig. 27.—BUDDING KNIFE.

THE GRAFTING-TOOL (figure 28) is much employed in cleft-grafting large stocks. It is used for splitting the stock, and has a sharp edge, curved inwards, to cut the bark in splitting. The wedge part is

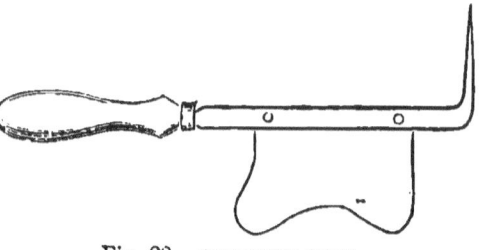

Fig. 28.—GRAFTING-TOOL.

used to keep the stock open while the scions are inserted.

THE LAWN-SCYTHE, with snath, is very necessary, to keep the grass smooth shaven and of that soft green, velvety appearance, so desirable. Those made of a thin plate of steel, welded to an iron back, are light and durable, and may be whetted until the blade is within half an inch of the back, without grinding. Where there is much extent of lawn, a Lawn-Mowing Machine, drawn by one or two horse-power, will be found convenient.

THE BUSH-HOOK (figure 29) is useful about old rose hedges, and is valuable for clearing up the undergrowth in opening new lands.

THE GRASS-EDGER (figure 30) is used for trimming the edges of grass plots. A long handle is attached, and it is pressed forward, guided by a line or the eye of the operator.

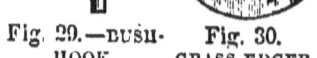

Fig. 29.—BUSH-HOOK.   Fig. 30. GRASS-EDGER.

3. Instruments for Designating, Watering, etc.

TALLIES.—Those for common use, to last a single season, are most readily prepared from the white pine of which most dry-goods boxes are made. The wood is very soft. For marking trees or grafts, a small tally, three-quarters of an inch wide by three inches long, notched at one end for attaching the wire, is commonly used. The name of the variety should be marked on it with a lead pencil, *immediately after* the tally has been brushed over with a thin coat of white lead. If marked while the paint is wet, it can be read as long as the tally lasts; otherwise it will soon be effaced.

Another kind is made, about six or eight inches long by an inch wide, of the same material, and marked in the same manner, to be stuck in the beds of flowers and vegetables, to mark the different varieties. Zinc labels are very durable. They may be cut in any desired shape out of sheet zinc. Write on it with an ink made of two parts fine verdigris, two sal ammoniac, one lampblack. After this is made fine in a mortar, add twenty parts water; bottle and shake it occasionally some days before using. It will keep for years, if the bottle is kept cork downward, to prevent the ammonia from escaping. The labels should be fastened to the limbs with a stout wire.

Fig. 31.—FOLDING LADDER.

Orchards should be mapped, that the names may be ascertained should the tallies get lost or become effaced.

FOLDING-LADDERS are very convenient in gathering fruit. The rounds are fastened by pivots at the ends on which they turn, and when the ladder is folded up, they lie in grooves made in the side-pieces. Figure 31 shows the ladder both open and closed.

THE STANDING-LADDER is also indispensable in the fruit garden. It should be made light, with flat steps. The supports are two sticks of light timber fixed to the top, with hooks and straps, to be expanded or contracted at pleasure. It should be six or eight feet high.

THE ORCHARDIST'S HOOK is a light rod with a hook at the end, with a movable piece of wood which slides upon the rod, as in figure 32. The branches to be gathered from are brought near by the hooked end, and retained in place by hooking the sliding-piece over another branch.

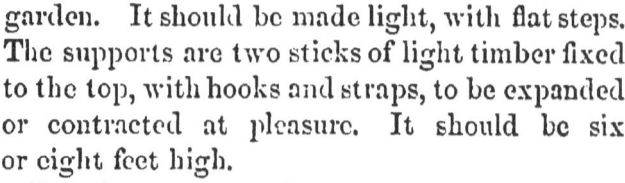

Fig. 32.

GARDEN ENGINES.—These are made of wood or iron in many forms, and act upon the principle of the forcing pump. The tubes should be made very strong, or they will be likely to burst in case of any obstruction. They are very convenient for watering on an extended scale, as in plantations of strawberries, etc.

WATERING-POTS are well-known implements, very necessary in a garden or green-house (figure 33). The best are of copper. There should be two or three roses of different fineness Hang them so the water can run out, when not in use. Tin ones should be painted occasionally, to prevent rusting. In the French watering-pot, figure 34, by the peculiar construction of the handle, the weight is more easily

Fig. 33.—WATERING POT.

Fig. 34.—FRENCH WATERING POT.

GARDEN IMPLEMENTS. 85

balanced in the hands, which enables the user to empty with far less muscular exertion than with a pot upon the old plan.

HAND SYRINGES are useful in watering plants in gardens or in pots. They will also be found very necessary in the pit or green-house, in washing the foliage of plants. They should be made of copper, with several caps of greater or less fineness. There should also be an inverted or gooseneck cap, for washing the under side of leaves. They are made of any desired size, up to a gallon. Insects may be expelled from plants by using an infusion of tobacco or sulphur-water for sprinkling them.

Fig. 35.—VINE SHIELD.

VINE-SHIELDS (fig. 35) are for protecting young plants from the cucumber and squash bugs. The top may be covered with millinet. They should be about eight or ten inches high, and made bevelled, so that one can be set within the other when put away. They are made with or without a pane of glass in the top. Put around any half-hardy plant, with a lock of hay in them, they afford a very good protection during winter. With a movable top, containing a pane or two of glass, they are a tolerable substitute for the next described.

Fig. 36.—HAND-GLASS.

THE HAND-GLASS.—The frame is made either of hard wood or cast iron. It is made in two parts, to give air readily to the plants. Its mode of construction is readily seen in figure 36. It is used for protecting and forwarding vegetables, etc.

BELL-GLASSES (figure 37) of different sizes are cheaper, and in protecting and forwarding small plants are as useful as the hand-glass.

PLANT-PROTECTORS.—These are made as follows: Cut up a three-fourth inch plank, at least a foot wide, into lengths of twelve or fifteen inches. These are the covers or tops, which are to screen your plants from sun and frost. Raise them above the plants you wish to protect, by nailing them at each end to a narrower bit of thick plank,

Fig. 37.—BELL-GLASS.

say nine inches in width, and of the same length as the width of the cover, as at *a*, figure 38. They are also made by tacking together at the edge two pieces of plank a foot square, as at *b*. They may be braced with strips of lath, where dotted, if desired. When you fear a frost, put these over the hills of beans, cucumbers, etc. It will protect them perfectly. If you wish to transplant your cabbages, or anything in your flower-garden, do not wait for a "season," but do it any day, just at night, in fresh-dug soil, giving the roots a good watering. Cover them daily with the protectors, taking them off at night, that they may be freshened with the dew. After a couple of days it will be sufficient to stand the protector on edge on the south

Fig. 38.—PLANT PROTECTOR.

side of the plants, to keep off the mid-day sun. In three or four days the roots will be established. They are also of use when the weather is so dry that hills of melons, squashes, etc., will not come up. Water the hills with a fine rose watering-pot, and lay the protector over the hills, and the young seedlings will soon make their appearance. When above ground, take off the protector and let the dew fall upon them at night, and in a day or two dispense with it entirely. They are excellent, also, to put over the patches of newly planted flower seeds, causing them to come up much sooner. Remove them when necessary to admit mild rains, and entirely when the plants appear.

Shingles, sharpened so as to enter the earth easily, are very useful to protect plants, newly set out, from the direct rays of the sun; two of them, inserted at right angles to each other, with the point of the angle to the south, and inclined so that the tops come a little over the plant, will screen it completely from the sun, and at the same time allow the night dews and gentle rains to refresh the plants.

CHAPTER IX.

PROPAGATION OF PLANTS.

There are two modes of propagating plants, viz., *by seed* and *by division*. Species are propagated by seed, but varieties, except in the case of annuals, generally by division, as they do not always continue true from seed. There are also two modes of *propagating by division;* in the one, the plants root in the ground as suckers, layers, and cuttings, and in the other they are made to unite with another plant, as in budding, grafting, and inarching. While all plants are naturally multiplied by seed, most kinds also allow of propagation by division, as by taking offsets, or parting their roots, by suckers, cuttings, runners, layers, etc. Propagation by seed often produces new varieties, which are only to be perpetuated by division of their roots, cuttings, layers, or by budding and grafting upon stocks.

Propagation by Seed.—The most healthy and vigorous plants are generally produced by seed, though many varieties can only be perpetuated by propagating by division The following conditions are necessary, says Thompson, for successful propagation by seed: 1st. That the seeds be perfectly ripened. 2d. That they have been properly kept until the period of sowing. 3d. That they be sown at the proper time; and, finally, that the sowing be performed in the proper manner. And it may be added that to accomplish the object of sowing, the seeds sown must be of just the kind intended to be used, and true to that kind.

The Maturity and Soundness of Seeds are necessary, to ensure the growth and perfection of the young plant. These can generally be determined by their external and internal appearance. If in cutting the larger seeds the substance of the seed be of the natural color, and the embryo be fresh and perfect, it will probably germinate. So if externally they have a clear color and a fresh, plump appearance, they will be likely to grow. The soundness of those that sink in water when good, (and most seeds do,) may be tested by putting them in warm water. Nearly all sound seeds will sink in this fluid in a short time. Of the finer seeds, a skillful eye will determine the quality with the microscope. But the surest test is, planting a few properly in a pot, protecting the surface from drying with a square of glass, and keeping it in a warm room, or plunged in a hot-bed or in a pit, giving it the heat naturally required by the species for germination.

Seeds are more often unsound from mouldiness or age, than from not having been properly ripened. They should be stored where they will be least affected by the presence of moisture and the changes of temperature. About 40°, but not lower, is said to be the best. Many oily seeds become rancid, and will not vegetate when sown.

Generally, seeds should be kept dry, but acorns and chestnuts thus kept soon lose their vitality and must be kept until planted in rather dry loam, or slightly dampened moss, well packed. Nearly all seeds keep better in closely packed dry soil, the air being thus mostly excluded, than hermetically sealed in bottles. In close stopped bottles or jugs, the air often becomes saturated with the moisture and exhalations from the seeds, which, in the impure, damp, close atmosphere, soon become completely spoiled. But peas, beans, and other seeds, where liable to insects, after they are well dried, should be put in bottles well corked, and a few drops of spirits of turpentine, of chloroform, or a bit of camphor, put in with the seeds. Either of these is fatal to these insects. For most seeds it is sufficient that they be gathered, when fully ripe, in dry weather, and thoroughly dried before they are threshed. If any moisture then appears, dry them further, and store in paper bags where they will be free from damp and vermin. In the first column of the following table is given the time that certain seeds will keep, according to Vilmorin; the second column gives the earlier table of Cobbet. It is generally best to select fresh seed, as seeds lose their vitality very soon.

	Years.		Years.		Years.
Artichoke	5— 3	Dock	3— 1	Pennyroyal	— 2
Asparagus	4— 4	Endive	9— 4	Potato (Sweet)	2— 3
Balm	— 2	Egg Plant	— 7	Potato (Irish)	— 3
Basil	6— 2	Fennel	5— 5	Pumpkin	5—10
Bean	6— 2	Garlick	— 3	Purslane	8— 2
" (Kidney)	3— 1	Gourd	5—10	Radish	5— 2
Beet	5—10	Hop	— 2	Rampion	5— 2
Borage	3— 4	Horseradish	— 4	Rape	— 4
Broccoli	5— 4	Hyssop	— 6	Rhubarb	2— 1
Burnet	2— 6	Jerusalem Artichoke	— 3	Rosemary	4— 3
Cabbage	5— 4	Kale	5— 4	Rue	— 3
Calabash	5— 7	" (Sea)	3— 3	Ruta-baga	5— 4
Camomile	— 2	Lavender	— 2	Sage	— 3
Capsicum	4— 2	Leek	2— 2	Salsify	2— 2
Caraway	2— 4	Lentil	— 3	Samphire	— 3
Carrot	4— 1	Lettuce	5— 3	Savory	2— 2
Cauliflower	5— 4	Mangel Wurzel	5—10	Scorzonera	2— 2
Celery	—10	Marjoram	2— 4	Shalot	— 4
Chervil	2— 6	Marigold	— 3	Skirret	2— 4
Cives	2— 2	Melon	5—10	Sorrel	2— 7
Corn	2— 3	Mint	— 4	Spinach	5— 4
Corn-Salad	5— 2	Mustard	5— 4	Squash	5—10
Coriander	— 3	Nasturtium	5— 2	Tansy	— 3
Cress	5— 3	Okra	— 4	Tarragon	— 4
" (Winter)	3—	Onion	2— 2	Thyme	2— 2
" (Water)	4—	Parsley	3— 6	Tomato	5— 2
Cucumber	5—10	Parsnip	2— 1	Turnip	5— 4
Dandelion	—10	Pea (English)	4— 1	Wormwood	— 2

The Time of Sowing all indigenous seeds in any locality is most favorable when they naturally fall from the plants. Hardy annuals, likewise, do much better if sown in autumn, or quite early in the spring. If not in the ground early, they flower late and badly. There are some exceptions, as in the case of haws and cedar berries, which hang until swallowed by birds, and sprout more freely after having undergone the digestive process. Some exotics of a hardy character likewise succeed best when sown at the time the seed falls, vegetating in autumn, growing slowly through the colder months, and progressing rapidly when spring opens. Others coming from a different climate, starting into growth in autumn, would perish during the winter months; but kept and sown when the temperature of the air and soil in spring is suitable for vegetating them, they will advance rapidly as the weather becomes more and more favorable to growth. In some cases where it might be best to sow at the natural period, if the aim was simply to continue the species, other motives render it necessary to sow at other times. A succession of flowers or a continued supply of vegetables during the season may, in the case of annual or biennial plants, make repeated sowings at proper intervals desirable.

Trees and shrubs it is well to sow, if practicable, at the natural period, but it is desirable the seedlings should not make their appearance above ground until a favorable season for growth. This is most readily secured in the case of seeds that do not keep well dry by *stratification* or mixing them with soil in autumn, but not encouraging growth until spring. This is done by placing a layer of seeds upon the surface of the soil, then a layer an inch or two thick of sand or light soil, and so on, the whole being laid so as to form a cone, over which is spread a covering of soil to protect from wet and frost. This should be done where least likely to invite the attacks of mice and other animals. Small quantities of seeds of this kind may be stratified in boxes and flower pots, covered from rats and mice and placed in a cool situation until spring. Holly seed requires to be kept thus two years. When vegetation begins to take place, the seeds, still mixed with the earth in which they have lain, can be sown in soil properly prepared. The larger seeds can be taken from the soil and planted out in the drills at proper distances.

Seeds must be sown in the proper manner.—Seedsmen are often blamed for selling bad seed, when the sole fault is with the planter. That seed may germinate, moisture, air, and a certain degree of warmth, varying with each variety, are necessary. Chickweed will vegetate at 32° F., but for most seeds of plants of temperate climates the best germinating temperature is about 60° F.; of half-hardy plants 70° F.; of tropical plants about 80° F.; but some require 100° F.

Light must also be excluded until the root can derive nourishment from the soil. The first effect of air, heat, and moisture upon the seed, is to change its starchy matter into the proper food of the embryo. If at this time the seed be withered by exposure to heat without sufficient covering, it will perish. It often happens that seeds are planted in a fresh-dug soil, and the above change in the properties of the seed takes place, but the earth not being *pressed* upon it, the seed dries up and the embryo perishes. Others, again, are buried too deeply, and though the seed swells, yet sufficient air and warmth are not obtained to give the embryo life. The seed should be just so far covered as to exclude light, and afford barely sufficient moisture for its wants. The first thing in sowing is a suitable preparation of the soil, so that the young roots thrown out may easily penetrate it. It must be made more or less fine for different seeds. Peas and beans do not require the soil to be as finely pulverized as small seeds. The seeds must also be firmly fixed in the soil, and pressed by the earth in every part, in order to retain moisture sufficient to encourage vegetation; but they should not be so deeply buried as to be deprived of air, or have their ascending shoots impeded by too much soil above. In all cases, seeds should be sown in fresh-dug soil, that they may have the benefit of the moisture therein, but they should never be put in when the soil is really wet, as the ground will bake and the seed perish. Moist weather in summer is excellent for putting in seeds, provided the ground is still friable. Just before a light rain is the best possible time for sowing turnips and other summer-sown crops.

Seeds of most kinds should be sown in drills or rows. In these they can be placed at any required depth, while if broadcast, some will be uncovered, and others too deeply buried in the earth. In drills you can know also where to look for the young plants; they can have the soil dug around them; they will thus grow much faster, and are much more easily thinned and cultivated. When the seeds are planted, the earth should generally be pressed upon them with a roller, by treading with the feet, in the case of large seeds, by smoothing the surface with the back of the spade, or by walking over them on a board for the smaller kinds. Pressing the earth upon them will retain the moisture about them, and hasten their vegetation. When they come up, keep them free from weeds, and thin them as hereafter directed in treating of each plant.

A great deal of the subsequent growth of the plant depends upon their not being sown too thickly, or at least thinned properly as soon as the young seedlings appear. A plant raised among a lot of crowded seedlings is very apt to die before it has made its fourth leaf. This seldom happens if the seeds are sown thin, and a little powdered charcoal is mixed with the earth.

Some seeds, which, like those of the carrot, adhere together, must be rubbed in the hands with dry sand to insure a more equal distribution in the drill. Others, like the beet, are covered with a hard shell, and others still with a tough skin. Both these may be soaked in water until it is somewhat softened, and by notching into the latter, germination is hastened. For broadcast sowing, very small seeds are often mixed with fine soil in order to ensure their being scattered more equally.

Among the other most frequent causes of failure in seeds are being sown in too dry earth and sowing them too deep. Excessive moisture is also to be guarded against, and giving them too much or too little bottom heat. M. Appelius observes that seedlings raised in hot-beds or frames frequently cause disappointment from bad management. Asters, Stocks, Phlox, Petunias, Pansies, etc., do better in a very gentle hot-bed, and produce stronger plants less likely to die off. When the dung of a hot-bed has given off its first heat, it begins to absorb moisture from the earth with which it is covered. And as the earth of the bed generally slopes to the south, the greater part of the water given runs off toward the front, and at the back of the bed the earth in which the seeds are sown is often too dry. Hence seeds that vegetate slowly and need constant damp, as Phlox and Pansy, should be sown at the front of the bed, and those that grow more readily at the top or back. The time required for certain seeds to germinate at a temperature from 52° to 65° is, according to M. Appelius: garden cress, 2 days; spinach, 3; cabbage, turnip, and lettuce, 4; peas, endive, poppy, melons, cucumbers, mustard, 5; lupine, lentil, horseradish, radish, onions, (often also in 15 days), leeks, 6; barley, rye, maize, broccoli, beans, beet, 7; wheat, thyme, marjoram, and some kidney beans, 8; marrowfat peas, 9; vetch, sugar beet, tobacco, hemp, 10; tomato, sea-kale, scorzonera, carrots, savory, basil, stocks, celery, 12 (turnip rooted celery sometimes 20); anise, fennel, 13; sunflower, artichoke, burnet,

14; balm, clover, 15; lavender, purslane, 16; sage, pepper, 20; parsnip, parsley, asparagus, 21; and potato in 28 days. It seems that seeds lighter than water do not germinate so soon as those heavier.

Though seeds will vegetate with due supplies of heat and moisture, a fertile soil is necessary for their further progress. Fine, light, rich mould favors the vegetation and early progress of most seeds, though many, after they are a little advanced, flourish best in strong, heavy loam. A compost of peat or leaf-mould, fine sand, and well rotted manure, should be prepared, and if all the finer seeds are covered therewith, one great difficulty in growing fine vegetables on stiff soils will be removed, as well as their early maturity secured. Even in dry weather one can generally bring up seeds by digging and finely pulverizing the earth; then soak it well with water that has been some time exposed to the air to raise its temperature; then sow the seed in drills of the proper depth, and sift over the bed a coat of this compost. In the case of large seeds, as corn, beans, etc., after the ground is prepared, only the hills or drills need to be thus soaked, and then covered with the compost.

Special directions for managing seeds requiring peculiar care will be given hereafter.

Seeds must not only be properly managed, but there is no pleasure in growing them unless of the right kind, as it is very vexatious to sow Early Yorks when you think you are sowing Drumheads, and *vice versa*. The way to avoid such mistakes is either to raise your own seed, carefully label them, or to know of whom you buy. Your own eye in the case of many seeds will not assist you at all in discriminating.

Seed must not only be of the right sort, but true to that sort. Early York cabbage seed may be sown, or Scarlet radish seed; yet, from having been planted near to some other varieties, the seed is crossed with them and the most valuable qualities of the variety lost. The cabbage may be late or long-legged, and not head at all, or the radish tough and misshapen.

Preserving Seed.—The very finest plants should be chosen for this purpose, that is, those most true to their kind and most perfect in shape and quality. In the cabbage, for instance, a small, short stem, well formed head with few loose leaves; in the turnip, large bulb, small neck, few, short and slender-stalked leaves, and solid flesh. In the radish, high color (unless white,) small neck, few and short leaves; and in the case of flowers, seed should be saved only from those most perfectly developed.

Great care should be taken to preserve the varieties unmixed, for, as just stated, if varieties of the same species, or very similar species, are planted near each other, they will cross and produce untrue seed. In this way, it is true, valuable varieties often originate, but the chances are that the produce will be worthless. There can be no cross between a cabbage and a carrot, because they are of totally different families, and there is no similarity; but all the varieties of cabbage will cross with each other, with Brussels sprouts, in short with all others of the genus *Brassica.* So of corn; in a few years the early varieties from the North, planted in Southern gardens, become so intermingled with the ordinary sorts, that the early character is lost. The difficulty of keeping seeds pure renders it advisable not to save seeds of two varieties of any species the same year, except in large gardens. Many kinds of seed it is more advantageous to buy of the regular seedsmen, than to grow and save them at home. The finest seeds in the world are grown where an amateur makes one or two species of plants, like Truffaut with Asters, a specialty, using every possible care for their improvement.

Crossing and Hybridizing.—These terms are used by many as meaning the same thing; strictly speaking, *hy-*

bridizing is when two distinct species are made to form a union, while *crossing* is where the same takes place with varieties of the same species. To make the matter plain, we must give the structure of the flower. The organs concerned in the production of the fruit or seed are the *stamens*, which correspond to the male organs, and the *pistil* or pistils, which are the female organs. These two are for the most part in one flower, and differ greatly in number in the

Fig. 39.—FLAX FLOWER.

different families. The simplest case is where both kinds are in one flower, as in fig. 39, which represents a flower of the flax split down, to show the arrangement of its parts. In figure 40 all of the flower is removed, except the stamens and pistil, which are enlarged. The central body is the pistil, and is surrounded by five stamens, which are shorter. It will be seen that each stamen is composed of two parts; a slender portion, the *filament*, which bears a two-lobed body, the *anther*, which produces a fine fertilizing powder, the *pollen*. The pistil has an enlarged base, the *ovary*, which contains the *ovules*, which are to become seeds; above this is usually a prolonged portion, the *style*. The styles may be one or several; in the case of the flax there are five, each one of which is surmounted by a *stigma*, that part which receives the fertilizing powder, or pollen.

Fig. 40.—STAMENS AND PISTILS.

The stamens and pistils are not always found together in the same flower. In Indian corn they are separated, but on the same plant the tassel containing the stamens or male organs, while the silk and ear are the pistillate parts; such plants are called *monœcious*. In other instances, as spinach, the flowers which contain the stamens are not found upon the same individual plant with those that bear the pistils. These are called *diœcious* plants.

Cross breeding, where both sexes are united in the same blossom, is accomplished by removing the stamens and dusting the pistil with the pollen of a different variety, a simple process; but from the resulting seed a new variety, partaking somewhat of the qualities of both parents, will be produced. Care is required in the process. A blossom must be selected not fully expanded, and all the anthers be cut out and removed. Protect the blossom with a loose bag of gauze to keep off the bees. As soon as the blossom is fully expanded, collect on a camel's hair pencil the pollen from a full blown flower of the variety selected for the male parent, and apply it to the stigma or point of the pistil. The conditions are a careful extraction of the anthers before they are advanced enough to fertilize the pistil, and to apply the selected pollen when in perfection, that is, in a powdery state, upon the stigma while still moist, and to prevent natural fertilization from pollen carried by insects or by the wind. Cross breeding often takes place naturally. If different varieties of corn are planted near together, often three or four kinds and colors of grain will be found upon one ear from natural intermixture.

But there are limits to the power of crossing plants. Those between two varieties of the same species, as between two kinds of corn or pear, are common enough, and these are fruitful and produce perfect seeds. In the same genera, also, certain nearly allied species are capable of fertilizing each other; the offspring in this case is called a hybrid, and does not always produce perfect seeds. Thus the different species of the strawberry, also those of the gourd and melon family, readily intermix. So also do those of the rose. But no one has succeeded in crossing the apple with the pear, or the gooseberry with the currant, though in both cases they are species of the same genus. Still less will such totally different plants as oranges and pomegranates intermix.

Our flower-gardens in modern times have been greatly enriched by cross breeding and hybridizing. Thus have originated a great number of new and beautiful roses, rhododendrons, azaleas, camellias, fuchsias, dahlias, etc., so beautiful in color and perfect in form and habit. There is no doubt of their great utility here. Cross breeding and hybridizing, it is claimed, are processes equally useful in fruit-growing; but it is certain that very few artificially cross-bred fruits are yet in cultivation, and of true hybrids it is doubtful if there are any which are valuable. It is certain that those most successful in producing improved varieties have not generally resorted to cross breeding.

True hybrids rarely produce perfect seeds, and those that do, revert to one of the parents after a few generations. From not being subjected to this drain on their vitality, they frequently bloom more freely, and the blossoms remain longer in perfection than those of plants that seed freely. Seed-bearing is the greatest tax upon the vigor of a plant to which it can be subjected. Hybrid varieties are increased and continued in existence by propagating them by division.

Propagation by Division.—Every other mode of propagating plants, except by seed, whether it be by bulbs, tubers, runners, suckers, parting the roots, layers, cuttings, budding or grafting, is effected by a division of the plant to be increased.

Bulbs.—Propagation by division, in the case of bulbs or tubers, is analogous to sowing seeds. The new bulbs may be separated when the leaves of the mother-plant decay. The onion, hyacinth, tulip, etc., are generally taken up and stored in a moderately dry, airy place, until it is the proper season for growth, and are thought to grow better in consequence of their surplus moisture being evaporated. The corms or bulbs of the crocus, thus treated, produce better plants and stronger flowers. Removal gives an opportunity for changing the soil before the bulbs are reset. There are, however, many scaly bulbs, as the lily, that are injured if long out of the ground, and if not planted again at the proper season, the strength of the plant is much diminished. Bulbs generally like a light, rich, sandy soil, well pulverized, and most bulbs and tubers require to be planted more deeply than seeds.

Tubers may be taken up when mature, and kept until the proper season for replanting. They may generally be cut into as many pieces as they have eyes, and each eye will produce a plant. The tubers of the Chinese yam have no visible buds, but if cut into pieces and planted, buds will push out from the wrinkles that appear upon its surface.

Runners are thrown out by the strawberry and many other plants. They spring from the crown of the plant, deriving from it their nourishment, and at a greater or less distance from the parent plant throw out a bud above and small projections or rudiments of roots, which, in favorable conditions, strike into the soil and help to nourish the young plant above. The growing point of the runner extends to form another new plant beyond. Runners cannot well take root in dry weather, but in contact with moist soil the roots soon strike. To facilitate the rooting, the joint is often pegged down, or a small stone placed over it a little behind the bud, which preserves the earth in a moist condition as well as keeps the joint close to the soil. If it is desired to obtain as many plants as possible, do not permit the parent-plant to waste its vigor in producing flowers and fruit, but cut off the flower stalks as they appear. If strong plants are desired, stop each runner after it has made one or two plants. The new plants, when well rooted, are ready for removal at the proper season.

Suckers.—These proceed either from the root or from the stem, or collar of the plant. *Root suckers* are produced from those plants which send out stray horizontal roots, as the sucker is in fact a bud from one of these roots which has pushed its way through the soil and become a stem. As this stem generally forms fibrous roots of its own above the point of junction with the parent-root, it may be slipped off and planted like a rooted cutting.

Root suckers are thrown up by some plants, like the currant, close to the main stem; by others, like the plum and paper mulberry, at considerable distance. Raspberries, poplars, roses, lilacs, and many other shrubs and trees, are thus readily propagated, the offspring with the roots that properly belong to it being carefully separated from the parent and replanted in suitable soil. The roots of the parent-plant should be injured as little as possible. Remove the soil, and if the sucker springs from a large root, detach a slice of it with the sucker instead of severing it. The supply of nourishment being diminished by separation from the parent-plant, the head of the plant removed must be cut in, except in the case of coniferous plants, to prevent evaporation.

The great objection to planting suckers is, that plants grown from them have a much greater tendency to throw out suckers, and thereby become exceedingly annoying in gardens, by encroaching on other plants, than if propagated by other methods.

Stem Suckers spring from the stem of the old plant where its base is beneath the surface. Shoots originating at this point frequently strike root and become rooted suckers. In plants in which this natural tendency is not sufficiently strong, it may be increased by earthing them up well with good mould, which may be kept moist by mulching. The quince and other plants are propagated in this manner.

Propagation by Slips.—This is the mode in which many small undershrubs, like box, sage, rue and lavender, are increased. They are dug up in spring or fall, and the young shoots, with some portion of root attached, slipped off with the thumb and finger, and if small, they are planted a year in nursery rows. Many kinds of plants grow from slips of the young branches with little or no root attached. The number of young plants to be obtained by division can be increased in some cases by sprinkling fine soil among them that the lower branches may strike root in it, or taking up the plant and resetting deeper than before. Box edging when overgrown, if taken up in spring, partly divided and replanted so that the base of each shoot is covered, can, after rooting, again be divided into as many plants as there were shoots. Stem suckers are often called slips.

Parting the Roots is the ordinary way of increasing herbaceous perennials with annual stems, such as phloxes, chrysanthemums, etc., which can be taken up in spring or autumn, and divided by hand, or with the trowel, knife or spade, into a number of plants with a portion of root to each.

Propagation by Layers.—A layer is a branch or shoot bent down into, and covered with, the soil, in order to make it take root. Meanwhile it is fed by the parent stock with which its communication is, however, partially obstructed to make the returning sap form roots, instead of going back into the stock. With some plants a sufficient check is given by simply bending and properly covering it with earth; the branch is held in its place by hooked pegs until it takes root. But in general this is not enough. The most common way of obstructing the return flow of sap is when the shoot is bent into the earth to half cut it through near the bend, the free portion of the wound being called a tongue. This is kept open by a bit of twig, or piece of crock. Such layers are in fact cuttings, only partially separated from parent-plants. The incision is made through the bark at the base of a bud. The object of the gardener is to induce the layer to emit roots into the earth at the tongue. There are other modes of effecting this.

With this view, he twists the shoot half round, so as to injure the wood vessels; he heads it back so that only a bud or two appears above ground, and when much watering is required, he places a handful of silver sand around the tongued part, then pressing the earth down with his foot, so as to secure the layer, he leaves it without further care. The intention of both tongueing and twisting is to prevent the return of the sap from the layer into the main stem, while a small portion is allowed to rise out of the latter into the former. The effect of this operation is to compel the returning sap to organize itself as roots, instead of passing downwards to form wood; the bending back is to assist this object, by preventing the expenditure of sap in the completion of leaves. The bud left on the tongue favors the emission of roots, as a tendency exists in nearly all plants to throw out roots at the joints, and the silver sand secures the drainage so necessary to cuttings.

The old mode of forming the tongue, and the best, unless the shoot is brittle, is shown in the figure, where the tongue is shown upon the underside of the layer. "A plan," says the Gardener's Monthly, " which is now much in vogue with the best propagators, is to cut the tongue *on the upper surface.* On bending down into the soil, the tongue is then twisted on one side, and the young shoot intended to form the future plant may then be lifted up and bent towards the parent as rapidly as one pleases, without any danger of it snapping off. There is another advantage in this way of layering. It is often necessary, in the stereotyped way, to place a chip or something between the tongue to keep it open. By this, the twisting of the tongue aside keeps it always separate from the old cut. Again, by this mode, very green shoots can be operated on,—magnolias, for instance, in June, and plants be got well rooted by fall, instead of waiting for the wood to ripen in August, when we have to wait for another year

Fig. 41.—LAYERING.

before our layer is sufficiently rooted to take from its parent. Another method of forming the tongue is to make the cut upon the side, as in figure 41.

Instead of forming a tongue to make a shoot throw out roots, the branch may be split in the centre for two inches, more or less according to its size, and the parts separated with a bit of wood. Roots will be thrown out along the edges of the split. The returning sap may also be arrested by ringing; in which case a ring of bark is removed from the branch for the purpose, or by a wire twisted tightly around it pinching the bark.

When the roots are thrown out naturally wherever a joint touches the earth, as in the verbena, the branches only require pegging down to make them form new plants.

Where it is difficult to get the shoot to be layered down to the soil, a portion of the soil may be raised to the plant, as the Chinese gardeners practice in a pot, the earth in which should be kept steadily moist.

Another mode of layering is by insertion of the growing point in the soil. When the shoots of a raspberry or gooseberry are of some length and firmness, if the growing points are inserted in well-dug soil, they will form a nice bundle of roots and a good bud ready for transplanting in autumn. This is worthy of trial with many other plants.

The grape is best layered by digging a trench and laying therein a thrifty cane in the spring; let remain until young shoots, three or four inches long, are formed; then gently draw a little of the soil into the trench covering the parent-cane, and as the shoots increase in strength, fill up the trench, and each young shoot will make a fine plant by autumn.

In general, the best season for layering is before the sap begins to rise in the spring, or from the last of June, during summer on wood of the same season's growth. A good time for roses is after the first bloom is over. Layered at this time, they will generally be fit to take up the ensuing winter, but most plants require twelve months, and some two years, before they will root. In nurseries the ground is prepared around each stool by digging and manuring, and the branches laid down neatly, so as to form a circle of rays around the stool, with the ends rising all around the circle to about the same height.

Cuttings.—A cutting is a part of a plant detached from the parent-stock, which, placed in proper conditions, will emit roots and become in its turn a new plant. It may be a portion of the stem, the branches, or the root, and sometimes even a leaf.

In a cutting, as in a growing plant, two forces are in constant activity, those of absorption and of evaporation.

Its life cannot be long continued, unless these correspond with each other. A cutting, from the lack of roots, absorbs feebly from the soil; hence evaporation must be diminished to correspond, and the base of the cutting must be in contact with a substance more or less humid. Evaporation is diminished by planting in a northern exposure, shading, the use of bell-glasses, etc. The more herbaceous or immature a cutting may be, the greater care is required to protect it from excessive evaporation.

Cuttings of hardy deciduous trees and shrubs should be taken off after the leaves fall, or before the sap rises in the spring. Those that strike readily in the open ground in mild climates may be planted out to form the callus, and be ready to enter into growth with the opening spring. In more northern climates they may be prepared for planting, and stored in moistened moss or damp earth, and kept from frost. The callus will be forming, and they will be ready to plant in early spring. Generally, cuttings should not be taken when the sap is in full flow, as moisture is then rapidly evaporated and the cutting exhausted before roots are formed. They should be taken when the plant is dormant, or when a new shoot has been made with leaves so fully formed and matured as to be in the act of forming abundance of woody tissue.

In selecting cuttings, they should come from healthy plants, from shoots of average strength, well nourished, but not over vigorous, as the latter are more quickly exhausted when deprived of their usual supply of nourishment. Horizontal branches growing near the ground, especially those which recline upon it, have a greater tendency to throw out roots. Upright shoots from near the summit are generally, but not always, less likely to succeed. The willow and poplar strike freely from old wood, and trunks of considerable size, if planted, will emit roots, but of most trees the best plants are made from well matured shoots of the current year's growth. In the case of hard-wooded plants that are hard to strike, it is a nice matter to select a portion of shoot in which the wood is neither too old and hard, from which roots will not be readily emitted, or too young and soft, as in this case they will damp off. Rose cuttings strike most readily when not quite fully matured. The proper state of firmness differs in different species. The age at which a cutting of any species will strike best or strike at all, is determined by experiment, but when once ascertained, it is invariably the same. The proper age of an untried species may be proximately determined from that of the most closely related species in which it is known, and will often prove to be right if the species are nearly allied.

Some cuttings require little preparation. A willow may be sharpened and driven into the soil and will take root, and in some instances has done so, if planted bottom upwards. Currants and gooseberries, cut into suitable lengths, will emit roots not only from the callus, but from any part beneath the soil. Of these, as of cuttings of all deciduous trees, the buds on the part of the cutting beneath the soil must be removed before planting, or they will push and become shoots. Cuttings of which the leaves have fully performed their office, and the wood is ripened early in the season, if made and planted out in warm, moist soil, will form roots before winter, and be ready to push into vigorous growth in spring. Such cuttings, planted in August or early in September, are nearly a year in advance of spring-planted cuttings.

Cuttings of plants, difficult to strike, may have a ring of bark taken out just beneath a joint, at mid-summer, which will cause a swelling of the branch above the ring. The branch is cut off in autumn at the base of the swelling, the top shortened, and it is planted as a cutting, or it is buried in the soil for the swelling to soften, and planted early in the spring. With plants that are not very free to strike, it is from the joints only that roots can be expected to grow; hence, in making cuttings, the shoot is divided just below a joint, and it is considered best to choose a joint between the young wood and that of the previous season. The cut should be quite smooth, for if the shoot be bruised, the returning sap will not be able to reach the wound in sufficient quantity to make it heal over and form the callus quickly, and the cutting will be likely to fail. When the callus is properly formed, there is little difficulty in striking cuttings. To form the callus, they may be mixed with damp sphagnum moss, or old tan, and kept in a dark cellar until about to push roots. Cuttings may be placed loosely in a common preserving bottle, with a wet sponge, the water drained out, and the bottle stopped with a cork, which has a half-inch hole in the top to admit air. This may be kept where the atmosphere ranges from temperate to summer heat, and the callus will form very quickly.

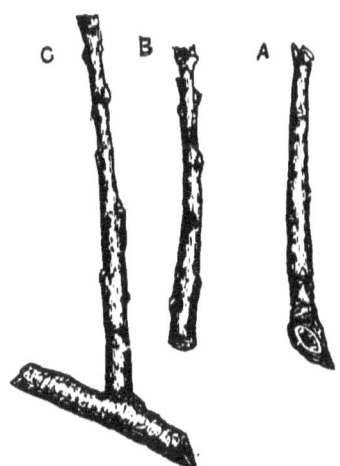

Fig. 42.—DIFFERENT FORMS OF CUTTINGS.

Preparation.—The way to prepare cuttings for planting is best shown by an illustration. Figure 42, *A*, shows a cutting formed from a lateral shoot, and has been cut off from the main branch with a *heel* attached. Such cuttings are sometimes torn out and the bottom smoothed with a sharp knife, and present a larger surface for the absorption of moisture. At *B* is a deciduous, woody cutting, as commonly prepared. At *C* is shown a mode in which grape cuttings are sometimes prepared; the two extremities of the fragment of branch at the base are furnished with buds. This is a mode which greatly favors the emission of roots. Figure 43 is a cutting of a geranium ready for insertion in the soil. In this case the lower leaves have been removed; they should be clipped but very little farther from the base than where

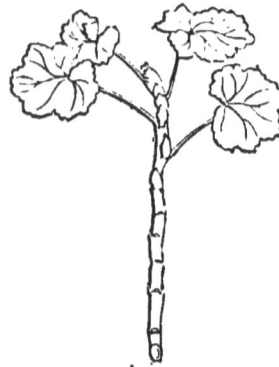

Fig. 43.—GERANIUM CUTTING.

the cutting is to be inserted in the soil. The leaves being kept near the moist surface, do not evaporate as rapidly as when elevated much above. The petiole (or leaf stalk) should be cut off as close to the stem as can be done without injury to the bark. If much of it is left and buried in the soil, it is apt to rot and produce decay in the cutting itself. If an old leaf or two is left, it will elaborate more sap for the formation of new roots than the very young ones. Cuttings of succulent plants, like the cacti, geranium, etc., require to dry a little that the wound may heal over before inserting in the soil.

The grape is often propagated from a single eye—a

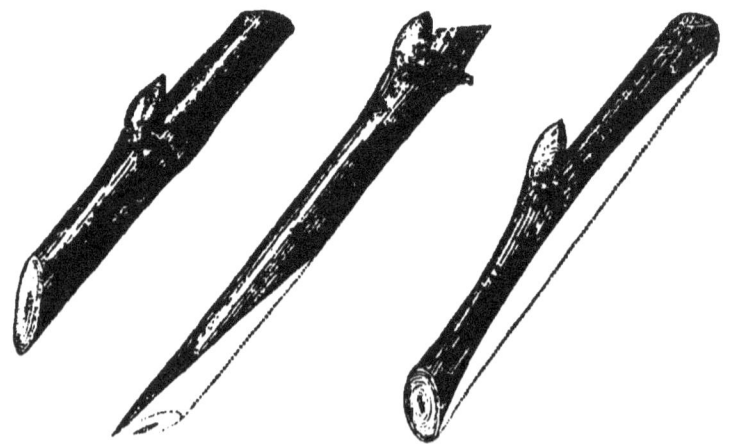

Fig. 44.—THREE FORMS OF GRAPE CUTTINGS.

mode now very much in use for new varieties. These cuttings, shaped in one of the forms shown in fig. 44, are planted in small pots under glass, the surface kept damp, and bottom heat applied. They soon take, and form the best vines.

The substances in which cuttings are struck are various. Many plants, as crysanthemums, currants, etc., will root in common garden soil. Powdered charcoal, brick dust, and even pure water are employed, but the most useful substance is pure silver sand, white, clean, and fine. Sea sand must not be used, unless all saline matter is washed out. Sand contains little food for plants, and they need little until the roots are formed, but it is free from matters which induce decay. It is porous and gives ready passage for the young rootlets, and, being fine, retains moisture by capillary attraction.

Some plants will strike roots if the ends of the cuttings are kept in water of the proper temperature. Bottles, vials, and jars, are used to hold the water, but as light is rather an obstacle to the ready formation of roots, if the vessel is transparent, it should be shaded. As soon as the roots begin to appear, the cuttings should be taken from the water and planted in fine soil, which must be kept moist, and the plants carefully shaded until they take fresh root.

Insertion.—Cuttings of hardy plants that strike readily in the open air are sometimes inserted with a dibble, but it is better to cut off by a line a straight edge in the dug soil, and place the prepared cuttings against it; press the soil closely around them. These are usually set perpendicularly. If the cuttings are long, they can be set in a sloping direction so as to be within reach of atmospheric influences. If not herbaceous, they should be inserted so deep that but two buds will be above the surface, and in the vine but one. Herbaceous cuttings are inserted less deeply.

When small cuttings are planted under glass, a pointed stick of proper size is used. Many kinds may be planted all over the surface of the pot, but most do better when inserted near the sides or bottom of the pot, and take root more readily. The soil in all cases about a cutting must be closely pressed against its extremity, or it will never strike root.

Temperature.—Many cuttings that rarely strike root in the open ground do so freely when moist bottom heat is applied. When the soil is but slightly warmer than the air, the roots grow in proportion to the top, but if the soil is constantly warmer, the disposition to produce roots will be greater than to produce tops. In striking cuttings, the object is to produce roots, and then leaves will follow; hence the temperature of the soil should be somewhat higher than that in which the species naturally commences growth, in order to secure good roots, without which there can be no vigorous leaf-buds. This stimulus should be applied to soft-wooded plants almost immediately; others may require some delay until the callus is formed. Deciduous shrubs in a dormant state should at first be placed in a temperature very little higher than would excite and swell their buds on the parent tree. Increase the bottom heat gradually, keeping the soil warmer than the atmosphere. From 50° to 60° is about right for the soil at this period, and about 50° for the atmosphere for hardy and green-house plants, increasing the bottom heat to 65° or 70° very gradually, when the roots commence growth, and care should be taken to prevent its falling lower until rooted, when it may gradually be lessened until but little above that of the air of the place in which they are growing.

Moisture.—The cutting, while rooting, must be kept in a suitable state of moisture. In vine cuttings, and others, nearly covered with soil, all that is required is to keep that in such an equable state of moisture that the cutting can have as much as it can appropriate, and no more. A cutting requires more moisture in the soil than if it were a rooted plant.

To recapitulate; the principal points to be attended to in making cuttings are to cut off the shoot at a joint, without harming the stem; to select shoots with well matured buds; to fix the end which is to send out roots firmly in the soil; to keep up an equable degree of heat and moisture; to cut off part of the leaves and shade the whole, to prevent evaporation, without too much excluding light, of which a portion is needed to stimulate the cutting into growth; to keep the soil moist but not too damp. It is well to transplant them into small pots, supplied with water regularly and moderately as soon as they begin to grow. Cuttings of slow-growing plants are those most liable to fail. An excess of heat, cold air, water, and light, are all injurious to tender cuttings.

Pipings.—Cuttings of plants with tubular stems, like the pink, are called pipings. The upper part of a shoot, when nearly done growing, is pulled out of the socket close above a joint, leaving the part pulled out with a pipe like termination. These pipings usually have their leaves or "grass" trimmed a little, and are struck in sand about an inch apart, with a bell-glass closely fixed over them. If well watered at first, they will not require it again for some time. They are planted about $\frac{3}{4}$ of an inch deep, and treated like other herbaceous cuttings. Under a north wall they succeed finely.

Root Cuttings.—Many shrubs and plants are in this way most easily increased. Pyrus Japonica, blackberry, rose, apple, pear, quince, elm, mulberry, osage orange, etc., if their roots are cut in pieces some three to nine inches long, and planted vertically with the end nearest the stem up, and covered slightly with earth, will soon form buds and throw up shoots. Many herbaceous plants, as sea kale, horseradish, Japan anemone, etc., are thus increased. Of these the cuttings are made short, and, except the second named, planted horizontally.

CHAPTER X.

BUDDING AND GRAFTING.

Budding is the art of making a bud unite to the stem or branch of another tree independently of its parent. It is a cutting with a single eye inserted in another tree called a stock, instead of in the ground. The operation may be performed at any time after the buds of the new wood are sufficiently matured. These must be perfectly developed, which is seldom the case until the shoot has temporarily ceased to lengthen, which is indicated by the perfect formation of the terminal bud. If the buds are desired very early, their maturity may be hastened by pinching the tops of the shoots.

The ordinary time for budding, north of Virginia, is from the middle of July to the middle of September, and the buds in general remain dormant until spring. Roses are, however, budded earlier, and allowed to make some growth. In the South, buds are inserted at any time when the bark will rise, from June to October. Those put in early will make a fine growth before autumn, in favorable seasons. A very necessary condition to successful budding is that the bark rise freely from the stock, and this must be in a thrifty, growing state, as when pushing into new growth a day or too after a fine rain. If the weather is too cold or the soil too dry, the bark will not rise. Such trees as make most of their growth early in the season must be budded before they cease to grow. Young shoots, when the buds are in a proper state, are cut below the lowest plump bud. If to be budded immediately, all the leaf is cut off, except the leaf stem, which is left for convenience of inserting, and in order to attract the sap into the buds. If the buds are to be preserved any time, the whole leaf with half of the leaf stem is removed to prevent evaporation. If this is done as soon as they are cut, they may be preserved several days in a closely covered tin box, or tightly corked preserve jar, if in a cool place, and indeed, if the wood is well ripened, though the footstalk of the leaf will drop, the bud will be in perfect condition some weeks. No water need be given if there are several cuttings in the box, as the air becomes sufficiently saturated with moisture from the cuttings themselves.

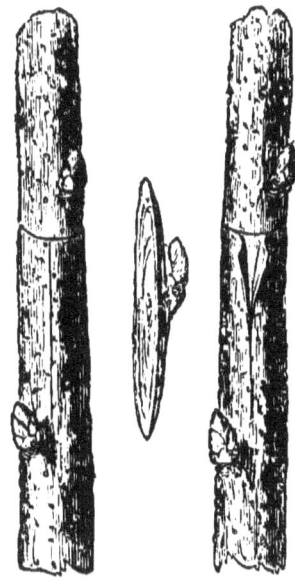

Fig. 45.—BUDDING.

The strings used for tying are taken from bass-mats, which should be wetted before use, until perfectly pliable. Better strings are made of white woollen yarn, as they are more elastic, and the color reflects the heat. The pruning and budding knives are the only implements required for the operation. The condition of the budding knife is of importance to success. It should be made thin, and the edge kept perfectly smooth and keen. It is figured in the chapter upon tools. The mode in which budding is performed is shown in figure 45.

Having the implements, stocks, and buds in the proper condition, take the shoot in the left hand, and the budding knife in the right. Insert the edge of the knife in the shoot, half an inch above the bud to be taken off. The bud is taken off with a drawing cut, parallel with the shoot, removing the bark and the bud attached, with a slight portion of the wood beneath the bud, half an inch above, and three-fourths of an inch below. The English remove this slight portion of the wood, taking great care not to injure the root of the bud; but it does not succeed so well in this climate as if a small portion of wood be left directly under the bud. Select, then, a small portion of the stock, smooth and free from branches, and make two cuts through the bark, one across the end of the other, in the shape of a T, as in the figure. Then raise the bark on the two edges of the perpendicular cut with the smooth ivory haft of the budding knife; insert the bud gently beneath the parts raised, not forcing it down like a wedge so as to rub off the cambium of the stock, but pressing very little against the stock until so fully inserted that its own cambium can be applied directly to that of the stock where it is to remain; cut off the top of the bark attached to the bud square, that it may fit the cut across the stock; then wind the bass pretty tightly about the stock, commencing below the end of the bud, and pass it closely around up to the bud. The shield should here be firmly pressed, that the base of the bud may closely rest upon the alburnum; bring the tie pretty close to the under side of the bud, making the next turn wider, so that the point of the bud and the leaf stalk may be seen between the turns of the tie; continue binding closely until the cross incision is covered, then fasten with a knot. Cover every part of the incision, except the bud and leaf stalk attached, which should remain uncovered. Do not tie it so tightly as to cut into the bark, but so as to exert upon it a moderate pressure. The bud is put upon the north side of the stock, when practicable, and when not, a little paper cap may be tied to the stock, to project over the bud, so as to admit the light, but exclude the direct rays of the sun. The success of the operation depends on its being performed rapidly, and with fresh, healthy buds; clean, smooth cuts; the bark rising cleanly and freely from the wood; the exact fit of the bud to the incision; and close, secure tying, to exclude the air and water. If the operation is performed in moist weather, and the bark of the bud is joined closely to the wood of the stock, success is almost certain. If the stocks are in a proper state, the upper edges only of the slit need be raised with the haft, and the bud being gently pushed to its place, will raise the bark smoothly before it, and the insertion be more firm than if the bark had been entirely raised with the haft. It is an operation requiring much exactness, but may be done in one minute; the point where a beginner will most likely fail is in the proper removal of the bud.

As soon as the bud has taken, the ligature may be loosened, and should be entirely removed when it begins to cut into the bark. If the leaf stalk, after a few days, drops off, it indicates the bud has taken; if it withers or adheres, the bud is likely to be dead or dying. The buds must be frequently examined, and the ties loosened, if becoming too tight, as they will in growing stocks. If it is desired to start the bud into immediate growth, soon after it has evidently taken, the stock may be shortened to within ten or twelve inches of the bud, and all shoots rubbed off as they appear, except that from the inserted bud. When this has grown three or four inches, the stock is cut off again near the budded shoot, and when this has grown some inches, the stock is cut off close to its base. When it is desired that the bud should remain dormant, cutting back the stock is delayed until just before the flow of sap starts in spring. Buds that are not permitted to push until spring soon overtake the others in growth.

Budding is the most rapid mode of increasing rare varieties, of which every bud is almost sure to make a good plant if the operation is quickly and skillfully performed. It is the easiest method of propagating apples, pears, and most other fruit trees. In the case of peaches it is almost universally applied, and also with those roses that will not succeed readily from cuttings. Budding and grafting can be performed only upon plants of the same, or nearly related, species. Thus a peach can be budded on a plum, as they are both stone fruits, and belong to the same natural group of plants, but no art could make the peach flourish on the apple or pear as a stock.

Grafting.—This differs from budding in its being the transfer of a shoot, with several buds upon it, from one tree to another, instead of merely employing a single bud. It is performed by bringing portions of two growing shoots together, so that the soft wood of the two may unite together. The shoot to be transferred is called the scion, and the tree which is to receive it is called the stock. The stocks are of all ages and sizes, but they must be sound and healthy. The scions employed are generally shoots of the preceding year's growth, which may be cut at any time after the leaves fall, and may be buried in a *dry soil*, with the upper extremities slightly projecting on the north of a wall. They must be protected from heavy rains, or the buds will start too early. Amateurs can best keep all they wish in a corked preserve jar, or a tin box, or closely covered bucket. Examine them occasionally, and if too much moisture is present, leave the cover off a few hours. The drier the better, if they do not begin to shrivel. Keep in a cool place.

Scions of healthy, close-jointed wood should always be chosen. If they are to be sent to a distance, those of rather large size and close joints should be selected, enveloped in a little thin paper slightly dampened, and the whole covered tightly with oiled silk. In this way, they will go a thousand miles in perfect safety. The but and extremities of scions should both be rejected. The tools required are, a grafting-knife, saw, and chisel; but, for whip-grafting, the knife only is employed. Two kinds should be used, one to prune and pare the stock, and the other to prepare the graft.

Grafting Wax.—A composition of very good quality is made of four parts rosin, two of beeswax, and one of tallow. Melt it altogether, turn it into cold water, and work and pull it thoroughly until it turns whitish; just as children do molasses candy. A wax for cold weather will work better with a little less rosin, and in warm with a little more. The stiffness of the wax is increased or diminished by employing less or more of tallow. In cold weather keep the composition in warm water, and in warm, in cold water. In putting it on, the hands must be slightly greased, to keep it from sticking to them, but grease the scion and stock in operating as little as possible.

In applying the wax, be careful to cover the scion on the sides and the cleft in the stock, forming a cap over the top, and press it closely and tightly around the graft, so as to cover every crack, and carefully to exclude the air and water. Cloth, saturated in a composition made a little softer by a greater addition of tallow and beeswax, is more convenient than the wax itself, especially for whip grafting. Take any thin, half-worn calico or muslin, tear it into narrow strips, roll them loosely into small balls, and soak them in the hot composition until every pore is filled. When wished for use, it is unwound from the balls, and torn into smaller strips, of the proper length and breadth required by the size of the stock; this, wound two or three times around the stock and graft, secures it perfectly, and is the most convenient way of applying wax.

Modes and Time of Grafting.—The modes of grafting most usually practised are whip and cleft grafting, and they are practised on the stem and branches, or the roots of trees. Root-grafting can be performed at any time in this climate, or from the fall of the leaf until the buds begin to open. The peach, grafted in this way early in the season, succeeds perfectly at the South, but generally fails north of Virginia. Stone-fruits of all kinds must be grafted earlier than apples, pears, etc., as their sap seems to lose all agglutinating properties after its first flow.

Graft them just as the buds are about to swell, but for most other species the best time for grafting, except in the root, where the scion will be protected by the earth covering it, is while the buds are swelling in the spring. If put in before that time, the alternate freezing and thawing to which they are exposed often destroys the vitality of the graft. Apples, pears, etc., may be grafted until they blossom, if the scions are kept perfectly fresh, and have not started. Grafting succeeds perfectly well just before the second growth, early in August, if the sap is thrown into the graft, by rubbing off the other shoots as they appear; but it is just as well to wait until spring, there being no gain in the growth of the graft over those put in at the usual season.

Whip, or Splice Grafting.—This mode is applicable to all small stocks, and succeeds best where the scion and stock are exactly the same size. Both stock and scion are cut off with a sloping cut about an inch and a half long on each, so as to match precisely, if of the same size; or, if not, at least on one side. A tongue is then made by slitting the scion upward, and the stock downward, which is raised on each and fitted into the slit of the other—holding the scion firmly in its place; bind it closely with the cloth covered with the composition. The engravings, figures 46 and 47, (next page,) show the different steps of the operation. It is the neatest, most expeditious, and most successful mode of grafting, where the stocks are of the proper size. Stocks, three-fourths of an inch in diameter, or even an inch, may be grafted in this way, but for inch stocks cleft grafting is preferable.

Cleft Grafting is the more common mode. It may be practised on large or small stocks, but for the latter whip-grafting only should be employed. The top of the stock is cut off carefully with a fine saw, and pared smoothly with a sharp knife. The stock is then split with the grafting tool, and held open with the chisel of the same, figure 48. A common knife will answer for splitting, and the split may be kept open for insertion with a wooden wedge or a large nail of which the point has been ground down to a wedge shape. Sharpen the lower part of the scion into a smooth wedge, one and a half inch long, more or less, according to its size and that of the split in the stock. The exterior side of the scion when sharpened should be slightly thicker than the other, that it may be sure to make a close fit there, figure 49. Let the scion have two or more buds, of which one should be on the wedge and inserted just below the top of the stock, figure 50. This often grows when the others fail. The main point is that the inside bark of the scion and that of the stock should exactly correspond, and meet at their edges at least in one place. To effect this, it is usual to set the scion so that its upper extremity falls a little without the line made by the continuation of the stock on the side in which it is inserted. It

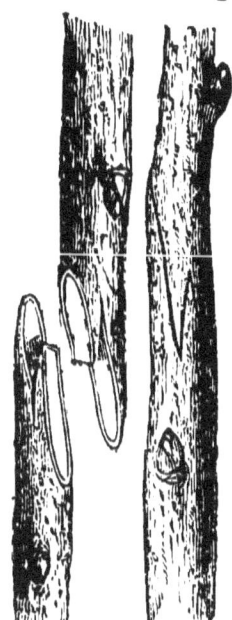

Fig. 46.   Fig. 47.
SPLICE GRAFTING.

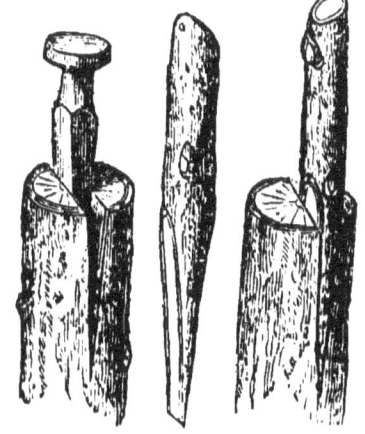

Fig. 48.   Fig. 49.   Fig. 50.

is better as in figure 51 to set it a little within or towards the heart of the stock, and the base of the scion a little out, and when the scion and stock cross each other, a meeting of the edges will be certain, and even a novice will thus succeed. One or two scions are set in the stock according to its size; the wedge is then withdrawn, and the whole carefully covered with the composition so as to exclude all air and moisture.

Fig. 51.

Root Grafting.—Both the whip and cleft modes are successfully applied in root grafting, but splice grafting is more generally in use. In root grafting fruit trees, the best stocks for the purpose are seedlings which are cut off at the collar and grafts inserted in one or the other of these modes, according to the size of the stock. If such stocks cannot be got, roots of thrifty trees may be employed, but are more apt to produce diseased trees. This work can be performed at any leisure time during the winter, and when the winters are mild and open, they should be set out in the open ground at once and covered about an inch above the point of junction with soil.

In colder latitudes they are packed closely in small boxes with sandy earth among the roots, and kept in a cool cellar until they can be planted in spring. In root grafting, either waxed cloth or twine is used to hold the scions in place.

In grafting, as in budding, always have sharp instruments; make the cuts clean and smooth; bring the inner bark, that is, the active young parts, of stock and scion in close contact, by a permanent pressure of the stock upon its scion; the top of the scion should be cut off next to a bud, and have a bud just beneath the shoulder where it unites with the stock; every portion of the wound should be perfectly covered with the composition, and the stock and scion must correspond, not only in their nature, but in their habits of growth.

Inarching, or Grafting by Approach.—This mode is 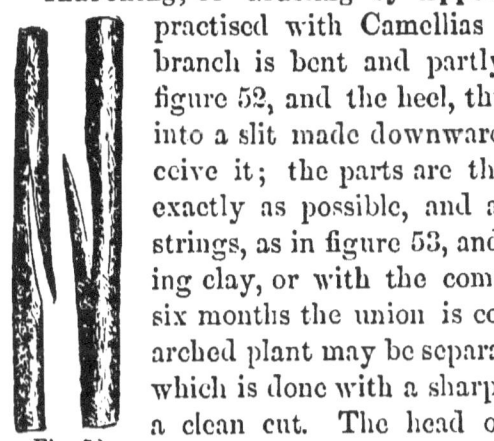 practised with Camellias and Magnolias. A branch is bent and partly cut through, as in figure 52, and the heel, thus formed, is slipped into a slit made downward in the stock to receive it; the parts are then made to meet as exactly as possible, and are bound with bass strings, as in figure 53, and covered with grafting clay, or with the composition. In five or six months the union is complete, and the inarched plant may be separated from its parent, which is done with a sharp knife so as to leave a clean cut. The head of the stock, if not removed before, is then cut away, and the plant is ready for removal.

Fig 52.

There are several other modes of budding and grafting, but the above are most useful and commonly practised.

The *advantages* of these operations are, the rapidity with which a valuable kind may be propagated, which will not grow from seed or cuttings: trees of worthless fruit may be changed into more valuable varieties; seedlings can be brought into early bearing; foreign, tender fruits may be rendered hardier on hardy, native stocks; a kind of fruit may be grown in a soil not congenial to it, as the pear by grafting on the quince; several varieties of fruit may be grown upon the same tree; and, finally, by grafting on dwarf-growing stocks the trees may be so dwarfed as to afford many ripening in succession within the limits of a small garden.

Fig. 53.

Experience shows the graft and stock mutually influence each other. The effect of the stock upon the graft in improving its product, is evident in such pears as succeed on the quince, their size and flavor being much improved. The graft in turn affects the stock, increasing or diminishing its vigor. The Newtown Pippin will roughen the bark of any other apple stock. A Collins pear, grafted upon the branches of another variety, is very likely to cause the death of the whole tree.

CHAPTER XI.

PRUNING AND TRAINING.

Pruning.—This operation is generally performed more at random than any other in gardening, yet is one of the most important and most delicate. Not even a twig should be removed from a tree without some definite object. This work above all others requires care, knowledge, and judgment, and should never be left to ignorant operators. In their hands the results can hardly fail to be injurious, but performed by those who base their practice on the laws of vegetation, it contributes to ensure a regular production of beautiful and perfect fruit, and still more to prolong the life and fruitfulness of trees.

The benefits of skillful pruning, as stated by Du Breuil, are:

1st.—It permits one to impose upon its subject a form corresponding with the place it is designed to occupy. Thus to standard fruit trees is given the pyramidal form, or that of the vase. Trees thus managed produce larger and more abundant fruits than those left to grow at random, and occupy less space. Trees upon an espalier or wall, and vines upon a trellis, are made to develop their wood with symmetry and regularity, and occupy usefully the whole surface they were designed to cover.

2d.—By pruning, all the main branches of the tree are furnished with fruit bearing branches duly exposed to air and light in their whole extent. An unpruned peach tree will produce fruit only at the extremity of each branch, but by pruning, all parts of the tree are made fruitful.

3d.—By pruning, fructification is made more equal. By suppressing each year the superabundant flower-buds, and thinning the branches themselves, one preserves for the formation of new flower-buds for the following year the sap which would have been absorbed by the parts removed.

4th.—Finally, pruning renders the fruit larger, and of better quality. A large part of those nourishing fluids which would have supplied the suppressed parts, are turned to the benefit of the fruit on the remaining branches.

Lindley adds that the time in which a fruit ripens may be changed by skillful pruning. If raspberry canes are cut down to three eyes in the spring, a late summer or autumn crop will be produced. By removing the flower-buds of remontant roses, fine autumn blooms are obtained.

Time for Pruning.—Pruning is performed at two periods during the year. Winter pruning is that given to trees while vegetation is in repose, and summer pruning includes all that a tree or plant receives in its stages of active growth.

Winter Pruning.—This may be performed at the South directly after the fall of the leaf, and in mild weather through the winter months, until vegetation is about to commence; at the North, from the time the severe frosts are over, until the sap begins to move, that is, in February and March. If pruned before the heavy frosts, the cut, being exposed to their severity, does not heal readily, and the terminal bud is often destroyed. Pruning must not be undertaken while the branches are frozen, as the wood cuts with great difficulty, and the wounds are torn and commonly heal badly, and the nearest bud generally perishes. If delayed until the shoots begin to start, all the sap from the roots, that has been absorbed by the parts of the tree cut off, is lost. A great many of the expanding leaf and flower-buds will be broken off, and finally the sap, in full flow, pours from the wounds and the tree is greatly weakened thereby.

Pruned at the proper season, the tree throws all its force upon the remaining buds, developing those which would else be dormant. Where, however, a tree is too vigorous to fruit well, a late spring pruning, when the shoots begin to lengthen, will check its vigor and cause the formation of fruit buds.

The vine, currant, and gooseberry, may be pruned at any time between the suspension of growth and the first flow of sap. In general, it is best to prune plants in the order in which vegetation commences; first apricots, then peaches, just as their buds begin to swell, plums and cherries, then pears and apples. Stone fruits should be lightly pruned, as they are apt to be injured by the issue of gum from the wounds.

Summer Pruning.—Shoots may be removed at any time, if the tree seems to be throwing its strength in a wrong direction. This is better accomplished by disbudding, that is, removing those buds which would produce unnecessary shoots, or pinching the extremities of those shoots which are making too much wood.

Pinching, or removing the growing point with the finger and thumb, is the most essential operation in the summer management, both of fruit trees and ornamental plants. The tendency of the sap is to the growing points, and especially to those more elevated and exposed to the light. The upper buds, if the tree or plant is near to and shaded by others, are the only ones to develop, and, consequently, it shoots upward rapidly, while the stem is not proportionally developed, and few side branches are thrown out. Such a tree must not only be cut back severely at the winter pruning so as to shorten the leader to perhaps one-third of its growth, but it needs looking to in summer, or it will push upward as strongly as before. To strengthen its side branches, then, it is necessary to pinch in early, while they are in active growth, the leader or any other shoot that is evidently receiving an undue amount of sap, which operation checks the flow of sap to that point, and directs it to where it is more needed. When a side shoot shows a disposition to outgrow the leader, the defect is remedied by pinching, with no loss of wood or growth to the tree. Pyramidal forms can only be secured in this way by summer pinching, keeping the lower limbs always the longest. In the same way early bearing is promoted, for the check given to the growing point concentrates the sap, and, unless the shoots again start into growth, it is likely to form fruit buds. Bushy specimen plants in the green-house and flower-garden are not to be seen in plants left to themselves. The stems are soon naked, and, if cut back, they soon grow up as bad as before. If the leading and other dominant shoots are pinched back, leaving the side shoots unchecked until ripe, when they may be cut back a little to make them branch, they will be as healthy and full of bloom as those at the upper part of the plant. Pinching should be performed at once as soon as a shoot shows itself out of proportion. Further directions as to the summer management of particular trees and plants will be given hereafter.

Implements.—The implements required in pruning are the common pruning knife, a small saw with very fine teeth, a socket chisel two or three inches wide, with a long handle, and a pair each of large pruning shears, pruning scissors, and pole pruning shears; these should divide the branch with a clean, smooth cut, and not bruise it on the side next the stem.

Mode of Operating upon the Branches.—They should be so cut that they will heal kindly. If it was desired to cut off a branch as at fig. 54, it is cut as near to the bud as possible, without injury to it. The knife is entered directly opposite to the base of the bud, and comes out even with the point of the bud. In this way the bud will not suffer, and the cut quickly heals. In fig. 55 the cut is so far above the bud that the shoot will die down to near the bud, and require to be again cut off that it may heal over. If the cut is made, commencing too far below the bud, as at fig. 56, the bud is badly nourished and will be less vigorous, and perhaps perish. In cutting off a branch it should not be cut so close to the stem as to wound it, or make the cut larger than the base of the branch, neither so long as to leave a snag to decay slowly for years, if it do not send out new vigorous shoots again requiring removal.

Fig. 54.   Fig. 55.   Fig. 56.

Considered mechanically, the great art is to make a clean, smooth cut, so as to leave the bark in a healthy state to cover the wound, and to prune so near a bud as to leave no dead wood. Hence, if the branch be removed with the saw, the cut must be smoothed over with the knife. In cutting off large branches, the wound should be covered with grafting wax, or painted over with Mr. Downing's preparation of shellac dissolved in alcohol, in order to exclude the air.

General Principles of Pruning.—The secret of pruning judiciously consists in 1st, "Calculating intelligently the proportion one ought to establish between the branches with fruit and those with none, and which serve only to nourish the tree. 2d, In establishing an equilibrium among the parts of the tree, so that neither side nor its leader may grow out of proportion so as to weaken the other side or the base by drawing to itself all the sap."

Pruning is most commonly intended either to *improve* the *form* of the tree by directing the growth from one part to another; to *renew* the *growth* of stunted trees; to *induce* or *diminish fruitfulness;* to remove *diseased* or decaying *branches;* and in cases of transplanting, to *proportion* the *head* to the *roots.*

In *pruning to improve the form of the tree,* whether fruit trees, or ornamental trees in pleasure grounds, the object is to preserve its natural shape, so that it may be an agreeable object on the lawn, or when combined with others in a group. Lawn trees should never have the stems trimmed up to bare poles, but the branches should proceed from near the ground, so that when covered with foliage they will nearly sweep the surface, and be one mass of green from the base to the top. So in all kinds of fruit trees, the branches should be allowed to proceed from the trunk about a foot and a half from the ground. Such trunks are screened from our burning sun, and are much more healthy and fruitful than those with naked stems five or six feet high. Every tree growing naturally has its trunk sheltered from the sun. If it grow in the open ground, this is accomplished by its own branches, while in the forest all the trunks are sheltered by the canopy of foliage above. If one part of the tree is disposed to outgrow another, and thus destroy the balance, it may be shortened in winter, and the shoots pinched off the next summer, until the sap is thrown in the right direction into weaker branches that were left entire, and the balance is restored. When it is desired that new shoots of a branch should take an *upright direction,* prune to an *inside bud.* If you wish an *open, spreading top,* prune to an *outside bud* of the branch. If the branches be cut at an inside bud, as at *A*, figure 57, the growth from the upper buds will be as in figure 58; but if the cut at an outside bud, *B*, figure 57, the new branches will spread apart, as shown in figure 59. To make a stem

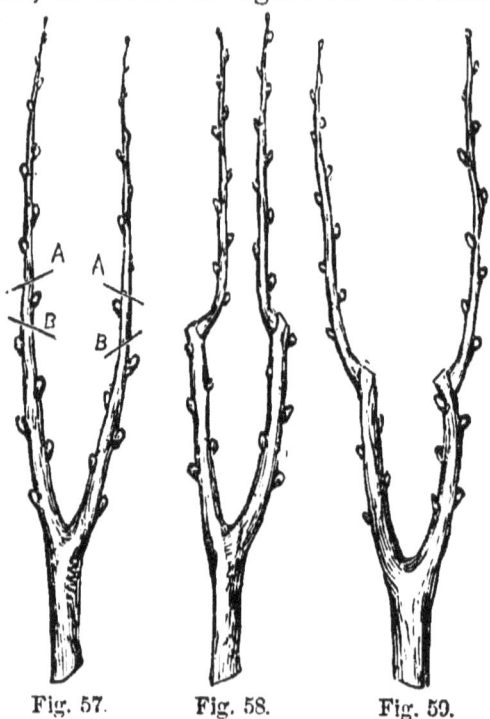

Fig. 57.   Fig. 58.   Fig. 59.
PRUNING TO IMPROVE FORM.

grow erect, in the annual cutting back which young trees require, select the bud intended for a leader on opposite sides each successive year, and the tree will grow upright. Selecting it two or three years on the same side, will cause the trunk to incline in that direction. Symmetrical growth is not only agreeable to the eye, but it assists in maintaining the equilibrium of vegetation, preventing the sap from being drawn more to one side than the other.

Pruning to Renew the Growth.—When a tree has

stopped growing, remaining stationary, it often happens that if it is cut back in winter to a few buds, the whole force of the sap being made to act on these few buds, vigorous young shoots will be produced, and these sending down new woody matter to the stem, new roots are formed, and the whole tree is renewed. In young trees where the growth has not been checked, an annual cutting back of the new growth is likewise necessary, and will strengthen the branches on the lower parts of the tree, and thicken up the trunk, enabling it to maintain an erect position.

Pruning to Reduce or Diminish Fruitfulness.—Everything that is favorable to rapid, vigorous growth, is generally unfavorable to the immediate production of fruit. Hence pruning, to induce fruitfulness, is performed after vegetation has commenced. If a tree be severely pruned immediately after its leaves have put forth, it is so checked as to be unable to make a vigorous growth the same season, the circulation of the sap is impeded, and the young shoots that would have made wood branches, had the growth been unchecked, will become fruit spurs. Pinching the extremities is, however, the usual mode of pruning to induce fruitfulness. The same result is produced by pruning the roots, which also lessens the dimensions the trees would otherwise obtain, by diminishing the quantity of food they receive from the soil.

Pruning at Transplanting.—At this time all bruised and broken roots and branches should be removed with a sharp knife. When trees are taken from the ground, a greater or less portion of the roots is destroyed or injured, and the natural balance between the root and top is destroyed, and the tree in this condition will either die or make a slow growth. In England, the climate is so moist that trees may be removed and leave nearly all the branches as they were; but under the hot suns and strong winds of an American climate, a vigorous shortening in is requisite.

As horticultural theorists strongly insisted that pruning at transplanting was injurious, J. J. Thomas, Esq., author of the Fruit Culturist, has settled the question by direct experiment. Of six apricots, two years from the bud, about seven feet high, five were cut back and one left uncut at transplanting. The most vigorous of the five made 21 shoots, from 6 to 21 inches long. The weakest had 9 shoots 6 to 7 inches long, not counting the shoots less than 6 inches in length. The unpruned tree had on 7 shoots all less than 2 inches, and not one-twentieth part of the amount of foliage to be found on other trees. Experiments upon cherry trees, planted at the same time, equally showed the necessity of pruning at transplanting. Trees unripened when transplanted are so checked that it requires years to restore them. In a southern climate they must be more severely cut back, when planted out, than in that of Macedon, N. Y., where the experiments were made.

It matters very little how closely we prune the top of the trees; only have good roots, and a single season's growth will restore the balance. Do not leave more than one or two buds to a branch of the previous year's growth if the tree is of much size at the time of transplanting. Coniferous trees, as the pines, firs, etc., are exceptions, for if cut back at planting, the leader being lost, the form of the tree is difficult to restore. Hence those only of this class should be planted which have been taken up and reset annually in the nursery until a mass of fibrous roots has been formed. These must be protected from the air until the tree is reset. Broad-leaved evergreens, like English Laurels, evergreen Oaks, may be cut back and a portion of the leaves removed to lessen evaporation, with the same advantage as deciduous trees. Indeed, many of the broad-leaved evergreens, taken from the woods, cannot be transplanted with any success, unless nearly all the top is removed. Nursery-raised trees are taken up and reset so often, that they can be replanted safely without cutting in so severely.

M. Du Breuil, from whose work we have already drawn, bases the whole theory of pruning fruit trees upon the following six general principles, which, in giving, we condense:

I.—*The vigor of a tree subjected to pruning depends in a great measure on the equal distribution of sap in all its branches.* That this equal distribution may take place—

1. *Prune the branches of the most vigorous parts very short, and those of the weak parts long.* The feeble parts being pruned long, present a great number of buds and a large surface of leaves, which attract the sap, and produce vigorous growth; while the vigorous parts being pruned short and the surface of leaves diminished, growth in those parts is also diminished.

2. *Leave a large quantity of fruit on the strong part, and remove the whole or the greater part from the feeble.* The sap which arrives in the strong part will be appropriated by the fruit, and the wood there will make little growth, while the feeble parts being deprived of fruit, the sap will be appropriated by the growing parts and they will increase in size and strength.

3. *Bend the strong parts and keep the weak erect.* The more erect the branches are, the greater will be the flow of sap and consequent growth; hence, the balance may be restored by bending down those disposed to make too much growth.

4. *Remove from the vigorous parts the superfluous shoots as early in the season as possible, and from the feeble parts as late as possible.* The fewer the young shoots are in number, the fewer the leaves, and the less the sap is attracted there; but leaving these standing on the feeble parts, these leaves attract the sap and induce vigorous growth.

5. *Pinch early the soft extremities of the shoots on the vigorous parts, and as late as possible on the feeble parts, excepting always any shoots which may be too vigorous for their position.* By this practice the flow of sap to that point is checked and turned to the growing points that have not been pinched.

6. *In training, lay in the strong shoots on the trellis early and leave the feeble parts loose as long as possible.* Laying in the strong shoots obstructs in them the circulation, and favors the weak parts which are at liberty. Giving also the feeble parts the benefit of the light in training, and confining the strong parts more in the shade, restores a balance.

II.—*The sap acts with greater force and produces more vigorous growth on a branch short pruned than on one long pruned.* The whole sap of the branch acting on two buds must produce greater development of wood on them than if divided among fifteen or twenty. Hence, to produce wood branches, we prune short, or if fruit branches we prune long, because slender and feeble shoots are more disposed to fruit. Hence, also, trees that are enfeebled by over-bearing should for a year or two be pruned short, until the balance is restored.

III.—*The sap tending always to the extremities of the shoots causes the terminal bud to push with greater vigor than the laterals.*—When we wish a prolongation of a stem, we should prune to a vigorous wood bud, and leave no production that can interfere with the action of the sap on it.

IV.—*The more the sap is obstructed in its circulation, the more likely it will be to produce fruit-buds.* Sap, circulating slowly, is subjected to a more complete elaboration in the tissues of the tree, and becomes better adapted to form fruit buds. If we wish a branch to bear fruit, we can obstruct the circulation of the sap by bending or making incisions around the branch, or if wished to change a fruit into a wood-branch, raise it into a vertical position and prune it to two or three buds, on which we concentrate the action of the sap and induce them to grow vigorously.

V.—*The leaves serve to prepare the sap absorbed by the roots for the nourishment of the tree, and aid in the formation of buds on the shoots.* All trees therefore, deprived of their leaves, are liable to perish. Hence, the leaves should never be removed from a tree under the pretext of aiding the growth, or ripening the fruit, as deprived of leaves trees cannot grow, neither can their fruit mature.

VI.—*When the buds of any shoot or branch do not develope before the age of two years, they can be forced into activity only by a very close pruning, and in some cases, as the peach, even this will fail.* Hence the main branches should be trimmed so as to secure a development of their successive sections, and so shortened in as not to allow the production of long, naked stems, leaving the interior of the tree bare of shoots, and consequently unproductive.

In order to induce trees to grow in any particular form, it is not so much labor as continued attention that is required. A thorough pruning once a year will not produce the desired effect, but a little attention two or three times a week during the growing season, will be sufficient to examine every shoot in an acre of garden trees, and the eye is very soon trained so as to detect at a glance the shoots that require attention. (*Du Breuil, Lindley, Barry, etc.*)

Training.—The principal objects of training are to render plants more productive of fruits and flowers than if left to grow voluntarily, also to form screens of various running plants to keep any unsightly object from view. The points to be attended to, are to entirely cover the wall or trellis, bending the branches backwards and forwards so as to form numerous deposits of returning sap, and ensure the full exposure of the fruit-bearing branches to the sun and air. The long shoots are shortened or pinched to make them throw out side branches, with which the trellis is covered, without permitting them to cross each other. Training flowering plants is necessary that they may appear in elegant and symmetrical form. It should be regulated by a knowledge of their habits of growth, and consists principally in checking over-luxuriance of growth and tying them to stakes or frames. Directions for training the grape, etc., will be given hereafter.

CHAPTER XII.

TRANSPLANTING.

In the operation of transplanting, the main points to be regarded are the proper preparation of the soil for receiving the plant; care in taking it up so as to avoid injury to the small, fibrous roots; setting it firmly so that its roots may take a secure hold of the soil; planting with as little delay as possible; and, lastly, maintaining the balance as far as practicable between the top of the plant and its roots, so that the former may not lose more by evaporation than the roots absorb, until again established.

Preparation of the Soil.—Plants, when removed, need a freshly dug soil which affords a moist situation in which the delicate fibers may be emitted, and therein quickly establish themselves. If also well drained and trenched, the effect upon present and subsequent growth is very decided: a tree or vine thriving much better in such a situation, than if the roots are put into a hole with none of the surrounding soil loosened. The soil ought also be enriched with fine manure, but no coarse, unfermented manures should be applied where they will come in contact with the roots. When the ground is in a suitable condition, holes should be dug for the reception of the roots of the plants. These had better be made square than round, as a large hole in that form can be sooner made. The diameter should be such that it will receive all the roots when fully extended. The holes should be made too large rather than too small. In digging the holes, throw out the best soil on one side and the poor on the opposite. If the ground has been prepared deeply, the holes may be made just deep enough to receive the roots, which, in some cases, are spindle-shaped and extend downwards to a considerable depth, and in others run along the surface. For most plants the hole should be deeper at the sides than at the centre, leaving the bottom convex and not basin-shaped. It should have the bottom soil loosened, and in dry weather be watered, but the water should be allowed to subside so as to be moist, not wet, at the time of planting. It should be left of such depth in all good soils, that the neck of the plant may be as near the surface as before, or but a trifle above; but in clayey soils, ill drained, let it be somewhat above on a broad, slightly elevated mound.

Taking up the Plants.—In this operation *avoid injury to the roots;* with the utmost care they will be mutilated. A little attention will save a year's growth to a tree. The roots are of two kinds, the main roots which support the plant in the earth, and the small branching or fibrous roots, the fresh tips and numerous fibrils or root hairs of which supply it with nourishment. These parts are of great delicacy, and if injured or broken off, the plant must throw out others, or perish for want of nourishment. These fibrous roots are the ones most likely to be destroyed or injured in taking up, and in replanting to be squeezed between stones and hard lumps of earths, so that the circulation is weakly and imperfectly carried on through diseased and defective organs. The roots of a tree therefore, when transplanted, must be examined, and all those injured, and all the small fibrous extremities in bad condition, should be cut back with a sharp knife to the sound parts before it is reset, in order to force the root to throw out new fibres, which, in many plants, are produced in great abundance from where a root has been cut back with a clean cut. Roots, matted with fibers, should be disentangled and soil introduced among them in planting, so as to separate them from each other.

While the plant is out of the ground, its roots should be protected from exposure to the air, and, if not planted immediately, should be covered with earth. Many trees are ruined by lying out exposed to the sun for hours while holes are being dug to receive them. Before the tree is reset, the top also should receive the necessary pruning.

Replanting.—After the holes are ready and the tree prepared, its roots should be laid upon the convex surface to see if the hole is of the proper depth, which may be judged by the eye, or more exactly by laying a rod across the hole close to the stem, resting on the level ground on each side. If the neck of the plant is too high or too low, make the necessary alteration, bringing the bottom to the proper height, and convex as before. Hold the tree lightly,—if it is in the same aspect as before, in respect to the points of the compass, it certainly can do it no harm, and many cultivators think it important. Let the roots be nicely spread over this convex surface, training out the leading roots at distances as near equal as possible, not bundling the small roots together, but separating them with particles of fine soil. Then holding the stem firmly and erect, save a slight inclination towards the side from which the heaviest gales or most constant winds are expected, throw the finest, lightest soil, from that reserved by itself, down near the stem, letting it fall down towards the extremities of the roots, and introduce it carefully with the hand among the roots. Having thus covered the lower roots, those above should also be adjusted and covered with the same care, and when all are well covered, water may be given with advantage, unless the soil and weather are moist. If not watered, when the roots are well covered, the earth should be moderately pressed upon them by treading the soil, (being careful not to injure them,) if the ground is light and friable, but by no means if wet. After watering or treading, the remaining soil should be put on, leaving the collar of the plant covered a very little deeper than before, (in the case of trees some two inches,) and the looser and drier this surface soil is, the better will it resist drought. If the body of the tree is held firm by tying it to a stake, it will prevent the loosening of the roots by the action of the wind upon the tops.

Checking undue Evaporation until the Plant is established.—The maintaining the balance between the top and root of the plant is best secured by performing the whole operation at the proper season, in mild, moist weather, and with as much despatch as possible, meanwhile protecting the roots from the air and sun; by *pruning severely* the tops of plants that admit the operation, thus lessening the evaporating surface; and by guarding with the greater care from injury the roots of conifers and other plants that do not. Removing a large portion of the leaves will likewise diminish the evaporating surface, and is very necessary in planting hollies and evergreen oaks. Shade from the sun those plants that require such protection, (and nearly all are thus benefited,) and water to supply the absorbing extremities of the roots with an abundance of food, that the increased quantity imbibed by each may, in some degree, make up for their diminished number. Mulching the surface thinly after a rain is also useful in preventing undue loss of moisture from the soil.

Preparation of Trees for Transplanting.—As a rule, there is little gained by planting out large trees. Small trees, as Downing remarks, can be taken up with a system of roots and branches entire, while the older and larger tree, losing a part of its roots, requires years to resume its former vigor. Trees, transplanted while small, will prove more healthy, vigorous, and enduring; but sometimes, for immediate effect, or to preserve a favorite tree, it is necessary to transplant it when of larger size. This is done by shortening in the leading roots at a distance from the trunk, varying with the size of the tree to be operated upon. A circular trench is dug in spring or before mid-summer around the whole mass of roots, partially undermining them and cutting off all that extend into the trench, which is dug at such a distance from the tree that it encloses a sufficient ball of roots; the trench may be filled with poor earth, or covered with plank. The tree will be checked somewhat, and will fill the ball around it with a mass of fibrous roots, and in the proper season can be moved with safety. Many trees naturally tap-rooted, and evergreens difficult to transplant, are, by being transplanted annually or biennially from their seedling state, compelled to throw out a mass of fibrous roots, retaining among them a ball of earth, and are thus ready to be moved at any time without danger.

It is often desirable to plant fruit trees before the leaves naturally fall, in seasons when autumn frosts are unusually late. A week or two before the trees are to be taken up, pluck from them every leaf, and allow them to remain and ripen their wood. After this time they can be taken up, packed, and sent safely long distances without shriveling. Meanwhile the ground should be prepared, the holes made, and, after pruning, plant them out, giving them a good watering before the last soil is thrown in. In this way, where much planting is to be done, a month's time in autumn is gained.

Transplanting Herbaceous Plants.—Most of these are easily transplanted as soon as they have done flowering, or before they begin to grow in the spring. For annuals, when the season is somewhat advanced, a damp, cloudy day, just before or just after a shower, or in the evening, is the proper time for the operation. Immediately after a very heavy rain is not the best season, as the soil, if moved while too wet, forms a crust about the plant. In the case of choice young plants, they should be taken up with a trowel, removing them with a ball of earth, and the plant will hardly be checked in its growth. Larger plants may be taken up in the same way with the transplanter or spade. Those not removed with a ball, may be grouted by mixing up a quantity of rich loam in water to a semi-fluid state, and inserting the roots therein. Plants that suffer little in taking up, like the cabbage, may have a hole made in the earth with a dibble and the plant inserted therein, when the dibble is again inserted a little obliquely near the stem, and the earth pushed up close to the root. All tap-rooted plants are moved with difficulty. Many herbaceous plants, sweet potato slips for instance, can be safely set out in dry weather in freshly moved soil, by making a hole for their reception, setting the plants therein, and just covering the roots with fine soil; then fill the hole with water about the roots and cover them at the surface with dry soil, to retain the moisture and keep the surface from baking. The operation must be performed in the evening.

All valuable herbaceous plants should be protected with sun shades or plant protectors, when just planted, if the sun comes out hot. These are described in the chapter on Implements.

CHAPTER XIII.

MULCHING, SHADING, AND WATERING.

Mulching.—Mulching is placing litter of various kinds, as leaves, pine straw, or strawy manure, upon the surface soil over the roots of plants and shrubs. If leaves are used, a little earth may be required to keep them in place. Mulching is used as well to prevent moisture from evaporating from the soil in summer, as to prevent frost from penetrating to the roots in winter. In summer a mulch is usually applied to trees and shrubs newly transplanted, and to herbaceous plants that are impatient of heat about the roots. Irish potatoes, mulched, produce more abundantly, and are of better quality. Strawberries, thinly mulched, with the crown uncovered, are much more productive and continue longer in fruit. Rhubarb and other plants, requiring a cool soil, can thus be more easily raised; and so with many other crops. Summer mulching should be applied directly after a rain, that the moisture in the soil may be retained. It should not be applied to potatoes or other tender plants until the danger of frost is over, as the increased evaporation from damp mulch will produce a white frost when there is none or little elsewhere formed. Fruit trees, by having their roots mulched, are kept in better health and vigor. Mulching not only wards off drought, but, in this way, by keeping the ground moist, and by the decay of the mulching substance, a good deal of food is conveyed to the plants. Some authors are of the opinion that ground will become continually richer by being shaded. A supply of small, fibrous roots is thrown out at the surface by mulched plants, and thus is prevented the formation of tap-roots, which are inimical to the production of blossom buds. But the great benefit of mulching is that a steady permanency of moisture is retained, in spite of adverse circumstances, and without stagnation. In general, the coat of litter for mulching must be thin, that the rain may not be prevented from reaching the roots of plants.

Many plants, nearly hardy, can be kept through the winter safely by a coat of dry litter over the roots, and especially the crown of the plant, to turn off a portion of the rain and to keep frost from penetrating to their roots. Verbenas, which would perish without this protection, are often kept over safely under a cover of two or three inches of leaves. So of other plants, where the object is to protect the root and crown, but not the foliage. Mulching has the disadvantage of being untidy in appearance, and of affording shelter to insects and mice, and damage also may occur from its being carelessly set on fire from a cigar, or in cleaning up the garden, thus destroying the plants it was intended to protect.

Shading.—In all glass structures during the warmer portion of the year, some provision must be made for shading. This may be done by thin sheeting, but as this is expensive from its rapid decay, it is usual to whitewash the glass externally as often as may be necessary. The autumn rains will soon wash it off when the season comes in which more light and heat is desirable. The lime of the whitewash, however, soon loosens the putty, so that a preparation of thin flour sizing, thickened with a little pipe clay, will be found better, though not as easy to remove. Where a glass is not needed, as for keeping camellias, and other plants, in pots through the summer, a sort of lattice, made by nailing laths upon a light, oblong frame made for the purpose will be found useful. Laths can also be tied together with coarse twine, being separated by one or more knots, as greater or less distance is desired. Mats and old salt and coffee sacks are often used, but they exclude too much light, and are best employed to prevent radiation, and thus keep out frost in winter.

Water is beneficial to plants as a vehicle for conveying all soluble matters, which form the food of plants, whether they be animal, vegetable, gaseous, or earthy.

Other elements being present in sufficient quantity, the growth and health of a plant will be more or less satisfactory in proportion as it is or is not supplied with all the water it can consume. The action of water is not, however, always beneficial. Injudiciously applied, it destroys more plants than almost any other item of mismanagement. In excess, it is always injurious. It fills the spaces in the soil which would otherwise be filled with air, and plants are choked and perish for want of this indispensable element. A superabundance of water, for a time, increases the growth of foliage and renders it tender and succulent; hence a good supply thereof is needful to plants, the leaves of which are eaten, as lettuce and spinach.

But by this excess the production of flowers and fruits is delayed. The odor of the former and the flavor of the latter are weakened and impaired. The size of the fruit is increased by abundance of water, and without it the strawberry, for instance, will not swell; but the increased size, unless it ripens in a bright atmosphere or the quantity of water is diminished as the fruit ripens, is partly at the expense of flavor. Fruit is not only impaired in quality, but is very liable to crack or burst from excess of moisture, as the plum, grape, or stanwix nectarine often do, or rot upon the tree while still immature, as the peach, plum, etc.

An excess of water softens the tissues of plants, and renders them much more liable to injury by frost. A frost directly after warm and abundant rains, when plants are full of sap, is much more fatal than the same temperature in dry weather.

The temperature of the soil, if wet, is greatly lowered, and its capacity for heat diminishes. The constant evaporation from wet soil so lowers the temperature of the adjacent stratum of air, that frosts occur when there are none on dryer soils. The constant dampness of the atmosphere, produced by excess of water in the soil, diminishes evaporation from the leaves of plants, and hence renders the process of assimilation slower, and less food is taken up by the roots. By diminishing the absorption of carbonic acid, it lessens the atmospheric supply of food. It creates a tendency in the organs of plants to vary from the normal type of growth, changing the flowers, for instance, into green leaves and ill-formed shoots.

Succulent plants, those with fleshy roots, and those with leaves that appear dry, and transpire but little, and in which vegetation proceeds slowly, are most subject to injury from excess of water. Plants growing in a clear light are less endangered by an over supply, than if growing in a shaded situation, as they can both assimilate and perspire more. Plants in pots are most likely to be injured by injudicious watering, at times being drenched with too much, and at others allowed to become too dry.

Where water exists in excess, it must be removed by drainage. This is indispensable in pot culture. It is particularly to be attended to in the case of plants which are to be kept through the winter in green-houses or pits.

The quantity of water that plants require varies with the species of plant and with its condition, whether in a state of growth or repose. A plant cultivated for its leaves requires more water than if grown for its flowers, and still less is needed if grown for its seeds or fruit. In proportion, also, as the roots of plants extend into the earth, the less water at the surface is required. Tap-rooted plants, like cotton, when once established, are not apt to suffer from drought; but those with roots at the surface only, need frequent watering. Perennial plants, also, in general require less the artificial application of water than annuals. The growth of the former is merely suspended by dry weather for the time being, to be resumed when moisture is supplied; but if water and the food of which it is the vehicle be withheld from annual plants, the double tax imposed upon them by nature of forming both roots and shoots at the same time, can no longer be met. Growth being suspended, the plant attempts to flower and ripen seed, and thus, while imperfectly developed, it reaches the limit of its existence and dies.

Plants with fleshy or fibrous roots are impatient of abundant waterings, yet do not well resist drought. Bulbous and tuberous rooted plants, and those with fleshy leaves, can support drought a long time and do well with rare but abundant waterings. Germinating seeds and young plants should have them light but frequent. In a state of free growth, water abundantly; while ripening fruit, water rarely; when transplanting, water freely.

The lighter the soil, the more frequent and copious must be the supply of water. So as the temperature in summer becomes elevated and the days are clear and the atmosphere dry, evaporation increases, while rains become less frequent; hence the more water will have to be artificially supplied. At such times it must be given copiously, for mere sprinklings bake the soil, and do more harm than good.

When at rest, as in the winter of temperate climates and in the dry season of the tropics, very little moisture in the earth is required by perennials, unless marsh plants. Bulbs in a state of rest will endure almost any amount of dryness, and may even be exposed to excessive heat, somewhat resembling, in this respect, a ripened seed. Bulbs that have been kept dry for some time, when again to be started into growth, should receive but little water at first. If much is given, it will be absorbed without being digested, and stagnating within, will destroy the bulb. Hence, we plant bulbs in a light soil and on raised beds, that the superabundant moisture may not destroy the roots.

But a moderate degree of water is needed when vegetation commences in the spring, for the earth is usually sufficiently moist; but when they have started into growth, plants should be abundantly supplied, and the quantity gradually diminished as the organization becomes complete. As autumn approaches, evaporation becomes less, and the supply of water should be diminished, both in the quantity and frequency of application. Withholding water gradually from plants that are to be kept through the winter will cause them to ripen their shoots, and they will be more likely to survive the cold season.

No plant, at any time, should receive more moisture than it can consume either by assimilation, or rejection in the form of perspiration. Plants with large, broad leaves, like tobacco, squashes, etc., expose more surface to the light and sun, perspire freely, and hence need more water than those with small, pinnate leaves, like the acacia, or than succulent, or fleshy plants, a class that requires but little water at any time, and is very impatient of an excessive supply, especially in winter.

Watering artificially is resorted to in order to maintain a proper degree of humidity in the soil. This is indispensable in hot-houses, etc., and with all plants in pots. With these the protection of the glass assists in keeping the air about the plants in a state of humidity.

But in open air culture, artificial watering can never be so beneficial as natural rain, and is often, indeed, a real disadvantage to plants.

Artificial watering, with all its disadvantages, must, to a considerable extent, be resorted to in hot climates, or the results of gardening will often be quite unsatisfactory. In giving it, the conditions of beneficial, natural watering should as far as possible be observed. The rains that are most refreshing to plants are those of mild temperature and which distil gently, bringing to the roots of plants not moisture only, but ammonia and carbonic acid. If rain did not bring with it fertilizing matters, it would

7

in time wash out all the fertility of the soil and leave it sterile. This is the effect of heavy, beating storms, which carry away more of fertility than they bring; while if the soil be stiff they puddle the surface, rendering it, when dry, impervious, preventing the access of atmospheric air and the moisture of the dew and of any gentle rains that follow.

Hence, in applying water, it should not be thrown upon the soil with force from a coarsely perforated watering pot, as its effects would be injurious in precisely the same way as a washing rain. To tender plants and germinating seeds it should be applied through a very fine rose. The rose to a garden watering-pot should not permit a common pin to enter its perforations. For delicate seedlings in pots it is better to give water by sprinkling gently from a wetted brush, both the plants and the soil. For larger plants in pots or in the ground, the leaves may be sprinkled, unless too succulent, but the main supply of water should be given by pouring it gently upon the sides of the pot or upon the surface of the earth, and let it flow gradually over and sink into the soil.

It is not best, in general, to water close by the stems of plants. The roots take up food only at their extremities, and generally extend as far as the branches. Both the roots and leaves of plants require water, and receive it in natural watering. But the rains that fall upon a tree do not fall upon its trunk, but roll off all around it, and drop precisely where the extending roots are ready to take it up. Watering directly at the base of a plant, close to its stem and collar, will be likely to rot or injure that vital part, and small, delicate plants are pretty sure to damp off. Thus applied, much of the water never reaches the absorbing extremities of the root. As a plant increases in size, the farther from the stem should the water be applied.

Vines trained to verandas, or growing up under the eaves of dwellings, often suffer from the want of water applied to the foliage. Trained against the walls, evaporation goes on very rapidly from the heat reflected upon them, and but very little rain falls upon the foliage. They also become covered with dust and their pores choked therewith. When the sun shines warm and brightly, plants should be watered only about the roots, for if applied to the foliage, the drops, remaining thereon, act as so many burning glasses, and scorch the leaves, covering them with brown spots wherever the water rests. But in the spring, when the earth is moist, if the air is dry, and indeed at all times when the atmosphere is dry, and particularly when plants become covered with dust, they will be greatly refreshed by syringing or sprinkling the foliage in the evening or morning, if their leaves are not susceptible of change by humidity.

Plants in pots should be watered frequently and little at a time. If the ball has become dry, do not deluge it at once, as it will flow directly through the pot or out at the sides, carrying with it the richness of the soil, while the ball still remains dry. Give it a little water, and when that soaks up, give, a few minutes after, a little more, until the entire ball is in a suitable state of humidity. The drainage must be good, or if much water is given to plants in pots, the soil will become heavy, water-logged, and impervious to the atmosphere.

The best water to use is rain water, caught in open cisterns, as it is well aerated and abounds in ammonia and fertilizing gases. If spring or well water must be used, add a very little guano, say a pound or two to twenty gallons of water, giving the smaller quantity to delicate plants, and the larger to gross feeders, and before using let it stand a few hours. Manure from the hen roost in double quantity may be substituted for guano. For sprinkling the foliage, pure water is better.

The temperature of water, too, must be regarded. The good effects of bottom heat in hot-beds, or of artificial heat in green-houses, are often entirely counteracted, and plant growth brought to a stand, by watering with cold water. It is not only the lowering the temperature of the roots of plants, but the suddenness of the change that is injurious and often fatal. Water should always be applied a few degrees warmer than the soil, that growth may be promoted and not checked.

As to the time of day at which water should be given, unless applied quite freely, it does little good in the heat of a summer's day, as the hot atmosphere drinks up the moisture before the plant can imbibe it. The effect of rain can be best secured by watering just at night, when the falling dew will, in some measure, prevent evaporation from the plants, and they get fully refreshed during the night. But in the spring of the year, to water in the evening in dry weather darkens the soil, and, therefore, increases radiation. Evaporation is also greatly increased; the temperature sinks rapidly, the plants are chilled, if not frozen, and make less growth than if not watered at all. So, also, in autumn, for the same reason, at those times water only in the morning, and the heat of the soil will not be materially lowered, the sun's rays communicating fresh warmth.

It should be the great object of the gardener to avoid the necessity of watering, by shading the earth or the plants themselves, by mulching, top-dressing, or sun shades. Seeds will come up much more satisfactorily in the open ground if shaded, than if one depends upon watering. If watering is resorted to at all, it should be given copiously and the supply kept up until the plants are established. After watering, the ground should be stirred about the plants, if up, as soon as it is sufficiently dry, and never allowed to become hard. A mulching of leaf mould is desirable, to keep the surface in a proper state, and if applied when the surface is wet, it will prevent the necessity of repeated waterings.—(*De Candolle, Lindley, Mc'Intosh.*)

Summer Cultivation.—If before seeds are planted, the

soil be deeply moved and finely pulverized, the labor necessary in the subsequent culture of garden crops is greatly diminished. Still the hoe cannot be dispensed with, and the soil is stirred therewith among our growing crops, in order that the earth may be kept in a light and permeable state, so that the roots of plants may extend freely through it in search of food. If kept in this condition, water deposited by rain and dew is imbibed more readily and sinks more deeply into the soil, supplying plants both with moisture and ammonia. Moisture from beneath is also more freely supplied by capillary attraction from the subsoil if the earth is kept in a light, porous state. The atmosphere, laden with nutritive gases, freely penetrates the soil and deposits nourishment within reach of the young rootlets of plants. By the same process weeds are destroyed, their growth prevented, and there is also a thorough pulverization and intermixture with the soil of the manures which have been applied.

Judgment as to the time and manner of hoeing must be exercised. Even hoeing may do harm—but there is more danger that it will not be done sufficiently often, than performed imperfectly. In a hot and a dry climate, hoe less deeply than in those that are cold and moist, as hoeing favors evaporation, and this may prove injurious where the sun is hot and the rains are not frequent. So in spring, hoe more deeply and frequently than when the season becomes advanced. A heavy, argillaceous soil should be more deeply moved than one more sandy. Where a poor soil has been recently manured, it should not be hoed too deeply, but the compost should be allowed to remain intermixed with the surface soil.

In practice the plants cultivated and their stage of advancement must also be considered. Plants with long tap-roots, like beets and carrots, are benefited by deep hoeing, which might be injurious to those with fibrous and spreading roots. Among the latter, deep culture between the rows is beneficial, so long as the plants are young and their roots not extended; but when they begin to shade much of the surface, and to occupy most of the soil with their roots, merely loosening the immediate surface, at the same time destroying all weeds, will be quite sufficient.

All garden crops, then, should be frequently and deeply hoed early in the season, and in the early stages of their growth. Even to suppress the weeds which spring up freely in the moist soil at that time requires frequent and thorough hoeing. Of course hoeing, or moving the soil in any way, is not to be undertaken while it is wet. When young seedling plants first appear, the earth must be lightly stirred about them, to break up any crust upon the surface that may have formed. Take care not to injure the young plants, though at this time the mutilation of a few roots, if the most of them are unhurt, is easily repaired; and the plant is not so much injured by their loss as benefited by that thorough pulverization of the soil, that permits the free extension of the roots, and opens it to the air and night dews.

At this time all weeds should be removed, and the plants thinned to an inch apart, so as not to interfere with each other. When they have made a little more growth, and there is less danger of insects and other disasters, they should be thinned to the proper distance and hoed more deeply, taking care not to cover or injure the young plants. After this continue to keep the soil light and open, of course destroying all weeds.

In heavy loams, watering or dashing rains will frequently puddle the surface, which bakes in the sun so effectually as to exclude the atmosphere. The rains that follow flow off without sinking into and moistening the soil. But a soil which, soon after each rain, while not too wet, is freshly hoed, will, at all times, present an open, porous, finely pulverized surface, ready for the absorption of plant food from the atmosphere, and easily permeable to the roots of plants in search of it.

As the plants increase in size, the ground is shaded by their foliage, which, in a measure, prevents the growth of weeds and protects the surface of the soil from being hardened by the sun. At this time hoeing is less required, nor can it be performed without considerable mutilation of the branches and larger roots, and thus cutting off in part their communication with the soil—injuries from which plants in an advanced stage of growth, and under the burning heat of summer do not readily recover.

It is not fully decided whether the soil should be frequently stirred during droughts. Our present opinion is, that in all warm climates it should, at such times, be undisturbed. If the earth be already loose and in fine tilth, the air that enters into its pores will deposit its moisture therein. At night the dews are deposited much more heavily upon freshly dug soil. But this deposit of atmospheric moisture will avail little if the surface is often stirred, as more water will be given off by day than is absorbed at night; and a plot frequently hoed during a drought would at length become quite dry to nearly the depth it was cultivated. However it may be in England, here no deposit of moisture from night dews, or supply brought up by capillary attraction from beneath, can make good the loss of water by evaporation from the soil in a hot summer day. De Candolle says that in most hot countries frequent hoeings are avoided, as they really have the evil of favoring evaporation of moisture from the soil at the time when, the heat being most intense, the water is naturally retained therein by the hardening of its surface, and would act with most activity in decomposing and dissolving the organic matters it contains. The true course is deep, thorough culture early in the season and while plants are young. But hoeing must not be performed in spring or autumn, at times when the indications are that frosty nights will follow, as tender plants are much more likely to be killed thereby from the increased evaporation at the surface of fresh dug soil. Through the summer, after each good rain, as soon as the ground will do to work, stir the surface and kill the weeds, leaving it in a light, friable condition, to be undisturbed, unless to destroy any weeds that appear, until another rain renders further hoeing necessary. Continue this until the plants approach blossoming, or begin to cover the ground, after which hoeing, if performed at all, must be as shallow as possible. A soil thus managed is always open to atmospheric influences, and what moisture it may have or receive is better retained.

CHAPTER XIV.

PROTECTION FROM FROST.

Late spring frosts are the terror of gardeners. In sections of country subject to them, tender plants should not be planted early. As mulched or newly dug soils are much more liable to the white frosts of spring, mulching should not be applied to Irish potatoes, etc., until danger of frosts is over, nor should tender plants be hoed when a change to cold may be anticipated. If a frost is apprehended, plants in hills are best protected with boxes, vine shields, or plant protectors placed over them. Rows of beans or potatoes can be secured by covering them with wide plank placed on blocks two or three inches above the plants. "Almost all the modes of protecting plants are founded on the doctrine of radiation, and hence the fact should be kept constantly in mind that all bodies placed in a medium colder than themselves are continually giving out their heat in straight lines, and that these straight lines, when the body is surrounded by air, may always be reflected back upon the body from which they emanate by the slightest covering placed at a short distance from them; while, on the other hand, if this slight covering be placed close to the body, instead of reflecting back the heat it will carry it off by conduction, that is, the heat will pass off through the covering closely applied, and be radiated from its surface." (*Daniel.*) Hence the covering or protection given is far more efficient if it enclose a stratum of air without actually touching the plant.

When plants are actually frozen, in many cases they may be saved if they can be thawed gradually without exposure to the sun. To effect this, if coverings are applied before sunrise, or the plants are sprinkled repeatedly with water until the frost is extracted, they generally escape without serious injury. If a frosty night is followed by a cloudy or foggy morning, injury to plants need not be apprehended.

Fruit trees and vines in blossom, or with young fruit set, are in some large districts so liable to suffer from late spring frost, that fruit bearing, in the case of those first to bloom, is the exception. The crop is lost perhaps two years out of three. It is seldom in the most frosty localities that they are endangered more than two or three nights in a season, all the fruit of the peach being rarely killed until it begins to enlarge, and the blossom is on the wane. Such trees are too large to admit of being covered. They can, however, be fully protected by smoke. Ordinary smoke in still, frosty nights, rises rapidly, and to be of any service, it must settle over the trees in a moderately dense cloud, acting as a screen and preventing radiation. A heavy, damp smoke, not rising rapidly, in which the trees are kept fully enveloped until some time after sunrise, is what is necessary to protect a fruit garden. A slight frost will do fruit blossoms little injury, and there are some, which, like those of the Forelle pear, will bear a good many more degrees of cold than others. When a severe frost is pretty certain, billets of short, dry wood, fat light wood, and piles of wet tan, saw-dust, or other damp trash, should be distributed about 2 rods apart over the fruit garden, and the most to the windward. The tan or trash should be distributed during the winter. About three o'clock in the morning is soon enough to start the fires, each of which is made with three or four of the billets, being kindled with the light wood. When well lighted, put on and nearly smother it with the wet tan. If it again break out into a blaze, apply more tan, and keep up damp, smouldering fires, and a curtain of smoke over the trees until the sun is well up and the frost fully extracted. If the fruit is frozen hard as bullets, have no fears, but keep up a dense smoke. By this mode of applying smoke the peach crop can be saved every year. There is no doubt about it. When a boy, thirty-five years ago, we ate of pears thus saved by an uncle of ours, and have ourselves since repeatedly practiced it and seen it tried by others. Our Gardening was the first English work, so far as we know, in which this mode of protection was published, though French authors, we find, allude to the process. Boussingault says it is as old as the Incas of Peru. The peach crop has thus been preserved with the mercury as low as 24° on the morning of March 27th, and the blossoms mostly fallen. Without such protection few good varieties of the peach are safe with the mercury below 30°. The expense of the operation is but a trifle, compared with the value of a fine crop of fruit in a locality where all, not thus protected, is cut off.

Winter protection is also necessary for the preservation of many valuable plants, the limits within which they are naturally found being much narrower than those within which they can be grown in perfection with a little protection. Besides ordinary bedding plants which are stored during the winter in pits or other structures, and again occupy the beds and borders when danger of frost is over, there is a large class of plants, that, with a slight protection where they stand, will pass the winter safely and throw up much more vigorous shoots than if taken up and replanted. A friend of ours succeeds perfectly with the fig in Pennsylvania by bending down the limbs yearly and covering them with earth; and with no protection, in Georgia, they are occasionally killed to the ground.

Ordinary herbaceous plants need no protection, unless they have been divided or transplanted in autumn. Those that are more tender may have their roots and crowns protected with moss, straw, or coarse stable manure, not placed so thick as to heat. Leaves, if employed, will require a little soil or brush thrown over to keep them in place. Tender bulbs are protected in the same way. If the foliage is evergreen, it must not be smothered with too thick a covering.

Shrubby plants may have their roots well covered thus, and their stems bound with straw or moss. For small shrubs, a few evergreen boughs thrown over them is a good protection; larger ones may have their branches drawn together and wound with straw. Tender roses may have tan-bark or saw-dust banked up about their stems, to be removed in spring.

Climbing plants, if tender, must be taken down and laid upon the soil to be covered with leaves or earth.

There is some danger, where much litter is used, of harboring vermin. Many things are better protected by bending a few hoops across the bed with three or four laths lying on them, on which is thrown a cloth or matting in severe weather. Pansies, carnations, and stocks, are thus generally protected, giving them light and air in mild weather. Flower pots, sun shades, vine shields, and wooden frames, covered with canvas or oiled paper, are all useful in protecting low plants. Boxes and barrels are convenient for larger ones. None of these must touch the plant they cover, as they would conduct the heat away from what they touched. The main object of these coverings is to confine the air and protect the surface from radiating heat.

All plants will endure more frost uninjured in a dry, well-drained soil. In low, damp locations, plants, elsewhere considered hardy, are frequently killed by frost. They are also much more easily injured directly after a mild term starts them into growth.

CHAPTER XV.

INSECTS AND VERMIN.

To these numerous and most destructive foes all our gardens are exposed. No plant and no part of a plant is exempt from their attacks. One devours its tender leaf as it issues from the ground; another preys upon the root, and the plant perishes; another burrows into the stem, boring it in every direction until it is broken off by the wind. The caterpillar preys upon the leaves when it gets more mature, while the black grub cuts off the young plant just as it is shooting into growth. Some feed upon the flowers, while others devour the matured fruit or seed.

Insects are on the increase in American gardens, partly from the fact that the destruction of forest trees and wild plants has driven them to the cultivated ones for food, (the apple tree borer, for instance, originally subsisting on the thorn,) partly from being constantly imported from all other countries from which seeds and plants are brought, and partly from the diminution of birds and other enemies by which they are naturally held in check.

Insects are the most extensive class of animals. They are destitute of an internal skeleton, but possess a sort of external one, serving both for skin and bones, and divided into numerous segments connected together by slender points of attachment. They all have six or more articulated legs, and are generally oviparous, or produced from eggs. They possess sight, hearing, smell, and touch at least,—senses in common with those of the superior animals. They do not breathe through the mouth or nostrils, but through vessels, for the reception of air, called spiracula, placed along each side of the body.

Nearly all insects have four stages of existence. First, eggs which hatch into larvæ; these change into pupæ, where they remain dormant for a longer or shorter period, and from which they emerge at last as perfect insects. Some insects, however, bring forth their young alive, as well as deposit eggs. In others, as the Orthoptera, or grasshopper family, the young has nearly the form of a perfect insect. Some insects are injurious to plants only in one stage of their existence, others at all times, when not in a dormant state.

A knowledge of the habits and transformations of insects is necessary to detect how and at what period of their existence they can best be destroyed, or in what manner vegetation can best be shielded from their attacks.

By many insects plants are at once destroyed; by others wounds are inflicted that end in a diseased condition of the parts affected, which is communicated to the whole plant. Plants in a weak or diseased state are far more liable to be attacked by insects than those which are healthy and vigorous.

Various remedies are proposed when plants are attacked by insects, among which those most generally applicable are dusting the leaves with quicklime, sulphur, snuff, soot, dust impregnated with the oil of turpentine. Also sprinkling or washing the plants with water heated to

130°; or with infusions of aloes, tobacco, quassia, China berries; also with soapsuds, especially that made from whale oil soap, guano dissolved in water, fumigating with tobacco smoke, etc.

A camphor and aloes preparation is also found serviceable for sprinkling plants, and was first recommended by Dr. Batty, of Georgia, in the Southern Cultivator, and is thus prepared: Put into a barrel of water a quarter of a pound of camphor, in pieces the size of a hickory nut; fill with water and let it stand a day, and with this water your plants, and fill the barrel for the next watering. The camphor is slowly dissolved, and will last a long time. If the camphor water is too weak, add to a barrel of water a cupful or more of strong lye, and more will dissolve. Add also a pound of cheap cape aloes to a gallon of lye (or water in which a pound of saleratus or potash has been dissolved); add a pint of this to a barrel of water, and use as the camphor water. Camphor and aloes (especially the former) are offensive to most insects.

Preventive measures are of more value than remedial, in protecting plants from insects. Among those most likely to be of value, are the following:

Rotation of Crops.—Each species of insect generally feeds on the same species of plant, or at least on plants of the same natural family; hence a constant change of crop prevents the forthcoming brood from finding their proper food, and many of them perish. This is, however, more applicable in the case of field crops, than in orchards and gardens.

Decaying Trees.—Destroy all decaying trees in the neighborhood of orchards and gardens, as they are often a refuge, and tend to propagate insects destructive to the neighboring crops.

Scraping of the rough bark of trees, and washing them with tobacco water, lime water, or a wash of lime, sulphur and clay, or a solution of potash, destroys the hiding places of insects, and many of the insects themselves, which infest trees.

Birds and other Animals.—The encouragement of insectivorous birds and other animals, instead of their thoughtless and injurious destruction, is one of the most promising methods of lessening the insect tribes. A single pair of breeding swallows, Bradley has calculated, destroy over three thousand worms in a week. Toads live almost entirely upon insects, and do not injure plants. A large class of insects also live entirely upon insects that are injurious to plants, and should be encouraged.

Lime and Salt.—Dressing the soil with lime, sowing in autumn six or eight bushels of salt to the acre, turning over the soil and exposing it to frost just before winter, or during the winter months when the ground is open, are all found to be beneficial. Rolling the surface soil smooth when crops are planted destroys the hiding places of many insects, and renders them less destructive.

Any insect peculiarly injurious must be watched as to its habits, mode of feeding, and its transformations, in order to discover where it may be most successfully attacked.

As healthy plants are less subject to attack, keep the ground in good order, sow good seed, cultivate thoroughly, and the crop will be less endangered.

Fires.—Insects also may be destroyed and their increase prevented by bonfires of brush, just after dark, which will attract and destroy immense numbers of moths and beetles.

"Erect a post in the centre of the garden, on which nail a platform of planks some thirty inches square, which cover with sand; on this build nightly a fire of fat light wood for some weeks, from the time that moths, millers, and butterflies begin to infest the garden. Large numbers will fly into the fire and be consumed."

Traps.—Hang up common porter bottles, though wide-mouthed bottles are preferable, during the insect season, with a few spoonfuls of sweetened water or molasses and vinegar in them, to be renewed every second evening, and hundreds of moths that would have been the parents of a new race of destroyers will be caught. This is the most promising mode of waging war also upon the melon-worm, as well as the corn and boll-worm, and many other insects. For filling the bottles, a better preparation still is a pint of water to half a pint of molasses, the water having as much cobalt dissolved in it as it will take up before mixing with the molasses. Put a wineglassful to each bottle, and empty once or twice a week. Mr. Downing mentions an acquaintance who, using the molasses and water only one season, caught and exterminated three bushels of insects in this manner, and preserved his garden almost free from them. Mr. Robinson, of New Haven, caught over a peck in one night.

Hand-picking.—In some cases, the only effectual mode is hand-picking. If the leaf-roller, the beetle, or the grub is crushed under foot, by preventing reproduction, a thousand enemies are destroyed at once.

Descriptions of the principal insects, and the means of destroying them will be found in that portion of the work which treats of the plants which they attack.

Mice may be caught in traps, or poisoned with arsenic; but the latter is dangerous if fowls or children have access to the garden.

Moles are often very troublesome in undermining beds of cuttings or young plants in search of worms and insects. They may be caught in various traps sold for the purpose, but by putting tarred sticks in their burrows they will be driven from them. Salting the soil is fatal to many insects that are the food of the mole.

Hares and Rabbits are very destructive to trees and

garden vegetables in all country places, and even in towns we do not escape; they can be repelled by a tight board fence, or a close hedge of the Macartney rose. Choice trees can be bound up in straw during the winter, or in an envelope of chestnut bark slipped over the stem.

CHAPTER XVI.

VEGETABLES—DESCRIPTION AND CULTURE.

ARTICHOKE.—(*Cynara Scolymus.*)

The garden artichoke is a perennial plant, a native of the south of Europe, where it has been in cultivation from the time of the Romans. Columella mentions it, and says its name—*Cynara*—is from *cinere* (ashes), because the soil for artichokes should be dressed with ashes. The plant resembles an overgrown thistle, but is more beautiful; has large pinnatifid leaves, three or four feet long, covered with an ash-colored down. The eatable portion is the undeveloped flower head, which is only fit for use before it begins to open its bloom; it is about the size and somewhat the shape of a small pineapple.

As the artichoke is a native of a hot climate, it is perfectly adapted to the temperature of the South, and is hardy throughout the Union. It adds a pleasant variety to our early summer luxuries, and should be in more general cultivation.

There are three varieties: the *Globe*, the *Oval Green*, and the *Purple*. The first has dull purplish heads with scales turned in at the top, and is most esteemed, the edible parts being larger. The Oval Green is the hardiest sort, and has a conical or ovate head, with pointed scales turned outward. The Purple is earlier than the others, the scales pointed, tinted with purplish red towards their points, but is not so good when cooked. There is also the large green, which grows larger than the common green, and is most esteemed at Paris under the name *Gros vert de Laon.* The base of the scales of this variety is quite thick and fleshy.

The ash of the artichoke has been analyzed, and it is found that potash and phosphoric acid are the most abundant constituents, indicating the application of ashes and bone-dust as the best special manures.

Fig. 60.—ARTICHOKE.

Propagation and Culture. — Artichokes are propagated by seed, or by offsets from the old roots. If by seed, sow in early spring when the peach is in full blossom, in very rich earth, in drills an inch and a half deep, and a foot apart; they do still better by sowing them earlier in a cold frame. Transplant them when from six to twelve inches high into a rich soil. If the beds are thinned out by transplanting, so that the plants are left a foot apart in the rows, the rest may remain in the seed bed until fall. The finest heads are produced in a rich, moist loam, and they should be transplanted into such a soil. The best compost is a mixture of three parts well-decomposed manure, and one of *leached* ashes. They require an open exposure, free from the shade and drip of trees, or the plants will spindle and produce worthless heads. The rows must be four feet apart, and the plants three feet in the rows. Plants from seed are better and more permanent than from offsets.

If propagated by suckers, these must be slipped off in spring from the parent plant, retaining as many fibrous roots as possible. They should be selected when the leaves are eight or ten inches high, and be taken only from those shoots which are sound and strong, and have already formed some roots. Uncover the old stools to the origin of the suckers, of which from six to twelve will be produced to each plant. Allow two or three of the best of these to remain; slip off the others with a heel, from which trim off the rough part smoothly, retaining the fibrous roots. Remove the large outside leaves, or their exhalations will exhaust the plant before it gets rooted. They are greatly invigorated if set in water three or four hours before they are planted. Set them in rows, the same distance as above, about four inches deep, in holes made with a trowel; press a portion of fresh soil about their roots and water freely. When this has settled away, fill up to the surface with soil. Keep sun shades or shingles upon the south side of them a few days, until established, giving water, if needed, until they begin to grow.

The only other attention they require during the summer is the frequent use of the hoe. They will produce heads the same year from June to October, and annually thereafter from April to June or July, according to the season. The quality is improved, though at the expense of the quantity, by allowing only the head surmounting the main stem to grow on each stalk, removing all the laterals of the stem while young. As often as the head is cut, the stem should be broken down close to the root, to encourage the production of suckers before winter. They should receive their winter dressing before the ground freezes deeply. Cut away the old leaves without injuring the centre or side shoots, dig the ground over, and throw the soil in a low broad ridge over each row, putting it close about the plants, but leaving the hearts clear. As soon as the shoots appear four or five inches above the surface, the ridges thrown up must be levelled and the earth removed from about the stock to below the part whence the young shoots spring. Remove all these shoots but two, or at most three, leaving the most vigorous, taking care to select those lowest down on the stock, as the strong, thick ones from the crown have hard woody stems, and produce but indifferent heads.

Although the artichoke is a perennial, yet after the fifth year, the heads grow small and dry. The beds should in consequence be broken up at this time, or as soon as they begin to fail, and fresh ones be formed on another site.

As the newly-made beds come into flower after the season for the old plants is over, those fond of this vegetable will prefer to make a new plantation every year.

Artichokes are made to attain a much larger size than they otherwise would by twisting a ligature tightly around the stem below each head, and thus preventing the reflux of the sap.

The artichoke is much benefited by the application of sea-weed or any other manure containing common salt. This is probably in a great measure because salt keeps the soil moist.

Chards.—After the best heads have been cut, when old plantations are to be destroyed, cut off the stems as low as possible, and the leaves within six inches of the ground. When the new leaves are two feet high, blanch them, as directed for Cardoons, which many think they excel.

For Seed.—Select a few of the finest heads and permit them to flower. Bend over the stalk and tie the head to a small stake, to prevent the water from settling among the expanded scales. When the flower has withered, the seeds will be ripe. One ounce of the seed will produce about six hundred plants, and for three and sometimes five years will vegetate freely if kept cool and dry. Put away in paper bags for use.

Properties and Use.—The artichoke is wholesome, yet it contains but little nutriment, and is cultivated merely to please the palate. The heads are sometimes pickled. It is eaten by the French as a salad, with oil and vinegar, salt and pepper; the bottoms are often fried in paste like the egg plant. The English gather them when they spread their scales and the flower appears about to open; the whole head is boiled and the scales pulled off, one or two at a time, dipped in butter and pepper, and the mealy part stripped off with the teeth. The bottom, when the leaves are disposed of, is eaten with the knife and fork. The flowers have the properties of rennet in curdling milk.

ARTICHOKE, JERUSALEM.—(*Helianthus tuberosus.*)

This is a hardy, perennial species of sun-flower, a native of Brazil, introduced into England in 1617, and was much esteemed as a garden vegetable until the Irish potato took its place.

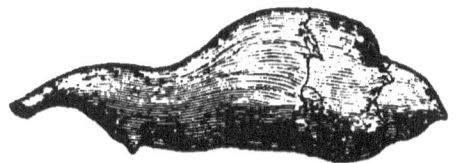

Fig. 61.—JERUSALEM ARTICHOKE.

The crops obtained in good soils are enormous. The salts found in the ashes are mainly potash and lime, the former very largely.

Culture.—It flourishes best in a rich, light soil, with an open exposure, but will thrive in almost any soil or location. Plant in spring or fall, either small tubers or the large ones, cut into sets of one or two eyes, four inches deep, in rows three and a half feet apart. Make the rows run north and south, to admit the sun, and put the plants eighteen inches apart in the rows. Keep the ground free from weeds and earth up slightly. They will be fit for use in the fall. Take care to dig them up thoroughly, as the smallest piece will vegetate. They will grow on land too poor for almost anything else. If the top be cut off one-half way down in August, it is said by some that the size of the tuber will be very much increased by the admission of air and light. This is doubtful.

Use.—The roots are eaten boiled, mashed with butter, and are considerably nutritive, nearly as much so as the Irish potato. It has a moist, soft texture, and a tolerably agreeable taste. It is, however, rather a second-rate dish. They are better pickled in vinegar. The plant is most useful in feeding cows and pigs, affording large quantities of food from quite poor soils.

ASPARAGUS.—(*Asparagus officinalis.*)

This plant has been cultivated as a garden vegetable for at least two thousand years. Cato, 150 years before Christ, gives a full detail of its mode of culture among the Romans. Its culture originated probably in Greece, for its name is pure Greek, and signifies a bud not fully opened; and it is known throughout Europe, by names derived or corrupted from the Greek.

The wild asparagus is found on the sea coasts of most parts of Europe. Its stem is not thicker than a goose-quill. From this wild plant, by the aid of manure and culture, our delicious garden varieties were raised. Miller has succeeded in effecting the same result in modern times.

There are only two varieties of any importance, the

green and the *red-topped*. The latter, with purplish green shoots, is the one principally cultivated. There are some sub-varieties, but these derive all their merit from superior cultivation. R. Thompson states there is really but one sort of asparagus.

An analysis of asparagus by Thomas Richardson shows the ashes to contain about $\frac{34}{100}$ of soda, and nearly $\frac{13}{100}$ of chloride of sodium, or common salt.

In other analyses the proportion of soda is considerably reduced. Asparagus, like some other plants, has the power of substituting the other alkalies, lime and potash, in the place of soda. All the analyses exhibit large proportions of chloride of sodium, or its elements, chlorine and sodium, also of phosphoric acid. In asparagus, over three-fifths of the inorganic elements of the plant are made up of these constituents. This explains why salt and seaweed are found useful, and shows that the application of bone manure, or superphosphate of lime, in connection with animal manures, may be beneficial.

Culture.—Asparagus is propagated only by seed, one ounce of which will produce a thousand plants. Sow quite early in spring on a bed of fresh and deep sandy loam, the richer the better—as free as possible from all shade of trees or shrubs. Draw the drills one foot apart, and with a dibble make holes six inches distant, in which drop two or three seeds. Let the seed be covered an inch deep, and press the earth upon it. If unable to sow early, shade must be given to the bed, for which purpose pine boughs are well suited. These should be removed at night and on cloudy days, and entirely as soon as the plants are up.

Care must be taken to keep the seed-bed light and free from weeds, though this operation must be delayed until the plants come up. If two plants appear in the same place, the weaker must be removed. Transplanted, these will make pretty good plants by fall. When the stems are withered, cut them down and spread well-rotted stable dung over the bed two inches deep, which will increase the vigor of the plants the next year, and also protect them from frost.

Let the plants remain in the seed-bed until they are about to grow early in spring. To have this delicacy as early as possible, choose a site where the bed can be fully exposed to the sun. If you wish to prolong its season, another bed may be planted on a northern exposure. The subsoil should be dry, and if not naturally so, must be well drained. It must be dug up thoroughly at least two and a half feet deep, the poor soil removed, and its place supplied with rich, light loam.

After taking out the soil, the bottom should be covered with at least six inches of well-rotted manure, as this can never be reached after the roots are once planted. Intermix as much more throughout the bed, except the top four or five inches, as the manure should not come in contact with the fresh roots. Bury your manure and mix it well throughout the whole depth, as you can hardly make the ground too rich. Asparagus will *grow*, it is true, without all this trouble, but the size, sweetness, and tenderness of the shoots, will pay for doing the work in the best manner.

The upper five inches should be light, rich, sandy loam mixed with leaf-mould, and the top left as light as possible. So manured and deeply dug, the plants will send down their roots too deeply to fear a drought. The plants should be carefully taken up with a fork, and the roots preserved uninjured. Select mild, cloudy weather, when the ground is in good working order, for it must not be wet. Lay the roots separately and carefully together, that they may not be entangled and injured while planting; keep them, while planting, in a basket covered with a little mould.

Plant your first row by straining a line eight inches

from the edge of the bed; then with the spade cut out a trench six inches deep with the side next the line perpendicular, in which set the plants twelve inches apart, if large heads are desired. Place the roots against the perpendicular side of the trench, and spread them out like a fan against the cut without any doubling, keeping the crowns all at the same level, at about two inches beneath the surface, and cover them by drawing back the light earth regularly over the plants. Draw the line again fifteen inches from the first, and proceed as above, leaving a path of two feet wide a little below the level of the bed, eight inches from every third row. Some plant lettuce and radishes between the rows, but it is not advisable, though a crop of cabbages may be made in the alleys. After the beds have been planted, rake them smooth, and do not tread between the rows. Keep the edges of the bed smoothly trimmed and even. The beds are made narrow to avoid the necessity of treading upon them with the feet, as they should be left as light as possible, for, lasting from ten to twenty years without working, the rains will render them compact, and walking upon them would be very injurious. If some of the beds are made with but two rows, these, being narrower, will warm through quicker and be earlier in the season.

Water them daily in dry weather until the plants are well-rooted. All weeds must be removed as they appear. As salt is an excellent manure for this plant, the weeds may be easily kept down by its application. Old brine or refuse salt, in which meat or fish has been packed, is better than any other, as it abounds in the blood and juices of the meat, which are a most valuable fertilizer. Asparagus is a sea-shore plant, and salt will not hurt it, but is life and nourishment to it.

Old beds have been covered an inch deep, and the plants continued to thrive; but a sprinkling just sufficient to make the soil look white is enough. As soon as the plants have turned yellow in the fall, cut them down close to the ground, but be careful not to do this early, or they will throw up new shoots and be much weakened. Remove the stalks and all weeds, cover the beds with three or four inches of good stable manure, and let it remain until time for the spring dressing. If you have charcoal dust at command, a layer of an inch thick over the manure will be found quite useful in preventing the loss of ammonia. When the weather grows warm and spring has fairly opened, and the ground is sufficiently dry, before growth commences, with an asparagus fork dig in the manure placed on the beds in the fall, and loosen the earth four inches deep, taking care not to wound the crowns of the plants. Give the beds a top-dressing of salt, 2 lbs. to the square yard, before growth commences, and water freely in dry weather. Applications of liquid manure are likewise very salutary. A good liquid manure for asparagus is an ounce of guano and four ounces of salt to two gallons of water. Guano or night soil composted with charcoal, so as to be entirely inodorous, is also beneficially applied at any time. Another slight covering of charcoal dust, after the spring dressing, will be of service, and make the shoots earlier. Until the bed is two years old, the alleys should be also deeply dug and well manured, as the plants will derive much nourishment from them. After that period the roots will extend so widely that they cannot be worked without injury.

When the bed is one year old, it may, if it has been well treated, be sparingly gathered from. The plants will not be injured if the shoots are of good size and but few are taken. They will yield a full crop when two years transplanted. Asparagus should be cut before the heads lose their compact form, when only four or five inches above the ground. Remove the earth to the bottom of the stalk, and cut it off sloping with a pointed knife, taking care not to wound any other shoots that may be near it, as they are constantly putting forth from the crowns. Too many shoots should not be cut from the beds, nor the gathering prolonged too late. Whenever the bed puts up weak and small shoots, these should be allowed to remain, which will increase the size of those remaining, and the future value of the bed. When green peas become plentiful, the asparagus bed should rest. After the cutting ceases, you may judge from the size of the summer shoots the productiveness of the bed the coming spring. These elaborate the food for the future crop. The manure applied in autumn has but little effect on the next spring's shoots, but from its influence the strong growth of the succeeding summer will prepare an abundant supply of large shoots the second spring. The spring and autumn dressings should be continued while the bed lasts, for the top soil must be kept perfectly free and light, that the shoots may readily push through it, and the surface left rough, that it may catch and retain the winter rains so as thoroughly to moisten the lower roots. Finally, good asparagus is not to be obtained without an abundant supply of manure. The beds will, if thus treated, remain productive twelve or fifteen years.

Asparagus can be forced by planting a hot-bed *thickly* with thrifty roots; it comes into bearing in four weeks, and affords asparagus for a month in the winter season. Give plenty of air in mild weather.

For Seed.—Reserve some of the best shoots in the spring, and mark them by placing a stake by each one, and let them run up and ripen their seeds. Take shoots with fine, round, close heads; fasten them, as they grow, up to the stake, and the seed will ripen better. Gather the seed when ripe, and wash off the pulp and husk, which will pass off with the water, if gently poured off, and the seeds will sink to the bottom. Dry them thoroughly, and store away for use. They are, for your own sowing, just as well kept and sown in the pulp. Asparagus seed will keep four years.

Use.—The tender shoots thrown up in the spring when from four or five inches long, are the parts in use, and are very delicate and much esteemed, though not very nutritious. They are excellent simply boiled, or as an addition to soups when in season.

BASIL.—(*Ocymum Basilicum*, and *O. minimum*.)

Two species are cultivated, Sweet Basil, (*O. Basilicum*), and Bush Basil, (*O. minimum*). Both are annuals, with small leaves and small white flowers, and natives of the East Indies. Sweet basil is the species most cultivated, and was introduced into England in 1548.

Culture.—Basil likes a rich, light soil, free from shade. The plants may be started early in March, under glass, in gentle heat. They should be thinned when the young plants appear, and transplanted when of sufficient size where they are to remain. Basil is rather difficult to transplant, but can be carefully lifted in tufts with the balls of earth attached, in a moist time, with complete success; give water and shade until established. It can also be sown on the borders where it is to remain, but if sown too early in the open air, the seed is apt to rot or the young plants to be killed by frost, as they are rather tender. April is the month for sowing in the open ground. Do not cover the seed deeply, but press the earth upon it. Make the rows ten inches apart, and thin the sweet basil to ten inches, and the bush, which is more dwarf, to five inches in the row. Weeds must be kept under, and the soil mellow, by frequent hoeing. Bush basil makes a very pretty edging. It should be cut not too closely just as it comes into flower, and hung up in small bundles in the shade to dry for winter use; thus cut, it will soon grow up again. When thoroughly dried, it may be pounded fine and kept any length of time in closely stopped bottles.

Seed.—Let some of the finest plants remain uncut, and gather the seeds as they ripen. They will keep for six years.

Use.—The leaves and small tops are the parts employed, and give a delightful flavor in cookery. They have a strong flavor of cloves, and are used in soups and sauces, and other high-seasoned dishes. They are much employed in French cookery. It is the most agreeable of the pot herbs, and the most useful, except parsley and sage.

A small sprig of basil, on account of its odor, is an agreeable addition to a bouquet of flowers.

BEAN, ENGLISH BROAD.—(*Vicia Faba.*)

The English Broad Bean is an annual from two to four feet high, with white, fragrant, papilionaceous flowers, with a black spot in the middle of the wings; seed pods thick, long, woolly within, enclosing large, ovate, flat seeds, for the sake of which it is much cultivated in Europe. It is a native of the East—some say of Egypt, but is probably from Persia, near the Caspian Sea—and has been cultivated from time immemorial.

VARIETIES.

Mazagan.—Sweet and agreeable in flavor, and produces well if planted early. Far the most productive variety with me. Pods contain three or four beans, which are small, oblong, and thick.

Long Pod.—Stems rise about three or four feet high; bears well; the pods are long, narrow, and generally contain four beans of good quality; remains in use later than the preceding.

Broad Windsor.—Stems 3 to 4 feet high; pods short, but very broad, containing two beans, very large, roundish, and flattened. Best for a late crop, as it is longest in use.

Dwarf Early.—This is very early and productive, but has a long tap-root, and is not suited to shallow soils.

Culture.—The early crops should be on a dry soil moderately rich and warm, to promote their growth during the winter. The latter crops should be on a deep, strong loam. They are to be sown in drills 2½ feet apart for the Dwarf and Mazagan, and 3 feet for the others; put the beans four inches apart in the row, and cover three inches deep with earth, which should be pressed upon the seed. If any miss, they may be supplied by transplanting. This bean will do well wherever the winters remain open, and the mercury does not, in ordinary years, fall below about 10° Fahrenheit, and should be planted from October to February inclusive. In Virginia, and where frosts are severe, they must be put in as soon as the ground opens in spring, but they are then not as productive as when they can be planted during the months above named. No ordinary frost will injure them. When two inches high, hoe between and draw the earth about the stems of the plants. Continue this during their growth. When the plants come into bloom, take off two or three inches of the tops of the stems, which will increase the crop and hasten its maturity. The crop should be gathered before they are full grown, while they are still tender and delicate.

To Save Seed.—Allow a portion of the crop to remain until ripe. Thresh for use.

Use.—The English use these beans while young and tender, as we do green peas. They must be cooked very young, and in the same manner; or may be boiled with bacon. They are not likely to come into general use.

BEAN, KIDNEY.—(*Phaseolus.*)

These are tender, Leguminous annuals, mostly natives of India, first cultivated in England in 1597. The species cultivated are *P. vulgaris*, Pole or Running Bean, with seed-pods long, straight, and pointed, brittle while young; *P. nanus*, the Bush Bean, is probably a sub-species of this, with more acuminate leaves and larger bracts; *P. multiflorus* is the Scarlet Runner; and *P. lunatus*, the large and small Lima Bean, with broad, compressed, scimetar-shaped pods, and seeds broad and compressed.

The Asparagus, or Yard-long Bean, is a species of *Dolichos*.

Of these species there are many varieties, which, for convenience, we will class as dwarfs and running beans. Those with edible pods, breaking crisply, are called snaps. Of Dwarf or Bush Beans the best are:

Early Mohawk.—Pods long, beans large, oval, with dark-colored specks; it bears very well, is one of the earliest varieties, and is least injured by frost. In good seasons, fit for the table about five or six weeks after sowing.

Early Valentine.—Pods round, and continue crisp longer than most other varieties. The beans are pink-speckled on a salmon ground; bears well. Sown with Early Mohawk, is about five days later.

Newington Wonder.—Very dwarf, pods of medium length, dark green color, thick and fleshy; seeds form slowly, and the pods continue long crisp and fit for use; seeds small, oblong, and light chestnut-colored when ripe.

Late Valentine.—Pods similar to Early Valentine, equally crisp and tender, color dark brown, speckled; a better bearer, and grows more thrifty than the early sort. One of the best. About ten days later than the Mohawk.

Royal Kidney.—Pods long, finely flavored; seeds white and large. Sown at the same time, is a fortnight later than the Mohawk. This is one of the best for winter use when ripe.

Yellow Six Weeks, China Red-eyed, and Turtle Soup, are likewise good varieties.

Of Running or Pole Beans, the best are:

Dutch Case Knife, with large, broad pods, and flattish, kidney-shaped, white seeds, and is a good winter bean.

Algiers or Wax Bean is an early, running kind, with pale yellow pods, free from any tough lining, very tender and soft when cooked; seeds medium-sized, roundish, black. Excellent, but at the South soon stops bearing.

London Horticultural is also excellent, the pods continuing tender until the seeds are quite large; the latter are large and roundish.

In Southern corn-fields are grown several excellent kinds, which are not described in our books. Three are particularly desirable, viz:

White Prolific is a medium-sized, white, oval, kidney-shaped bean, with roundish tender pods, and exceedingly prolific; desirable green or for winter use.

Dark Prolific resembles the last, but the seeds are of a very dark dun color.

Black Speckled has the pods more flattened; seeds roundish, of a dull white, black speckled, and skin rather thick, but the pods are excellent to use green. Of very vigorous growth, and best endures the summer heats. Not over two plants should remain to a pole.

Lima Beans are from the East Indies. There are the green, the white, the speckled, and the small white or Carolina. The white Lima is not quite so large as the green, but, bearing with greater abundance, is to be preferred. It is also not quite so hardy and productive as the Carolina, but is much larger and richer flavored, and is the most grown for city markets.

Carolina or Butter bean closely resembles the white Lima, but is smaller, earlier, hardier, and bears much more abundantly, and though not quite so rich, is for general culture the best running bean.

Wood-ashes and bone-dust, or superphosphate of lime, will supply the soil with the most necessary elements for the bean crop, which, by the way, like most legumes, draws most of its sustenance from the atmosphere.

Culture.—As beans are very easily destroyed by spring frosts, there is no use in planting the main crop too early. A few of the Extra Early or Mohawk may be planted at the same time with early corn, and if there is danger, protect them when they come up, by placing wide planks over the rows an inch or two above the plants, supported on blocks or bricks every cold night. The main early crop is planted in Georgia the last of March, or early in April; at New York City, about the first of May. Planting may continue until about eight weeks before the autumn frosts occur. The soil for the early crop should be dry and light; if wet or tenacious, the seed often decays without germinating, or comes up spindling and unproductive. For the summer-sown crop, a soil slightly moist, but still inclining to a sand, is to be preferred.

Plant in drills eighteen inches or two feet apart, and the seed two inches apart in the row. Cover the seeds about an inch and a half deep. A pint of seed will plant about one hundred and twenty-five feet of rows. When the plants come up, thin them gradually to six or eight inches in the row, and they will be much more vigorous and productive. The Late Valentine does best in hills eighteen inches apart. Plant four or five beans to a hill. Keep them always clean, and the soil light and mellow with the hoe. Draw the earth carefully about their stems when about to flower, making broad, low hills to protect the roots from heat and drought. If well cultivated, the same plants will continue to bear a long time. Do not hoe any of the kidney beans, whether dwarf or runners, when the foliage is wet, as the plants will rust and be greatly injured, if not destroyed. Choose dry weather for working them, and hoe shallow when the plants get large. The value of the crop depends greatly upon their being properly thinned in the drills while young.

Pole or running beans for snaps may be planted when the main crop of bush beans is put in, or a few days later; and at the South, a few hills should be planted monthly, until July, to give a succession, for which nothing is better than the corn-field varieties described. They should be planted in rows about four feet apart, and the hills from two and a half to three feet in the row. The hills should be broad and raised some three inches above the ground level. Put in the poles before planting, let them be uniformly about ten feet long, and inserted well in the ground. Put five or six beans around each pole, and cover them an inch and a half deep, and when up, reduce the plants to three in a hill, and where there are less than that, plant again.

Lima beans require a rich, strong soil, and will thrive on heavy loams, where the other running beans and snaps would not flourish. They are still more tender than snaps, and should not be planted until settled warm weather, as the seed will rot in cool weather, and the slightest frost will destroy them if they chance to vegetate. The tenth of April is early enough in Middle Georgia; near New York City they plant a month later. They may be forwarded by planting in small pots in a hot-bed to be transferred, by breaking the balls, to the open ground when three inches high. Lima beans will not thrive if too much crowded; the rows must be five feet apart, and the hills three feet in the row. The space between may be cropped early in the season with Irish potatoes, etc. When the plants begin to run, give them a little assistance, if not inclined to cling to the poles. If these are too high, the vines are later in bearing, and the crop out of reach in gathering. When they blossom, pinch off the tips of the leading shoots, to hasten the maturity of the crop.

In planting Lima beans, place the eye downward and the narrow end the lowest, as the bean always rises from the ground in that position, and if not planted right, it has to turn itself over in the soil, and if prevented by any obstruction from turning over, it is sure to rot in the ground. Planted in this way, they come up sooner, better, and more evenly. A quart will plant about four hundred hills. The subsequent culture consists in keeping the ground frequently hoed when the vines are dry. They will continue in bearing until cut off by the hard frosts.

For Seed.—Gather both the Lima and kidney beans when ripe and dry them thoroughly. The seed should be kept pure by planting the varieties at a distance from each other. Where subject to be destroyed by bugs, if saved in paper bags, put them up in glass bottles or earthen jugs well corked. Into each one pour, before corking, a teaspoonful of spirits of turpentine. The turpentine odor will destroy the bugs, if the vessel is tightly corked, without injuring the vitality of the bean.

Use.—The tender, fleshy pods of snap-beans are a favorite summer vegetable, very delicate, wholesome, and moderately nutritive. They are boiled while green, and may be preserved for winter use, by cutting them into pieces and laying them down in salt. They will make their own brine, and must be kept covered by it, or they will spoil. Cook in two waters to extract the salt. The Lima beans, and the snaps also, when full grown, are shelled, and may be preserved for winter use, and afford in proportion to their weight, more nutrition than most other vegetables. Wheat contains but 74 per cent of nutritive matter, while kidney beans contain 84 per cent. They abound in the constituents that produce muscle and fat, and will supply better than most vegetables the place of animal food. Gather them in their green state when full grown, and dry them carefully in the sun. They are better gathered thus than if delayed until ripe, and are also free from bugs. Soak them over night before being boiled. They can also be laid down with layers of salt like snap-beans. They are very good gathered when ripe, and dried carefully in an oven in order to keep them free from insects, which, at the South, are quite destructive. Snap-beans are also pickled, while young, in the same way as cucumbers.

BEET.—(*Beta vulgaris*, and *B. Cicla*.)

The **Common Beet,** *Beta vulgaris,* is a biennial plant, a native of the sea coasts of the south of Europe, and is said to have been cultivated for its beautiful red roots long before its edible properties were discovered.

It was introduced into England by Tradescant, in the year 1656. Its name is said to come from the resemblance of its seed to the letter *Beta*, of the Greek alphabet.

The best varieties are the following:

Extra Early Turnip, or Bassano Beet.—The root is oval; color, pale red. Downing truly says "it is the sweetest, most tender, and delicate of all beets;" but the color boils out, so that it is not as beautiful as some others, yet it is the best early beet and one of the easiest grown.

Early Turnip-rooted is a week or two later; the exposed part of the root is brownish, red below ground, and flesh of purplish red, which becomes lighter in boiling; apparently coarse, but really tender, sweet, and well-flavored.

Long Blood is the kind most grown for winter use. It grows a foot or more in length, and four or five inches in diameter, mostly beneath the earth. It is a good keeper and very sweet.

Early Long Blood resembles this; but about half the root is above ground, and if not gathered and stored early, is more exposed to injury from frost.

The London Horticultural Society, after a comparison of many kinds, prefer the following:

Nutting's Selected Dwarf Red.—Leaves 9 to 12 inches high, dark red. Roots, under ground, $9\frac{1}{2}$ inches around; flesh dark red, and when baked, deep crimson; of smooth, close texture, sweet and well-flavored, of no earthy taste; the best sort.

Short's Pineapple.—Leaves 6 or 7 inches high, dark purple stalks, tinged with dull orange. Roots 8 inches in circumference; flesh, deep crimson. Baked, of a dull, deep crimson, tender, mild, sweet, and well-flavored, but with a slight earthy taste. Both these are small kinds. The large-growing, coarse beets are never good.

Culture.—The beet, being a native of the sea-shore, abounds in soda, which can be supplied, when deficient, by an application of common salt the autumn before planting. This, and leached or unleached ashes, will afford nearly all the inorganic elements of the crop.

The main summer crop of beets should be planted when the peach and plum are in full blossom. A few Bassano or Early Turnip should be planted a few weeks earlier, and of other kinds successive beds may be made whenever the soil is in a suitable state, from January until the summer droughts come on. Advantage should be taken of the rains that usually occur about the last of July, or early in August, to put in a crop for winter. This crop should be put in earlier the farther northward the locality. At New York, the main crop is planted as early as the middle of June, about three and a half months before killing frosts. This last planting often proves a failure in the dry autumns of a Southern climate. It generally will succeed in rich, fine soil.

When the surface soil is rich and the bottom poor, it will be difficult to make the beet, carrot, and other taprooted plants produce fine, smooth roots. This difficulty will cease if the ground be deeply and thoroughly worked, mingling the soil and making it uniform throughout, and taking care to place at the depth of one foot below the surface a layer of good manure.

The best beets grow in sandy bottom lands, but any soil will answer for them if deeply and thoroughly worked and well manured. This is necessary with all tap-rooted plants, and especially with the beet. Beet seed is somewhat slow in vegetating, and the later sowings may be soaked in water twenty-four hours before planting, and the drills well watered upon the seed, which is then covered with light soil pressed gently upon the seed; a good method of planting all summer crops. Make the beds four or four and a half feet wide, for convenience of cultivating; spade them up at least a foot deep,—eighteen inches is still better; mix in a good supply of well-rotted manure throughout, if the ground requires it. Rake the ground even and smooth, and mark out the rows twelve inches apart across the bed; draw the drills an inch and a half or two inches deep, in which drop the seed two inches apart, and press the earth gently upon it. When the plants are up, thin them to eight or nine inches apart, fill any vacancies by transplanting, and keep the ground around them loose and free from weeds until matured.

In planting crops of beets, carrots, and parsnips, particularly the two latter, sprinkle *a few* radish seeds, if you like, and the ground is rich, in the rows to distinguish them. The radishes will be up in a week, and the ground can be hoed or weeded without any danger of destroying the young plants. Drills can also be made between every two rows of beets, making a drill every six inches, which can also be sown with radishes or lettuce plants, which can thus be grown abundantly between other crops without loss of room. But a rich soil is required to bring forward both crops to perfection.

For early beets it is well to prepare a good bed under glass in which the rows should be marked out a foot apart. The ground should be deeply spaded and thoroughly manured. Mark out your rows for the beets, and between the first two draw a drill in which you can sow your early York cabbage; between the next two you can raise all the Butter-lettuce you wish to set out for heading. In the rows of beets themselves, you may sprinkle a few radish seed; then a row of later head-lettuce, tomatoes, egg plant, peppers, etc. The drills retained for the beets should be sown in this climate with the Bassano beet about the tenth of January. By the time the hard frosts are over, the beets, cabbages, etc., will be fit to transplant. Thin out to six inches apart, planting out those pulled up in the open ground. In transplanting the beet, a deep hole should be made with a dibble, and the root not bent. Those that remain in the bed will soon come into use, and by the time they are gone, the transplanted ones will come on for a succession.

The winter crop should be secured as soon as the first killing frosts occur, as the sweetness is lost by remaining in the soil. The roots should be taken up, dried a little, and stored away in casks with layers of dry sand, where they will keep in good condition until spring. The mangel wurtzel beet is much cultivated in some countries for feeding stock, and is very good for the table when young and tender, but in our long season it loses its sweetness before winter. Here the sweet potato, rutabaga, and other turnips, are more promising.

The Swiss Chard, or White Beet, *Beta Cicla,* is also called the Sea Kale Beet. There are two varieties, the white and the green, which receive their names from the color of the foot-stalks of the leaves. Either of these is good. The plant very much resembles the common beet, but the leaves and their stalks are much larger, thicker, more tender and succulent, and less capable of resisting frost.

Fig. 62.—SWISS CHARD.

The root of this plant is small, coarse, and of no value; only the leaves and their stalks are employed, especially the latter, which are cooked and eaten as asparagus.

The culture is exactly the same as the common beet, except the plants should be twelve or more inches apart. The soil may be richer and not so deep, and the plants are more benefited by copious watering, especially with liquid manure. For winter use, the leaves may be covered with litter and afford blanched leaf stalks all winter. If the soil be moist and kept mellow and free from weeds, it will yield bountifully. Salt is a beneficial manure for this crop, applied while preparing the ground, as it keeps it moist. It is singular that a plant of so easy culture, and yielding during the entire season after May a supply of the most delicate greens, has not come into more general cultivation.

For Seed.—Select a few of the finest looking roots, those smooth and well-shaped. Plant the different varieties as far apart as possible; indeed, it is better to save the seed of only one kind the same year for fear of intermixture and degeneracy. Keep them free from weeds, and tie the seed stalks to stakes to support them. Gather and dry the seed as soon as ripe, and put away in paper bags. Keep dry, and it will be good for ten years.

Use.—The young and tender tops of the common beet, and the leaves and stalks of the chards, are boiled as summer greens, or of the latter the midrib and stalk may be peeled and boiled separately from the rest of the leaf and prepared as asparagus, for which they are an excellent substitute. In gathering, the largest outside leaves should first be taken, and the inner ones left to increase in size, taking care to gather them while still perfectly green and vigorous.

When common beets are thinned, the young beets pulled up, if cooked, tops and bottoms, are very sweet and delicate. When well grown, the roots give an agreeable variety to our table vegetables, being tender, sweet, and considerably nourishing. They also make an excellent pickle. If eaten moderately, they are wholesome, but in too large a quantity produce flatulence and indigestion.

When old, the addition of a little powdered sugar to the roots, when prepared for the table, restores some of their lost sweetness. The leaves are said to abound in nitre; the roots are full of sugar, and a variety, the Sugar Beet, is largely cultivated in France for its manufacture.

BORECOLE.—(*Brassica oleracea, var. acephela.*)

This plant, known also as Kale and German Greens, is the easiest cultivated, and one of the most valuable of the cabbage tribe. It has large curled or wrinkled leaves, forming an open head, and such a hardy constitution that it resists the severest frosts, which serve only to improve it. It remains green and eatable all winter without the least protection at the South, and in the Northern States requires only a slight covering. The best varieties are:

Dwarf Green Curled, very popular in northern climates, because from its small size it is completely protected by winter snows, and gives a good crop in a small space.

Buda Kale, with purplish leaves, somewhat glaucous, cut and fringed; very hardy; may be blanched like Sea Kale; taller than the preceding.

Turner's Cottager's Kale is a new kind, very popular in England, and promises well here; it stood the winter of 1859–60 at Philadelphia; grows two and a half feet high; leaves green, not so much curled as the Dwarf.

Culture.—Raised from seed, like the rest of the cabbage tribe, which may be sown in April with the winter cabbages and treated in the same manner. Transplant, if the Dwarf Green Curled, into rows eighteen inches apart and twelve inches in the row. Give it a good soil. The other sorts require about the same space as winter cabbages. Borecole may be sown as late as the middle of August in the place where it is to remain, and managed like the Ruta-baga turnip. Like the cabbage, it is visited by the Aphis or Cabbage-louse, and caterpillar, for which see Cabbage.

Seed.—Manage some of the best plants as cabbage.

Use.—The outside leaves can be cut off for use when from 7 to 9 inches long, but they will be coarse and rank until mellowed by frost. The better way is after frost to cut off the hearts, not square across, but with a sloping cut, in order to throw off the rain, and the stem which is left will throw up fresh sprouts for a succession. For winter and spring greens this vegetable is nearly equal to the Savoy cabbage, after the frost has rendered it sweet and tender.

BROCCOLI.—(*Brassica oleracea, var. Botrytis cymosa.*)

This is a biennial plant of the cabbage tribe, resembling cauliflower, from which it differs in its undulating leaves, its larger size, and the color of some of its varieties.

It is supposed to have originated from the cauliflower; it is a hardier plant, but not so delicate in flavor. It has been cultivated about two hundred years, and was introduced into England from Italy. Broccoli is raised more easily than cauliflower. The Early Purple Cape broccoli, producing large, brownish heads, very close and compact, is the best of over 40 sorts.

It requires the same special manures as cabbage and cauliflower, and for cultivation sow, transplant, and manage like late cauliflower. To protect from insects, see Cabbage.

Use.—The same as cauliflower, to which it is inferior and where that succeeds, will hardly be worthy of culture.

BRUSSELS SPROUTS.

(*Brassica oleracea, var. bullata gemmifera.*)

This plant is a hardy variety of the Savoy cabbage, producing an elongated stem, often four feet high and crowned with leaves similar to the Savoy. Small, green heads like cabbages spring from the axils of the stem leaves, which, dropping off, leave the little heads arranged spirally around the stem as the plant proceeds in growth. Brussels Sprouts are raised from seed, which may be sown in April. Set the plants in rows two feet by one and a half feet apart, and treat in all respects as directed for winter cabbage. Cut off the leaves at the top of the stem some ten days or a fortnight before the little heads are gathered, and use for greens.

It will stand the winters without protection south of Virginia, but the product is rather small, and the plants are very subject to the Aphis during the winter.

For Seed.—Cut off the top of the stem and permit the flower stalks to spring from the little heads only. Keep at a distance from all the other varieties of Brassica, in order to have pure seed.

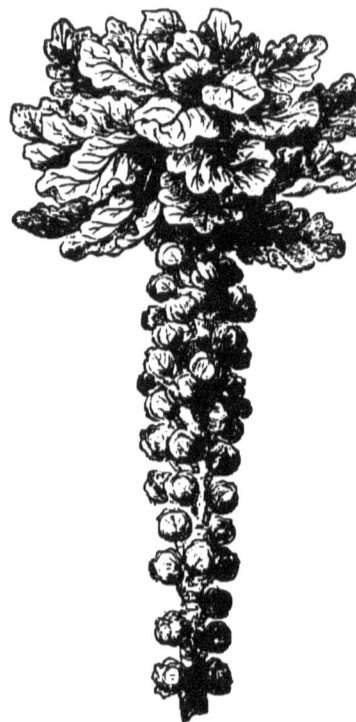

Fig. 63.—BRUSSELS SPROUTS.

Use.—The top boiled for winter greens is very delicate in flavor and similar to the Savoy. But the little sprouts after they have been touched with frost, which very much improves them, are the parts most used. The sprouts are fit for use all winter.

BURNET.—(*Poterium sanguisorba.*)

A hardy, perennial, Rosaceous plant from Britain, of which the young leaves taste and smell like cucumbers, and are put into soups and salads. The leaves are green all winter. Propagated by seeds or parting the roots. Sow in autumn or early in spring, in drills eight inches apart, and thin to six inches in the drill. Make new plantations once in three years by dividing the roots. Seldom cultivated.

CABBAGE.—(*Brassica oleracea, var. capitata.*)

This is a Cruciferous biennial plant, quite hardy, found wild on the coasts of England, France, and many other parts of Europe. The wild variety is known as Sea Colewort, bears but a few leaves, and is far from palatable, unless boiled in two waters to remove its saltness. The cultivated variety was probably introduced into England by the Romans, and the common name doubtless comes from the Latin *Caput*, or head. This is one of the most useful crops in cultivation. Cabbages are eatable almost from the time they leave the seed-bed until they have acquired a hard, close head; it is a crop that can be put on every bit of otherwise idle ground. They can be planted between beds and rows of anything and everything else, to be eaten as greens when young, or left to head on the coming off of other crops, and if there should be a superabundance above the wants of the family, nothing is better for the cow and the pig. For early cabbage it is necessary to rely upon English seed, as the seed of the early varieties saved in this country grow later by our culture, soil, and climate. For late cabbage, the American seeds are superior to the imported, and produce finer and larger heads. No seed for late cabbage is better than our own, if saved from fine, large heads. But all the late cabbages in hot climates, without proper care, are prone to run into coleworts or "collards."

The best varieties are as follows:

Early York, which has been in use over a century as the best for the earliest crop. Stem short, head oval, a little heart-shaped, very firm, and of fine, delicate flavor; its small size enables it to be grown in rows a foot apart each way, giving over 40,000 heads to the acre.

Large Early York, or Landreth's Large York, succeeds the above. It is of larger size, not quite so early, and more robust, and bears the heat better, and will often continue in eating all summer.

Early Battersea has a very short stem, is about 3 feet in circumference, or about 26 inches when the outside leaves are removed. The ribs boil tender. If cut close to the ground, the sprouts it throws up, if all but one or two are removed, will form new heads late in the season. Early Sugar Loaf, Early Emperor, Early Nonpareil, and Early Vanack, are nearly allied to this.

Early Winnigstadt.—Stem dwarf, head large, broad at the base, sharply conical, heart firm, boiling tender. Sown late, it proves a good winter cabbage.

Early Wakefield and Early Oxheart are also excellent, quite early sorts, and like the Battersea.

Early Dutch is an excellent variety that connects the early and late sorts, and is one of the very best in culture. It is succeeded by the winter cabbages, such as

Flat Dutch, which is a large, spreading, short-stemmed variety, flat on the top, close headed, firm in texture, and if headed late, keeps well, and is of better flavor than

Bergen, which is also a drumhead cabbage, but larger, and a little coarser; one of the best for late keeping.

The Drumhead resembles the Flat Dutch, but is less dwarf.

Green Glazed, in this climate, is more capable of resisting the caterpillar and other insects, but it is a coarse variety with very loose heads.

Red Dutch is used principally for pickling, and should be sown at the same time with the drumheads. Early York and Flat Dutch are the best of the above kinds.

SAVOY CABBAGES.—(*B. oleracea, var. bullata-major.*)

These differ from the preceding in their wrinkled leaves. The varieties are hardy, being rendered more sweet and tender by frost. The only two worthy of culture are:

Curled Savoy.—An excellent winter variety, much improved in sweetness and tenderness by frost. It does not head firmly, but is very fine flavored, and even the outside leaves are tender and palatable.

Drumhead Savoy is almost as large and firm as the drumhead cabbage, and keeps very well. The head is round, flattened at top. It is nearly as delicate as the curled variety.

The Savoys are not as certain a crop as the other cabbages, but far superior in delicacy. They are nearly equal to cauliflowers.

Culture.—An analysis of different varieties of the cabbage shows them all to contain a very large proportion of nitrogen; after evaporating the water, drumhead cabbage gives of nitrogen 17.899 parts in a hundred; Savoy, 20.763; red, 16.212; turnip-rooted, 19.052. We also find this plant remarkably rich in phosphorus and sulphur; hence its unpleasant smell in decay, like that of animal matter. It abounds also in soda and potash. Hence, common salt, to yield soda and chlorine, wood ashes for potash, bone for phosphoric acid, and gypsum, to add sulphur and lime, together with a soil saturated with manure of animals, especially the liquid excretion, all come in play in making fine cabbages. Frequent stirring the soil, too, will rob the atmosphere of its ammonia for the same purpose.

The genus to which the cabbage belongs, (*Brassica*,) embraces also the Turnip, Borecole, Broccoli, Cauliflower, Brussels Sprouts, etc., and the following observations apply to the whole of them.

For the seed-bed the soil should be a moist loam, but more dry in the case of plants which are to stand the winter. For final production most plants of this genus like a fresh, very rich, moderately clayey loam. A moist, cool bottom suits them admirably; such of them as are to stand the winter in the open ground should be grown in a lighter soil, not over rich. Good, well-decomposed stable manure is usually employed in preparing the soil for this genus. Pure hog manure is by some considered objectionable, as it is said to cause any of the cabbage tribe to become clump-rooted and lose their regularity of shape. A plentiful application of salt the autumn before planting, say at the rate of eight or ten bushels per acre, is very beneficial to this tribe, as it destroys the cutworm and keeps the soil moist and cool. Bone-dust, and especially superphosphate of lime, has a very surprising effect upon them, far more than analysis would lead one to suppose.

The ground is advantageously dug twice the depth of a spade, and should be well pulverized by the operation. All of the cabbage tribe are particularly benefited by frequent and deep cultivation; they especially like to have the soil about them thoroughly worked *while the dew is on them*. There will be a very great difference in the growth of two plots of cabbages treated alike in other respects, one of which shall be hoed at sunrise, and the other at midday; the growth of the former will surprisingly exceed that of the latter. But the cabbage tribe cannot be hoed too much for their benefit even if daily. The situation must be open and free from all shade or drip of trees; if shaded from the midday sun, it is an advantage, but it must not be by trees. In the shade of trees and other confined situations, they are much more subject to be infested with caterpillars, and to grow weak and spindling. In planting out, any of which the roots are knotted and clumped should be rejected.

Early York cabbage seed may be sown early in September or October in the open ground, watering in the evening when dry, as it usually is this month. The seed should be sown in drills, six inches apart, and one inch deep, and the ground deeply dug; water the drills before covering the seed, unless the ground is moist. Cover with fine, rich soil, pressed lightly upon the seed. The plants will appear in about a week, and a little soot should be scattered over them to prevent the attacks of insects. When large enough to transplant, they can be set very thick in a cold frame or box, to stand over the winter. Cover over with glass, or boards if you have not glass, during severe weather, but give air every mild day, and set out when the weather grows mild in the spring.

From Washington southwards, a still better way than putting the plants in a frame, is to throw a piece of ground into high ridges, two feet apart, running east and west. On the south side of these ridges, set out the plants a foot apart, so that they will be shielded from the cold north winds, and enjoy the full warmth of the sun. Plant on the sides of the ridges and not in the trench. When the weather grows severe in December, cover slightly with straw or litter; remove it when mild weather returns, and cultivate as usual, gradually levelling the ridges, and you will have cabbages earlier than by any other mode; the ground should be good. If you raise your plants in the cold frame, they will be ready to transplant from the 20th to the last of February. They will be very liable to be eaten off by the cutworm when transplanted. There are two modes of preventing this. The best method is to sow the ground intended for cabbage, the autumn after being spaded up, with salt at the rate of eight bushels per acre. If you have not already sown your cabbage plot with salt, there is another plan to keep off the cutworm, equally successful. Throw your ground into ridges and trenches sixteen inches apart; let these trenches be at least six inches deep. In the bottom of these transplant your cabbages, one foot apart. Some use a dibble, but a trowel is much better, as it does not leave the soil hard. Prepare your ground in dry weather, but choose a moist day for transplanting. It is a good plan to wet the roots before planting out. When they get rooted, stir the soil gently about them, but do not fill up the trenches until the plants are so large that there is no danger of the worm. This method of protecting cabbages was pointed out to me by a negro gardener several years since, and I have tried it repeatedly. The worm will not go down into the trenches to destroy the plants.

When the plants get strong, the ground should be deeply and repeatedly hoed. Do this while the dew is on, and retain its ammonia in the soil. The cabbage is partial to moisture, so hoe it frequently, and when you go out in the morning, you will find the plot moist with dew, while the unstirred soil around is dry as ever. The only secret in raising early cabbage is, set your plants in rich ground and *stir the soil*. On poor ground (and even on rich, if half tended) they will run into collards. *Stir the soil*, and less manure is required.

If the fall sowing has been neglected, sow the seeds in January or early in February, in a cold frame, as directed in the article on the Beet; or they may be sown in the open ground when the heavy frosts that freeze the soil are over, covering them with litter, if protection is needed against unseasonable frosts, to be removed when the danger is over. Transplant and cultivate as above.

For the middle crop to last through the summer, the seed can be sown as above, or any time until the middle of April. The cultivation is the same, except that the plants should be set about sixteen to eighteen inches apart. The varieties are the Large York, Battersea, and Early Dutch. These will not head unless the ground be rich, rather moist, and, above all, diligently worked.

The late crop, Red Dutch, Savoys, Flat Dutch, etc., sow about the first of April. It is sown the 1st of May near New York, but, sown at that season in the South, it is not certain to come up. If seed of any of the cabbage tribe be sown after the weather grows warm, it must be watered in the drill, or covered with rich, fresh earth, which must be pressed upon it by walking on a board, and it must be shaded by a covering of boards or pine brush during the day, removing it at night, until the plants get a little established. If the weather is warm and wet, the covering may be dispensed with. They should not be transplanted until July or August. Let the ground be well spaded, and thoroughly manured. They must be *set in the ground up to the first leaf, no matter how long the stem may be*, or they will not head. They also require a rich soil, but not from fresh manure. The manure for the cabbage crop should be thoroughly decomposed, or the plants will be covered with aphides or cabbage lice. The best way is to throw the ground into ridges from two to two and a half feet apart, making the trenches between more or less deep, according to the length of the stems; wet the roots thoroughly, and transplant in moist weather, doing it carefully with a trowel, and when the ground gets dry, draw the earth level, which should just reach up to the lower leaves, not all at once, but gradually. If you have not late plants, sow Early and Large Yorks, or Winnigstadts, in July here, or June northward, and good heads of a smaller size can be produced.

After the late cabbages are transplanted, let them be well cultivated by deep and frequent hoeing, and do not strip off the lower leaves if you wish them to head.

Insects.—Many remedies are employed to keep off the green worm, so destructive to the cabbage tribe. An infusion of tobacco or of the ripe berries of the Pride of China tree, sprinkled on them once or twice a week from a water-pot, is said to be effectual. Sprinkling with ashes is a good practice; also to coop a brood of chickens near, as they destroy the worm without injury to the cabbage. Break off a leaf at night and place it on the top of the head. In the morning early, most of the worms will be on the under side of this leaf. Brush them off into a dish of soapsuds. Repeat this daily until the worms are destroyed. Aphides are not so apt to be troublesome when the plants are in vigorous growth; an application of strong soapsuds generally destroys them. Wetting the leaves with water raised to the temperature of 130°F., it is said, will kill them without injury to plants. Dry charcoal dust mixed with Scotch snuff and dusted over them is another remedy. Air-slaked lime in which a few drops of spirits of turpentine have been diffused, will generally drive away both the aphides and the green worm.

The small, black Flea-beetle, or Turnip-flea, frequently attacks the young plants, and it is sometimes nearly impossible to drive them away. In some localities the plants have to be raised in boxes elevated five or six feet from the ground to escape them.

To preserve Cabbage.—Heel them in in a dry situation, up to their lower leaves on the north side of a fence or building, and cover slightly with plank, straw, or pine brush, to keep them from freezing and thawing during the winter. It is not the frost, however, but the sun upon them, while frozen, that does the injury. In Virginia and northward, dig a trench on a gentle slope, and lay two or three bean poles in the bottom; on these, beginning at the upper end, lay the cabbages, head downward, a little sloping, so that the water may run out from the heads. Cover now with earth a few inches thick, forming a sharp ridge about their roots, which should be made firm by treading or beating. Begin at the lower end and dig out as wanted for use.

Seed.—Set out some of the best *heads* in the spring at a distance from turnips and all other members of this family, or they will intermix. Of the late varieties, home-grown seed, if pure, is the best. Support the stems as they rise by stakes, and gather the seed before it scatters. Seed will keep four years.

Use.—Cabbage, as an article of food, is not so remarkable for its fattening properties as for its power of supplying strength for labor by producing muscle and bone, which it owes to its richness in blood-forming material, abounding in nitrogen, phosphates, and sulphur. Hence it is very nutritious for, and much relished by, laboring people in all parts of the world, but is apt to disagree with those of quiet and sedentary habits. *With the latter it is more wholesome and digestible if eaten uncooked.* Many persons can eat "cold slaugh" with impunity that are unable to use boiled cabbage without great inconvenience. It is by many much relished when made into sauer-kraut, and is also pickled.

CARDOON.—(*Cynara Cardunculus.*)

The Cardoon is a perennial plant, a native of Candia, introduced into England in 1658. It resembles, and is a species of artichoke, but is of larger size, some five feet in height, with the leaves spreading out widely. In continental Europe, it is considerably cultivated, but it is a fancy vegetable, raised mostly as a curiosity, and of no great merit as an esculent. In France the Tours Cardoon, a very spiny, thick or fleshy-ribbed variety, is most cultivated, and, being the least liable to run to seed, is the best sort. The common spineless variety is the only one of which seed is usually offered in America.

Sow in drills five feet apart when the spring frosts are over, and at intervals until within four months of killing autumn frosts, as the early sown ones may run to seed. Other crops may at first occupy the space between the drills. Plant the seed an inch deep, and thin the plants gradually until they are eighteen inches apart in the drills. Those taken up may be reset to fill vacancies or to enlarge the plantation. The soil must be light, deep, well pulverized, and tolerably rich. Keep the ground loose about them, hoeing up all the weeds. When the plants are eighteen inches or two feet high, they must be blanched. The decayed leaves must be removed, and the rest closed together by strings or bass matting. Then bind up the plant carefully with twisted bands of hay or straw, beginning at the root. Select a dry day, or the plants will rot. Bind up two-thirds of the height of the stem; then dig and break the ground and earth up to nearly the same height. As the plants grow, continue to tie and earth up. Watering liberally in hot weather is the only way to keep them from seeding. When the plants are blanched eighteen inches or two feet, they are fit for use. They will blanch fully in about two or three weeks. Do not let the earth get between the leaves or they will decay.

For Seed.—Leave a few full-grown plants unblanched to stand the winter, and they will shoot up to seed the next season.

Use.—The stalks rendered white and tender by blanching are used in stews, soups, and salads, the leaves and stems being white and crisp for two feet in length. The plant is not very nutritious.

VEGETABLES—DESCRIPTION AND CULTURE.

CAULIFLOWER.—(*Brassica oleracea, var. Botrytis cauliflora.*)

This plant is a biennial, and was introduced into England from the Island of Cypress, in the early part of the seventeenth century. It is a kind of cabbage with long, pale green leaves, surrounding a mass or head of white flower buds—in short, "a giant rose wrapped in a green surtout," but much more like a mass of fresh curds than a rose. Since its introduction, it has been much improved by the skill of the gardener. The seed is generally imported from Europe.

There are several varieties, of which the Walcheren is the best; a dwarf, rather broad-leaved variety, which resists better summer droughts and winter's cold than the others. The London and Asiatic are also cultivated.

Cauliflower requires the same manures as cabbage. There is much less difficulty in its cultivation near the sea-shore than inland. The ground should receive a dressing of common salt.

Culture.—Cauliflowers are sown at two periods for the early and late crop. For the former sow early in September thinly in drills six inches apart, in rich, light soil, and if the ground is too dry and hot, water the seed in the drill before covering; cover with fine, light soil, and shade with a mat until the seeds are just *beginning* to come up, (not longer.) When the plants are three inches high, in the colder localities, they are taken up carefully and potted singly in small pots, three in a pot where the quart size is used. Instead of potting, they may be set out in a cold frame or pit four inches asunder, to remain until spring opens, giving them meanwhile all the air the weather will admit to harden them. They will stand light frosts without injury. As early as safe, remove the sashes entirely a few days, take them up from the bed with a transplanter with balls of earth, or, if in pots, divide the ball carefully if it contains more than one plant, and set them out in very rich ground 20 by 24 inches apart, inserting their stems in the earth nearly to the first pair of leaves; shield them with plant protectors from heavy frosts.

In milder localities, as the coast and middle section of the more Southern States, the plants, when taken up, are set out in rows where they are to remain, four inches apart in the row and the rows four feet apart; they are protected during frosts and heavy storms by hoops and mats, or by a covering of four planks a foot wide to each row. These are supported by rafter-like supports, every 5 or 6 feet, to which one of the planks is nailed on each side, while the others are movable and are taken off in all mild weather, but the plants are kept covered in severe frosts and storms. The ends are closed with plank. Instead of plank, white cotton cloth, prepared with linseed oil, affords a suitable covering. They must have air and light at all times when practicable. Slugs must be watched, whether wintered thus or in a hot-bed. They may be driven off by sprinkling the soil and plants with quicklime. As early as may be safe in February, prepare the soil between the rows, which, during the winter, should have been protected from treading by a coat of leaves, or a few old plank, and plant another row therein with the plants 20 inches apart. Thin the plants that were wintered to 20 inches, taking them up with a transplanter, and plant out those not required for the intermediate row in a plot prepared for the purpose. Shade a little with plant protectors until established, if there is danger of their flagging; afterwards cultivate them as cabbages.

For the late crop sow in the manner above directed, at the same time with winter cabbage, from April to July. An ounce of seed will yield three or four thousand plants. The seed-bed should be of light, rich soil, and when the plants are two or three inches high, they should be taken up and set out in a bed four inches apart, shading them until again established, or, if the weather is too dry and hot, thinned to that distance in the seed-bed. They should be taken up with balls of earth in a transplanter and planted out at the same time with winter cabbage, in rows 20 by 24 inches apart. Protect them from the cut-worm and insects in the same manner. If possible, give them a plot of moist bottom soil, made very rich with well-decomposed manure. Water freely when needed, which, in dry weather, is every other day at least; if with liquid manure, so much the better. Let them never suffer from drought; they will show when they need water by their drooping leaves. Soapsuds is an excellent application. Keep the ground hoed thoroughly about them, especially the day after each watering, that it may not bake.

The hills should be hollowed about the cauliflower like a shallow basin, to retain moisture. The head may be blanched by bending the leaves and confining them loosely with a string. They will head in succession during the autumn. To protect them from insects, see cabbage.

When a cauliflower has reached its full size, which is shown by the border opening as if about to seed, the plant should be pulled, and if laid entire in this state in a cool place, may be kept several days. It should be pulled in the morning, for if gathered in the middle or evening of a hot day, it boils tough. When there is danger of severe frost injuring the cauliflowers that have not already headed, they may be protected by pine boughs or empty boxes or barrels where they stand, or pulled up with the earth attached to the roots, and removed to a cellar or out-building, where they will flower in succession. In the low country this will hardly be necessary, and the spring crop is, I believe, more certain with them.

For Seed.—Set out, in spring, some of the finest heads, with fine, close flower-buds, and proceed as with cabbage. It is very liable to intermix with the other Brassicas; so that it is best to depend upon foreign seed. Seed will keep three or four years.

Use.—The heads or flowers boiled, generally wrapped in a clean linen cloth, are served up as a most delicate dish. "Of all the flowers in the garden," says Dr. Johnson, "give me the cauliflower." It is one of the very best of vegetable products, and so prized wherever known. It is nutritious and wholesome even for invalids, beside being a very ornamental addition to the table.

To Cook.—Cut off the green leaves, and look carefully that there are no caterpillars about the stalk; soak an hour in cold water, with a handful of salt in it; then boil them in milk and water, and take care to skim the saucepan, that not the least foulness may fall on the flower. It must be served up very white, with sauce, gravy, or melted butter.—*Mrs. Hale.*

CARROT.—(*Daucus Carota.*)

The carrot is a hardy, Umbelliferous biennial, found wild in Great Britain, as well as in this country, growing in sandy soil or by road-sides. The root of the wild plant is small, white, dry, woody, and strong flavored; while that of the cultivated variety is large, succulent, and generally of a reddish yellow or pale straw color. The cultivated carrot is, however, thought to have been brought into Europe from the island of Crete, where it was early cultivated. It was carried to England by Flemish refugees in the days of Elizabeth, and the leaves were thought beautiful enough to be used in ladies' head-dresses. Cultivation has changed a wild, worthless plant into a most nutritious root.

M. Vilmorin, of Paris, has done the same in our day, and from the wild plant by selecting seed, in three generations produced roots as large as the best garden carrots, the flavor of which, by most of those who have tasted them, is considered superior to the old varieties.—(*Bon Jardinier.*)

The best varieties for the garden are:

Early Horn, which is very early, high colored, and sweeter than other varieties. It does not grow very long, and may be known by its conical root shortening abruptly to a point. It will grow closer together, and is better on shallow soils than other kinds, except

Early French Short Horn, which is an earlier and superior variety of the above, and for an early crop the best.

Altringham.—Color, bright red, and growing with the top an inch or two above ground, which sometimes freezes in very severe winters, if left in the ground, as is usual with this crop in Southern gardens. Of excellent quality.

Long Orange.—Is paler in color, and of great length, the root not above the ground. It is next in quality to the above, and best for winter use where the crop is to be left in the ground.

Analysis shows that lime, potash, soda, sulphuric acid, and chloride of sodium or salt, abound in the ashes of this plant. The salt and lime mixture, composted with leaf-mould or swamp muck, a little plaster of Paris, bone-dust, and wood ashes, are the special manures needed.

Culture.—Carrots like a light and fertile soil, dug full two spades deep for the long varieties, as they require a deeper soil than any other garden vegetable. The manure should be put as near the bottom as possible, not less than eighteen inches from the surface; but the soil should be fertilized by a previous crop, if fine, smooth roots are desired.

In the Southern States carrots, for the early crop, may be sown in October or the first of November, and again from January to April inclusive, after which the seed comes up badly. At New York, the late crop is sown in June for winter use, and for the early crop they sow in September, and protect it a little with litter through the winter.

Late sown seed do not vegetate freely. Sow in drills fifteen inches apart; cover the seed half an inch deep with fine soil, and for the late crop, if the ground is dry, water the seed before covering, and after a few hours press the earth upon the seed with a roller or plank. Thin the young plants to six inches apart. In short, the culture of the carrot is just that of the beet, which see. Six hundred bushels have been produced from one acre. The carrots need not be pulled at the South, but may be left safely in the ground to draw as wanted for use during the winter. In severe weather, they may be protected by a covering of litter; but it is hardly necessary, except for the Altringham. At the North, they are stored in cellars or in piles, covered with straw and earth, like the potato.

For Seed.—Leave some of the finest roots, protected with litter, where raised, to blossom and seed the next summer; save only the principal umbels. Each head should be cut as it turns brown, dried in the shade, rubbed out, and dried in paper bags. The seed will not vegetate if more than two years old.

Use.—The carrot is a very wholesome food for man or beast. It is a valuable addition to stews and soups, and is also boiled plain, pickled, and made into puddings and pies. Boiled or grated, it is an excellent poultice. The grated root is often added to cream to improve the color of winter butter. One carrot, grated into cold water, will color cream enough for eight pounds of butter, without any injury to the flavor. One bushel of boiled carrots and one of corn are said to be worth as much as two bushels of corn to feed to pigs. They are excellent for feeding horses and milch cows, and for this purpose are the most profitable of all roots in deep, fertile soils.

CELERY.—(*Apium graveolens.*)

Celery is a hardy, biennial, Umbelliferous plant, a native of Britain, where the wild variety, called Smallage, is found growing in low, marshy grounds, and by the sides of ditches, and is a coarse, rank weed, with an unpleasant smell and taste.

There are several varieties, some of which have hollow stalks. None but those which are solid are worthy of notice; among the best are:

Red Solid.—The hardiest variety, for winter use, withstands frost, and is distinguished by its color from the

White Solid, which is more crisp and delicate in flavor, and a general favorite, on account of its color.

Seymour's White seems to be an improvement on the old Red and White Solid, producing larger and finer stalks, which are solid, flat at the base where they overlap, and form a crisp, well blanched heart; quality best.

Curled White.—Leaves dark green, curled, resembling parsley, and, like that, useful in garnishing; hardy for winter use, but not as fine flavored. Useful to stand over the winter to use for soups in the spring.

Early Dwarf Solid White. — Dwarf, thick-stemmed, with a full heart, blanching promptly; quality excellent, and giving more well blanched substance than the taller sorts.

The soil for fine celery must be rich in potash, lime, phosphoric acid, and chloride of potassium. But it will not do to depend upon special manures alone, without the addition to the soil of well rotted animal manures.

Celery flourishes best in a soil moist, friable, and rather inclining to lightness. It must be quite rich, without the application of heating manure. It likes a cool, moist, but not wet soil. There are several modes of cultivation. The common mode is to sow the seed in April thinly in drills eight inches apart. As celery is a long while vegetating in the open air, it is desirable to sow the early crop under glass. Let the seed-bed be very rich, and if not sufficiently moist, sprinkle the drills well before covering, and cover thinly with light, sifted soil. Shade the bed on sunny days, but admit mild rains and warm dews, but keep all close in cool weather until the young plants make their appearance. Unless managed as directed for fine flower seeds, celery will not readily come up. Water must be given from a fine rosed pot if the soil is dry.

[The manuscript of the author gives no directions for the cultivation of celery. The old way is to plant in trenches, a foot deep, well manured at the bottom, and to earth up gradually, as the plants make their growth. This plan is now abandoned by our best growers, and in the lack of Mr. White's directions, we give those of a well-known authority, Mr. Peter Henderson, taken from his valuable work called "Gardening for Profit."—*Pubs.*]

Celery may be planted any time from middle of June to middle of August; but the time we most prefer is during July, as there is but little gained by attempting it early. In fact, I have often seen plants raised in hot-beds and planted out in June, far surpassed both in size and quality by those raised in the open ground and planted a month later. Celery is a plant requiring a cool, moist atmosphere, and it is nonsense to attempt to grow it early, in our hot and dry climate; and even when grown, it is not a vegetable that is ever very palatable until cool weather. This our market experience well proves, for although we always have a few bunches exposed for sale in August and September, there is not one root sold then for a thousand that are sold in October and November. Celery is always grown as a "second crop" by us, that is, it follows after the spring crop of Beets, Onions, Cabbage, Cauliflower, or Peas, which are cleared off and marketed, at latest, by the middle of July; the ground is then thoroughly plowed and harrowed. No additional manure is used, as enough remains in the ground from the heavy coat it has received in the spring, to carry through the crop of Celery. After the ground has been nicely prepared, lines are struck out on the level surface, three feet apart, and the plants set six inches apart in the rows. If the weather is dry at the time of planting, great care should be taken that the roots are properly "firmed." Our custom is, to turn back on the row, and press by the side of each plant gently with the foot. This compacts the soil and partially excludes the air from the root until new rootlets are formed, which will usually be in forty-eight hours, after which all danger is over. This practice of pressing the soil closely around the roots is essential in planting of all kinds, and millions of plants are annually destroyed by its omission. After the planting of the Celery is completed, nothing further is to be done for six or seven weeks, except running through between the rows with the cultivator or hoe, and freeing the plants of weeds until they get strong enough to crowd them down. This will bring us to about the middle of August, by which time we usually have that moist and cool atmosphere essential to the growth of Celery. Then we begin the "earthing up," necessary for blanching or whitening that which is wanted for use during the months of September, October, and November. The first operation is that of "handling," as we term it, that is, after the soil has been drawn up against the plant with the hoe, it is further drawn close around each plant by the hand, firm enough to keep the leaves in an upright position and prevent them from spreading, which will leave them as shown in fig. 64. This being done, more soil is drawn against the row,

Fig. 64.—CELERY AFTER "HANDLING."

(either by the plow or hoe, as circumstances require), so as to keep the plant in this upright position. The blanching process must, however, be finished by the spade, which is done by digging the soil from between the rows and bank-

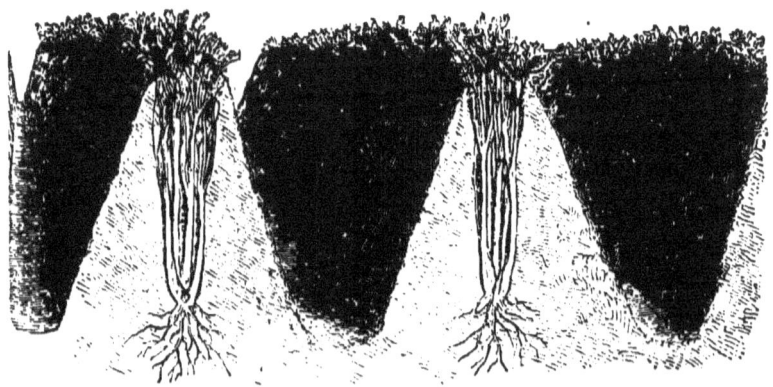

Fig. 65.—CELERY EARTHED UP.

ing it up clear to the top on each side of the row of Celery, as in fig. 65. Three feet is ample distance between the dwarf varieties, but when "Seymour's Superb," "Giant," or other large sorts are used, the width between the rows must be at least 4½ or 5 feet, which entails much more labor and loss of ground. For the past eight years I have grown none but the dwarf varieties, and have saved, in consequence, at least one-half in labor, and one-third in ground, while the average price per root in market has been always equal and occasionally higher than for the tall growing sorts.

My neighbors around me have at last got their eyes opened to the value of the dwarf sorts, and I think that a few years more will suffice to throw the large and coarse-flavored sorts, such as "Seymour's Superb," and "Giant," out of our markets.

The preparation of the soil and planting of Celery for *winter use*, is the same in all respects, except that, what is intended for winter need never be "banked up" with the spade. It merely requires to be put through the handling process, to put it in a compact and upright position preparatory to being stowed away in winter quarters. This should not be done before the middle of September, or just long enough before the Celery is dug up, to keep it in the upright position.

We have, however, another method which we have found to answer very well for the late crop, and it is one by which more roots can be grown on the same space and with less labor than by any other. It is simply to plant the Celery one foot apart, *each way*, nothing farther being required after planting, except twice or thrice hoeing, to clear the crop of weeds until it grows enough to cover the ground. No handling or earthing up is required by this method, for, as the plants struggle for light, they naturally assume an upright position, the leaves all assuming the perpendicular instead of the horizontal, which is the condition essential before being put in winter quarters. This method is not quite so general with us as planting in rows, and it is perhaps better adapted for private gardens than for market; as the plant is more excluded from the air, the root hardly attains as much thickness as by the other plan.

Our manner of preserving it during the winter is now very simple, but as the knowledge of the process is yet quite local, being confined almost exclusively to the Jersey market gardeners, I will endeavor to put it plain enough, so that my readers "may go and do likewise." In this locality we begin to dig up that which we intend for winter use about the end of October, and continue the work (always on dry days) until the 20th or 25th of November, which is as late as we dare risk it out for fear of frost. Let it be understood that Celery will stand quite a sharp

Fig. 66.—CELERY STORED FOR WINTER.

frost, say 10 or even 15 degrees, while 20 or 25 degrees will destroy it. Hence experience has taught us, that the sharp frosts that we usually have during the early part of November, rarely hurt it, though often causing it to droop flat on the ground, until thawed out by the sun. It must, however, never be touched when in the frozen state, or it is almost certain to decay. The ground in which it is placed for winter use should be as dry as possible, or if not dry, so arranged that no water will remain in the trench. The trench should be dug as narrow as possible, not more than 10 or 12 inches wide, and of the depth exactly of the height of the Celery; that is, if the plant of the

Celery be 2 feet in length, the depth of the drain or trench should be 2 feet also. The Celery is now placed in the trench as near perpendicular as possible, so as to fill it up entirely, its green tops being on a level with the top of the trench. Figure 66 represents a section across a trench filled with Celery in the manner just described. No earth whatever is put to the roots other than what may adhere to them after being dug up. It being closely packed together, there is moisture enough always at the bottom of the trench to keep this plant, at the cool season of the year, from wilting. That which is put in trenches about the 25th of October is usually ready to be taken up for use about the 1st of December, that a couple of weeks later, by 1st of January, and the last (which we try always to defer to 15th or 20th November) may be used during the winter and until the 1st of April. For the first lot, no covering is required, but that for use during the winter months must be gradually covered up, from the middle of December, on until 1st of January, when it will require at least a foot of covering of some light, dry material—hay, straw, or leaves—the latter perhaps the best. I have said the covering up should be gradual. This is very important, for if the full weight of covering is put on at once, it prevents the passing off of the heat generated by the closely packed mass of Celery, and in consequence it to some extent "heats," and decay takes place. Covered up in this manner, it can be got out with ease, during the coldest weather in winter, and with perfect safety. These dates of operations, like all others named throughout, are for this latitude; the cultivator must use his judgment carefully in this matter, to suit the section in which he is located.

To save Seed.—Leave some plants where grown; in the latter part of February, take them carefully, cut off the outside leaves, and remove the side shoots, and plant them out in moist soil, one foot apart. Select those which are solid and of middling size. Tie the seed-stalks to stakes, to preserve them from being broken off by violent winds. After the flowers open, while the seed is swelling, if dry weather occurs, water at least every other night. When the seed is dry, it may be rubbed out and stored in a dry place. They will keep good four years.

Use.—Celery has some little nutriment, but is cultivated chiefly as a luxury. The sweet, crisp stalks, used raw, with a little salt, form a most grateful salad. It is also used as a seasoning, and is a great improvement to soups and gravies. A few plants for this purpose are as necessary and wholesome as onions. The unblanched leaves and seeds are sometimes employed in flavoring. The blanched stalks form a pleasant conserve, with the addition of sugar.

CELERIAC.—(*Apium graveolens, var. napaceum.*)

Celeriac, or Turnip-rooted Celery, is a variety of celery which forms at the base of its stem an irregular knob, which is the part used, either cooked or raw, in salads. The roots have been grown to three or four pounds weight. It is sweeter, but not so delicate as common celery, and is not much in use, except in climates so cold that the common sort can not be easily preserved through the winter, while this can be stored like turnips.

The young plants of celeriac are raised exactly like those of celery. When six inches high, they are fit for final transplanting. Set them in rows two feet asunder, and eight inches apart in the rows upon the level ground, or in drills drawn with the hoe three inches deep, as they require but little earthing up. When arrived to nearly their full size, they must be covered over with earth to the depth of four inches. In dry weather they should be watered plentifully every evening, as they like even more water than celery. The only additional attention required is to keep them free from weeds. The plant is more easily cultivated than celery.

Saving Seeds.—The directions for celery are in every respect applicable to celeriac.

Use.—The stalks are used for seasoning soups, etc., the same as celery, from which they can hardly be distinguished. The roots are nice boiled tender, cut in slices and dressed like turnips. They are often made into a salad, after boiling them, and are used in seasoning soups or meat pies.

Fig. 67.—CELERIAC.

CHICK-PEA.—(*Cicer arietum.*)

This is an annual Leguminous plant from southern Europe, of which there are three varieties, one with white and one with yellow seeds, both of which have white flowers; and a third variety has red seeds, and rose-colored flowers. It is sown like peas early in spring, in drills three feet apart. The pods should be gathered before they are quite ripe. The seeds are largely used in soups, purées, etc., in France and southern Europe. They are less nourishing than the common pea, and not very digestible. In shape they somewhat resemble a ram's head. They succeeded quite well in Georgia, as far as growth was concerned, but on gathering, they were found each to contain a worm which made them worthless for use when ripe. Seeds of this plant were distributed under the name "Garbanza" by the U. S. Patent Office.

CHIVES, or CIVES.—(*Allium Schœnoprasum.*)

A hardy, perennial plant of the onion tribe, growing wild in the meadows of Britain, as some varieties of the same genus do in this country. The bunches are made up of a mass of little bulbs, and produce pretty purplish flowers early in summer.

Culture.—Any common soil will answer. Divide the roots in autumn or spring, and plant them on a bed or border, in little bunches of ten or twelve offsets, in holes made with the dibble ten inches apart. If kept free from weeds, they will speedily make large bunches, a few of which will supply a large family. Cut the tops smoothly off near the surface, when wanted, and fresh ones will soon spring up. Chives make a very pretty edging for beds in winter and spring. Renew every four years by taking up and dividing the roots.

Use.—It is an excellent substitute for young onions in winter and spring salading, and is also used like leeks and onions in seasoning soups, gravies, etc. The leaves, cut up fine and mixed with meal and water, are often fed to young chickens as a preventive of disease. The little bulbs may be taken up and stored, and are a tolerable substitute for small onions.

CHERVIL.—(*Scandix cerefolium.*)

An annual Umbelliferous plant, a native of southern Europe, with finely divided leaves, somewhat resembling parsley. Formerly it was much cultivated. There are two sorts, the plain and curled.

It is propagated from seed, which is sown early in spring, and every three or four weeks until autumn. The summer sowings must be in a shady situation. Make the drills very shallow and nine inches apart, and cover lightly with the back of the rake. When the leaves are three or four inches high, they are fit for use. Keep them closely cut, and they will afford a succession for some time. Keep the soil light and free from weeds, and let a few shoots remain uncut to run up to seed.

Use.—The young leaves have a milder flavor than parsley, and are used in soups and salads, and also boiled. "Chervil should be eaten," says an old writer, "with oil and vinegar, being first boiled, which is very good for old people that are dull and without courage; it rejoiceth and comforteth the heart and increaseth the strength." It is now nearly out of use.

CORN.—(*Zea Mays.*)

Indian Corn, or Maize, is a native plant, found distributed in all the milder climates of America at its discovery. It is of more universal culture than any other plant on this continent, and can be made to produce more food per acre than any other grain. The best garden varieties are:

Extra Early—with short ears, small cob, and large grains, which are of excellent flavor. It can be grown fit for the table in six weeks from the time of planting.

Eight-rowed Sugar.—Ears of larger size, grow two or more on a stalk, remain in a milky state, and fit for the table a long time; grains, when dry, are small and shrivelled; of very sweet and excellent flavor when boiled.

Stowell's Evergreen Sweet Corn.—A twelve-rowed variety with ears larger than the Eight-rowed. The grains resemble the Sugar Corn, but are thinner when dry. It produces well, and is quite as good.

The common Dent corn of the South better endures intense summer heat, and will supply green corn for the table when the preceding sorts fail from drought. It is less injured by the corn-worm, which eats into the end of the ear, than Sweet or Sugar corn.

Maize likes a soil abounding in soluble silica. Gypsum and ashes, experience has proved the best special manures. Sweet corn has much less starch than the other varieties, but much more sugar and extract. It has also a greater portion of dextrine and gum.

Culture.—In the Northern States, a dry soil and a hot season are required to produce large crops of corn. At the South, we raise far better crops in moist seasons, and on moist bottom lands. Rich, deep loam affords the plant plenty of moisture and nourishment, which the corn likes. The Extra Early and Sugar corn will bear thick planting. Plant the first crop in the open air when the peach is well in bloom, and every three weeks thereafter to July at New York, and until August in Georgia, selecting the early sorts for the first and last plantings.

The early crop may be forwarded a month, by planting a few hills in pots under glass, on a large scale, in boxes, thus: "Prepare boxes about 4 feet long, 3 feet wide, and 5 inches high. Make one of the sides so that it can be easily removed. Fill these boxes with loam mixed with some manure. Then prepare some strips of board $2\frac{1}{2}$ inches wide, 5 inches long, and as thin as the blade of a hoe. Put these down endwise into the loam, so as to divide the loam into squares, $2\frac{1}{2}$ inches square and 5 inches deep. (As these squares are each to contain a hill of corn, it will be seen that the thin strips are to prevent the roots of one hill from interfering with those of another.) Place these boxes in a sunny place, well protected from the west wind, and about a month before the usual planting time, plant 4 kernels of corn in each one of these squares. By planting time, that corn will be 5 or 6 inches high. Having prepared the ground and opened the hills, take the hills of corn from the boxes in the hand, put them into the prepared hill, press the earth around them, and the corn is at once planted and hoed the first time. It would be well to use some phosphate of lime or hen manure, so as to cause the corn to start immediately. In a short time the corn will be as large as usual when hoed the second time."—(*New England Farmer.*)

The ground for corn should be deeply plowed or spaded, then laid off in hills three feet apart each way, for Sugar and Early corn, leaving three or four plants in a hill, while two plants in hills five feet apart is near enough for large Southern corn. If the ground is not rich, place a shovelful of decayed manure to each hill. Fresh dung can be immediately applied to corn, if spread before plowing, and well turned in. Plant four or five grains to a hill, and cover two inches deep. When they are up, thin as above. Hoe deeply and often while young, and draw the earth each time a little about the stalk; but after the plant is six inches high, shallow surface culture, killing the weeds and loosening the surface without cutting the main roots, is all that is needed.

Corn is a gross feeder, and cannot get too much manure. A sprinkling of guano about the hill is beneficial, if it does not touch the seed. Growth is much improved by giving the plants, at their first hoeing, a teaspoonful of gypsum to each hill, or a pint of ashes, or as much of the charcoal *poudrette*. Chickens, birds, and squirrels can be prevented from pulling up the corn, by soaking it in water twelve hours before planting, then stirring the seed briskly in a vessel containing a little tar mixed with warm water; thus giving each grain a thin coat. After which, for convenient handling, it is to be rolled in as much ashes, gypsum, or lime, as it will take up. One-half bushel of corn requires a pint of tar and a gallon of warm water, with as much ashes as will stick to the grain. It is effectual against birds, squirrels, etc., while the seed vegetates freely, if previously soaked.

The Corn-worm, (*Heliothes?*) comes from the egg of a tawny yellowish moth deposited in June, and after, in the silk or apex of the ears of Indian corn while in the milk. The caterpillar, at first scarcely visible, increases rapidly, and, sheltered by the husk, feeds voraciously upon the tender grains at the end of the cob. It is thought to be identical with the boll-worm of the cotton plant. Injury may probably be warded off by catching the first brood of moths in wide-mouthed bottles, or plates, containing a gill or more of molasses and vinegar. These, being set upon a board some six inches square, fastened upon a stake, raised above the plants, are found to attract the moths from a great distance, and, alighting on it in their eagerness to feed, its adhesive nature prevents escape.

The light wood fires would also probably serve the same purpose.

Where the worm has eaten the ear, a secure retreat is afforded to many other insects, and as the dampness from the exuded sap favors the growth of mould, the remainder of the ear is thus destroyed.

The worms are brown, or green striped with brown, and from half an inch to over an inch in length. They are in some seasons quite destructive in the South, preferring the Sugar corn to the ordinary field varieties.

THE BILL-BUG, or CORN-BORER, (*Sphenophorus*), is about half an inch in length, of a reddish-brown or reddish-black color. The head is furnished with a long bill or trunk, whence its name. It is destructive to Southern corn crops, where abundant. The bug eats into the cornstalk just at the surface of the ground, and deposits its egg. The grub, when hatched, devours the substance of the stalk, and at length is transformed into the pupa, or chrysalis state, remaining in the stalk until spring. The best remedy is to burn the cornstalks and roots, by which their number, the succeeding year, is greatly lessened.

For Seed.—Select the best ears from stalks that bear more than one.

Use.—Indian corn is prepared in a greater variety of ways for the table than any other grain. In fact, the modes of preparation alone would almost fill a volume. That from the garden is mostly boiled green. Green corn can be very easily preserved for winter use, by cutting off the kernels after boiling, and drying in a shaded, airy place. Or, cut the corn off the cob, and put it in a stone jar, with a handful of salt to a pint of corn. When the jar is full, put a weight on it. When you wish to use it, remove a little of the top, and wash and soak it over night. Sugar corn is the best for this purpose.

CORN SALAD.—(*Fedia olitoria.*)

Corn Salad, Fetticus, or Lamb's Lettuce, is a small annual plant, a native of English wheat-fields. It has long, narrow leaves of a pale glaucous hue, and very small, pale blue flowers. It has long been cultivated in English gardens as a winter and spring salad. There is also a round-leaved variety with leaves thicker, and of a darker green.

Culture.—Corn salad likes a loam of moderate fertility, not too heavy. It is raised from seed, one quarter of an ounce of which will sow a bed four feet by fifteen. Sow seed of the preceding year's growth, at intervals from August until frost, in drills six inches apart. Thin the plants as wanted for consumption to four inches in the drills, and keep free from weeds by frequent hoeing. Gather the leaves to eat while young, taking the outer ones, as with spinach. It will be fit for use all winter, where the ground keeps open. A spring sowing may be made among the earliest crops, put in for later use when desired. Allow some of the plants to shoot up to seed, which, as they shed easily, is shaken out upon a cloth spread under the plants. It keeps six years.

Use.—It is used during winter and early spring, to increase the variety of small salads, and as a substitute for lettuce. In France it is boiled like spinach. There is a species (*V. eriocarpa*) with larger leaves, cultivated solely to use in this way.

COW-PEA.—(*Dolichos.*)

Several species of Dolichos are largely cultivated in most southern climates, the vines of which are used for forage, and the seeds employed not only for stock feeding, but the finer kinds are used largely as substitutes for kidney beans as food for man.

Of these the most in use are *Dolichos Sinensis* and *D. sesquipedalis*, Asparagus or Yard-long beans with edible pods from one to two feet in length, cultivated like pole beans; and *D. unguiculatus*, under which the cow-peas are included. These have either erect or twining stems, according to the variety, and are mostly grown in the field, either broadcast or between the rows of corn when last worked. None of them are much in use north of Virginia, they being a Southern institution.

CRESS, AMERICAN.—(*Barbarea vulgaris*).

A biennial Cruciferous plant with yellow flowers, the radical leaves of which are lyre-shaped, and the upper ones pinnatifid, and cultivated in some gardens as a winter salad. Often called water-cress at the South.

Sow either in drills or broadcast in a moist place, the last of August, September, or early in October, giving water in dry, hot weather. Let the plants remain six or eight inches apart. Preserve a few good plants for seed.

Use.—It is generally liked as a winter or early spring salad, somewhat like the water-cress, but more bitter.

The Winter Cress, *B. præcox*, resembles the foregoing, but is a perennial plant with larger leaves. The use and culture are the same. Less bitter than the former.

CRESS, GARDEN.—(*Lepidium sativum.*)

Cress, or Peppergrass as it is called, from its pungent taste, is a hardy Cruciferous annual, probably from Persia, and has been cultivated in England since 1548.

There are three sorts, of which the common Curled and the Normandy are the best; the broad-leaved sort is coarse and inferior.

Culture.—Cress likes a light, moist mould, and in summer a shady border is to be preferred. It is propagated from seed, which, to keep up a succession of young and tender plants, must be sown every week or two. Give it rich earth, that it may grow rapidly. It is best when an inch high, but is generally allowed to get two or three times as high before cropping. Begin to sow for winter and early spring use in September and October, in a sheltered situation; and again as soon as spring opens, sow in the open ground, in drills six or eight inches apart; cover lightly, and pat over the bed with the back of the spade to press the earth upon the seed. Keep the ground clear, and water in dry weather. It can be had all winter by the use of the cold frame or hot-bed; give plenty of air. A few rows left uncut will produce seed abundantly.

Use.—The young and tender leaves give to salads a warm, pungent, and agreeable taste. It is generally used in connection with lettuce and other salads.

CUCUMBER.—(*Cucumis sativus.*)

This is a tender, trailing annual, with rough, heart-shaped leaves, and yellow flowers, growing wild in the East Indies, etc. It is one of the earliest garden products mentioned in history, and was cultivated from the earliest times in Egypt.—(*Numbers* xi., 5.)

It has always been a vegetable peculiarly grateful and refreshing to the inhabitants of warm climates. It was probably early brought into Europe from the East, as it was in high esteem among the Romans, who so well understood its culture, that it appeared on the tables of the wealthy in winter. In England, it was introduced as early as 1573. The best varieties are:

Early Cluster, named from the fruit growing in clusters. The fruit is about five inches long, very productive. Early Russian is a smaller and earlier variety of this.

Early Short White Prickly, growing five or six inches long, with white prickles, remaining green longer than most other varieties; productive.

Early Frame.—Six to ten inches long, much used for forcing; productive and good.

White Spined, or **White Spined Long Green,** is of fine form, deep green color, which it retains well; a good bearer, and of the best quality.

Long Green Prickly.—Dark green color with black spines, grows about ten inches in length and bears abundantly; excellent for pickles.

Gherkin.—*C. Anguria*, a different species with small and prickly fruit, and leaves much divided, or palmated; a great bearer, but used only for pickling.

There are many other varieties, some of which grow two feet long, crisp and well flavored, but the foregoing are the best for family culture.

Culture.—The seed may be planted here about the first of April, or as soon as it can be done with safety, as this plant is very tender and will not bear the least frost. If the soil be deeply trenched, the plant is much less susceptible to drought. After the ground is prepared, dig out holes fifteen inches deep and the same in diameter, six feet apart each way, and partly fill them with well-decomposed manure. A little guano, or fowl manure, sprinkled in the bottom of the hills, will be very beneficial. Do not use fresh manure, or the plants will die out. Cow manure and leaf-mould are excellent. Cover over the manure with rich, mellow loam. Raise the hills a little above the surface, and put eight or ten seeds in the hill; cover an inch deep, and when they get rough leaves, pull up the poorest plants, and leave but three in the hill. Old seed is much better than new, as the plants will run less to vines and bear better.

As soon as the vines get rough leaves, nip off the extremities, to make them branch out, and they will fruit the sooner. This is called *stopping*. Cucumbers are very subject in cool, dry seasons to attacks of insects, especially the striped bug and the cucumber flea. Dry wood ashes or air-slaked lime, dusted thoroughly upon the plants when the dew is on, will generally repel them, and bring the plants forward. But warm rains will soon bring up the plants beyond the reach of the depredators, or, if not, put over the hills boxes covered with millinet. Hoe frequently, until the plants cover the ground. The Early Cluster should have the hills about four feet apart.

After the first planting, succession crops for pickles are put in up to July near New York City, and in Georgia until August. At the South, the melon worm makes its appearance in July, and unless the cucumbers are gathered while small, they will be injured by this insect.

Cucumbers can be very much forwarded by planting them in boxes covered over with glass. Two seven-by-nine panes are large enough to cover a hill, and such hills will not be troubled by the bugs, while the seed can be put in four or five weeks earlier than otherwise. The seed can also be planted in pots under a frame, or in a green-house, to be turned out, when the weather gets favorable, into the open air, and they will scarcely show they have been moved. Or they can be raised wholly without removal, in hot-beds made as directed in a former chapter. They do best when started in pots placed in a small hot-bed, and transplanted when the leaves are two or three inches broad into new beds of a larger size. They must have plenty of air, and be placed near the glass, or they will be drawn up. If they begin to grow long-legged, give them more air. The temperature of the seed-bed should range between 65° and 85°. Always water the plants with tepid water, about noon, unless in mild days, when it may be done in the morning.

Liquid manure, especially guano water, is very beneficial. In planting in the bed for fruiting, do not break the ball of earth; take them out of the pots carefully at night, water gently, keep the sash down the next day, and shade at noon-day, to keep them from withering. It is necessary the beds should be shaded with a mat, during the middle of the day, when the sashes are kept down, until the plants get well established.

Stopping in the frame is still more important than in the open air. The temperature now must be kept between 70° and 90°, by external coatings of fresh dung, if necessary. The shoots must be trained regularly over the surface of the bed. Leave only two or three main branches to each plant, removing the others as they appear. If the plants that have been stopped have extended their runners three joints without showing fruit, they must be stopped again. The vines should blossom in a month from the time of planting. Impregnate the pistillate or female blossom (which may be known by its having fruit attached,) by taking the staminate blossom and placing its centre within that of the pistillate blossom. They may be gathered in about two weeks after impregnation. Three plants are sufficient for one sash of the usual size.

For Seed.—Choose some of the finest fruit of each variety growing near the root. Do not raise the plants near other varieties, or the seed will mix and deteriorate. Let them remain until they turn yellow, and the footstalk withers; cut them off and keep in the sun until they begin to decay; then wash the seed from the pulp, and spread it out to dry. It will keep eight or ten years, and is even better when three or four years old, as the plants are less luxuriant and more productive.

Use.—Cucumbers are a very popular, but not very wholesome vegetable. They are of a cold, watery nature, and many persons of weak constitution cannot eat them without positive injury. They possess scarcely any nutritive properties, but their cooling nature renders them to most palates very agreeable, and persons in good health do not find them injurious. They are eaten raw, fried, stewed, and pickled.

CHINESE YAM.—(*Dioscorea Batatas.*)

A perennial plant brought from China to France in 1850 or 1851 by M. de Montigny, the French Consul at Shanghai. It has annual stalks or vines, and perennial tuberous roots. The leaves are heart-shaped, triangular, pointed above, and seven or eight nerved. The length and breadth of the leaf are about equal; it has a smooth and glossy surface, and is of a deep green color. Its footstalks are half the length of the leaf, furrowed, and of a violet color. Its flowers are diœcious, and of a pale yellow color. The twining stems turn from left to right, and grow, if staked, at least ten or twelve feet high, and develope from the axils of the leaves small tubers, the size of a large pea or kidney bean, which drop from the stem at maturity.

Culture.—The small, axillary tubers afford the readiest mode of propagating the plant, though the largest product seems to have been obtained where the root tubers were cut in sections an inch or an inch and a half long. These should be planted in rich ground deeply trenched, the deeper the better, and then laid off in low ridges or beds eighteen or twenty inches from centre to centre. On the top of this ridge a furrow, three inches deep, is made with the hoe, in which the sets are planted. This should be done early in the spring, and where the seasons are short, the plants should be started in pots to be planted out when danger of frost is over. Keep the young plants free from weeds, and cultivate like sweet potatoes, except no earthing up is required. The plant likes moisture, and growth is arrested in dry weather. It is found to produce larger roots if not staked, and the plant is allowed to fall upon, and shade, the ground. Watering in dry weather is beneficial. The crop should not be gathered until after the autumn frosts, and roots will be found somewhere between ten and thirty-six inches below the surface. The whole root should be extracted, as the lower part is always the largest and most starchy. This should be reserved for the table, while the upper or slender part should be kept for propagation. It is a difficult matter to take them up without breaking, as they often grow three feet long. If not required for immediate use, the roots may safely remain in the ground until spring, or may be taken up and stored. The deep trenching required in preparing the soil, and the great labor in gathering the crop, will prevent its extensive cultivation.

Use.—The roots, which are oblong and tapering, are the edible part. The maximum size to which they grow is two inches in diameter, the larger end tapering upward to the size of the finger. They are covered with a brownish-fawn-colored skin, pierced by numerous rootlets. Under this is a cellular tissue of a white opal color, very crispy, filled with starch, and a milky, mucilaginous fluid, with scarcely any woody fiber. When cooked, it boils or bakes quickly, and becomes dry and mealy, and is generally preferred to the Irish potato, which it resembles in taste. Each plant often produces several tubers, but generally only one, ranging in weight from eight ounces to three pounds. It is more nutritive than the Irish potato, which it may possibly rival in esteem wherever labor is cheap and it is desirable to obtain a large amount of food on a little space.

The other yams, *Dioscorea sativa* and *alata*, are cultivated on the Gulf coast to some extent, and in the same manner as the sweet potato, except that the vines are supported by a stake or pole.

D. aculeata sometimes grows three feet in length, and often weighs thirty pounds. The roots are cut up into small sets and planted in rows two feet apart and eighteen inches in the row, and by forwarding them in pots upon hot-beds have been grown in Europe as far north as Paris.

EGG PLANT.—(*Solanum Melongena*.)

The Egg Plant, or Guinea Squash, is a tender annual from Africa, introduced into England in 1597. It derives its most common name from the white variety, which, when small, bears a close resemblance to an egg. When first introduced, it was not regarded with much favor, but is now rapidly working into general esteem.

Large Prickly-Stemmed Purple is the largest variety, often growing to a diameter of eight inches, shape slightly oval, and dark purple color.

Long Purple is perhaps the best kind for family use, as it is ten days earlier than the other varieties, and though not growing so large, is very prolific in fruit.

Striped Gaudeloupe is a variety the French cultivate, which has a white fruit, striped and marbled with violet. A large, white, edible variety has just come into use in Philadelphia. The New Scarlet, with tomato-shaped, scarlet fruit, and the common White, are only grown for ornament, not being considered wholesome.

Culture.—Egg plants require a light, loamy, rich soil, to bring their fruit early to perfection. They like the soil manured with half decayed leaves, well dug in. To have them early, sow in a hot-bed, or in a cold frame under glass, the latter part of February, or early in March. The rows may be six or eight inches apart, made shallow and the earth pressed upon the seed. Keep the sash carefully closed until the plants are up, and then give air in warm days. They succeed best with a small frame to themselves, as they like a higher heat than is desirable for other plants. As very few plants are required, they may be planted in a small box without bottom, placed on the ordinary hot-bed and covered with a square of glass. Prick them out, when two inches high, into small pots, and afterwards transfer them to larger ones, as directed for the tomato. They can thus be planted out with the ball of earth entire. Do not put them out until settled warm weather, for if the plants get chilled while young, their growth is so checked that they may never fully recover.

The plants, when young, are often destroyed in a day or two by a minute flea. Keep them closely covered until well out of the seed-leaf, and, if attacked, sprinkle them with a solution of aloes or quassia, and dust them with lime and sulphur.

It is hardly worth while to sow the seed in the open ground, as they would be so late in coming into use. Prepare the final bed for egg plants by making trenches three feet apart, burying in them old cabbage stumps, corn stalks, and other vegetable refuse, and covering them with soil twelve inches deep, in which plant out the egg plants two feet apart in the row. Water abundantly until established. Keep the ground well hoed and free from weeds, and earth up the plants a little from time to time. Twelve to twenty plants will be enough.

For Seed.—Allow one of the largest fruits from a prolific plant to ripen seed. It will keep three or four years.

Use.—Egg plant is used by the French in various ways in soups and stews, but generally cut in thin slices, and fried in batter. They are not commonly liked at first, but after a few trials become very agreeable to most tastes, and are esteemed a delicacy. They are fit for use when some two or three inches in diameter, and continue so until the seeds begin to change color. They are not unwholesome, but cannot be very nourishing, as they contain a very large proportion of water. Before frying, they should be cut in slices a quarter to a half of an inch thick, and piled on a plate with alternate layers of salt, in order to remove the acrid taste.

ENDIVE.—(*Cichorium Endivia*.)

Endive is a hardy annual, a native of China and Japan; first cultivated in England in 1548. The root leaves are numerous, large, sinuate, toothed, and smooth. The stem rises about two feet high, producing generally blue flowers. The best varieties are:

Large Green-Curled.—A fine, hardy variety, with long, beautifully curled leaves. It is the best for salads.

Broad-leaved Batavian has thick, plain, or slightly wrinkled foliage. It is principally used for cooking, and making a larger head is preferred for stews and soups, but is not much used for salads.

White-flowered Batavian is a new variety which blanches very white and tender; flowers white. These two sorts are also called Scaroles. Besides the above, there is another species, chicory or succory (*C. Intybus*,) a good deal used as a winter salad in Europe, but it is mainly cultivated for the root, which is dried and ground for the purpose of adulterating coffee. It is a hardy perennial, which in many places is a common weed.

Culture.—Endives delight in a light, rich soil, dug deeply to admit its tap-roots, and to serve as a drain for any superfluous moisture in the winter standing crop. The situation should be open, and free from the shade of trees.

If desired in summer, sow as early in the spring as possible. The main crop is sown near Philadelphia the 1st of July; here in August or September for fall and winter use. Sow at this season, if possible, everything just before a shower; draw a furrow the depth of the hoe, in the bottom of which scatter the seed thinly, and cover slightly with earth, pressing it upon the seed. Plant in the evening, if dry, and before covering water copiously with the fine rose of a water-pot in the drill; do not press the earth upon the seed until morning; shade during the day, and continue watering in the evening until the plants get rooted. The drills should be twelve or fifteen inches apart. Hoe freely and keep the ground free from weeds; thin the plants when two inches high; those removed may be transplanted to another location; choose moist weather for this purpose, trim the leaves a little, and water moderately every evening, until the plants get established and during very long droughts. Those left in the seed bed make the best plants. They should be thinned to 12 or 15 inches in the drill, or planted out that distance apart, the *Batavian* requiring the most space.

In about three months after sowing, as they grow stocky and full in the heart, the leaves being about eight inches long, tie up the leaves of a few every week or so to blanch, and render them tender and remove their bitter taste. Perform this in dry days. The curled sort will sometimes blanch pretty well if neatly earthed up without being tied, but it is better to tie it. The broad leaved from its loftier and looser growth needs a bandage. Fold the leaves round the heart as much as possible in their natural position, and tie them up with a string or shred of bass; then cover them entirely with sand in the form of a cone, making the surface smooth and firm. This must be done in dry, but not frosty weather, as the plants will rot if the leaves are wet or frozen. They may also be blanched under garden pots like sea-kale, or by merely tying them closely, winding the string several times round the plant and closing the top, so as to exclude the rain, drawing the earth around the base to support it. This is the best mode in hot weather; in autumn they will blanch in ten days, in winter they require nearly twice that time. Succory to blanch is taken up and planted in boxes of mould, which are carried into a cellar or dark room and watered when necessary. The blanched leaves will be supplied all winter. Endive needs no protection in our Southern winters. At the North it is taken up with earth about the roots, and wintered in frames.

For Seed.—Let some of the best and most vigorous plants remain till February, and transplant if you wish to use the ground, in rows eighteen inches apart. Support the stems by stakes, and gather the seed vessels as they ripen. Dry them thoroughly on a cloth, thresh, and preserve in paper bags. The seed will keep four years.

Use.—Endive is cultivated for its stocky head of leaves, which, after their bitterness is removed by blanching, are used in autumn and winter for salads and stews. It possesses a good deal of the virtues of the dandelion; it never disagrees with the stomach, but suits every constitution. The French use it in a variety of forms, raw, stewed, boiled, etc., but it is chiefly employed as a salad.

GARLIC.—(*Allium sativum.*)

This is a hardy perennial from Sicily and the south of France; it has been cultivated at least three hundred years. There are two sorts, one with large and the other with small bulbs; each bulb consisting of a half dozen or more small bulbs or cloves.

Culture.—Garlic likes a dry, light, rich soil, but not freshly manured; the manure should be put on the preceding crop. Prepare the ground as directed for the rest of the onion tribe, and mark it off into drills eight inches apart. Plant the cloves four inches distant in the drills, and two inches deep, and see that they are put in right side up. Keep the ground free from weeds, and light by frequent hoeing; plant from October to March.

A few roots may be taken up the latter part of May for use as required, but do not lift the crop until the leaves are withered. Break down the seed stalk if it rises, to prevent it from running to seed, which would lessen the size of the bulbs.

When the leaves turn yellow, take up the bulbs and dry them thoroughly in the shade, tie them together by the tops, and lay them up for winter in a dry loft as you would onions. If the ground is not needed for another crop, they may remain to be drawn as wanted.

Use.—This plant has a well-known, strong penetrating odor, which is most powerful at midday. In medicine it is an excellent diaphoretic and expectorant; a diuretic when taken internally, and has a reputation as an anthelmintic or worm destroyer. Some nations use it very extensively for seasoning soups and stews, and indeed it enters into almost every dish; but in this country it is not very much liked. Still, a *very slight*, scarcely perceptible flavor, or, as the French have it, a *soupçon* (suspicion) of garlic is not repugnant, but rather agreeable to most tastes. The juice is a good cement for broken china.

GROUND PEA.—(*Arachis hypogœa.*)

This plant is likewise known as the Ground-nut, Pindar, and Pea-nut. Although not exactly belonging to the kitchen garden, a few hills should be allowed a place for the sake of the little folks. It is a trailing, annual, Leguminous plant, a native of South America, from whence it was transported to Africa and our own country. It is one of the few plants which ripen seed under ground. The yellow, pea-shaped flower springs from the part of the stem near the surface of the earth, and after being fertilized, the flower stem elongates, growing from four to eight inches, turning downward until the small tubercle which is to be the future seed-pod reaches and penetrates the earth. The seed of the ground pea abounds in a fine oil, which is sometimes expressed for table purposes. This oil renders it a very valuable crop for fattening hogs, being for this purpose fully equal to, and probably better than corn. The vines are greedily eaten by most farm animals.

Culture.—The ground pea thrives and produces best on a light, sandy, tolerably fertile soil, with a good clay subsoil. Like clover, it possesses a long tap-root, which extends deep into the earth, drawing thence the nutriment which is beyond the reach of many of our cultivated crops. The soil should be deep and mellow and well broken up, so as to be ready for planting soon after the heavy frosts are over. The last of March or the first of April is a suitable time. They succeed well as far north as Virginia, beyond which they may be started early in hot beds, and transplanted to the open ground when the weather becomes mild.

For field culture, they may be planted in the pod, two in the hill; but for the garden should be shelled. It is best to drop about four in a hill on the level ground, the rows being laid off three and a half feet wide and the hills two feet asunder; cover them two or three inches.

When they come up, thin them to two in a hill, and, if there be any vacancy, transplant. It is better to plant them level than on ridges, as they are less liable to suffer from drought. As they continue growing all the season, it is well to get them started as soon as the severe frosts are over. The only after-culture they require is to keep the ground clean and mellow, and a slight hilling up when they are laid by. They will produce from twenty-five to seventy or eighty bushels per acre, according to soil and culture, and are as easily cultivated as corn.

HORSE-RADISH.—(*Nasturtium Armoracia.*)

Horse-radish is a Cruciferous perennial plant, growing naturally in moist places in England, and various other parts of Europe. Its flowers are white, and appear in panicles in May. It has long been an inhabitant of the garden.

Culture.—Horse-radish delights in a deep, rich mould, moderately and regularly moist; the roots are never of good size if grown in poor soil, or under the shade of trees. It seldom produces seed, and hence is propagated by sets provided by cutting the roots and offsets into lengths of two inches. The tops and crowns of the roots make the best sets, as they are earlier and make a finer growth than those from the centre of the root. Each set should have two eyes. The finest crops are made by trenching the ground two feet deep, and planting the cuttings with a long, blunt-pointed dibble. It may be done late in the fall, or if in spring, the earlier it is planted, if the ground is suitable, the better. The rows should be eighteen inches apart, the plants twelve inches in the row, and planted eight or ten inches deep. After the beds are planted, smooth the surface and keep clear of weeds, and avoid treading upon the beds, as they should be kept as light as possible. If planted in March, a crop of radishes or lettuce may be taken off the ground before the plants make their appearance. They speedily root and send up long, straight shoots, those appearing in April that were planted in autumn. The only cultivation is to keep them free from weeds, and remove the decayed leaves in autumn. Hoe and rake the bed over in autumn, and also the following spring. By the next fall, the roots are ready to take up as wanted. If the plants throw up suckers, they should be carefully removed as they appear.

If any manure is applied to horse-radish, it must be put at the bottom of the trench before planting, or the plant will send out side shoots in search of the manure, which would greatly injure the crop.

To take them up, a trench is dug along the outside row down to the bottom of the upright roots, which are cut off nearly level with the original planting. The earth from the next row is turned over upon them to the desired depth, and so on until finished. The pieces of roots left will send up new shoots, and the same bed will produce well in this way five or six years, when the site of the plantation should be changed; when this is to be done every piece of root should be taken up, for the smallest of them will vegetate and prove troublesome if left. The best roots come from fresh plantations.

Use.—Horse-radish scraped into shreds with vinegar is a well-known and desirable accompaniment to roast beef. It is also used in fish and other sauces and chicken salads, and is thought to assist digestion. The shreds pickled in strong vinegar and closely stopped in glass bottles will keep for years.

HOP.—(*Humulus Lupulus.*)

The hop is a plant of the Hemp or Nettle Family, with a perennial root, throwing out many herbaceous climbing stems, and is found growing wild on the banks of rivers in Europe, Siberia, and our own country. It was cultivated in England, in or before 1525, when the old doggerel states:

> "Hops, heresy, pickerel, and beer,
> Were brought into England in one year."

A few roots should be in the garden, as they are useful in making yeast and beer.

Culture.—It is propagated by dividing the roots in autumn and spring. It being diœcious, care should be taken to get sets from the pistillate plants; to produce the crop in perfection, there should be a male plant in the vicinity. Give the plant a deep, rich soil; put two or three plants, six inches apart, in a hill, making with the plants, when set, a triangle, and the hills six or eight feet apart. Keep the ground free from weeds, and well stirred. Manure them every year. Give them poles twelve or fourteen feet long, and two or three poles to each hill. Gather when of a straw color, and the inside of the hop is covered with a plentiful yellow dust, and the seeds are brown; dry thoroughly, and put them up in bags for use.

Use.—The principal use of the hop is in the preparation of yeast, etc. The young shoots and suckers are boiled and eaten as asparagus. It is very largely cultivated in fields, to be used in the manufacture of ale and strong beer. Its medicinal qualities are tonic and soporific. In gardens it is often grown as a screen, to hide unsightly objects, the plants being set twelve inches asunder in a row, and staked, or trained on a trellis.

JAPAN PEA.—(*Soja hispida.*)

This is an erect-growing, rough-hairy, annual Leguminous plant, with a woody stem, growing some three feet high, branching near the ground, with ternate leaves, resembling those of the Kidney bean. There are three varieties; those with white, red, and yellow seeds.

They are planted at the same time with Kidney beans in rows 3 feet apart and 2 feet in the row, leaving but one plant in the hill; cultivate as corn. The peas, when ripe, after soaking over night, are prepared for the table like Kidney beans, and are largely used for preparing the soy sauce of Japan and China.

KOHLRABI.—(*Brassica oleracea var. Caulo-rapa.*)

This plant, called also Turnip Cabbage, from the turnip-like form of its stem, is but yet little cultivated. The edible part is the enlarged short stem, which is of a globular form, with a few leaves on top. Its culture is the same as the cabbage, except that in hoeing care must be taken not to throw dirt into the heart of the plant, or the bulb cannot form. Keep the soil flat in hoeing.

The Early White Vienna, and Early Purple Vienna, are the best for the garden. It is cultivated exactly like the Ruta-baga turnip, for which, when cooked young, it is an excellent substitute. When full grown, it is used for feeding stock. It is very hardy, and needs no winter protection in the more Southern States.

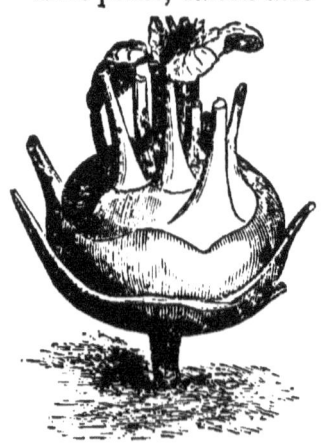

Fig. 68.—KOHLRABI.

LEEK.—(*Allium Porrum.*)

The leek is a hardy biennial of the onion tribe, found wild in Switzerland, but has been cultivated in gardens from the earliest times. It is mentioned in the Scriptures with the onion as one of the vegetables of the Egyptians; and at the present day is often associated with the name of St. David, the patron saint of the Welsh. This plant endures the extremes of heat and cold without injury.

Ashes, bones, gypsum, and common salt, will supply the requisite inorganic materials for this or almost any other garden crop. A compost of guano, gypsum and charcoal would be very beneficial.

Varieties.—There are two in common use; the Scotch, which is the larger and hardier, and the London, which by many is considered the better of the two, both tall, with thick stems, and broad leaves. The Large Rouen Leek, with dark green leaves and a short stem, sometimes grown to the thickness of a man's arm, is now most liked in France. Its stem is said to grow large enough for use sooner than any other, and it is now much esteemed.

Culture.—The leek is raised solely from seed, which may be sown at any time during autumn, winter, and spring, until the middle of April. February is the best month for the purpose, if but one crop is raised.

The soil for leeks, as for the others of the onion tribe, should be light and rich,—the blackest and most fertile soil of the garden—but the manure applied must not be rank. The same guano compost may be applied as for onions. They are generally sown broadcast, but it is a much neater method to sow in drills. Make the drills in the seed-bed eight inches apart, and about an inch deep, and scatter the seed rather thinly. Press fine earth upon the seed, as directed for onions. Some gardeners thin them out, and allow them to remain in the seed-bed, but the leek is so much improved by transplanting that this plan cannot be recommended. When the plants are three or four inches high, they must be weeded and thinned to one or two inches apart, and frequently watered in dry weather. The seed-bed must be kept clean and light by weeding, or the use of the hoe whenever required, until the plants are six or eight inches high, when they will be fit for transplanting. They must then be taken away from the seed-bed, the ground being previously well watered, if not already soft and yielding.

Having prepared beds four feet wide by spading in a quantity of well-rotted manure, lay it off in little trenches twelve inches apart, and as deep as the hoe will conveniently go. Dibble holes three inches deep, and nine inches apart in the bottom of the trenches, in which set out the plants. Press the earth to the roots and neck only, and not to the leaves. The tops and roots may be slightly trimmed and shortened. Some prefer planting them, as is best for shallow soils, on the level surface of the prepared bed, by inserting them in holes made with the dibble nearly down to the leaves, with the whole neck beneath the surface, that it may be well blanched. Choose a moist time for transplanting, and give a little water should they droop. A portion may remain in the seedbed, six inches apart in the rows, but they do not grow as large as the transplanted ones.

The beds must be hoed occasionally, to keep them free from weeds and loosen the soil. In dry weather they should be freely watered. By cutting off the leaves a little about once a month, the neck will swell to a much larger size; earth them up gradually, if they stand on a level ground, and, if in the trenches, the earth should be drawn by a hoe, little by little, into the trenches, as the plants increase in growth.

If a very early crop is desired, they may be planted in September, and the plants will be ready to set out the middle of February ensuing, and will come into use in

June or July. Leeks can be planted between almost any other crop by giving six inches extra room.

For Seed.—Some of the finest roots of last year's growth may be transplanted in February eight inches distant in a row. When the seed stems arise, they must be supported by tying them to stakes. The heads should be cut when changed to a brownish color, with about a foot of the stalk attached, for the convenience of tying them into bundles of three or four to dry. When dry, they may be hung up in a dry place, and kept in the head until wanted, or threshed out and stored in paper bags; the seed will keep two years.

Use.—The whole plant is much used in soups and stews, but the most delicate part is the blanched stems. From its mild, agreeable taste, it is esteemed by many above the onion.

LENTIL.—(*Ervum Lens.*)

The garden lentil is an annual Leguminous plant cultivated in France for its flat seeds, of which two are contained in each pod. Lentils are planted at the same season with snap beans, in warm, sandy soil. If planted in one too rich, they grow vigorously, but produce few seeds. Sow in drills 20 inches asunder, covering lightly, and manage them like the snap bean. Harvest when the stems begin to turn yellow, and the pods of a dark color, but do not beat them out of the pod until required for use, as in this condition they remain longer fit for use and sowing.

Green or dry they are cooked like beans, and when dry, should be boiled two hours and a half. Soak in water before boiling. When done, add butter, pepper, and salt.

They are an excellent addition to soups, being very nutritious. Like beans and peas, but in a greater degree, they are apt to be unwholesome for those of weak digestion.

LETTUCE.—(*Lactuca sativa.*)

Lettuce is a hardy, annual, Composite-flowered plant, generally considered a native of Asia. The Cos lettuce, however, came from the Greek island of Cos, in the Levant. It has been cultivated in England since 1562.

Of the two great families of lettuce, the Cos varieties, which grow upright and of an oblong shape, and require blanching, though more esteemed in England, do not generally succeed so well in this country, except at the South, where they may be sown early in October. The cabbage varieties are more hardy and free growing, and better adapted to our common gardens.

The following are good cabbage lettuces:

Hammersmith, or Hardy Green.—Leaves thick, dark green; the wrinkled and concave seeds, white; stands the winter better than any other sort, but in summer soon runs to seed.

Butter, or Early Cabbage.—Heads small, white, crisp, and closely cabbaged; leaves pale yellowish green; excellent for hot-bed culture, or open air; early and hardy.

Brown Dutch (yellow seeded).—Heads much larger; equally tender and excellent, and closely headed; with brownish green leaves.

The next three varieties, if sown at the same time with the above, will come into use about two weeks after them:

Royal Cabbage.—Black seed; heads larger, and leaves of a darker green than the early cabbage; equally firm and crisp.

Philadelphia Cabbage.—Of the same season as the preceding, and equally good.

Victoria Cabbage.—Withstands the heat rather better than the two preceding, and produces large, white, crisp heads; perhaps the most desirable of the three.

After these come on:

Curled India.—Leaf of a light yellow green, and very much curled; a very distinct sort; heads large and close, but not so fine and crisp as the other varieties, but will continue to head much later.

Neapolitan.—Very dwarf; leaves curled and serrated on the edges; head large, firm, blanching white, crisp and excellent; seeds white. It soon begins to head, and does not run to seed as readily as most kinds. In England it is considered the best summer cabbage lettuce.

The best Cos lettuces are:

White Paris Cos.—Very large; leaves pale green, obovate, hooded at top, closing over and blanching a large heart without tying; becoming white, tender, crisp, and excellent; seeds white. Seeds should be saved only from those with leaves round, concave, and inclined to hood or turn inwards. The best summer sort.

Paris Green Cos.—Very like the last, but the leaves are of a darker green until blanched; but the heart is white, crisp, and excellent. Hardier and better for autumn sowing than the last, and by some thought of equal excellence. These two lettuces scarcely require tying for blanching, and are always good.

Culture.—In raising good lettuce three things are necessary—good seed, good soil, and frequent hoeing; and of these the first is perhaps the most important. There is generally no difficulty in making lettuce seed vegetate, but if it is not saved from good heads it will not produce heads, even with the best culture. Lettuce likes a good mellow soil, enriched with well-rotted manure. Good heads will not grow on poor ground. Lettuce may be sown in autumn for six or eight weeks before the hard frosts come on, and transplanted into frames for winter cutting, or, protected with a little straw, it will stand through the winter in the open air and be planted out for heading in early spring. Hammersmith and Paris Green Cos are best for autumn sowing, and at the South yield small salad in mild weather through the winter. A second sowing should be made at the first opening of spring, and then at intervals until the summer's heat comes on.

If there has been no fall sowing, a little should be sown the latter part of winter under glass, for which select Hammersmith or Early Cabbage. Give it plenty of air, but keep it covered nights and cold days, and as the weather grows mild, leave off the glass altogether a little while before setting out in the open air. Fall-sown Butter lettuce may also be transplanted under glass at nine inches apart, and the table be kept supplied in this way with fresh heads all winter. Plenty of air must be given them, and they should be covered in freezing weather only. For a fall heading, a crop can be sown at the same time with turnips, in a shady situation, which being transplanted, will give good heads. The fall and summer sowings do much better if thinned to a suitable distance, and allowed to head where they stand, as lettuce plants are impatient of transplanting in hot weather; but they may be safely moved if shielded by sun shades.

Lettuce should be sown in drills eight inches apart. An ounce of seed will produce about ten thousand plants. Let the seed be very lightly covered, and if dry weather, press the earth upon it by walking over it on a board, or patting it with the back of the spade. Beds about four feet wide are most convenient. If the lettuce comes up too thickly in the drills it must be thinned, as the plants begin to crowd, to two inches apart. Transplant into the ground where they are to remain, when the plants show four leaves. The Early Cabbage may be planted nine inches apart each way; but the other varieties will not do with less than a foot. The soil into which they are to be removed to head must be rich, light, and mellow. Transplant in moist weather with a trowel, disturbing the roots as little as possible. Water the plants until established. Rabbits are very fond of lettuce, but can be kept off by dusting the young plants with ashes. After the young plants get established, give them frequent hoeings; and if good seed was sown, there can be but little danger of not being rewarded with beautiful crisp heads.

Seed.—Some of the finest and most perfect heads of the early sown crops should be selected. Each variety must be kept separate, and all imperfect heading plants near them destroyed. Tie them to stakes, and gather the branches as fast as they ripen. Dry the seed in the shade, and thresh and store in paper bags. Lettuce seed cannot be relied upon when more than two years old.

Use.—Lettuce is the most popular of all salads, and it is also sometimes used in soups. Boiled, it is quite equal to spinach. It is fit to boil from the time it is large enough until the seed stalk begins to shoot up. Its juice contains a narcotic principle somewhat like opium, which is in small proportion when young, but increases with the age of the plant. This principle has not the constipating effects of opium. A tea prepared of lettuce leaves is sometimes used in cases of diarrhœa. For a common salad, let the leaves be carefully picked early in the morning, washed and drained before sending to the table, and provide salt, oil, sugar, and vinegar, that each person may season to his taste. The finer salads require hard-boiled eggs, mustard, and other condiments.

MARJORAM.—(*Origanum Onites,* and *O. Marjorana.*)

There are four species, two of which are sufficient for the garden.

Pot Marjoram, *O. Onites,* is a perennial Labiate plant from Sicily. It is propagated generally by dividing the roots early in the spring, and may be by seed. Plants should be set in rows twelve inches apart, and ten inches in the row, in a light, dry soil, and a warm situation.

Sweet Marjoram, *O. Marjorana,* is a tender biennial commonly grown as an annual; a native of Portugal, and has been cultivated in England since 1573. It has small, acute leaves, and flowers in small, close heads. Sow in a slight hot-bed early in spring, and transplant when the frosts are over into rows nine inches apart and six inches asunder in the row; or it may be sown in shallow drills in the open air after the ground becomes warm. As the seed is small, cover lightly with fine earth and thin out the plants to the proper distance. The leaves, green or dried, are used for seasoning soups, stuffings, etc.

MARIGOLD, OR POT MARIGOLD.

(*Calendula officinalis.*)

A hardy annual, a native of France, Spain, and the south of Europe. Its bright yellow flowers give it a place in the flower-garden. A few plants only are needed by any family.

There are two varieties, the single and double; the former of which is a little the higher flavored. Sow in autumn or early in spring on a good mellow soil, in drills one foot apart, or broadcast; when the plants are up, thin them to twelve or fifteen inches apart, or transplant them that distance, if more plants are desired. Water until established. The flowers, during the summer, must be gathered, dried thoroughly in the shade, and put up in paper bags. Leave a few fine flowers for seed. The darkest colored ones are the best. The flower is a valuable ingredient in soups. The plant is now but little used.

MELON. (*Cucumis Melo.*)

The melon, or musk-melon, is a tender, trailing annual, of the same family as the cucumber, squash, etc. It is supposed to be from Persia, but has been cultivated in all warm climates so long, that it is difficult to assign, with certainty, its native country. It has been cultivated in Southern Europe at least four hundred years. It is the richest and most delicious of all herbaceous fruits. In England its culture is a difficult and expensive process, but in this country the most luscious melons are raised almost without trouble.

Melons may be arranged in two classes, the green-fleshed and the scarlet-fleshed, the colors of the latter shading through orange to yellow. The varieties are very numerous. The best for garden culture are the green-fleshed.

Beechwood.—One of the best and most productive of its class; ripens quite early, about twelve days after the Christiana. Fruit medium size, oval, netted; skin, greenish yellow; flesh, pale green, rich, melting, and very sugary.

Citron.—"Small, roundish, flattened at the end, regularly ribbed, and thickly netted; skin, deep green, becoming pale greenish yellow at maturity; rind moderately thick; flesh, green, firm, rich, and high flavored. Pretty early." (*Downing.*) Best for general use.

Skillman's Fine Netted.—"Earliest of the green-fleshed melons. Small, rough-netted, flattened at the ends. Flesh green, very thick, firm, sugary, and of the most delicious flavor." (*Downing.*)

Hoosainee.—A Persian melon. Fruit oblong, oval, and of good size; skin, light green, netted; flesh, pale greenish white, tender, sweet and rich; bears well; rather late.

The pine-apple is one of this class, and one of the best for forcing. Good and productive.

Christiana.—Scarlet-fleshed; an orange-fleshed variety from near Boston; a week or ten days earlier than the citron; round; skin dull yellow when ripe; very good, but inferior to all the green-fleshed sorts, though valuable from its earliness.

Netted Cantaloupe.—Fruit rather small, round, pale green, netted; flesh, orange red, sweet and rich; the best of the scarlet-fleshed, which are never equal to the others.

There are also several varieties of winter melon cultivated in Spain. The best of these are said to be *Melon d'hiver à chair blanche*, which will keep in a dry room until February; green-fleshed, juicy, sweet and good: *Melon d'hiver à chair rouge;* like the last, but red-fleshed, and does not keep so well: *Melon de Valence;* large, egg-shaped, thin rind, shaded green, white-fleshed, juicy, and very sweet, and an excellent keeper.

An analysis of the melon shows it to contain about $^{99}|_{100}$ of water.

Culture.—The melon likes a rich, sandy soil, well manured, and deeply dug. If the soil is clay, it should be corrected by the addition of charcoal-dust, sand, or leaf-mould from the woods. The most luscious melons are grown on new land, fresh from the woods. They like, also, soil manured by cow-penning. In selecting seed, get the oldest to be had, and take great care to get that which is perfectly pure, for the seed of melons raised in proximity to gourds, cucumbers, pumpkins, etc., will produce new varieties, destitute of flavor. All plants of this family are exceedingly liable to intermix, to their great detriment. They will deteriorate, if planted within one hundred feet of each other.

Plant in the open ground when the frosts are over, a little later than the general corn crop is planted. In sections where the seasons are too short for it the melon is planted in pots in a hot-bed, and the maturity of the crop may be hastened every where in this way. When the ground is warm, the balls are taken from the pots, and set where they are to remain, protecting them with sunshades a little at first, or with hand-glasses, if cold. Have about three plants to each pot. In the open ground, plant in hills six feet apart, and ten seeds to a hill, an inch deep. Thin to three, and finally two, in a hill. Make the hills as for cucumbers. Superphosphate of lime has an almost magical effect in improving the size and hastening the maturity of the melon. The insects are the same as attack the cucumber, and a little guano sprinkled around the hill, not too near the plants, and intermingled with the surface soil, will also by its pungent smell drive off the bug and flea, and also prove a very valuable fertilizer of the plants. Watering with guano water for the same purpose is very beneficial. Until the vines touch, keep the ground about them fresh dug, mellow, and free from weeds. When the vines begin to run, and show the first blossom, they must be stopped by pinching off the extreme bud, as in the cucumber. This will render them earlier and more prolific in large fruit. Their whole culture is like that of the cucumber, and they may be forced in the same manner. In sections where the melon worm destroys the later grown fruits, get them into bearing as early as may be. This is a green worm, the progeny of some moth, which crawls up from the ground, eating its way into melons, squashes, cucumbers, etc., admitting the air, and causing them to decay at once, and fill the atmosphere about them with a most disagreeable and sickening odor. I know no remedy; but when the first fruit is attacked, early in August here, the vines are removed and other crops put in.

To Save Seed.—Select of each variety some of the earliest and best melons; wash the seed from the pulp, dry them in the shade, and put away in paper bags. They will keep ten years. Old seed is more prolific in fruit than new. Be sure and plant the oldest seed to be had, if it appears well preserved; seeds will not be true if the varieties are within one hundred feet of each other.

Use.—The melon as a palatable and luscious fruit, very cooling in hot weather, maintains a high rank. It is usually eaten with salt alone, though many like the addition of sugar and spices. That it is wholesome is proved by its constant use while in season as an article of food among the people of Southern Europe. The musk-melon contains but a trifle more water than the beet, and is quite as nourishing. It contains albumen, casein, dextrin and sugar, which, combined with citric, malic, and tartaric acid, give its peculiar rich flavor. The green fruit may be cooked like the egg-plant, and is also made into mangoes.

MUSHROOM.—(*Agaricus campestris.*)

"The mushroom," says Loudon, "is a well-known native vegetable, springing up in open pastures in August and September. It is most readily distinguished when of middle size, by its fine pink or flesh-colored gills and pleasant smell. In a more advanced stage the gills become of a chocolate color, and it is then more apt to be confounded with other kinds of dubious quality; but the species which most nearly resembles it is slimy to the touch, having a rather disagreeable smell; further, the noxious kind grows in woods, or in the margin of woods, while the true mushroom springs up chiefly in open pastures, and should be gathered only in such places."

Some of the species of this genus are very poisonous. The mushroom is remarkable for its close assimilation in taste to animal matter. It is beginning to be extensively cultivated in this country near our large cities.

Culture.—Beds may be readily constructed at any time of the year, except between April and September, when the temperature is rather too high for successful culture, unless in the cool cellar of some outhouse. But November and December are the best months for the purpose. Mushrooms are propagated by spawn, which may be obtained for commencing from the seedsmen of our large cities. After a little spawn is obtained, it may be increased as follows:—Take a quantity of fresh manure from high-fed horses, mixed with short litter; add one-third cow's dung, and a good portion of loamy mould. Incorporate them thoroughly, mixing them with the drainings of a dung heap, and beat them until the whole becomes of the consistency of a thick mortar. Spread the mixture on the level floor of an open shed, and beat it flat with a spade. When it becomes dried to the proper consistency, cut it into bricks about eight inches square; set them on edge and turn frequently until half dry, then dibble two holes about half through each brick, and insert in each hole a piece of good spawn; close it with a moist composition similar to that of which the bricks were made, and let them remain until nearly dry. Then somewhere under cover place a bottom of dry horse-dung six inches thick, and place the bricks, spawn side up, one upon another. The pile may be made three feet high; cover it with warm horse-dung sufficient to diffuse a gentle heat through the whole. The heat should not be over 70°, and the pile should be examined the second day to see that it does not overheat. When the spawn is diffused entirely through the bricks the process is finished. The bricks should then be laid separately in a dry place, and if *kept perfectly dry*, retain their vegetative power for many years. One bushel of spawn will plant a bed four feet by twelve.

Beds for mushrooms may be made anywhere in a dry situation under cover. Make them four feet wide and from ten to fifteen feet long, according to the wants of the family. A small shed might be erected for the purpose, but the back of a green-house is a very good situation, as they do not need much light. Space must be left for an alley, and if the shed be ten feet wide, it will admit of a bed on each side.

Mushrooms, like other fungi, abound in nitrogen; hence this substance is necessary to their nourishment, and unless substances, like horse dung, rich in nitrogen, are supplied, it is useless to attempt their culture. Earthy materials are added to prevent the escape of ammonia, which would pass off in fermentation, and the substances used are beaten and trodden to render the mass compact, that fermentation may be slower and more lasting. The process of making the beds is as follows.

A sufficient quantity of the droppings of hard-fed horses, pretty free from litter, must be obtained, which, while collecting, must be kept dry, and spread out thinly and turned frequently to prevent violent heating. When the rank steam has escaped, the bed may be built. The site should be dry. Dig out the earth six inches deep, the size of the bed, and if good lay it aside for use. Fill this trench with good fresh dung for the bottom, and lay on this the prepared dung, until the whole is six inches thick above the surface; beat it down firmly with the back of the fork, and build up the sides with a slight but regular slope. Let the bed slope downwards towards the walk, lay over it three inches of good clayey loam; place another layer ten or twelve inches thick of prepared dung, and in the same manner continue until the bed is two and a half or three feet thick. Cover the bed with clean litter, to prevent drying and the escape of the gases, and let it remain ten days, or until the temperature becomes mild and regular; about 60°, and certainly not less than 50°, is the proper degree of warmth. Here skill and practice are most required, for on the treatment at this precise point, the success of the bed depends. If the manure has a brown color, and is so loose and mellow that when pressed it will yield no water, but has a fat, unctuous feel, without any smell of fresh dung, the bed is in a right state. If it is dry and hard, or sloppy and liquid, it is not in the proper condition. In the first case moderate watering may restore it, but in the latter the superabundance of water will probably spoil it, and it is better to commence anew. When the bed is ready, break the bricks of spawn into lumps the size of a walnut, which plant regularly six inches apart over the surface of the bed, including its sides and ends, just beneath the surface of the manure. Level the surface by gently smoothing with the back of the spade. Fine rich loam, rather light than otherwise, is then put on two inches thick. Lastly a covering of straw from six to twelve inches, according to the temperature. If the bed gets too hot, take off most of the covering. When the bed appears too dry, sprinkle it gently with soft tepid water in the morning. The water should be poured through the rose of a watering-pot upon a thin layer of straw, laid on for the purpose, and when the earth becomes a little moistened, the straw should be removed, and the dry covering replaced. In warm weather it will need frequent sprinkling, but in winter very little.

As cow-manure, though it contains less ammonia, retains

its heat longer than that of the horse, a mixture of the two may be safely employed.

In four or five weeks after spawning, the bed should begin to produce, and if kept dry and warm will last several months. A gathering may take place two or three times a week according to the productiveness. If it should not come on in two or three months, a little more warmth or a sprinkling of water will generally bring it into plentiful bearing, unless the spawn has been destroyed by overheating or too much moisture. In gathering the mushrooms detach them with a gentle twist and fill the cavity with mould; do not use a knife, as the stumps left in the ground become the nurseries of maggots, which are liable to infest the succeeding crop. Gather before they become flat, when half an inch or more in diameter, and still compact and firm.

Use.—This "voluptuous poison" has been cultivated and in high esteem among epicures since the time of the Romans. They are employed in catsups, pickles, and rich gravies, and considered by those accustomed to them very delicious. Dried and powdered they are preserved in closely stopped bottles for times when they are not to be procured fresh.

MUSTARD.—(*Sinapis alba, and S. nigra.*)

The leaves of the White Mustard, (*S. alba*) are used for salads; and the seed of the Black Mustard, (*S. nigra*) furnishes the well-known condiment. Both are hardy annual Cruciferous plants, and succeed in any good common loam, but where sown in September to stand the winter, as is common in the South for early greens, the soil should be rather dry. White Mustard may be sown any time of the year for a salad, in the same manner as cress, which see. It must be used when the seed-leaf is just expanded, for if it gets into the rough leaf it is fit for nothing but greens. For use, cut them off with a sharp knife. They should be used soon after gathering. Mustard for greens or for seed should be sown broadcast or in drills eighteen inches apart, to be finally thinned to about a foot in the drill. The leaves at the South are gathered the latter part of winter or in early spring. Keep the ground free from weeds. When grown for seed, gather when the pods change color, and thresh when dry.

Use.—The tender leaves of both species are used for salads, and should be more cultivated for this purpose. They are also much cultivated for greens. The seeds of the white variety, ground, form the Durham or London table mustard, but the flour of the black sort is that from which our American table mustard is, or ought to be, made. The seeds may be ground in a common spice mill or crushed by a roller on a table. In this country the flour is usually sifted after grinding, but the French do not separate the husk, and thus make a brownish flour, more powerful and palatable than the other. Mustard is a very agreeable condiment, assisting digestion and promoting appetite. The seed used whole is an excellent seasoning to various kinds of pickles. It is also much used in medicine, both by the faculty and in domestic practice. It is an acrid stimulant, and in large quantities acts as an emetic. The proper dose for the latter is from a teaspoonful to a tablespoonful in a glass of water. Mustard is a local excitant applied to the skin in a cataplasm, made of the ground meal with vinegar or lukewarm water; *if mixed with boiling water the acrid principle will not be developed.*

NASTURTIUM, or INDIAN CRESS.

(*Tropæolum majus* and *T. minus.*)

There are two species, the Large Nasturtium (*T. majus*) and the small Nasturtium (*T. minus*) both from Peru, where they are perennials, but are here treated as annuals. The large species was introduced into England in 1681. The stalks are long and trailing; the leaves have their petioles fixed at the centre. Flowers helmet-shaped, of a rich, brilliant orange, and continue from their first appearance all summer; and if not so common would be thought very beautiful. The small sort is preferable for the garden, being productive and needing no support.

Culture.—Nasturtiums flourish in a moist soil, but do best in a good, fresh loam. If the soil is too rich, the plants are luxuriant, but do not bear so abundantly, and the fruit is of inferior flavor. Give them an open situation. Sow in spring when the ground gets warm; put the seeds an inch deep and four inches apart, covering them three-fourths of an inch. The seed must be of the preceding year's growth. They may be sown by the side of a fence or trellis. If more than one row is sown, they should be at least four feet apart. Thin the plants, when they are well up, to a foot in the drill. Hoe the ground well, and keep down the weeds. If sown in the open ground, support them as you would peas with lattice or brush. Give the plants a little assistance in fastening themselves to the trellis. Water in dry weather. Gather the fruit when full grown, but while still fresh and green.

For Seed.—Let some of the berries mature, gather them as they ripen, spread them to dry and harden, and store in paper bags.

Use.—The flowers and young leaves are used in salads, and have a warm taste like water cress. The flowers are used in garnishing dishes. The fruit, gathered green and pickled, forms an excellent substitute for capers.

OKRA.—(*Hibiscus esculentus.*)

This is an annual Malvaceous plant, a native of the West Indies, and much esteemed and cultivated wherever its merits are known. There are several varieties—the round, smooth green, and the long fluted or ribbed white, which grow tall; also the dwarf. There is no great difference in quality, but the dwarf sort is best for gardens.

Okra likes a good, dry soil. Any soil will produce it that is good enough for the cotton plant, which belongs to the same natural family. The pods are not as pleasant or early on over-rich soil. It is not planted until the frosts are over, as it is tender, though it often comes up from self-sown seed. The time of planting cotton or snap beans is a very good guide, though some may be put in as an experiment two weeks earlier. Make the drills three feet apart, sow the seed rather thinly, and thin out to two feet apart in the drill. Those thinned out may be transplanted and will make productive plants. No seed should be allowed to ripen on those stalks from which the pods are gathered for eating. As fast as the pods become hard or unfit for use, cut them off, for if left on, the stalk will cease to be productive. If not allowed to ripen seed, the plants will continue bearing through the season. The dwarf okra may stand about fifteen inches apart in the drill, and it is well when any plant begins to fail in productiveness to cut it down to a foot from the ground and it will soon throw up bearing shoots.

To Save Seed.—Leave some of the earliest plants to ripen seed, if you would have this vegetable in good season. Shell out the seed, and stow away in paper bags.

Use.—The pods gathered in a green state, and so tender as to snap easily in the fingers, are the parts employed in cooking. If old, they are worthless. They are very wholesome, considerably nutritious, very mucilaginous, and impart an agreeable richness to soups, sauces, and stews. They are also simply boiled in salt and water, and served up with butter, pepper, &c. Okra can be preserved for winter use, by putting down the pods in salt like cucumbers, or by cutting them into thin slices and drying like peaches. When dry, put up in paper bags. The seed is sometimes used as a substitute for coffee, which it is not very likely to supersede.

THE ONION.—(*Allium Cepa.*)

The genus *Allium* contains several of the most useful plants of our gardens. In it, besides the proper onions, are included the Garlic, Leek, Rocambole Shallots, and Chives, which are treated of in their several places.

VARIETIES.—There is a great number of varieties of onions, among which are:

Large Red, a hardy variety raised abundantly in the Northern States for export. It is deep red, medium size, rather flat, and keeps well, and is the strongest flavored.

Yellow Strasburg.—Large yellow, oval, often a little flattened, very hardy; keeps exceedingly well. Best for winter use at the South. Flavor strong.

Yellow Danvers.—Middle size, roundish oblate; neck slender; skin yellowish-brown; early and good; keeps well.

Silver-skinned.—Of smaller size but finer flavor, silvery white, flat, and very much used for pickling on account of its handsome appearance and mild flavor.

Potato Onion.—This derives its name from forming a number of bulbs on the parent root beneath the surface of the soil. It ripens early, but does not keep until spring. A sub-variety with smaller bulbs is said to produce bulbs on the stem like the Top Onion. It is very prolific, and affords a supply before other kinds are ready. Plant the offsets in rows a foot apart and ten inches in the row, three inches deep, from October to March.

Fig. 69.—POTATO ONION.

Top or Tree Onion.—(*Allium Cepa. var. viviparum.*) Is said to have originated in Canada. It produces little bulbs ("buttons") at the top of the seed stems; hence its name "Tree Onion". This is the easiest to manage of any of the onions, is of good, mild flavor, early and productive with little care, so that it is a favorite in climates too cold and too warm for the other varieties. Plant the buttons from October to March in drills one foot apart and six inches in the drill. Plant the apex of the button just beneath the surface of the soil. The small top bulbs are fine for pickling.

Ciboule or Welsh Onion, (*Allium fistulosum*).—Of two kinds, white and red; is quite distinct from the common onion and does not bulb. It is sown in September for drawing early in spring. Flavor strong, very hardy.

Fig. 70.—TOP ONION.

Thompson describes 20 sorts of onion, of which the foregoing are the best. Of these the first two and the Top Onion are to be preferred for general use.

Culture.—Onions are raised from seed or sets, which may be planted from October to April, but February is the best month for the purpose. They all require a rich, friable soil and a situation enjoying the full influence of the sun, and free from the shade and drip of trees. If the soil be poor or exhausted, an abundance of manure should be applied some time before planting and thoroughly incorporated with it; for rank, unreduced dung is injurious, engendering decay. If applied at the time of planting, the manure must be thoroughly decomposed, and turned in only to a moderate depth. If the ground be tenacious, sand, or better still, charcoal dust, is advantageous; ashes and soot are particularly beneficial. Common salt, at the rate of six to eight bushels per acre, is an excellent application to this family of plants. In digging the ground, small spadefuls should be turned over at a time, that the texture may be well broken and pulverized.

The common onion, *A. Cepa*, a Liliaceous plant, is probably a native of Asia and Egypt, has been cultivated from the most remote antiquity, and is one of the most useful of our garden crops.

Ashes, bone-dust, gypsum, and the salt and lime mixture will supply nearly all the inorganic constituents of this crop; and where they do not already exist in sufficient quantities in the soil they may be supplied in addition to animal manure. An experienced cultivator states that when sufficient manure cannot be obtained, four hundred pounds of Peruvian guano composted with five bushels of bone dust, dissolved in sulphuric acid, and enough charcoal dust to divide the mass, will be found to produce a maximum crop. Guano water and spent lye well diluted are excellent liquid manures. They do not require a change of soil, being an exception to the general rule that plants like a rotation, as they have been grown in Scotland a century in the same spot without any diminution of the crop.

The onion can be grown in great perfection at the South. In the hot climates of Spain, Portugal, and especially Egypt, the finest onions in the world are produced, the roots being milder and of greater size than in most countries.

It is a good plan to make the beds just wide enough for three rows, say thirty inches wide, with a narrow alley between, which may be filled with sweet corn or cabbages, after the crop is laid by.

But in common gardens beds four feet wide and the rows thereon twelve to fourteen inches wide are most convenient. The soil of the beds must be finely dug, the surface rolled smooth, and all the clods beat fine that may have escaped the spade. The drills should be drawn very shallow, as the best onions grow upon the surface of the ground. For this reason, it is well to roll the bed, or beat it smooth with the back of the spade, before making the drills. Some soak the seed twenty-four hours before planting, but to little advantage. Do not sow very thickly— only one or two seeds in a place. A seed every inch is quite thick enough, as thinning out, when too thick, is apt to injure the remainder. Cover the seeds about half an inch with fine sifted soil, and press down the earth upon them by a roller, or walking over them on a plank.

When they come up, thin them out gradually in the drills, to six inches apart. Keep the bed clean and free from weeds, and stir it frequently, but not deeply, with a hoe. Do not hill the earth up against the bulbs; but draw it away from them with the fingers, as they keep better if grown pretty much above the ground. There is no crop more easily raised or preserved, if the ground is rich enough, and the bulbs made to grow upon the surface. After the young onions have got a good start, it is best to drop the hoe entirely and resort to hand-weeding. In dry weather, a thorough drenching in weak liquid manure, or soapsuds, is excellent. For pickling, the white kind should be sown much more thickly, and thinned out until about one or two inches apart in the row, which will cause them to ripen early, before they have become too large.

If onions grow thick-necked, and do not bulb properly, bend down the stems about two inches above the neck, to the ground, without disturbing the roots. This is needful only in very wet seasons.

When very large bulbs are desired, the seed may be sown quite thick, in pretty good soil, and not thinned out at all. Little bulbs or sets will form about the size of the button onion, which may be taken up when the tops die, and preserved in a dry loft until time for preparing the bed, and then may be planted, instead of the seed, eight inches apart in the drills. If they throw up a seed stalk, it must be promptly broken off, or they will form no bottoms. These sets, planted out early in the year, will form fine large bulbs in May or June; while those raised from the seed do not ripen until July. Hence the latter are better keepers. Besides, they are better flavored, and more solid. The little bulbs of the top onion are managed like these sets.

When the crop is ready for harvesting, it is known by the drying up and change of color of the stems.

The Onion-fly, (*Anthomya ceparum,*) is a native of Europe, of late years becoming common in many American gardens, and wherever found is very destructive to the crop. The parent insect is a small ash gray fly, about half the size of the common house fly. The female lays her eggs on the leaves, when they are very young, close to the earth. As soon as the maggots hatch, which is when the young plants are about the size of a quill, they descend between the coats of the onion to its base, feeding upon the bottom part of the bulb, which soon becomes rotten, when the worm leaves it, to enter the earth and complete its transformations. Figure 71 represents the larva of the natural

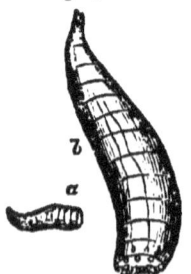

Fig. 71.

VEGETABLES—DESCRIPTION AND CULTURE. 263

size at *a* and at *b*, magnified several times. Figure 72 shows the way in which the insects work upon the young plant. In figure 73 the perfect insect is given, the natural size of which is indicated by the cross lines, and in the same figure the magnified pupa or chrysalis is shown at *d*, and the actual size at *c*.

Fig. 72.

These insects increase so rapidly that unless destroyed at their first appearance, which is shown by the leaves drooping and turning yellow, it is almost impossible to eradicate them. Such plants should be at once pulled up, and with the soil in which they grew, burned, which will prevent their increase. Applications of soot or salt upon the beds, of lime-water, stale urine, and tobacco water, are also employed, and beds strewn with fine charcoal are said to be less liable to attack. It is difficult, however, to reach the insect, except by pulling up the bulb. It is said that

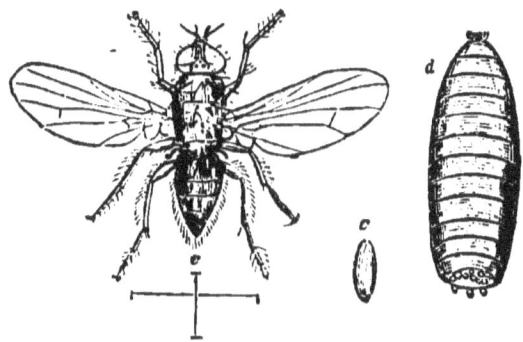

Fig. 73.

removing the earth from the onion bulbs as soon as growth has well commenced will prevent the fly from depositing its eggs, and the onion, being nourished by its fibrous roots, ripens and keeps better.

To preserve them.—Pull them on a dry day, dry them thoroughly in the shade, and stow them in a loft where they can have plenty of air. When thoroughly dry they can be strung in ropes, made by braiding the tops together. From two to five hundred bushels per acre is the usual crop.

For seed.—Select the largest and finest bulbs and plant out in the fall, about twelve inches apart, in beds of common garden soil, not too rich. Keep them free from weeds; and when they throw up seed stalks, support them by poles laid horizontally on stakes, six or eight inches above the surface of the beds. Home-grown seed from good bulbs is as good as the best imported. It will keep three years, but the fresh grown seeds are preferable. Onion buttons are grown in the same manner upon the Top Onion.

Use.—Onions are among the most useful products of the garden. They are used especially as a flavoring ingredient and seasoning for soups, meats, and sauces; for which purpose they have been employed from time immemorial. They contain considerable nutriment, and are tolerably wholesome, especially if boiled. Onions, like *all other vegetables*, need to be slightly salted *while cooking*, or their sweetness will be mostly lost. Raw, they are not very digestible, and they are the same if fried or roasted. Eating a few leaves of parsley will destroy in a measure the unpleasant smell they impart to the breath.

ORACH.—(*Atriplex Hortensis.*)

A hardy annual, of the same natural family as the beet and Jerusalem Oak, (*Chenopodiaceæ*) a native of Tartary, and was first cultivated by English gardeners in 1548. The stem rises three or four feet high, with oblong, variously-shaped leaves, cut at the edges, thick, pale green, and glaucous, and of slightly acid flavor; flowers of same color as the foliage. There are two varieties, the pale green, and the red or purple leaved, the latter of which is just now coming into fashion as an ornamental plant, on account of the fine color of its foliage.

Culture.—Orach flourishes best in a rich, moist soil. It is raised from seed sown in drills, fifteen to eighteen inches apart. Sow very early in spring, or in October, which is a good time in mild climates. Two or three sowings may be made in spring for a succession. The plants soon make their appearance; when an inch high, thin them to four inches asunder. Those removed may be replanted, being watered occasionally until established. Hoe them in a dry day, keeping the ground loose and free from weeds. Once established, it sows itself.

Use.—The leaves and tender stalks are cooked and eaten like spinach, to which they are preferred by many. They must be gathered while young, or they are worthless. The seed should be gathered before fully ripe, as they are liable to be blown away by wind.

PARSLEY.—(*Petroselinum sativum.*)

Parsley is a hardy, biennial, Umbelliferous plant from Sardinia. There are two varieties used in garnishing: the Common Parsley, with plain leaves, which is the hardier sort, and the Dwarf Curled, which is much handsomer and longer in running to seed.

The Neapolitan or Celery-leaved is grown by the French for the leaf-stalks, which they blanch and use like celery.

The Hamburg Parsley (*var. latifolium*) is cultivated for its fleshy roots, which are eaten like parsnips.

Parsley is raised only from seed, which may be sown

in autumn or spring, until the weather and soil are too dry and hot, when it will come up readily. It is best to sow it pretty early, as the seed remains long in the soil before vegetating. The beds must be made annually, if the plants are allowed to run to seed; but if the seed stalks are cut down as often as they rise, the plants will last many years. Many sow parsley as an edging to other beds or compartments. If in beds, it is better to sow in drills ten inches apart. Any good garden soil is rich enough for this plant. Pulverize the bed by thorough spading, and rake it level before making the drills. Sow the seed moderately thick in drills half an inch deep, and press fine soil upon it. The plants will not come up in less than three or four, and sometimes six weeks. If sown late give it a shady border. Should the bed get weedy before the parsley appears, pull the intruders out by hand. As soon as the rows can be seen, hoe between them, and draw a rake crosswise to break the crust which has been formed, and the plants will grow vigorously. They will be fit for use when two or three inches high. When they get strong, thin them out to three inches, and finally to nine inches apart, being careful to reject all plants from the seed bed that are not nicely curled. If they grow too rank in summer, cut them near the collar.

Soot is the very best manure for parsley, but it should be sparingly applied. A bed six feet long by four feet wide is large enough for almost any family. It is best to appropriate to it such a bed, where it will sow itself and yield a constant succession of new plants. The plants should have the stems cut down, if growing rank, three or four weeks before heavy frosts are expected, that fresh growth may be thrown up for winter and early spring use. It is well to protect the plants with a little coarse litter in cold climates, but this is not necessary south of Virginia.

Hamburgh Parsley is grown in drills one foot apart, the

plants ten inches in the drill, in a good deep soil, and is otherwise managed like carrots.

Neapolitan Parsley. The seeds are sown in early spring, and when the young plants are four inches high, they are planted out in rows or shallow trenches two feet apart, and the plants nine inches in the row. They are otherwise treated like celery, but need less moisture.

To save Seeds.—Allow some of the finest curled plants to throw up seed-stalks; let them stand eighteen inches apart; when the seed ripens it may be stored in a dry place. It will keep good several years, and it is singular that seed four years old will come up more quickly than that gathered six months before sowing.

Use.—Parsley is a very agreeable and useful plant, affording a beautiful garnish. It is also used for its aromatic properties in seasoning soups, stews, and meats. The green leaves eaten raw diminish the unpleasant smell of the breath after eating leeks and onions. It can be dried in summer, pounded fine, and put away in bottles; but this is of no use in mild climates, where fresh, green parsley can be had all winter from the garden.

PARSNIP.—(*Pastinaca sativa.*)

This is a hardy, biennial, Umbelliferous plant, of which the wild variety is found in various parts of Europe, and it is not rare in this country as a weed. It has long been cultivated. In its wild state, it is said to have poisonous properties; but it is rendered by cultivation sweet, palatable, and very nutritious for man and beast. The garden parsnips have smooth and light-green leaves, while those of the wild variety are dark-green and hairy; but the two do not differ so much as the wild and cultivated carrot. By ten years' culture, Prof. Buckman in England succeeded in producing the garden variety from the wild sort. This plant is of the hardiest nature, being improved by remaining in the ground exposed to frost during the winter. The best variety for the garden is the Hollow-crown or Sugar Parsnip. Its roots are smoother, more handsome, and better flavored than the other varieties. It is distinguished by the cavity which crowns the root.

Parsnips like a rich, sandy loam, the more deeply dug the better. They do exceedingly well on rich bottom lands, but do not succeed well in stiff clays. The manure should be applied to a previous crop.

Parsnip seed can be sown any time in spring before the hot, dry weather comes on, which will prevent it from vegetating freely. Scatter the seed thinly in drills fifteen inches apart, and when the plants appear, thin them to ten or twelve inches asunder. The culture in other respects is the same as that of the beet. The roots in cold climates are taken up and stored, if required for use in frosty weather, but the flavor is improved by exposure to the winter frosts, and they are commonly left where grown until spring, when if taken up before growth commences they will keep some weeks.

For Seed.—A few of the best roots may be taken up and set out two feet apart in a border; but they do better to remain undisturbed. The seeds cannot be depended on for more than one year.

Use.—The parsnip is a very wholesome and nourishing root, though its peculiar sweetish taste is disliked by many persons. It is, however, an agreeable addition to our supply of winter vegetables. Its fattening properties are great, and it is therefore an excellent root for feeding all kinds of farm stock. Cows fed upon it will yield milk abundantly, and butter of the best quality.

PEA.—(*Lathyrus Pisum.*)

This is a hardy Leguminous annual, probably from the Levant, where the gray field variety is found wild, but it has been cultivated from time immemorial. It is a climbing plant, producing its seeds in pods, which usually grow in pairs. The pea is now one of the most desirable culinary plants. Numerous varieties have been originated, differing in the color of the blossoms, height, time of ripening, and also in productiveness. Among the best are:

Prince Albert, or Early Kent.—Grows about $2\frac{1}{2}$ or 3 feet high. A small, white, very early pea, bearing moderately well; pods containing from eight to ten peas in each. The true sort is the earliest variety grown.

Extra Early.—This celebrated early pea comes into use about five days after the preceding, and with the *Cedo-Nulli*. The whole crop ripens at once. It is tolerably productive; $2\frac{1}{2}$ feet high.

Daniel O'Rourke, as I have received it, is very similar to this. Sangster's No. I is said to be the same as Daniel O'Rourke.

Cedo-Nulli comes into use with the preceding, and is a much finer pea. It has a longer pod, which is better filled. The vines are taller, and it bears about twice as many pods to the stalks as the Extra Early; the most prolific of early peas, and continues long in bearing; 3 feet high.

Early Emperor; said to be as early as Prince Albert; the pods and peas somewhat larger, and a more productive sort.

Early Frame, known also as Early May, Early Warwick, Michaux de Hollande, etc., grows about 4 feet high, with small, round pods, containing some five or six peas of fine quality, which when dry are small, very round and white. This is the parent of the preceding sorts, not quite so early, but more productive, and one of the two hardiest for planting in late autumn, to grow through the winter, in mild climates.

Early Charlton.—Also called Early Hotspur, Michaux Ordinaire, is of more vigorous growth, and larger foliage; 5 ft. high, with broad, flat pods, containing six or seven peas of excellent quality and larger size than the *Early Frame;* just as hardy and fit for use a few days later.

Early Tom Thumb is the most dwarf sort known, being only ten or twelve inches high, and of good flavor; it requires no sticks.

Bishop's New Long-Pod is also a very productive dwarf sort, of excellent quality; grows 1½ to 2 feet, with straight, cylindric pods, containing six or seven large peas.

The foregoing are for the early crop; for the middle season:

Fairbank's Champion.—This is the very best large pea; a wrinkled marrow, of the highest excellence; grows about 4 feet high, and bears very well. Pods long, somewhat curved, slightly flattened, and containing seven or eight large, sugary peas, which when dry are somewhat shrivelled and of a bluish cast.

Dwarf Blue Imperial.—About 3 feet high; pods long, curved at the extremity, and containing eight or nine good peas, of a bluish cast.

Victoria is an early, fine flavored, white, wrinkled marrow, about 3 feet high, and productive of fine large pods.

Napoleon is a fine blue, wrinkled marrow; the earliest of this class, and quite productive.

The most desirable late sorts are:

Large White Marrowfat, growing 4 or 5 feet high, with broad pods, containing about eight large peas of excellent quality; round and white when dry. The Tall White Marrowfat grows over six feet high.

Black-eyed Marrowfat seems to bear the summer heat better than most kinds, and is of good flavor.

Hair's Dwarf Mammoth grows 2 feet high, with a large, wrinkled seed, of a bluish green color, and the highest flavor. Like Bishop's Long-pod, and Allen's Dwarf, the peas should be planted from four to six inches apart in the row, as they branch much. An improvement on Knight's Dwarf Marrow.

Knight's Tall Marrow.—This sort grows 6 or 7 feet high, with large, dark glaucous green leaves, large, broad, well-filled pods; seed large, thin skinned, tender, and sugary, wrinkled, and of a bluish cast; productive. The rows should be six feet apart.

The Sugar Peas are without the tough interior lining to the pod when young, and they will snap in two as readily as the pod of the kidney bean, like which they are prepared for the table. There are two sorts: the Dwarf Sugar about 3 feet high, with small crooked pods; and the Large Crooked Sugar, with large, broad, flat, crooked pods. The stems grow about 6 feet high.

As some families prefer white, others blue, some dwarf, and others tall sorts, it will not be difficult to make a selection from the foregoing list. There are some fifty sorts in the catalogues, but many of them are synonyms.

Potash and phosphoric acid are large constituents of the ash of the pea. Ashes and bone-dust, or superphosphate of lime, especially the former, are likely to be the special manures most needed.

Culture.—A moderately rich and dry calcareous loam is best suited for the early pea and the dwarf varieties. The late peas and the lofty growers do better in heavier soil, and a cool, moist situation. The manure should be applied early the preceding autumn, to be well reduced by the time the crop of peas is ready to feed upon it. In poor ground, fresh stable manure is better than none.

If the ground, however, be extremely rich, there will be more vines than fruit. The soil must be deep, so that the roots may penetrate deeply to obtain moisture in time of drought, that the vines may not mildew. If the vines mildew or get too dry after they begin to blossom, the pods will not fill well. On this account it is found to be of advantage to plant in a furrow some six inches deep, as they continue much longer in bearing than when planted shallow.

The early crop may be planted as soon as the ground will do to work in the spring. And in the Cotton States, where the winters are mild, Early Frame and Charlton Peas may be planted from the last of November until March; Prince Albert, etc., in February; and the later kinds until early in April, and for a fall crop in August, to come into use in October.

Near New York City they are planted from as early in March as the ground opens, until late in May. The distance of the rows apart will depend upon the variety. They should not be nearer to each other than the height to which the sort planted generally attains. Tom Thumb may be planted only fifteen inches apart from row to row, but as it is a branching sort, the plants may be five or six inches in the row. It is usual to plant in double rows, from nine to twelve inches asunder, leaving the distance above directed between each pair of rows. The sticks are set midway between the double rows, supporting the vines of both. It is maintained by many that from its more full exposure to the air and sun a single row will produce as much as two. The tall later sorts are far more fruitful if the rows are put twenty or thirty feet apart, and the space between occupied with other crops.

It is best to plant the early crop in rows running east and west, that the sun may warm the ridge of soil drawn up to the roots; but the rows of the main crop should run north and south. Early peas should be planted in the drills, about an inch apart; the medium growers an inch and a half; while for the tall kinds, as Knight's Tall Marrow, and the Mammoth, two inches are not too much. A quart of seed of these varieties will plant not quite fifty yards of double rows, while a quart of early peas will plant nearly seventy yards twice as thickly. The soil with which they are covered should be chopped fine, if lumpy, and in planting pressed upon the seed. Better delay a little than plant when the ground is wet. After the peas are about two inches high, hoe them well, drawing the earth a little toward them, and loosening the soil between the drills, destroying every weed. Repeat this once or twice, before brushing, which should be done when the plants are six or eight inches high, or as soon as the tendrils appear. This may be done by sharpened branches of trees prepared fan-shaped, and of a height proper for the pea to which they are to be applied, or stakes may be driven down every six feet each side of the drills, and lines of twine stretched from one to the other. Pea brush is, however, the best, as the vines lay hold of it more readily. It should be placed firmly in the ground, between the drills. After brushing, draw up the earth on each side, to help support the vine. Market gardeners do not employ brush or twine, but let them fall over and bear what they will. This does tolerably well with the early varieties, if the spaces between the rows be filled with straw or leaves.

Peas are forced by planting under glass in pots, to be transplanted, when the season permits; but in mild latitudes this is needless, as the pea when young will survive a temperature but two degrees above zero if not in a state of rapid growth. If a hard frost occur when the plants are in bloom the crop is lost.

Seed.—The plants of the rows intended for seed should not be gathered from for any other purpose. When the pods begin to dry, gather and dry them thoroughly, and store the seed in bottles, pouring into each a little spirits of turpentine, as directed for preserving beans. The bean and pea bugs belong to the genus *Bruchus* of Linnæus, a family devouring the seed of many Leguminous plants, and the eggs of both species are deposited by the parent beetle in the soft pods, and directly over the seed. The maggots work their way into the seed, where they obtain their perfect form. The pea bug does not usually destroy the germ, but its congener, the species that infests the bean, is much more destructive, several often inhabiting a single bean, and leaving nothing but the outer skin and a mass of yellow dust. Spirits of turpentine appears to be fatal to them.

Some think that peas are earlier if the seed has been obtained from a more northern locality than the one in which they are planted. The garden pea is very wholesome, and an almost universal favorite. To have them in perfection, they should be freshly gathered, and by no means allowed to stand over night before use. They can be shelled and dried in the shade, and form a tolerably agreeable dish in winter, but they are much inferior to those freshly picked. Green or dry they are very nutritious, abounding in flesh-forming constituents.

PEPPER.—(*Capsicum.*)

This genus (*Capsicum*) of plants belongs to the Solanum family, and several species are in cultivation, all of which are natives of tropical regions. Some of them have been cultivated in England 300 years, *C. annum*, or Guinea Pepper, having been introduced there in 1548. Those most in use are:

Bell Pepper.—This was brought from India in 1759; of low growth, with large, red, bell-shaped fruit.

Its thick and pulpy skin renders it best for pickles; more mild than most varieties. It is a biennial.

Cayenne, or Long Pepper.—Is a perennial, with small, round, bright red, tapering fruit, extremely pungent. Of this there is a large and small fruited sort, both excellent for pepper sauce, and to grind as a condiment.

Large Sweet Spanish is a large, mild variety of annual pepper, much used in pickling.

Tomato Pepper is of two sorts, red and yellow, both tolerably mild; fruit tomato shaped.

Culture.—Capsicum likes a rich, moist loam, rather light than otherwise. Guano and fowl manure are excellent fertilizers for peppers.

For early plants, sow the seed in drills, one inch deep and six inches apart, under glass, in February, at the South, or in March and April in the Northern States, and transplant after the frosts are entirely over, when three or four inches high, into good soil, in rows eighteen inches apart each way. Sow at the South, also, in the open ground, as soon as the settled warm weather comes on, say the last of March or first of April, and thin them out to the proper distance. An ounce of seed will give two or three thousand plants. They should be transplanted in moist weather only, and must be watered until well established. Shading a few days at midday, after transplanting, is very beneficial. Cultivate and earth up their stems a little.

Seed.—A plant bearing the earliest and finest fruit should be selected. The varieties should be grown as far apart as possible. When ripe, the pods are hung up to dry, and kept until the seed is wanted for sowing.

Use.—These plants are very much used in all hot climates, where they enter as a seasoning into almost every dish. The large kinds for pickling should be gathered when full grown, and just before turning red. They are also dried when ripe, and used for seasoning. Cayenne and the other small kinds are ground for table use, or made into pepper sauce by the addition of strong vinegar. Peppers are often rubbed upon meat to drive away insects. The daily use of this plant in hot climates is decidedly a preventive of bowel complaints, for which reason it is so universally cultivated in tropical regions.

POTATO (IRISH.)—(*Solanum tuberosum.*)

The Irish potato is a perennial plant, with a tuberous, subterranean stem, of the same genus with the egg-plant, and nearly allied to the tomato. It is reported to have been brought into England from Virginia by Raleigh, in 1586, but as he never visited Virginia, he probably obtained it from some other portion of this continent. Though called the Irish potato, it is really a native of the western coast of South America, where it is still found wild, both "on dry, sterile mountains, and in damp forests near the sea," whence roots have recently been obtained differing very little from the cultivated varieties. Notwithstanding its excellence and complete adaptation to the English climate, it appears to have come slowly into use. Raleigh planted it on his Irish estate near Cork, but it is only within about a hundred years that its culture has been general, even in Ireland. In 1780, very few individuals in America raised as large a crop as five bushels. Of the numerous varieties at this time, the best, perhaps, for garden culture we name below. Varieties, however, run out after a few years' culture, and those newly raised from seed take their place, and there are many the popularity of which is local.

Fox Seedling.—A medium-sized, round, white potato, of fine flavor when it first matures, but does not keep for winter.

Ash-Leaved Kidney.—Kidney-shaped, thin-skinned, of good form, with few eyes. In planting, cut it lengthwise through the centre; very early.

Mercer.—Long, kidney-shaped, flattish, full of eyes, and often knobbed, spotted with pink at the small ends. It is early and productive.

Prince Albert.—Oblong, a little flattened, yellowish, white eyes, few, and scarcely sunk in the smooth skin; ripens with the Mercer. Several varieties have been directly imported from South America, and others originated from these, by Rev. C. E. Goodrich, of Utica, N. Y. We cultivated several of his kinds for some years, and were pleased with their quality and freedom from rot. Among them were the Black Diamond, Garnet Chili, Pale Blush Pink Eye, New Hartford, and Rough Purple Chili. They are more hardy than the old sorts, but none are entirely free from rot. [The Early Goodrich, one of Mr. G's. seedlings, and the Sebec, are among the most prized early varieties at the North, and the Early Rose, a descendant of the Garnet Chili, is of excellent quality, and the earliest yet known.—*Ed.*] At the South a potato is required that will continue growing through the long summer. The common sorts ripen early, and commence new growth, so that it is very difficult to keep them in their dry, mealy state. Starting the buds has the same effect upon these tubers as upon the grains of wheat which lose their starch by conversion into sugar and dextrine, making both the flour and tuber, when cooked, far less palatable and nourishing.

Potash and phosphate of magnesia are indicated by analysis to be the most important inorganic elements of the plant. Wood ashes will furnish most of the constituents required from the soil.

Culture.—The Irish potato likes a cool, moist climate and soil like those of Ireland. The soil should be well enriched with vegetable and not with animal manure. The best potatoes in this country are grown in the cool and hilly sections of the North, and the best there are grown by simply turning over a meadow sward; upon this the rows are laid off shallow, and the clover sods are often so tough with matted roots when planting (having been newly turned over), that earth is with difficulty obtained to cover the potatoes. Soon decomposition commences, a gentle heat is given out, and by the time the potatoes are ready for the first working they can be plowed with ease. At the second working, when the plants are laid by, the soil is mellow as an ash heap, the young plant the meanwhile being supplied with moisture and the very food required to perfect its tubers and render them farinaceous and nutritive. In our gardens we cannot obtain such a soil, but we can very much improve the yield, and especially the quality of our Irish potatoes by imitating it as nearly as possible. We can dig into the soil vegetable matter to decompose, such as leaves, garden refuse of all kinds, and pine straw. Even tan bark is not a bad application to the potato crop, but if used must be accompanied with plenty of ashes or lime to correct its acidity. One reason for the application of vegetable manure to this plant is the superior quality of the tubers produced. Liebig first remarked that ammoniacal manures injure the quality of the potato, though they increase the size and quantity. If manured with strong animal manure the tubers are moist and waxy, while if grown upon a soil manured with ashes, lime, and an abundant supply of carbonaceous manures, such as decaying vegetable matter, the produce is far more starchy and nutritive. Potatoes enriched with strong dung are far more liable to rot than if manured with leaves, ashes, and lime.

The rows should be from two to two and a half feet

asunder, and the sets from six to twelve inches in the row, the greater distances for the tall-growing sorts. Experiments in England have proved that there the best crops are secured when the sets are planted six inches deep, or in light sandy soil not less than seven inches. The sets should be cut a week before planting, and allowed to dry. A medium-sized tuber will make five or six sets. After the ground has been well prepared by plowing or spading, dig a trench eight inches deep, the width of the spade, and in the bottom of this form a slight furrow with a hoe, that the sets may be in a line. In this furrow the sets are placed (for Mercers eight inches apart). Cover with a good coat of manure of the kinds before directed, to which manipulated guano, or superphosphate of lime and gypsum, may be added with advantage. The earth is hauled over them, leaving the surface some two or three inches below the general level, that the plants may receive and retain near them all the rain that falls. After the plants come up, hoe them well, but do not disturb the ground if there is any apprehension of even a slight frost. When all danger of frost is over, they should, if possible, receive a good mulching of leaves directly after a good heavy rain, and some trash may be laid over to keep the leaves in place. The leaves must not be put on too early, as if applied before the frosts are entirely over the evaporation from a bed of damp leaves so lowers the temperature at their surface that a frost scarcely perceptible elsewhere may prove fatal to tender plants thus mulched.

If the leaves are not to be obtained, keep the soil free from weeds by flat culture, until the tops cover the ground. The early crop may alternate with Lima beans, making the rows five feet apart in this case, and they will be ready for digging when the beans are fit for use which are planted in hills between the potato rows. This crop should be planted as early in the spring as possible. At the South, in January or February, and at the North in

March or April. The main crop may be put in three or four weeks later, but if they escape spring frosts the early planted crops are best. In colder climates the sets are often kept in a warm room covered with damp moss until they have grown a half inch, and then if planted out without being dried, in a warm situation, are considerably earlier. A teaspoonful of gypsum dusted over the plants when they appear above ground is very beneficial. Never work the crop after the blossom buds appear.

When the tops begin to die, dig the crop, and store in a cool, dry place. Sprinkle them with lime when dug, and they are less in danger of rot. This disease often attacks them while growing, beginning at the haulm, and descending to the tubers, which soon become a mass of rottenness. It is caused by the fungus, *Botrytis infestans*, but is thought to be gradually disappearing. If potatoes are allowed to remain in the ground until they begin to grow, they become waxy and worthless, and those that are stored will not remain eatable, unless the sprouts are rubbed off as they appear.

Use.—The tubers of the Irish potato, consisting chiefly of starch, and having no peculiarity of taste, approach nearer in their nature to the flour of grain than any other root. Hence the potato is almost universally liked, and can be continually used by the same individual without becoming unpalatable. It is a good supporter of respiration, and adapted for the formation of fat, but is deficient in nitrogenous or muscle-forming elements. Sustained labor cannot be performed on this diet without the addition of other food better adapted to the formation of flesh. Potatoes are boiled, baked, roasted, or fried. When long kept, the best ones are selected, boiled, and mashed, before going to the table. Starch can be manufactured from potatoes, as may ardent spirits.

POTATO, SWEET.—(*Convolvulus Batatas.*)

This valuable plant, first cultivated in England in 1597, by Gerard, is the potato mentioned by Shakespeare and his cotemporaries, the Irish potato being then scarcely known. "Let the sky rain potatoes," says Falstaff, alluding to this vegetable, which was at that time imported into England from Spain and the Canary Islands, and considered a great delicacy. The sweet potato is a tender perennial plant, of the Morning Glory family, a native of China and both Indies. It has small leaves, with three to five lobes, according to the variety, with herbaceous vines which run along the ground, taking root at intervals. Its roots are long, spindle-shaped or oval, often very large, and abounding in starch and sugar. Its nutritious properties and agreeable flavor have brought it into general use in all parts of the globe, where the climate is warm enough to admit of its successful cultivation. The following are the most common varieties, and perhaps as good as any.

Small Spanish. — Long, grows in clusters, purplish color, very productive, and of excellent quality, but if not well grown, is fibrous; flesh white.

Nansemond is a larger variety, and good at every stage of growth; the best for the North.

Brimstone.—Sulphur-colored, long, of large size, and productive; keeps well with us, and is one of the best sorts; very dry, and excellent.

Red Bermuda is of the Yam family; leaves, many-lobed; the best early potato; productive.

Common Yam. — Leaves many-lobed; root yellow, large, oblong, and somewhat globular; the best long-keeper, and very productive. Has something of the pumpkin flavor.

Hayti Yam.—Larger in size, white flesh, not so sweet, but more farinaceous. Keeps equal to the last, and is dry and floury; the most prolific of all.

Culture.—Sweet potatoes like a rich, sandy loam, perfectly friable, and, as indicated by analysis, abounding in potash. The soil should be well enriched. A dressing of wood ashes would be very beneficial to this crop. Next to potash it demands a supply of the phosphates. They do well on fresh lands, if well broken up and friable. At the South, the Spanish potatoes are generally planted where they are to remain, like the Irish potato, whole or cut up into sets. But both these may, and the yams must, be propagated by slips, as they grow larger and yield more abundantly.

To raise slips, select a sunny spot sheltered by fences or buildings, and lay it off in beds four feet wide, with alleys of the same width between them; slope the beds a little towards the sun, dig them well, and add plenty of well-decomposed manure, if not already rich. Do this in Georgia in February, or early in March. At the North, a gentle hot-bed will be required, and it will be found very useful in every locality, in order that the slips may be ready as soon as all danger of frost is over.

Choose smooth and healthy-looking potatoes, and lay them regularly over the bed an inch or two apart, and cover them about three or four inches with fine soil; rake the bed smooth, and it is done. In large operations, ten bushels of potatoes should be bedded for every acre of ground.

While the slips are sprouting, prepare the ground to receive them. It should be rich, or made so with well-rotted manure, and thoroughly and deeply broken up with the plow or spade. Lay it off just before the slips are ready, in low, parallel ridges or beds, the crowns of which are three and a half feet asunder, and about six inches high, on which plant out the slips with a dibble eighteen inches apart, one plant in a place. Choose for this operation such a day as you would for cabbage plants, or do it in the evening. The sweet potato is readily transplanted, and if holes are dug in the mellow bed, deep enough to admit the plant, and the slips, set upright therein, have the earth washed in about their roots by pouring water upon them from the open spout of a water-pot, finishing the operation by covering over with a coat of dry, mellow earth, brought up and pressed pretty closely about the slips to keep the moistened earth from baking, very few will die, even if they are set out at mid-day; but as the plants would be checked, a cloudy day, or just at night, should be selected for the operation.

This is an excellent mode of transplanting all plants, and is of great use both in the vegetable and flower-garden. If the slips are not washed in as above when taken up in dry weather, it is of great advantage to grout them, as well as all other plants you wish to transplant. This is done by immersing the roots in water thickened with rich earth. It refreshes the slips, and gives them a thin coating of earth as a protection against the atmosphere. Draw the slips when about three or four inches high, by placing the left hand on the bed near the sprout to steady the root, and prevent its being pulled up with the sprout, which is loosened with the right hand, taking care not to disturb the fibrous roots of the mother potato, for this continues to afford a succession of slips, which may be successfully transplanted in Georgia until the first of July. At the North, they should not be put in later than the first of June.

After the piece is planted, go over it again in a few days to plant over any place where the slips may have failed. As soon as the ground gets a little weedy, scrape it over, loosening the earth and covering up the weeds, but be careful not to injure the young slips. Faithful cultivation and frequent moving the soil are as beneficial to this crop, while young, as to any other. At one of the hoeings just before being laid by, the ground should be deeply moved with the plow or spade, but not close to the plants. They should be laid by before the plants run a great deal, after which they should be undisturbed. Be careful not to cover the vines, but if they become attached to the soil, loosen them up from it, so that the vigor of the plants may be thrown into the roots and not into the running vines. Make the hills large and broad, not pointed. In hoeing, draw the vines carefully over towards you while you draw up the earth and cover the weeds; then lay them carefully back, and finish the other side in the same manner. At this time fill the spaces between the rows with leaves and litter while the ground is wet, to retain the moisture. After the vines have covered the ground too much to use the hoe, any large weeds that appear should be pulled up by hand.

The Yam potato can also be raised from seed, but the Spanish variety, like the sugar cane and many other plants long propagated by division, rarely produces seed.

Just as soon as the tops are killed by frost, the potatoes should be gathered. In field crops they can be plowed up and gathered by hands which follow the plow, depositing the potatoes in small heaps, but in the garden the potato can be gathered with the hoe or the potato hook, an implement much used in gathering crops of the Irish potato. It is better to do this in a dry day, and many prefer to dig their potatoes just before the frost kills the vines, thinking they keep better.

To keep sweet potatoes, it is necessary, at the North, to store them in a dry, warm place, in well-dried sand. At the South, they are safely stored in hills containing thirty or forty bushels each. Let the potatoes, when dug, dry in the sun through the day, and in digging and handling, they should not be bruised. Elevate the bottom of the intended pile about six inches with earth, furnished by digging around it a circular trench. On this put pine straw two or three inches thick, or dry leaves, on which place the potatoes piled in a regular cone. If the weather is good, cover them only with pine or other straw for two or three days, until the potatoes are well dried, before their final earthing up. Let the covering of straw be three or four inches thick; then cover it over with large strips of pine bark, commencing at the base, and cover as shingling unto the top, leaving a small aperture. Cover four or five inches thick with earth over all, except this aperture, which must be left open for the escape of the heat and moisture generated within.—(*Peabody*.)

Some cover this opening with a piece of pine bark, to keep out the rain, but a board shelter is preferable. It is well to protect the hills from rain by a temporary roof of plank. When the weather gets warm, in the spring, take up the potatoes, rub off the sprouts, and keep on a dry floor. If put up with care, they will keep until July. One important step toward their certain preservation is to gather them carefully from the ground, as the least bruise produces rapid decay.

For Seed, some of the finest roots of the most productive hills can be packed in barrels, and covered with sand, in a dry, warm place, free from all exposure to frost. A small garden crop is best kept in barrels with dry sand or leaves; if the latter, a layer of leaves at the bottom, then a layer of potatoes, then a layer of leaves, and so on until the cask is filled. Use dry leaves, and store in a dry place.

Use.—This root is deservedly a favorite at the table, and the most wholesome grown. In nutritious properties, it excels all other roots cultivated in this country, except the carrot. Weight for weight, it contains more than double the quantity of starch, sugar, and other elements of nutrition, that are found in the best varieties of Irish potato. For feeding stock, three bushels are equal to one of Indian corn, yielding, on the same land, five or six times the food that is produced by this most profitable grain.

A good baked sweet potato is almost as nutritive as bread. They are better baked than boiled. They are also used for pies and puddings, and sweet potato rolls are excellent. In short, the modes of cooking this valuable vegetable are innumerable, but perhaps the very best is Marion's mode of roasting in the hot ashes.

PUMPKIN.—(*Cucurbita Pepo.*)

A trailing annual, from India and the Levant, with globular or cylindrical fruit. It has become so crossed that it is difficult to say of some varieties to which species they should be referred.

The best variety for family use is the Cashaw, a long, cylindrical, curved variety, swollen at one extremity, of fine, creamy yellow color, very solid and excellent to use as a winter squash, and quite as valuable as any for the other purposes. Pumpkins are not as particular about soil as melons and cucumbers, but will grow well on any tolerably rich ground. It is not best to grow them in the garden, as they will mix and corrupt the seed of the other varieties. They like a soil freshly reclaimed from the woods; the field is the proper place for their cultivation. Plant when the main crop of corn is put in; let the hills be ten feet apart. Hoe frequently and keep clean. Let only one plant remain in each hill. Do not earth up the plants, but keep the soil about them light and loose with the hoe, until the vines prevent further culture.

Use.—In France, as well as in New England, the pumpkin is much used for stews and soups. The best, such as

Cashaw, are good substitutes for the winter squash, and make an excellent pie. They are also a valuable food for cattle. They can be preserved by boiling and drying the pulp in an oven, or by cutting in strips and drying by the fire, or will keep very well whole, if in a cool, dry place, free from frost.

RADISH.—(*Raphanus sativus.*)

This is an annual Cruciferous plant, grown in England as early as 1548, being one of the plants mentioned by Gerard. The lower leaves are lyrate; stem about two feet high, with pale violet flowers; the root fleshy, spindle or globular-shaped, of various colors. There are two kinds of radish, the spindle-rooted, and the globular or turnip-rooted. These are again divided into early and late varieties, among which we will notice:

Early Scarlet Short-Top.—Root long and spindle-shaped; leaves very short. It is the earliest, most crisp and mild-flavored, and requires less space than the other varieties. Much esteemed for its bright color. The root grows partly above ground. Long Scarlet Early Frame, and Salmon, differ very slightly from this.

Scarlet Turnip-rooted.—Turbinate; scarlet-colored; flesh white and tender; not equal to the last, but bears the heat better. A sub-variety has rose-colored flesh. Another, the *Purple Turnip-rooted*, differs only in its external skin, which is purple.

White Turnip-rooted has a white exterior, and a round bulb, terminating in a small, fibrous root. Flesh, white and mild.

Oval (or Oblong) Rose-colored.—Root oval or oblong;

crimson skin, and tender, rose-colored flesh. The best of all in quality; good for forcing and the early crop.

Yellow Summer.—This is a turnip-rooted variety, named from its color, and will stand the heat better than any other variety.

Black Winter or Spanish.—Turnip-shaped, black, and very large; sown in August or September with turnips. It can be gathered and stored for winter. The flesh is white, hard, and hot. The White Spanish is white outside, and the flesh milder than the Black.

Chinese Rose-colored Winter.—Conical; bright rose-colored; flesh solid; texture fine; rather hot.

White Chinese.—Outside white; bulb inversely turbinate; flesh milder than the last three, tender, and excellent; the best winter sort. The Scarlet Oval Rose and White Chinese are the best sorts.

Culture.—Radishes like a rich, sandy loam, dug a full spade deep, but succeed in any good garden soil. Their culture is very simple. If manure be freshly applied, it should be at the bottom of the soil, or the roots will fork. They are often sown in beds four or five feet wide, thinly broadcast; but it is better to put them in drills about eight or ten inches apart, an inch deep, scattering the seed thinly, which may be in beds devoted to this crop, or made between the wider rows of beets, parsnips, onions, carrots, as well as spinach, peas, beans, Irish potatoes, yielding large crops, and taking up no room available for other purposes.

From the first of November until March a succession of the Oval Rose, or Scarlet Short-top varieties, can be grown under glass. All that is required is a bed of good, rich loam, watering them occasionally, and giving air every day, when it does not absolutely freeze. Let the sash be off every mild rain, and let the earth come within seven or eight inches of the glass. On open ground crops can be made for fall use, if desired, by sowing in succession, after the summer heats are over, until about the time of the first frosts. With the first opening of spring, commence planting in the open ground, and sow every week or two until the dry, hot weather comes on. In the low country South, they may be grown all winter, with no other protection than a little litter thrown over the beds in severe frosts. As birds are very fond of the seed, it is sometimes necessary to protect the beds with nets. Radishes are of such rapid growth, that they will generally take care of themselves after planting in a good soil, but hoeing once will hasten their growth.

For Seed.—Some of the finest and earliest can remain where grown, or be removed to another bed and inserted up to their leaves. Water frequently until established, and while the flowers are opening. Let the roots be three feet apart, and do not permit any others to flower near them, if pure seeds are desired. When the pods turn dry, gather, dry, thresh out, and save in paper bags. The seed will keep three years.

Use.—The tops used to be boiled for greens. The seed leaves, when they first appear, are used as a salad, with cress and mustard, and the seed-pods, gathered young, form a good pickle, and are a substitute for capers.

There is a species, *Raphanus caudatus*, or Rat-tailed radish, of which the pod grows a foot or more in length, with a peculiar pungent but delicate flavor, and it may be eaten like the root, or pickled. It is from Java.

But of the common species the roots are the parts mainly used. They are much relished, while young and crisp, for the breakfast table. They contain little beside water, woody fiber, and acrid matter; so they cannot be very nourishing or wholesome. When young, and of good varieties, they are much more digestible than when older and more fibrous.

RAMPION.—(*Campanula Rapunculus.*)

This is an English biennial plant, related to the Canterbury-bell, with a long, white, spindle-shaped root, lower leaves oval lanceolate, with a panicle of blue bell-shaped flowers in June. It has a milky juice.

Culture.—Sow the seed in April or May in a rich, shady border. It likes a moist, rich soil, not too stiff. The seed must be very slightly covered, but fine earth should be pressed upon it. As the plants grow, thin them to four inches apart, and pull them before they run to seed.

To save seeds, allow some of the best plants to remain.

Use.—The root is eaten raw like a radish, and has a pleasant, nutty flavor. Cultivated only by those in search of variety.

RAPE, OR COLZA.—(*Brassica Napus, var. oleifera.*)

Rape, or Colza, is a biennial plant of the cabbage tribe, a native of England, with glaucous radical leaves and yellow flowers, appearing early in spring. It is often called Kale.

Culture.—Sow at the same time with cresses and mustard in late winter and spring. Sow in drills or beds, and follow the culture directed for white mustard. Rape, sown like turnips the first of September, will survive the frosts and afford an abundance of fine greens the latter part of winter and early in spring, wherever the turnip will stand the winter.

Seed.—A few plants sown in August and September, and kept over, will flower and seed the next year abundantly.

Use.—The seed leaves are gathered young for a small salad with cresses and mustard. Later it is used like mustard for greens. This plant is much cultivated in Europe for the oil expressed from its seeds.

Rape, Edible-rooted, or French Turnip, *B. Napus, var. esculenta,* is another variety with edible roots, sometimes cultivated as a substitute for the turnip. The root is white, carrot-shaped, about the size of the middle finger. It is much grown in Germany and France. [This is not the French Turnip of the North, and is the Teltow of the Germans.—ED.]

Culture.—It is raised from seed, which may be sown in August or September, and requires the same treatment as turnip. It likes a sandy soil, and if grown in too rich earth, it loses its sweetness. In dry weather, the beds must be watered regularly until the plants get three or four leaves. To save seed, see "Turnip."

Use.—It is much used in continental cookery, and enriches all the French soups. Stewed in gravy, it forms an excellent dish, and being white and carrot-shaped, when mixed with carrots upon a dish, it is very ornamental. In using, there will be no necessity of cutting away the outer rind, in which the flavor chiefly resides. Scraping will be quite sufficient.

RHUBARB.—(*Rheum.*)

The garden Rhubarb, or Pie-plant, is a perennial of the same natural family as the common dock. The varieties now cultivated are hybrids, and have supplanted the original species, *Rheum Rhaponticum, palmatum,* and *undulatum,* excelling them in size, earliness, and delicacy of flavor. The best sorts are the Early, which is of but medium size; Myatt's Linnæus, rather early, and yielding large crops of large leaves, and the best flavored of all; Myatt's Victoria, which is two weeks later; stalks very large, and good; Downing's Colossal, and Cahoon's Mammoth, very large varieties, of good flavor.

Rhubarb is remarkable for the quantity of phosphates and soda it extracts from the earth. Crude soda might be added to the soil. Guano and bone-dust are very beneficial.

Rhubarb succeeds best in a rich, deep, rather light loam, and in a situation open to the air and light. Trench the ground two spades deep. It may be raised from seed, but thus grown, sports into new varieties. It is best propagated by dividing the roots, reserving a bud to each piece. These may set about two inches deep in rows three feet apart, and from eighteen to thirty inches (according to the sort) in the row. All the culture required is to keep the surface soil light and free from weeds. The plantation may be made in the fall, after the leaves are killed by frost, and protected by litter, or as early in the spring as the weather and soil permit. It should not be disturbed after growth commences. Pluck no leaves the first year, after which the crop will be abundant. Make a new plantation about once in five years. If a plant or two in summer dies out, as it is apt to do in the South, it is best to remove the next autumn the old plant together with soil in which it grew, and supply fresh soil. New plants to reset the vacancy can be obtained by uncovering an old crown and cutting from it a bud with a piece of root attached.

To obtain the largest product, the flower stems should be broken off when they appear, for the plant is weakened by permitting it to seed. A yearly surface dressing of well-rotted manure should be given, for the stalks, to be good, must be quickly grown.

Forcing.—This plant is forced by placing a large flower pot over the roots, and covering with stable manure. The more common way is to surround the plant with a small barrel without a head; a cover is placed over it at night and in cold days, and it is then surrounded with a pile of stable manure built up in as sharp a cone as it can be made to form. If the root is good, it will soon fill the barrel with shoots. The plant should be permitted to rest after this crop through the season, and others be selected for the purpose the next year. This operation, at the North, is common enough, but at the South it is generally death to the plant.

Use.—The leaf-stem, or petiole of this plant, when the external skin is removed, is cut up in thin slices, and having an agreeable acid, is used exactly like the apple for pies, tarts, and sauce, at a time that fruits cannot be obtained. Gather them while young, just as they attain their full size, before they lose their fine flavor. They should be gently slipped from the root without using a knife.

This plant is in almost universal use in England, France, and the Northern States, and succeeds perfectly well in Middle Georgia. We hope to see it common in Southern gardens wherever it will succeed.

ROCAMBOLE.—(*Allium Scorodoprasum.*)

This is a hardy, perennial, Liliaceous plant, of the onion tribe, from Denmark, and is sometimes called Spanish Garlic, and Great Shallot. It has its bulbs and cloves growing in a cluster, forming a kind of compound root. The stem also bears bulbs at its summit. These are often sold for onion buttons.

Culture.—It is best propagated by the root-bulbs, those

of the summit being slow in production. The planting may be made at any time in the fall, winter, or spring. Insert the bulbs in drills eight inches apart and six inches in the drill, with the dibble, about two inches deep. Keep clear of weeds, and cultivate and store like garlic. A very few roots are sufficient for any family.

Use.—The bulbs are used in the same manner as garlic, and are preferred for cooking, being of much milder flavor.

ROQUETTE.—(*Brassica eruca.*)

This is an annual plant from France, of which the leaves are used as a salad. Sow thinly in drills a foot apart, as soon as spring opens; here in February and March. Water frequently, if necessary, which will lessen the acrid taste of the young leaves; gather young. Not much cultivated.

SALSIFY.—(*Tragopogon porrifolifolius.*)

Salsify, or Vegetable Oyster, is a hardy, tap-rooted biennial, a native of various parts of Europe, with long tapering root of a fleshy, white substance, the herbage smooth and glaucous, the flower-stem three or four feet high, and the flower of a dull purple color. It belongs to the Composite Family.

VEGETABLES—DESCRIPTION AND CULTURE. 295

Salsify likes a light, mellow soil, dug very deeply, as for carrots and other tap-rooted plants. Sow early in spring, and for a succession until the summer heats come on, rather thickly, in drills an inch deep and a foot apart. An ounce of seed will sow a square rod. Scarlet radish may also be sown thinly in the same drills. When an inch high, thin the plants, and continue by degrees until the plants are six inches apart. If the soil is deep and moist, they will grow all summer and not run up to seed. Watering in dry weather, especially with guano water, will greatly invigorate the plants. Cultivate the soil, and keep it free from weeds, as for beets and carrots. The roots may be drawn and stored in sand, but where the winters are open should remain in the ground all winter, to be pulled as wanted.

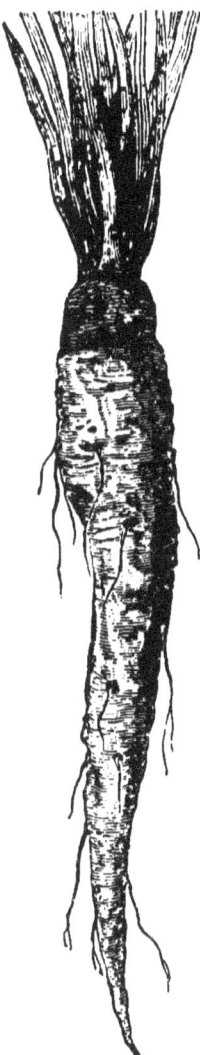

Fig. 74.—SALSIFY.

For Seed.—Leave, or transplant some of the best plants in spring, which will produce seed abundantly. Gather and dry in the heads, where they may be kept until wanted.

Use.—The stalks of old plants are sometimes cut in the spring, as a substitute for asparagus. The roots are boiled or stewed like carrots, and have a mild, sweet flavor, being wholesome, palatable, and tolerably nutritive. They are mostly cooked to imitate oysters, to which the flavor has some resemblance.

SAVORY.—(*Satureja.*)

This is a genus of Labiate plants of which there are two species in cultivation; the Summer Savory, *Satureja hortensis*, a hardy annual; and Winter Savory, *Satureja montana*, a shrubby perennial—both natives of Italy, and cultivated for their warm, aromatic flavors.

Both may be propagated by seed. Sow in spring, as soon as the ground is a little warm, moderately thick, in shallow drills, and cover lightly. For Summer Savory, the rows should be twelve inches apart, and the plants thinned to six inches; the thinnings may be transplanted to the same distance. Winter Savory requires more room; the plants should be a foot apart, in drills fifteen inches asunder. This can be propagated also, by slips, cuttings, or division of the roots. All the care required is to keep free from weeds. Seed can be gathered as it ripens from a root or two left uncut for the purpose.

Use.—The leaves of these herbs are much employed in soups, salads, stuffings, &c., on account of their agreeable pungent flavor. They are also said to possess the desirable power of "expelling fleas from a bed." Formerly, they were much used in medicine. Gather when they come into bloom, and dry for winter use in the shade, pound in a mortar, pass through a sieve, and put up in bottles closely stopped, and they will retain their fragrance any length of time.

SCORZONERA.—(*Scorzonera Hispanica.*)

Scorzonera is a hardy, tap-rooted perennial, a native of Spain, and cultivated in England since 1576. The stem is two or three feet high, few-leaved, branched at the top. The flowers are yellow.

Culture.—It is raised from seed, which must be sown yearly. The soil, like that for most root crops, must be mellow, deep, and fertile. Sow any time in spring, in drills a foot apart, and cover the seed half an inch deep. In the South it is better to sow two or three different times, as the early sown may run to seed, and the late sown may not vegetate. When the plants are three inches high, thin them to eight inches in the drill. In short, to cultivate and save seed, see Salsify.

Use.—The roots are carrot-shaped, but with a black skin. They are white within, are agreeable to the taste, and nutritive, but before use, the bitter outer rind must be scraped off. They are then boiled and used like salsify or carrots. The roots continue good all winter. The plant is too similar to salsify to render its cultivation an object where that is grown.

SCURVY GRASS.—(*Cochlearia officinalis.*)

A hardy, Cruciferous, annual plant, found near the sea shores of most temperate climates.

It is propagated by seed sown as soon as ripe, or very early in spring. Sow in shallow drills, eight inches apart, and thin to four inches. Keep free from weeds, and water in dry weather. Used as an addition to salads, like cresses, and medicinally in scurvy.

SEA KALE.—(*Crambe maratima.*)

This is a hardy, Cruciferous perennial, a native of the dry, shingly shores of Great Britain. The plant is smooth, of a beautiful glaucous hue, covered with a fine meal, and with large, sinuated radical leaves. The flower is of a rich white appearance, and a honeyed smell. It has probably been cultivated in gardens one hundred and fifty years, but not very generally until the beginning of the present century, though the English peasantry have been in the habit of gathering the blanched shoots as they pushed through the sand, and boiling them as greens, from time immemorial. Though a native of a cool climate, it succeeds perfectly in middle Georgia.

Culture.—The native soil of sea kale is a deep sand, mingled with matter from the sea. It likes a deep mould, or sandy loam, and if poor, well-putrified dung and half-decayed leaves may be added. Upon the richness and proper preparation of the soil the luxuriance of the plant depends. The situation must be free from all shade of trees. Sea kale is propagated by seeds, or offsets, or cuttings of the root; but the best plants are raised from seed. Sow the seed in a well-prepared soil, rich, or made

Fig. 75.—SEA KALE.

so with well-decomposed manure, and shaded by a fence, or building, from the midday sun. Draw the drills one foot apart, and scatter the seed thinly along the drills. The beds should be about four feet wide, for convenience. Sow very early in spring. If the outer coat of the seed be bruised, not injuring the latter, the germination will be accelerated. The plants are very slow in appearing; never less than three weeks, often four or five months, and sometimes a full year. Water plentifully in dry weather, and keep the seed-beds free from weeds during the season. Thin the plants, as they appear, to an inch apart, and, as they grow strong, to two or three inches, and keep free from weeds. In the autumn, when their leaves decay, clear them away, and earth them up about the crowns with an inch or two of soil from the alleys, or leaf-mould from the woods, and cover over the whole bed, four inches deep, with long litter, and leave it to stand until the time of transplanting.

As early as possible the spring ensuing, prepare the permanent bed for those you wish to transplant. Those raised where they are to remain succeed best.

Let the soil be light, and well enriched with good compost. Leaf manure is better than hot dung. Dig it up deeply and thoroughly, at least two feet deep, and lay it off in beds three feet wide, with alleys between, two feet in width. Upon each of these beds plant two rows of plants eighteen inches apart, and the same distance in the row. Take up the plants very carefully with the trowel, so as not to disturb the roots. If you plant cuttings of old plants, put two in each place, to guard against failures. In all cases, be careful in transplanting that the roots are not broken or dried by exposure to the sun and air. During the dry, hot weather of summer, the beds should be liberally watered, the first season after replanting, as upon their summer growth depends the next season's crop. Keep the soil clean, and after the plants get well rooted, dig over the ground between the rows, making the soil as fine as possible.

The coming autumn, the earthing-up must be a little increased; give a coat of leaf-mould, or compost manure, and over this a thick coat of leaves, which will bring the plants on early in the spring. The next spring remove the litter, and dig in some of the manure into the alleys, and then, if you blanch with pots, spread over the beds about an inch deep of clean sand. The shoots may be blanched, and a few cut for use, but sparingly, as the plants must not be weakened. The better way is not to remove the covering of leaves until you have gathered what you desire. On a portion of the bed to produce early, the winter covering of compost and leaves must be yearly applied.

Another portion must be left uncovered until the shoots begin to rise, and then covered with eight or ten inches of sand, for a later crop. Each spring give it a dressing of salt, like asparagus, and dig over the surface of the bed, as before. Retain for each plant only four or five of the best suckers, at regular distances around the stem; suffer none of these to seed, if you would not greatly injure the next year's growth.

Sea kale, though eatable without blanching, as spring greens, is vastly improved when blanched. This may be done by earthing-up the crowns eight or ten inches with sand, or light mould, or by retaining the coat of dry leaves put over the beds in autumn.

This covering may remain until the cutting ceases in the spring, when all covering must be removed at evening, or in cloudy weather. The shoots will raise the covering when in a fit state for cutting. The courses of leaves should be from five to twelve inches thick, according to the age of the plants, and as directed above, may remain on all winter. But a large flower pot, with the hole in the bottom stopped, and light at the edges carefully excluded by a coat of litter, is the best of all modes of blanching.

For Seed.—A plant that has not been blanched or cut from must be allowed to run to seed in the spring. A single plant will produce an abundant supply.

Use.—Sea kale comes on early in March, when vegetables are scarce, and affords a very wholesome and agreeable table luxury. The young shoots and leaf stalks, before unfolding, are boiled and dressed like asparagus, are employed in soups, and also make an agreeable salad.

SHALLOT, OR ESCHALLOT.—(*Allium Ascolonicum.*)

This is a plant of the onion tribe, which derives its botanical name from growing wild at Ascalon, in Syria. It has a strong taste, but as the strong flavor is not offensive, like the garlic, and does not remain so long upon the palate as the onion, it is often preferred. The root is bulbous, similar to that of garlic in being divided into cloves, included in a membrane. It rarely sends up a flower-stock, and hence is often called the barren onion.

The best sorts are the Common and the Long-Keeping, of which last the bulbs have been kept two years. The "Big Shallot" of our gardens is Rocambole.

Culture.—It is propagated from the offsets of the roots. Prepare the beds as for the rest of the onion tribe, but it will do with not quite as rich a soil. Let the soil be made perfectly light and friable. The last of September is the best time for planting the early crop, but they may be planted any time during the autumn and winter. The early planted ones come into use early in May. Make the beds four feet wide, and mark them off in drills an inch deep, ten or twelve inches distant, and put the offsets out six inches apart in the drills. Do not cover deeply; leave the point of the clove just even with the surface of the earth, and press the soil around. Keep the ground free from weeds, but be particular, in hoeing, not to earth up the bulbs. The leek is the only member of the onion tribe that is not injured by gathering the earth about its stem. Take up the bulbs when ripe, dry in the shade, and preserve as garlic. They may be kept until the next spring.

Use.—The shallot, though more pungent than some members of the onion family, is preferred by many in seasoning gravies, soups, sauces, and other culinary preparations, and is by some considered almost indispensable in the preparation of a good beefsteak. It can be pickled in the same manner as the onion.

SKIRRET.—(*Sium sisarum.*)

Skirret is a perennial Umbelliferous plant from China, known in Europe since 1548. It grows a foot high, with pinnate lower leaves. The root is composed of several fleshy tubers, the size of the little finger, joined at the crown.

Culture.—Skirret likes a deep, rich, rather moist soil, with the manure applied at the bottom. The situation should be open. It is propagated by seeds, or by offsets of established roots. Seedlings produce the best roots. Sow in spring, when the ground becomes warm, in drills an inch deep and ten inches apart. When the plants are an inch or two high, thin to six or eight inches apart. Cultivate like salsify, and keep clear from weeds. They will be fit for use in August, but can remain in the ground, to use as wanted, all winter. Slips of the old roots may be set out nine inches apart and cultivated in the same manner. Leave some of the plants in the ground, and they will throw up seed-stalks and ripen seed during the summer following.

Use.—The tubers are boiled and are very sweet, somewhat like the parsnip, and are thought more palatable by some, but are disagreeable to many. They are boiled, and served up with butter, or cold, with vinegar and oil, and are also cooked, like salsify, in batter. It was formerly esteemed as "the sweetest, whitest, and most pleasant of roots."

SORREL.—(*Rumex.*)

The sorrels are perennial plants belonging to the same family as dock and rhubarb. There are three species cultivated, viz: *Rumex acetosa*, or common English garden sorrel, of which the Belleville variety is best; *R. scutatus*; French or Round-leaved Sorrel, a trailing plant, with more acid leaves than the last; *R. montanus*, Mountain Sorrel, like the last, a native of France. Of this last there are two varieties, the Common Mountain, and the Green Mountain Sorrel. The first has pale green, blistered leaves, less acid than the common English, and does not run quickly to flower. The Green Mountain Sorrel is earlier than this, and is the latest to flower, producing freely dark green leaves of considerable acidity. The flowers of the first and last species are diœcious.

Sorrel will grow from seed, or dividing the roots early in spring. Sow in drills fifteen inches apart, and as they come up, thin them to one foot in the row; or part the roots in the autumn or spring, and set them out at the same distance. Water them occasionally until well established. Keep the plants free from weeds; cut down the stalks occasionally in the summer, and cover the crowns with a very little fresh earth, that they may send up large and tender leaves. When, in two or three years, the plants begin to dwindle, replant them in fresh soil. For seed, let some of the stalks run up, and gather when ripe.

Use.—Sorrel is much used by the French in soups, sauces, and salads, and also cooked as spinach, and when cooked in this way with turnip tops is thought to improve their flavor. Some use the leaves in pies as a substitute for rhubarb.

SPINACH.—(*Spinacia oleracea.*)

Spinach is a hardy annual of the same family with the beet, *Chenopodiaceæ*, and has been cultivated in English gardens since 1568, and probably long before. Some refer its origin to Western Asia. The leaves are large, stems hollow, and the male and female flowers produced on different plants. Its name, *Spinacea*, is derived from the Latin, *spina*, a thorn, on account of the prickly seed of one variety.

There are four sorts, three of which are smooth seeded, and the other prickly.

Round-leaved has large, roundish, and fleshy leaves, and is the sort commonly used for spring and summer crops, but late in the season it soon runs to seed.

Flanders has smooth seeds, and large, hastate leaves, six inches broad; a hardy, good, winter sort.

Lettuce-leaved.—Leaves rounder than the last; fleshy, or thick, and of a dark green color; nearly or quite as hardy as the last.

Prickly-seeded, or Winter Spinach.—Leaves smaller and thinner than the other sorts, triangular shaped, and very hardy.

Culture.—For the winter crop, a light, dry, but fertile soil is preferable; while for spring sowings, to have them long in use, a rich, moist loam is desirable. The lime and salt mixture with superphosphate of lime will supply most of the inorganic elements required by spinach. Give them an open situation. The earth should be well pulverized before sowing, as fine tilth greatly promotes vigorous growth. Spinach is propagated from seed so easily, and is so valuable for winter greens, that no garden should be without it.

The first crop is sown at the South the first of October, and in succession until winter sets in, and on the coast through the winter months the sowings are continued. At New York the first of September is the proper season. For this crop the prickly is the hardiest, but the Flanders and Lettuce-leaved are the best. Another sowing should be made as soon as spring opens, and they may be continued until the summer heats come on, when the plants will quickly run to seed. Use the smooth-seeded kinds for the later crops.

Sow thinly in drills an inch deep, about fifteen inches apart, or eighteen inches for the larger varieties. Sow in moist weather, or if dry, water the seed in the drill before covering, for if moisture be wanting during the early stages of vegetation, not half the seed will come up. Thin them by degrees, separating them at first only an inch or two as the plants grow fit for use. Thinning should commence when they attain four leaves an inch or so in breadth. The plants must finally stand for the prickly spinach, five inches, and the round leaf, eight inches in the drill. Keep the rows frequently hoed and free from weeds. Hoe in dry weather. Spinach kept clean and thinned properly is not so liable to die out in winter. During severe weather a thin covering of straw or evergreen brush is essential for the protection of the winter crop north of Washington, and is very beneficial south of that point. Regular gathering greatly promotes the health of the plants. The outer leaves only should be used, leaving the centre uninjured to supply successive crops. At the end of the winter, the soil between the rows of the winter standing crop should be gently stirred, to assist their production in early spring. For summer spinach and all other plants cultivated for their leaves, the soil cannot be too rich.

For Seed.—Some of the latest plants of the standing crop should be allowed to run up to seed; let these plants be eight or ten inches apart. Spinach is diœcious, and the male plants may be removed when the seed begins to form. When ripe, pull the plants, dry thoroughly on a cloth, and beat out and store the seed in paper bags. Spinach seed will keep three years.

Use.—Spinach and German Greens are the best plants to raise for a supply of early spring greens. Spinach eaten freely is laxative and cooling; it is not very nutritive, but very wholesome. It is so innocent that it is permitted to be eaten in diseases where most vegetables are proscribed. The leaves are very tender and succulent, and of a most beautiful green when boiled. The juice is often used for coloring various culinary preparations.

SPINACH, NEW ZEALAND.—(*Tetragonia expansa.*)

An annual plant brought by Sir Joseph Banks from New Zealand, in 1772, with thick, succulent, pale green, procumbent, deltoid leaves, and with small, green, inconspicuous flowers. It grows four or five feet high, and is of the same natural family as the ice plant.

Culture.—New Zealand Spinach may be sown early in April. The best soil is loam, deeply dug, and enriched by a liberal supply of manure. Make the drills three feet apart, and scatter the seed about six inches apart in the drill, and cover them an inch deep. Thin out the plants to twenty inches apart. Keep the ground thoroughly tilled and free from weeds, that the plants may make a luxuriant growth. In five or six weeks the young leaves will be ready to be picked. Preserve the leading shoot, and the branches will continue long in bearing, as in autumn they survive a pretty heavy frost. Twenty plants are enough for a family. Seed may be gathered as it ripens, dried carefully in the shade, and put up in paper bags.

It is used as a substitute in summer for the common spinach. Swiss Chard is a better one. The seed vessels make a good pickle.

SQUASH.—(*Cucurbita Melopepo.*)

The squash is a tender trailing annual, and was first brought to England in 1597. It is a native of the Levant. It is a much esteemed garden vegetable, and in some of its varieties can be had for the table the greater part of the year.

Summer Squashes.—The best are the Early Bush Scollop, which is small, and either white or golden yellow in its two subvarieties; both good; the Summer Crookneck, also a bush variety; bright yellow, covered with warts; Bergen, small, bell-shaped, striped dark green and white; used green, like the preceding, and when the shell hardens, becomes still better, being very dry and rich, and keeps well.

Winter Squashes are of many varieties; as Valparaiso, or Cocoanut, as it is named from its shape. It has a rough, grayish coat, flesh deep orange, very dry, and sugary; it is the best of all, but a great runner, and bears but moderately. Boston Marrow, Bell, Canada Crookneck, and Hubbard, are all good winter sorts. The last is a new variety of great excellence, related to the Valparaiso. The Cashaw Pumpkin is a good substitute for the winter squash.

Vegetable Marrow Squashes are in England the favorite sort, and used from the time the blossom drops until matured. The Custard Vegetable Marrow is now the kind preferred there. From a single trial they do not appear productive.

Culture.—The squash is planted at the same time as the cucumber and melon. Put six or eight seeds in a hill, and thin out to two or three when they get up. The bush squashes should be five feet apart, and the winter varieties at least ten. For cultivation, see Cucumber. Squashes are much better grown in rich soil; do not plant them near the cucumber or melon, if you would not have worthless seed from all the plants in their vicinity. Gather summer kinds while the finger nail can easily penetrate the rind; they must be plucked as soon as fit for use, or the fruitfulness of the vines will be much impaired. To keep winter squashes, they must be put away in a cool, dry place, free from frost.

The Squash Bug, *Coreus tristis.* This insect is of a rusty black color above, and yellowish beneath; of a foul, disgusting smell; of quick motions. It eats the leaf and stem, and at length destroys the stem. It lays its dark colored eggs in patches upon the under surface of the leaf, to which they adhere strongly. As soon as hatched, the young enemy in little swarms commence feeding upon the leaf, upon its under side, which soon withers. They are quite timid, but may be found in the cool of the day concealed under the leaves or clods of earth, and should be sought for while the vines are young, daily, in the morning, and crushed before they become numerous. (*Harris.*)

Another squash bug is the *Coccinnella borealis*, a species of Ladybird, which with its larva feed upon and destroy the leaves. Most of the ladybirds are beneficial in freeing plants of Aphides, but this is an exception. The color is dull yellow, and upon the thorax and wing cases are nineteen black spots, counting as two those divided by the suture of the wing. The eggs are laid in groups upon the under surface of the leaf. Successive broods are hatched through the summer. The remedy is hand picking.

The squash vine borer is the larva of *Ægeria cucurbitæ*, an orange-colored moth, with black spots, which deposits its eggs near the roots of cucumber and squash vines, often several upon a single plant. When hatched, the larva is a small, white worm that bores into the substance of the vine and soon destroys it. It is very troublesome in Southern gardens. A few ashes placed about the roots of the vine are said to be the best remedy.

Use.—The squash is a very wholesome and tolerably nutritious vegetable, prepared for the table in the same manner as the turnip for which it is an excellent substitute to eat with fresh meat. To be fit for use after being boiled tender, the summer sorts must be squeezed between two plates, for when full of water, as often served, it is not fit to be eaten. The winter squashes should be boiled dry; they make a good pie, like the pumpkin and the sweet potato.

TANYAH.—(*Calocasia esculenta.*)

This is a large-leaved, tuberous rooted, perennial plant of the Arum family, much cultivated at the Sandwich Islands, and forms the principal ingredient in the favorite *poi*, a food much in use there, and remarkable for its fattening properties.

It is cultivated somewhat near Charleston, and along the coast, and is perfectly hardy here, and probably near the coast as far north as Washington. The foliage is quite striking.

Culture.—It may be planted in any rich, well-drained, low spot. Select the eyes or buds, and plant like the potato. The small roots are the ones generally reserved for this purpose. There are two distinct kinds, named from their color the pink and the blue, of which the latter is thought by many to be the most farinaceous, but others prefer the taste of the pink variety. The sets may be put out in March or early in April, and the most attention required is to keep the soil clean and mellow. The rows may be three or four feet apart, and the plants two feet in the rows. It comes to maturity the autumn after planting, and may remain in the bed until wanted. It keeps better than either the sweet or Irish potato. It is prepared for the table by simple roasting, and eaten with salt. By many they are much liked, as they are quite farinaceous.

TARRAGON.—(*Artemisia Dracunculus.*)

This is a perennial plant, of the same genus as the wormwood, but its fragrant smell and warm aromatic taste have introduced it into the kitchen garden.

Culture.—This plant does not require a rich soil, and as it is a native of a cold climate, it is best to give it a bleak winter exposure. Poor, dry earth is necessary to perfect its flavor. Tarragon is propagated by seed, slips, cuttings and parting of the root. The latter is the easiest mode and most generally practiced. It may be planted in early spring, the plants being ten inches apart. Give a little water in dry weather until they are rooted. As they run up, if seed is not desired, cut down the seed stalks and they will shoot up afresh. Keep them free from weeds. It has been cultivated here with success. It must be taken up, divided, and reset every year, or it will die out.

Use.—Tarragon is used in salads, to correct the coldness of other herbs. Its leaves are excellent pickled, or for flavoring vinegar to be used for fish sauces, or with horse-radish for beefsteaks.

THYME.—(*Thymus.*)

Common Thyme, *Thymus vulgaris,* is a low, evergreen undershrub, a native of Spain, Italy, and Greece, cultivated in English gardens since 1548, and probably earlier. Its name, *Thymus,* comes from the Greek word for courage; as it was thought to renew the strength and spirits. It has a pleasant, aromatic smell, and a warm, pungent taste. There are two varieties, the broad and narrow leaved.

Lemon Thyme, *Thymus citriodorus,* is also a low, trailing, evergreen shrub, seldom rising above four or six inches high. It has a strong smell of lemons, which gives it its common name, and is preferred for some dishes.

Culture.—Thyme is raised by seed, cuttings, and dividing the roots. A light, dry soil is suitable. The root slips may be set out in rows six inches apart each way. The seeds are very small, and should be sown in moist weather in spring, the soil for their reception made very fine, and the seed raked in lightly with the back of the rake. Press the surface gently with a board or the back of a spade. Make the drills six inches apart and very shallow. Water lightly in hot, dry weather, both before and after the plants are up. Let them remain in the drills, or transplant when two or three inches high. Thin the plants to six inches apart, and keep free from weeds while the plants are small.

Thyme is often used as an edging. A very small plot is enough for any family.

For Seed.—It bears seed abundantly, if permitted. The spikes should be gathered as it ripens, before it is washed out by the rain. Dry upon a cloth in the shade.

Use.—The young leaves and tops are used in soups, stuffings, and sauces. They can be dried and preserved like other herbs; but in mild climates this is unnecessary, as it is evergreen.

TOMATO.—(*Lycopersicum esculentum.*)

The Tomato is a tender annual, a native of South America, and some say of Mexico, and of the same natural family with the Egg-plant and Irish potato. It was introduced into England in 1596, and was long cultivated in the flower garden for its beautiful red and yellow fruit, which was not used for food, but by many considered poisonous. "As an esculent plant, in 1828–9," says Buist, speaking of its use in this country, "it was almost detested; in ten years more, every variety of pill and panacea was 'extract of tomato.'" It is now one of the most popular vegetables in cultivation, and springs up self-sown in all our gardens. There are many varieties.

The Large Red is one of the best. It is patty-pan-shaped, and extra large specimens are sometimes six inches in diameter, or as large as a common bush squash. One of the best flavored.

Gallagher's Mammoth is a variety of this, of larger size, having few seeds, and of good flavor.

Large Yellow resembles Large Red in form, but is of a somewhat different flavor and is a good sort for preserves.

Large Smooth Red is a new variety of the Large Red, equally well flavored, and a favorite in the kitchen, as it grows regular and free from knobs.

Fejee Island, a rather later variety with more solid flesh, said to be a new kind from the Fejee Islands, came to this place from Naples twenty years ago and is a good sort.

Cherry is excellent for pickling. It is named from its size and shape.

Pear-shaped is of a pink color, firm flesh, and few seeds. Much used for pickling, and excellent for the table.

Early Red is a new French subvariety of Large Red, at least ten days earlier.

The tomato likes a light, loamy soil, of moderate fertility, as in a soil too rich it runs to vine, and the fruit ripens late. For the early crop, sow at the first indications of spring, some six weeks before corn planting time (early in February here and at the North in March) in a hot bed, or in boxes in the house.

Sow in drills eight inches apart, and when the plants come up, thin to two or three inches, and transplant into the open ground when the frosts are over. While in the seed bed give air at all times when there is no danger of frost. It is better to sow quite early and transplant when ready into small pots, and a couple of weeks after, when these are full of roots, shift them into five-inch pots, in which they may be kept until they blossom, if a late spring or apprehension of frost renders it necessary. Transfer them with the ball to the hill in the open ground in a cloudy, damp time, in fresh-dug soil. If the weather is dry they may be planted, the fresh soil pressed closely about the ball, a plentiful watering given, finishing with a covering of light soil to keep the ground from baking, and shade during the day until established. The Early Red should be selected for the first crop, and when planted out a warm exposure chosen. Let the rows be about three feet apart and the plants eighteen inches in the row. In poor soil less room is required between the rows. As they are very tender, do not plant out until danger of frost is over, and protect them by large flower pots or boxes, if there is any fear of frost. For a succession, sow in the open ground about corn planting time in a rich, sheltered spot, water with tepid water in dry weather, shield them with a mat or box in cold nights, and thin the plants while young to three inches, and carefully transplant these, when ready, with a trowel and ball into their final situation. Another sowing or two should be made, to keep up a full succession in the long summer of our Gulf States. The Large Smooth Red is a good sort for the main crop.

As soon as the lower fruit is half grown, cut off the upper part of the plant above the larger fruit, that its growth may be stopped, and the fruit below will be larger, and several days earlier. Ninety per cent of the fruit grows within eighteen inches of the ground, but a large portion of the vines grow above that height. Tomatoes like the soil about them well hoed, and free from weeds. Plants grown in the open air are more abundant in bearing than those forwarded under glass. In well-trenched ground, they will continue bearing until frost.

To Save Seed.—Select the largest early fruit, mash with the hand, and wash the seed from the pulp; spread out upon plates and dry in the shade; when dry, put them in paper bags.

Use.—Few vegetables are prepared in as many different forms as the tomato. It is pickled when green, and preserved when ripe; it is eaten raw or cooked; it enters into soups and sauces, and is prepared in catsups, marmalades, and omelets. The French, and the Italians, near Rome and Naples, raised them by the acre, long before used by other nations, and, it is said, prepared them in an almost infinite variety of ways. There are very few preparations into which it enters, which are not improved by the addition. A good supply should be prepared when in season by stewing and putting up in patent cans for winter use. On account of the acid of the fruit, earthen or glass jars are best.

TURNIP.—(*Brassica rapa.*)

The turnip is a hardy biennial of the cabbage tribe, a native of many parts of Europe, and has been cultivated for centuries. It was held in considerable estimation by the Romans. Cato is the first writer that mentions it. "Sow it," says he, "after an autumnal shower, in a place that is well manured, or in a rich soil." Columella recommends its cultivation, "because that portion of the crop not wished for the table will be greedily eaten by the farm cattle." It is cultivated in all temperate climes, and is now extensively grown as a field crop in England, for feeding stock, and is considerably raised for the same purpose in our Northern States.

Early White Dutch (Strap-leaved).—A round, flat turnip, with short, narrow, strap-like leaves; is the earliest kind.

Early Red-Top Dutch (Strap-leaved,) differs from the preceding only in the red color of the portion of the roots which is above ground. Both of these, in a moist, cool fall, are fit for the table six weeks after sowing.

The above are best for spring sowing, and also very useful for the autumn crop.

White Globe is a beautifully shaped, globular root, of the largest size.

White Norfolk is another large field sort; both are good varieties, and much cultivated South, both for their roots and for winter greens.

Yellow Dutch is very hardy, more so than the foregoing. Sweet, fine-flavored, and very nutritious. It is of a yellow color, round, handsome shape, firm and sweet, and keeps well.

Yellow Aberdeen is perhaps the same as the last.

Ruta Baga, or Swedes Turnip is a different variety, (*Brassica campestris var. ruta baga*,) of which the foliage differs from those preceding in being smooth and covered with glaucous bloom. There are several varieties, all hardy and good.

Purple-topped Swede.—The roots are very large, of an oval, tapering form, and the greater their size, the sweeter and more nourishing they become. It keeps until spring.

Skirving's Improved Swede.—This is of still better form than the foregoing, the leaves not so large, less smooth, and free from bloom; flesh fine, yellow, and very nutritious.

Sweet German Turnip.—Called also White Ruta Baga and Cabbage Turnip, (*Brassica campestris Napa Brassica, D. C.*,) resembles the last two, but the flesh is white, very sweet, with somewhat of the cabbage flavor, and is a good keeper. Roots large, but not as regular as the preceding.

It is found that the most important fertilizer is phosphate of lime. Either bone dust, superphosphate of lime, or guano, all rich in phosphoric acid, seems to supply everything this crop requires. Manured with either of these, it is soon beyond the reach of insects and casualties. For the spring crop guano or manures rich in ammonia are essential, but for the autumn crop the superphosphate of lime seems to act more beneficially than any other application. Manipulated guano, honestly prepared, is valuable at both seasons, and still better is the mixture of guano and superphosphate of lime.

Culture.—The turnip likes a rich, sandy soil. If raised on ground manured by cow-penning, the crop rarely fails, as the urine deposited in the soil affords the phosphates so necessary for this crop, and in such places it is far less infested with insects. Soil fresh from the woods also suits it. For the early crop seed grown north of the locality in which it is sown is generally preferred, but for the main crop, pure seed from handsome shaped roots of home growth is sufficiently good. In the more Southern States, sow early turnips late in January, or through February, and farther North as soon as the ground is in a suitable condition, and the danger of its becoming again frozen is over; that is, when the atmosphere begins to feel like spring. Sow in drills fifteen inches apart, in fine, light, well-manured soil, in drills one inch deep, covering the seeds half an inch, with fine soil pressed thereon. Keep the soil free from weeds. As soon as the plants get a little strong, thin out to two inches, and finally to six inches in the row. If the ground is not kept light and well worked, and the plants properly thinned, it is a mere waste of time and seed. The Early White Dutch is the kind to be preferred. They do much better in drills than broadcast.

For fall turnips, sow the Early White Dutch, etc., any time in August and September, broadcast, or better in drills, as directed above. If broadcast, thin them to about twelve inches apart or more. If sown just before a rain, they will come up at once. Soot, wood ashes, and unslaked lime are all useful to promote growth and drive away insects. The Red-top is an excellent variety for a general fall crop, and may be sown in October even, with success in the more Southern States. The last of July or the first of August is the time for sowing the main crop of common turnips, while in Georgia the last sowing for greens is made the first of November.

The varieties of the Ruta Baga and the Sweet German are the best when planted for late winter use. These are sown at New York the last half of June, or early in July; in Georgia, from the 1st to 20th of August. Sow in very rich, fresh-prepared soil. Let the drills be two feet apart, and thin the plants by degrees until twelve or fifteen inches in the row. As soon as the plants appear, loosen the earth about them. It requires a richer soil than the other varieties. Fill any vacancies in the row by transplanting; these plants will make nearly as large roots as the others. Keep the soil light and mellow by the use of the hoe. Large crops can be tended with the plow and cultivator to great advantage. In good soil the yield is immense. The crop may be drawn as needed. Some should be taken before they begin to grow up to seed and stored in a cool place for *late* keeping.

The Turnip Flea Beetle, *Haltica nemorum.*—This is a small, hard-shelled insect, of a smooth, shining, brassy, or greenish-black color, about an eighth of an inch in length. There are two yellow stripes down the wing cases. The hinder legs are formed for leaping. It attacks the turnip, and other plants of the same family, both in its perfect and larva states. When the plants have attained some size the injury to the crop is slight, but they generally take the young plants while in the seed leaf, and destroy the crop entirely in a few hours, whether it be a small bed, or a large field.

The best remedies are preventive, such as to roll the surface smoothly, so that the insects may find no hiding places in the soil, to sow the seed in drills, and in a fine, rich soil, and apply superphosphate of lime upon the seed in the drills, to apply plenty of seed, and thin out the plants when in the rough leaf. Any thing that will accelerate growth will soon place the crop out of danger from these little insects. Some sow radish seed with turnips, as the flea prefers the young radish leaf. If they once attack the plants, dusting them with lime ashes and soot is sometimes useful, but when in great numbers, it is scarcely possible to save the young crop.

To Save Seed.—Select a few of the best roots, shorten the tap-root, and plant them two feet apart. Tie the stalks to stakes, and keep them at a distance from all other members of the cabbage tribe. Seed of the turnip should be changed every few years, as the plant degenerates. It keeps three years.

Use.—This is one of those useful vegetables, that can be enjoyed with everything. The tops gathered in winter and spring make the greens so much prized by us all in early spring. The roots are wholesome, though they disagree with some stomachs. They are considerably nutritious also; four ounces of White Dutch containing eighty-five grains of nutritive matter, and four ounces of Ruta Baga containing one hundred and ten grains of the same. Any over-supply of this crop may be fed with great advantage to cows and swine.

WATER CRESS.—(*Nasturtium officinale.*)

This is a hardy, perennial, English, Cruciferous plant, growing in running streams. There is but one variety in use.

The Water-cress likes a clear, cool, running stream, fresh issuing from a spring, the nearer its source the better, with the water about an inch and a half deep, with a sandy or gravelly bottom. It must, of course, at first be raised from seed, which can be sprinkled at the source of some gravelly stream. If once established, it will soon propagate from self-sown seed. If the stems get choked with mud and weeds, they must be taken up and the beds cleared and replanted. The shoots ought always to be *cut*, as breaking injures the plants.

They grow best in water not over two or three inches deep, and if plants can be got, should be set in rows parallel with the stream, eighteen inches apart.

Use.—Water-cresses are generally liked for their warm, pungent taste, and are used alone or in mixed salads.

WATER MELON.—(*Citrullus vulgaris.*)

This is a trailing annual, a native of the tropics, and of the same natural family as the cucumber and musk melon, but belongs to a distinct genus. It is a large, succulent, and refreshing, but not high-flavored fruit, and is probably the melon mentioned in the Bible. The varieties are numerous, and many of them not known out of a limited locality.

Imperial.—Medium size, nearly round, skin pale green and white, marbled; rind thin, flesh solid, light red, crisp, rich, and high-flavored; seeds small, reddish-brown; productive.

Spanish.—Round, very dark green, thin rind, bright red flesh, and black seeds; rich and sugary. (*Buist.*)

Mountain Sweet.—Large, oval, striped with light and dark green; sometimes with a neck; flesh light red, quite solid, and of fine flavor.

Ice Cream.—Large, round, early, and productive; skin light green, rind half an inch thick; flesh white, crisp and sugary, excellent; seeds white.

Clarendon.—Large, mottled gray, with dark green stripes; rind half an inch thick; flesh scarlet, sugary, and exquisite; seeds yellow, spotted with black, and with a black stripe about the edge.

Souter is striped with pale and dark green, rind thin, flesh red, and of best quality; seeds white, with a russet stripe about the edge; form oblong to roundish.

Ravenscroft is oblong, dark green, faintly striped with lighter green; rind thin, flesh red and sugary; seeds white, with a brown stripe about the edge. The last three are fine varieties of Southern origin. The others are more cultivated in the North. The varieties intermix if grown near each other. The Citron watermelon is a small, round, pale-green, marbled sort, liked by many for preserves. Seeds red.

Culture.—The watermelon likes a deep, rich, sandy soil. Where this plant is most successfully cultivated, it always grows upon sand. The hills should be not less than ten or twelve feet apart in warm climates, and seven or eight at the North. Do not plant until the ground is warm, and cultivate exactly in the same manner as the muskmelon and cucumber. It should not be grown within one hundred feet of other melons, gourds, etc., if you would gather pure seed. Protect from insects as directed in the article, "Cucumber." The melon worm does not annoy the watermelon.

Use.—This is a wholesome fruit, very popular in summer from its beauty and the refreshing coolness of its juice. It is not very nutritious, as it contains ninety-five per cent of water. It is not by any means as nourishing as the muskmelon, and lacks its peculiar rich flavor. The outer rind is used for preserves. In many parts of Europe the juice is boiled into a pleasant syrup, or made into beer.

MEDICINAL HERBS.

A few roots of the most useful of these should be found in every garden. The medicinal properties of many of them depend upon their aromatic qualities, and they are never so fragrant and full of virtue when grown upon ground highly manured. Chamomile, lavender, rosemary, rue, wormwood, and many others, lose much of their strength when forced into rank growth. Common garden soil, without manuring, is quite good enough. Whenever the plants begin to decline, take away the old surface soil, and apply fresh, or set out new plants in fresh ground.

Medicinal, pot, or sweet herbs, as a general rule, should be gathered when in *bloom*, and dried carefully and thoroughly in the *shade*. When thoroughly dry, press them closely into paper bags, or powder them finely; sift, and keep in closely-stopped bottles.

Angelica, (*Archangelica officinalis,*) is an Umbelliferous biennial plant, growing from three to five feet high, and a native of many parts of Northern Europe. The whole plant is powerfully aromatic. Its roots have a fragrant, agreeable odor, and at first a sweetish taste, which soon turns acrid in the mouth. Its medical properties are aromatic, stimulant, and gently tonic.

Its stalks were formerly blanched and eaten like celery, but it is mostly cultivated to make a sweetmeat from them when young and tender. They are also candied by the confectioners.

Sow the seed one foot apart in August or September, and when they get about four inches high, the next spring, set them in rows two feet apart each way. Though the plant is only a biennial, yet by cutting down the seed-stalk whenever it rises, the same plant may be preserved several seasons. Angelica likes a moist, cool soil, such as the banks of ditches.

Anise, (*Pimpinella anisum,*) is an Umbelliferous annual, a native of Egypt. It is cultivated for its seeds, and its leaves, which are occasionally used as a garnish, and for seasoning like fennel. The seeds have a fragrant, agreeable smell, and a sweetish, pleasant taste. They are useful wherever an aromatic stimulant is required.

The plant grows about 18 inches high. Sow the seed where it is to stand in spring, in a dry, light soil, and thin out the plants, if too thick, to three or four inches apart.

Balm, (*Melissa officinalis,*) is a hardy, Labiate-flowered perennial, native of Switzerland and the south of France, but has long been cultivated in gardens. It has an aromatic taste, and a grateful, fragrant smell, a little like lemons.

It is a square-stemmed plant, rising about two feet high. It is used in making balm tea, a grateful drink in fevers, and for forming a pleasant beverage called balm wine. It is a great favorite with the bees.

Any garden soil will do for balm. It is readily propagated either by slips, or by parting the roots in spring. Plant ten inches apart, giving water if dry weather.

Bene, (*Sesamum orientale,*) is an annual plant, and a native of Africa and India. Introduced into this country by the negroes. It grows from three to six feet high, bearing numerous pods, filled with smallish seed. These are used for food in many parts of the world, and are also cultivated for the oil with which they abound. It resembles that of olives, and is nearly as good. The leaves abound in mucilage; one or two stirred in a half pint of water will form a bland mucilaginous drink very useful in cholera infantum, dysentery, and summer complaints generally. The leaves should be freshly gathered, and enough may be added to make the water ropy without affecting its color or taste.

Sow a row in spring, on the edge of a plot or border, and thin out as the plants require room. A few plants will furnish all the leaves desired.

Boneset, or Thoroughwort, (*Eupatorium perfoliatum*,) is a Composite-flowered perennial, a native of most of the United States, which, if not found growing wild in the vicinity, should be cultivated, as it is one of the best herbs in family practice. It has a faint odor, an intensely bitter taste, and is slightly astringent. Its medi-

Fig. 76.—BENE.

cinal virtues are diaphoretic, tonic, and in larger doses, emetic and aperient. It is principally used as a diaphoretic in colds, catarrhs, and rheumatism, in intermittent, remittent, and inflammatory diseases, or given cold as a tonic in dyspepsia.

Boneset can be raised by transplanting the roots, or sowing the seed in spring.

Borage, (*Borrago officinalis,*) is an annual European plant. The tender tops, young leaves, and flowers, are sometimes used as a salad by the French, and boiled by the Italians.

Medicinally it was formerly thought endowed with very great virtues, and numbered among the four cordial flowers.

Old Gerard says: "Those of our time do use the flowers in salads, and to exhilarate and to make the minde glad. There be many things made of them used for the comfort of the heart, to drive away sorrow and increase the joy of the minde." The plant is not much used now except as an ingredient in the drink called "a cool tankard," made of wine, water, lemon-juice, and sugar, to which a few of the tender leaves seem to give additional coolness.

Sow early in spring, broadcast, and a little thinning and weeding is all the attention that will be needed.

Caraway, (*Carum Carui,*) is a native of England and various other countries of Europe. It is a biennial, Umbelliferous plant, well known to the ancients. Pliny mentions it. Caraway is cultivated for its aromatic seeds, which are useful in confectionery, as in cakes, comfits, etc., and the leaves are sometimes used in soups. The roots are said to excel those of the parsnip, being formerly cooked and used in the same manner. Medicinally the seeds are used in an infusion for flatulence. Sow in autumn, or early spring, and thin so as to give each plant ten inches of room.* Keep free from weeds. Plants sown in autumn will give seed the next season.

Chamomile, (*Anthemis nobilis,*) is a hardy, Composite-flowered perennial, a native of England, cultivated for its flowers, which have a bitter, aromatic taste, and are in small doses a useful tonic, but given largely, act as an emetic. An infusion of them improves digestion and gives tone to the disordered stomach. The flowers are sometimes chewed as a substitute for tobacco.

It is best propagated by dividing the roots in spring. Keep the ground free from weeds. Plant nine inches apart. As to varieties, the single-flowered has the most virtue, but the double-flowered is most cultivated, from its greater productiveness.

Clary, (*Salvia sclarea,*) is a Labiate-flowered biennial from Italy. The leaves of this plant were formerly used in soups, and its flowers are now made use of in a fermented wine.

The medicinal virtues of the plant are cordial and astringent, and it is used either in its fresh or dried state. For propagation and culture, see "Sage," which belongs to the same genus. Clary, however, must be yearly renewed by fresh sowing. Thin the plants to 15 inches apart each way.

Coriander, (*Coriandrum sativum,*) is an Umbelliferous annual from the East, and also grows naturally in the south of Europe. Some like its tender leaves for soups and salads, but it is raised mostly for its seeds, which have a pleasant aromatic taste, though the smell is disagreeable. Coriander seed is carminative and stomachic. It is often used to disguise the taste of medicines, but it is principally employed in confectionery.

Sow the seed in spring or autumn, where they are to remain, in drills twelve inches apart. Thin the plants to four inches, and keep free from weeds.

Dill, (*Anethum graveolens,*) belongs to the same genus with Fennel, and is a biennial, Umbelliferous plant, a native of Southern Europe, cultivated for its seeds, which have an aromatic odor, and a warm, pungent, and somewhat bitter taste. Medicinally, they are good for flatulence and colic in infants. The leaves are sometimes used for culinary purposes, and the seeds are occasionally added to pickled cucumbers to heighten the flavor.

Sow the seeds either early in the spring, or soon after they are ripe, in a light soil. Thin, if crowded, and keep clean. The plants should be 8 inches apart.

Elecampane, (*Inula Helenium,*) is a native of England and Japan. It is a Composite-flowered, perennial plant, cultivated for its thick, fleshy, carrot-like root, which is useful as an aromatic tonic and expectorant. Cut up fine and fed with their corn, the root is a great relief to the distemper in horses.

It is propagated by offsets, or by parting the roots in autumn or spring, but may also be grown from seeds sown in the fall. It likes a moist soil, and the plants should be fifteen inches apart.

Fennel, (*Fœniculum vulgare,*) is a hardy, aromatic, perennial, Umbelliferous plant from the south of Europe, growing wild on the banks of rivers, and perhaps quite as properly belongs to the culinary as to the medicinal department of the garden. It has a finely divided leaf, and tall, umbel-bearing stems, crowned with small yellow flowers.

Culture.—Fennel will grow in almost any soil. It is propagated by offsets, parting the roots, or by seed; all which modes may be successfully practised at any time in autumn or spring.

The best season, however, for sowing the seed is when it ripens in the fall, in drills twelve inches asunder. The seed may be sown moderately thick, about half an inch deep, and the earth pressed upon them. When the young plants are four or five inches high, thin them out to twelve inches. Those taken up may be planted out to enlarge the bed. Water them freely, if the weather is dry. Keep the plants free from weeds, which is all the cultivation required. If the seed is not desired, the stems should be cut down as often as they run up; for if allowed to ripen seed, the old plants will last but a few years. But this is of little consequence, as plenty of self-sown seedlings will be ready to take their place. Eight or ten roots are enough for any family. It should be kept within proper limits, as it is much inclined to spread.

Use.—Fennel is a good deal used, in continental Europe, in soups, fish-sauces, garnishes, and salads. It is also considerably used in England, but less with us. The Italians blanch and eat the stalks of one variety called Finochie, like celery. A little fennel seed sometimes gives an agreeable variety in flavoring apple-sauce and pies. But it is most used medicinally. The seeds are carminative and stimulant, and in an infusion are excellent for the flatulent colic of infants.

Horehound, (*Marrubium vulgare,*) is a hardy, Labiate-flowered, perennial plant, a native of most parts of Europe, growing in waste grounds, among rubbish, in warm, dry situations. It has a strong aromatic smell, and a bitter, pungent taste, which is permanent in the mouth; medicinally, horehound is a tonic, somewhat stimulant and diuretic, and, in large doses, laxative. It enters largely into the composition of cough syrups and lozenges.

Sow the seeds in the spring, in any common soil. It scarcely needs any attention. It may also be propagated by dividing the roots. Plant eighteen inches apart.

Hyssop, (*Hyssopus officinalis,*) is a Labiate-flowered, hardy, evergreen undershrub, from the south of Europe, of which the leaves and flower-spikes are the parts used medicinally. It has an aromatic odor, and a warm, pungent taste. It is stimulant and expectorant.

Hyssop is propagated by slips, or dividing the roots, or

by sowing the seed in the spring. Transplant the young plants to where they are to remain, or you may thin them to six inches apart, and leave them in the seed-bed until autumn before transplanting. It likes a dry, sandy soil, and about eighteen inches space should be given to each plant.

Lavender, (*Lavandula vera*,) is a Labiate-flowered undershrub, a native of the south of Europe, and hardy south of New York. It is cultivated for its fragrant spikes of flowers, which are used for the distillation of lavender-water. Being dried, and put up in paper bags, they are also used to perfume linen. Both flowers and leaves are very aromatic. It has an agreeable pungent bitterness to the taste, and its medicinal properties are stimulant, cordial, and stomachic. There are three varieties—the *narrow-leaved*, one sort with blue and the other with white flowers, and the *broad-leaved* lavender.

Lavender may be propagated by seeds, slips, or cuttings. Sow the seed in drills ten inches apart, in spring, and transplant the next spring to a dry soil of but medium richness, and it will be more highly aromatic. Give each plant about two feet of space; for drying, gather the flowers before they begin to turn brown at the lower part of the spike.

Liquorice, (*Glycyrrhiza glabra*,) is a Leguminous, hardy perennial, from Southern Europe, the saccharine juice of the fleshy root of which is useful in catarrhs, fevers, &c. Its taste is sweet and mucilaginous, and it is much used as a demulcent, either alone or combined with other substances.

A few roots of this plant, when once started, will be of very little trouble in the garden. The plant is propagated early in spring, by cuttings of the roots. Dig the soil at least two feet deep. Take the horizontal roots of established plants, five or six inches long. Every shoot planted should have at least two eyes; make the rows three feet apart, and the plant twelve to fifteen inches in the rows, and cover the roots well with mould. Onions, lettuce, or radishes, may be grown between the rows the first year; afterwards keep the soil free from weeds, dress the surface with manure every autumn, and at the end of the third year take up the crop as soon as the leaves are fully decayed, and dry the roots thoroughly. In shallow or poor ground, it will not succeed.

Mint, (*Mentha.*)—Three species of this genus of Labiate plants are cultivated, all hardy perennials, natives of Britain.

Spearmint, (*Mentha viridis,*) belongs rather to the culinary than the medicinal department of the garden. It is employed in sauces and salads, as well as dried for soups in winter. A few sprigs of mint, boiled a little time with them, and then withdrawn, are thought by some to improve the flavor of green peas. It is also used in preparing mint-julep. Its medicinal properties are aromatic, stimulant, and stomachic. The leaves, boiled in milk, are useful in diarrhœa. Its infusion is good to prevent nausea. There are two varieties, the broad and narrow leaved, equally good.

Peppermint, (*M. piperita,*) has a strong, agreeable odor, a pungent, aromatic taste, giving a sensation of coldness in the mouth. Its medical properties are aromatic, stimulant, and stomachic. The essential oil and essence are the forms in which it is employed in medicine, and they are also largely used in confectionery and cordials.

Pennyroyal, (*M. Pulegium,*) is more acrid than the other mints, and its taste and smell are less agreeable. It possesses their warm, pungent flavor, and other general properties, but is not so good a stomachic. The American pennyroyal belongs to a different genus, *Hedeoma.*

All these species require a tenacious soil, which is all the better if moist, or even wet.

A border sheltered from the midday sun, but not entirely secluded from its influence, is always to be allotted them, as in such a situation they are most vigorous and constant in production.

They are readily propagated by dividing the roots in the winter or spring, or by cuttings planted in moist soil during summer. Plant in rows nine inches apart each way, and cover the roots about two inches deep. In autumn clean off the old stems, and add two inches of mould to the raked surface. Through the summer remove grass and weeds. Make new beds every three or four years.

Rosemary, (*Rosmarinus officinalis*) is a Labiate-flowered, hardy, evergreen undershrub, a native of the south of Europe. It has a fragrant, grateful odor, and a warm, aromatic, bitter taste. Its medicinal virtues are tonic.

It was formerly believed that this plant gave strength to the memory. The tender tops are the parts used in medicine.

Rosemary may be raised from seed, or by planting slips or cuttings in the spring or autumn. Sow the seed in drills sixteen inches apart. Transplant the next spring or autumn. Two or three plants will be enough.

Rue, (*Ruta graveolens*,) is a perennial evergreen undershrub of the Rue Family from the south of Europe. It flowers all summer, and is very well known from its peculiar strong, unpleasant smell. Its taste is bitter and pungent, and the leaves so acrid as to blister the skin. It is a very powerful medicinal agent, too much so to be generally used in family practice.

Rue is propagated by seeds, cuttings, or slips. It must not have a very rich soil, nor be suffered to run to seed. Sow the seed and cultivate as hyssop.

Sage, (*Salvia officinalis,*) is a Labiate-flowered, hardy evergreen undershrub, a native of the south of Europe. It has been cultivated from the earliest times, was classed among the heroic remedies, and considered the best of medicines for prolonging human life. An old Latin adage is "Cur moriatur homo cui salvia crescit in horto?" "Why should a man die while sage is growing in his garden?" It grows about two feet high, with wrinkled ashy green leaves, and terminal blue flowers in long spikes. It has a fragrant smell, and a warm, bitterish, aromatic taste.

Culture.—Sage is raised from seed, slips, or cuttings. It likes a dry, fertile soil. Sow the seeds on a gentle hot-bed, or in the open ground, early in spring, in shallow drills, eight inches apart. Press the earth upon the seed, covering them not over half an inch deep. Thin the plants, when well up, to half a foot apart, planting those taken up at a similar distance. Keep the soil light and free from weeds. In the autumn, or the next spring, plant them out in rows eighteen inches each way. Layers and rooted offsets may be set out at once at this distance. Cuttings of the outward shoots of the current year's growth, planted out in a shady border, in moist weather, readily take root; set them in rows six inches apart. In autumn or spring, take them carefully up and set them out in their final stations. Trim the plants to a round, bushy head. Gather and dry the leaves for winter use, but do not trim the plants too closely, especially in autumn or winter.

Use.—The leaves are used for seasoning stuffings, sauces, and many kinds of meat, as well as to improve the flavor of various other articles of cookery. Medicinally its infusion is given warm as a sudorific, or mingled with vinegar and alum is an excellent gargle in sore throat. It is stated by Bomare, that it was exported formerly by the Dutch to China, and it was so much preferred by the Chinese to their own tea, that they willingly exchanged two boxes of it for one of sage.

Southernwood, (*Artemisia Abrotanum,*) is a hardy evergreen, with fragrant, finely-divided leaves, nearly allied to wormwood, both being species of the same genus, and similar as to medical properties. Like that, it has a grateful odor, but it is not much used in medicine from its nauseous taste. As an ornamental evergreen, it is worth cultivating.

For culture, see "Hyssop."

Tansy, (*Tanacetum vulgare,*) is a hardy, Composite-flowered perennial, a native of Europe, long cultivated in gardens. It was formerly used to give flavor to puddings and omelets.

Its medicinal properties are tonic and stomachic. It is also a vermifuge. It was formerly of very general use in the preparation of alcoholic bitters.

Divide the roots, and set out a few slips in autumn or spring. After it is well rooted, be careful you do not get too much of it. There are two varieties, the common and the curled.

Wormwood, (*Artemisia Absinthium,*) is a native of Europe, and is a hardy, Composite-flowered perennial, cultivated much in gardens. Its odor is strong and fragrant, and its taste aromatic, but intensely bitter. It is cultivated for the tops or extremities of the branches. Its properties are tonic and diuretic, and it is a vermifuge.

Wormwood likes a calcareous soil, and may be raised either by cuttings, seeds, or dividing the roots. Cultivated same as hyssop, the roots being eighteen inches apart. A dry, poor soil is necessary to bring out the peculiar virtues of this plant.

Roman Wormwood, (*A. Pontica,*) is less nauseous than the preceding, and generally preferred.

CHAPTER XVII.

FRUITS.—VARIETIES AND CULTURE.

ALMOND.—(*Amygdalus communis.*)

The almond is a native of Asia and northern Africa. It is a tree of medium size, nearly allied to the peach in habit and general appearance. The leaves are similar to the peach, having glands like some varieties of the latter fruit, and flowers of similar shape, but much larger and more ornamental, varying in color from pure white to a fine blush. The chief difference is in the fruit, the stone of the almond being flatter, not so hard, and covered with a woolly skin that opens spontaneously when the kernel is ripe.

In southern Europe, the almond is much cultivated, and large quantities of nuts exported. The kernel is the part used; the sweet varieties, whether green or dry, form a very nutritious article of food, and a most agreeable addition to the dessert. Almonds are used in confectionery, cooking, perfumery, and medicine. The bitter almond is the kind used in perfumery and flavoring; it contains prussic acid, which, though a violent poison, is not thought injurious in the small quantities required for these purposes.

Cultivation.—A warm, dry soil is most suitable for the almond, which is cultivated exactly like the peach, and is subject to the same diseases; it may be budded on the almond, peach, or plum stock. The varieties are:

Common Almond. — Nuts one and one-fourth inch long, hard, smooth, compressed, and pointed, with a kernel of agreeable flavor. The hardiest and most productive variety, and is the common hard-shelled almond of the shops; flowers open before the leaves appear.

Long Hard-Shelled.—Nuts of the same size as the former, with a larger kernel and better flavor; flowers large and rose-colored. The tree is quite ornamental, when in bloom.

Ladies' Thin-Shelled.—The soft-shelled almonds of the shops; flowers are of a deeper color than the foregoing variety. Nut oval, one-sided, pointed, with a porous, light-colored shell, so tender that it may be crushed with the fingers. Kernel sweet, rich, and highly esteemed.

Bitter Almonds.—Are of several varieties, differing in the hardness of the shell, closely resembling the others, except in the bitter kernel; blossoms pale pink; leaves larger, and of a darker green than the other varieties.

THE APPLE.—(*Pyrus Malus.*)

The apple probably originated from the European Crab, but centuries of cultivation and reproduction from seeds of new and improved varieties have brought it to its present state of perfection in quality, size, and beauty.

Where the apple can be grown and preserved in perfection, it is the most useful of fruits. Varieties can be selected which will afford a succession through the entire year.

They can be thus preserved in our own mountain region, from which excellent fruit is brought as late as the month of May. The best varieties are excellent dessert fruits. For the table, they are prepared in many ways, as baking, stewing, in pies, tarts, puddings, dumplings, jellies, and preserves. They are also dried for winter use.

The best mode of propagating the apple is by budding or grafting on seedling stocks. For the raising of stocks, the seed should be sown in the fall, or early winter, in good soil, in rows eighteen inches apart; transplant them in rows four feet apart, and one foot apart in the row. If any of the plants become infested with woolly aphis, wash them with tobacco water. The young grafted trees should be planted in the orchard when one or two years old, at distances of twenty-five to thirty feet apart.

Analysis shows that one-half the ash of the bark of the apple, and over one-sixth of that of the sap-wood, is lime. When this mineral is not abundant in the soil, the tree cannot be kept healthy. Swamp muck or leaf mould, composted with lime and bone-dust, or ashes, are the best manures for the apple tree. The best soil for the apple, in this climate, is a deep, cool, moist loam; a northern, or north-west aspect, is preferable to any other. One of the greatest difficulties to be encountered in the cultivation of the apple is the sun-burning of the trunk, which can be prevented by training the trees with low heads, so as to shade their trunks from the rays of the sun.

By shortening in the branches of the young trees, when transplanted into garden or orchard, they can be made to put out branches about two feet from the ground, which is about the proper height to form a good top. The apple tree needs but little pruning; removing the water-sprouts and such limbs as cross each other is about all that is required.

INSECTS INFESTING THE APPLE TREE.

Many insects injure the apple tree by attacking the root, bark, wood, leaves or fruit. Of these only the most important can be mentioned, with the remark that many of them attack other fruit trees and even forest trees.

Apple Root-blight, (*Pemphigus pyri.*)—Upon the roots of the apple, wart-like excrescences are found growing, in the crevices of which are contained minute, yellow lice, often accompanied with larger winged ones of a black color, having their bodies covered with white, cotton-like matter. The wounds made upon the root by these insects produce an increased flow of sap to the spot affected, and these morbid enlargements are the result. Nursery trees affected should have their roots soaked in soapsuds before planting. Trees affected in the fruit garden may have their roots partly bared, and a liberal application of charcoal dust, ashes, or soapsuds, poured upon the warty excrescences. Their presence gives the affected trees a yellow, unhealthy appearance.

Woolly Aphis, or Apple-tree Blight, (*Eriosoma lanigera,*) is found upon the apple tree. The female is a small, egg-shaped, dull reddish-brown insect, with a black head, dusted with white powder, and with a tuft of white down growing from the hind part of the back, which makes a colony of these insects look like a small patch of white down. Each tuft contains a female and her young, which last are of a pale color. In Europe, trees are often white with these insects. Here they are generally found at the base of twigs and suckers from the trunk, or where a wound in the bark is healing. Scrape the bark of the tree, if rough, and wash the tree, filling every crevice with a solution of 2 pounds potash to 7 quarts of water, or Harris' Composition, 2 parts soft soap and 8 of water, with lime enough to make a thick whitewash. Sulphuric acid, mixed with ten times its bulk of water, is also recommended. This is the "American Blight" of English authors.

Apple Bark-louse, (*Aspidiotus conchiformis.*)—An oblong, flat, brown, oyster-shell shaped scale insect, fixed to the smooth bark, which it sometimes nearly covers. Its length is about one-eighth of an inch. Under each of these scales are from a dozen to a hundred minute white eggs, which hatch in spring, and the young lice disperse themselves over the smooth bark, to which they attach themselves and suck its juices. The females remain affixed, and when dead, their dried relics protect the eggs during the winter.

The Apple-tree Borer, (*Saperda bivittata.*)—The perfect insect is a cylindrical, butternut-brown, long-horned beetle, hoary white beneath, with two milk-white stripes above, running the whole length of its body; length from three-fifths to three-fourths of an inch. The larva is one of the worst enemies of the fruit grower. It is a large, cylindrical, white, footless grub, broadest anteriorly; its head chestnut-brown; mouth black. The insect appears early in summer, and deposits its eggs one at a time upon the bark near the earth. As soon as hatched, the minute worm mines through the bark, feeding upon it first and then upon the sap-wood, and finally upon the heart. At first it pushes out its excrement through a hole in the bark, which it afterwards closes. Trees are so weakened by this insect that they are easily blown down by the wind.

Remedies.—Wash the lower part of the trunk with soft soap just before the beetle makes its appearance, or with lye early in August, to kill the newly hatched grubs. If the presence of the grub is manifested in the trunk by the sawdust-like castings on the soil close to the tree, insert a wire or small twig into the hole, pushing it gently forward until the crushing of the worm is felt at the extremity. Piling leached ashes or lime about the base of the tree is beneficial. Unleached, they will sometimes kill young trees. The various species of woodpecker destroy thousands of these insects, and their presence in the fruit garden should be encouraged. Trees that branch low are less likely to be attacked by this insect.

The Apple Buprestis, or Thick-legged Apple-tree Borer, (*Chrysobothris femorata,*) is another quite destructive insect, infesting not only the apple, but the peach and white oak. The beetle is about half an inch long, flattened; color greenish-black, with a brassy polish; two very distinct metallic spots on the wing cover; eye prominent; head broad; antennæ short; thighs of the hind legs thickened and dilated. The insects make their appearance from about the time the apple blossoms, and continue some two months. They may be seen running up and down the trunk of the tree, and the eggs are deposited on the bark. The larva has nearly the same habits as the common borer, but differs greatly in appearance. It is a pale yellow, footless grub, with its anterior end enormously large, round, and flattened. The remedies are the same as for the common borer.

The Apple-tree Caterpillar, or Tent-caterpillar, (*Clisiocampa Americana,*) is a black, hairy caterpillar, with white lines, and along each side a row of blue spots. They live in societies in large, cobweb-like nests in the forks of the apple and wild cherry, which they form when the tree comes into leaf. From these, after having perhaps deprived the tree of all foliage, they finally disperse and spin oval white cocoons, which they place in a sheltered situation. The moth appears some eight weeks after the caterpillar first comes, and is dull brownish-red, with its fore wings crossed by two white bands parallel to the hind margin. The moth lays its eggs in large rings on the branches of trees, which are hatched the ensuing spring. If any of these clusters of eggs are found at pruning time, cut them off and burn them. If any caterpillars appear in the spring, they may be removed by a round bush fastened to a pole, which is put into the nest, and with a few turns, web and all are removed to be crushed by the foot. It is best to search for and destroy the nest and its contents when very small. Evening fires in the orchard will attract and destroy the moth. This insect is very injurious.

The Handmaid Moth, (*Datana ministra,*) is a brown,

hairy moth, which deposits its eggs in June upon the under sides of the leaves. The caterpillars are very destructive to the foliage.

The Palmer Worm, (*Chætochilus pometellus,*) is another very destructive insect in the orchard.

Apple-Worm, or Codling Moth.—(*Carpocapsa Pomonella.*)—The parent moth drops its eggs singly on the calyx end of the young fruit, from which the young worm, when hatched, eats its way to the centre. The worm, when small, is white, with a black head; the larger ones are flesh-colored, with brown heads. The wings of the perfect insect are marked with large brown spots, and shades of brown and gray. The worm gnaws a hole through the side of the apple, and thrusts out of it the refuse of its food. The fruit usually falls prematurely, and the worm escapes into the ground, or if not, crawls out upon the tree, hiding in crevices of the bark, and, in either case, spins its cocoon and is transformed into a pupa, in which state it remains through the winter. The remedies are—scraping the bark in the spring and burning the scrapings; allowing swine to run in the orchard to consume the fallen fruit; or gathering all that fall, and feeding them out or using them, destroying the insects within the fruit when cut open. A hay rope or cloth wound around the limbs, or placed in the forks of the tree, will attract the worms, which can be removed towards spring, and the chrysalids burned. Small fires in the orchard, early in summer, will attract and destroy thousands of these moths.

Gathering the Fruit.—Those intended for keeping, or sending to market, should be carefully picked from the tree, and handled with care, to prevent bruising. Those that fall of themselves must be kept separate, as the least bruise will cause decay. They must be frequently looked over, and every one the least decayed must be removed, or it will infect the others. They should be kept at a uniform temperature, in a dry, cool situation. Choice specimens may be wrapped in absorbent paper, and laid singly on shelves. They should not be exposed to much frost, and still less to extremes of heat. Specimens may thus be kept in good condition until March. A fruit room should be kept as cool as possible, and if the temperature could be uniformly at 32°, no decay would take place.

In selecting varieties for cultivation, preference should, as far as practicable, be given to those of southern origin. Of northern varieties, those classed as summer apples succeed very well here. Some of the early autumn varieties also do well, and, of course, are summer apples with us. But the winter apples, as a class, are entirely unsuited to the Southern States. The last ten years have developed, with us, a very large number of as choice and beautiful varieties of winter apples as can be found anywhere, so that, at this time, we can have an abundant supply during the entire year.

VARIETIES.

Early May.—Fruit small, round; skin thin, yellowish-green, when ripe, with sometimes a brownish-red cheek; stem short, in a shallow cavity; calyx small, closed, in a shallow basin; flesh yellowish-white; flavor mild acid, but rather astringent; begins to ripen from the 10th to the 20th of May.

Fig. 77.—EARLY MAY.

Early Harvest.—Fruit medium to large size, round, sometimes flattened; skin smooth, with a few white dots, and of a pale yellow color; stalk half to three-fourths of an inch long, slender, in a moderate cavity; calyx in a shallow basin; flesh white, tender, juicy, crisp; flavor rich, sprightly, and sub-acid. One of the best northern varieties; ripens from the 15th to the 20th of June.

Red June.—Fruit medium size, generally oblong in form; skin smooth, green in the shade, changing rapidly,

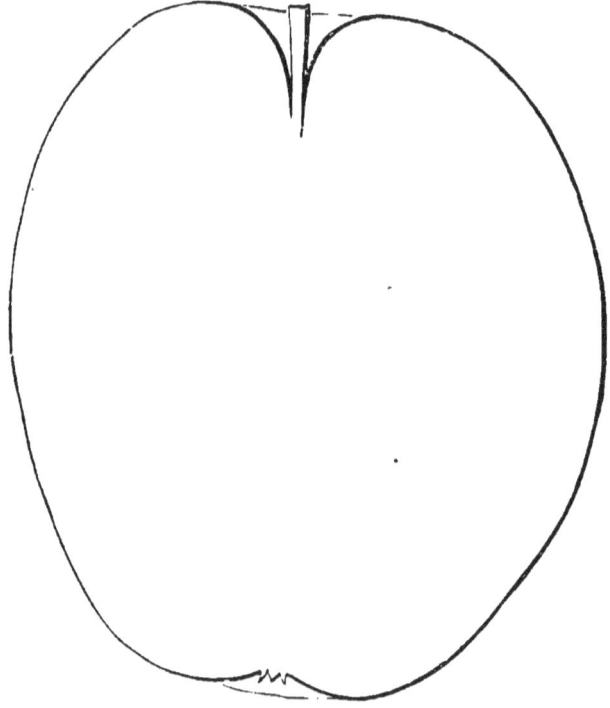

Fig. 78.—RED JUNE.

at maturity, to a fine dark crimson; stem half to three-fourths of an inch long, inserted in a moderate cavity; calyx in a shallow basin; flesh white, tender, mellow, and digestible, fine grained, slightly acid, moderately juicy, but not rich. A fine fruit, and very productive; tree very liable to be attacked by the borer.

Julien.—Fruit medium size, roundish, tapering somewhat to the eye; calyx small, in a narrow basin; stem short, in a moderate cavity; skin thin, yellowish-white, beautifully striped and marbled with carmine; the fruit is of a delicate, waxen appearance; flesh white, tender,

Fig. 79.—JULIEN.

juicy, and fine flavored. The best summer apple known; tree a fine grower and very productive; ripens the middle of July; rarely affected by worms.

Maiden's Blush.—Fruit medium size, flat, smooth, and fair; skin thin, clear lemon yellow, with a fine blush to the sun; stalk short, in a wide, deep cavity; calyx closed, in a moderate basin; flesh white, tender, sprightly, subacid. Excellent for drying and culinary uses, and a fair dessert fruit. Ripens the 1st of July.

Bough.—Large size; oblate in form; skin bright yellow, thickly dotted with russet specks; stalk rather long, in a deep, narrow cavity; calyx deeply sunk; flesh white, juicy, and very sweet; tree a poor grower.

Yellow June.—Fruit medium size; form rather flat; stem short, in a deep cavity; calyx large and open, in a moderate basin; skin thin, and of greenish-yellow color;

Fig. 80.—YELLOW JUNE.

flesh yellowish, tender and juicy. An excellent variety, and worthy a place in every garden. Ripens from the 15th to the 20th of June.

Cane Creek Sweet.—Medium size; ovate in form; skin pale green; stem long and slender, in a deep cavity; calyx closed, in a narrow basin; flesh white, tender, and sweet; when in perfection, juicy, but becomes mealy when over ripe. Quality very good. Ripens July 15th.

Toccoa.—Above medium size, conical; skin yellow, shaded and striped with red; flesh yellow, with a brisk Spitzenburgh flavor, moderately juicy; core large. A native of Habersham County, Georgia. Ripens August 1st. A fine fruit, and healthy tree.

Aromatic Carolina.—Fruit large size; oblate in form, tapering to the eye; stalk short and fleshy, in a deep,

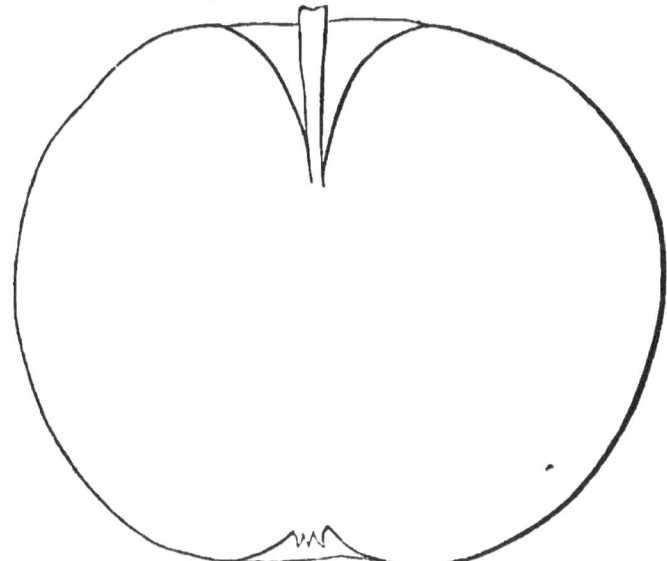

Fig. 81.—AROMATIC CAROLINA.

wide cavity; calyx in a wide, shallow basin; color green, striped with dull crimson, and covered with a white bloom; juicy, and of a fine aromatic flavor. Tree a vigorous grower, and very productive. Ripens July 15th to August 1st.

Fall Pippin.—Fruit very large, roundish, flattened, obscurely ribbed; stalk three-fourths of an inch long, in a deep, narrow cavity; calyx small, in a deep, narrow basin; flesh tender and mellow, with a rich, aromatic, sub-acid flavor. A splendid apple here. Ripens in August.

15*

Horse.—Size medium to large; conical in form; skin thick, golden yellow, when thoroughly ripe, with a blush cheek on the sunny side, a little russeted about the stem; stem short, and rather large, in a shallow cavity; calyx in a narrow basin; core large and hollow, seeds few;

Fig. 82.—HORSE.

flesh yellow, firm, coarse grained, with a rich acid flavor. Best known variety for drying. Ripens August 1st. Tree vigorous, and very productive.

Disharoon.—Fruit large, nearly round; skin thin, pale green; stem about three-fourths of an inch long, slender, inserted in a moderate sized cavity; calyx open, of common size, in a small basin; flesh yellowish, tender, juicy, and of an excellent mild, acid, aromatic flavor. Ripens in September. A native of Habersham County.

Buff.—Fruit of the largest size, roundish and somewhat ribbed and angular; skin thick, ground color yellow, but striped and shaded with dull red, marked with a few greenish russet spots; stem three-fourths of an inch long. in a medium cavity; calyx in a large, irregular

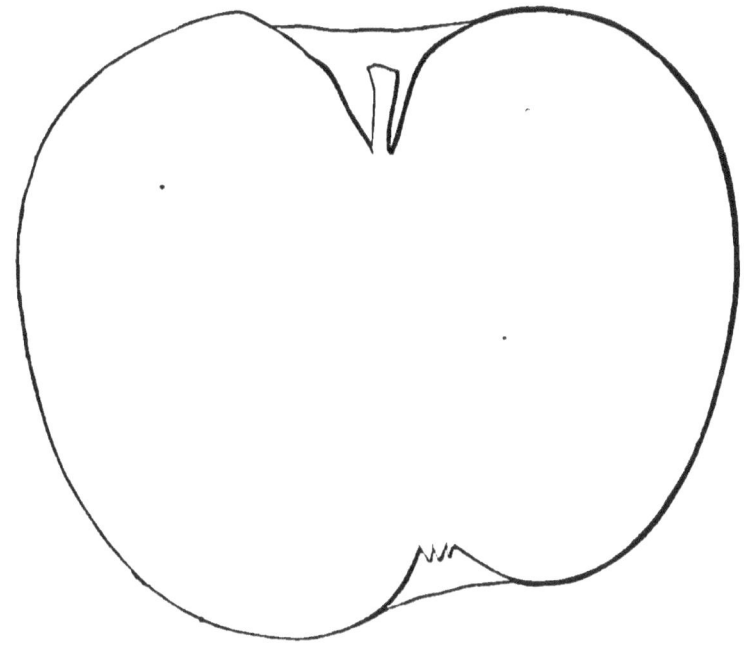

Fig. 83.—BUFF.

basin; flesh yellowish, and, when well ripened, tender and good, sometimes indifferent. Ripens October to March.

Habersham Pearmain.—Fruit medium sized, and of ovate form; stem short and slender; calyx of moderate size, in a slight basin; color bright crimson, and very fair and beautiful in general appearance; flesh white, rather dry, of firm texture, and of a brisk, sub-acid flavor. Ripens middle of September. Tree of upright growth, and very symmetrical.

. **Meigs.**—Fruit large; regular oblong, narrowing to the eye, sometimes slightly ribbed; skin yellow, but mostly

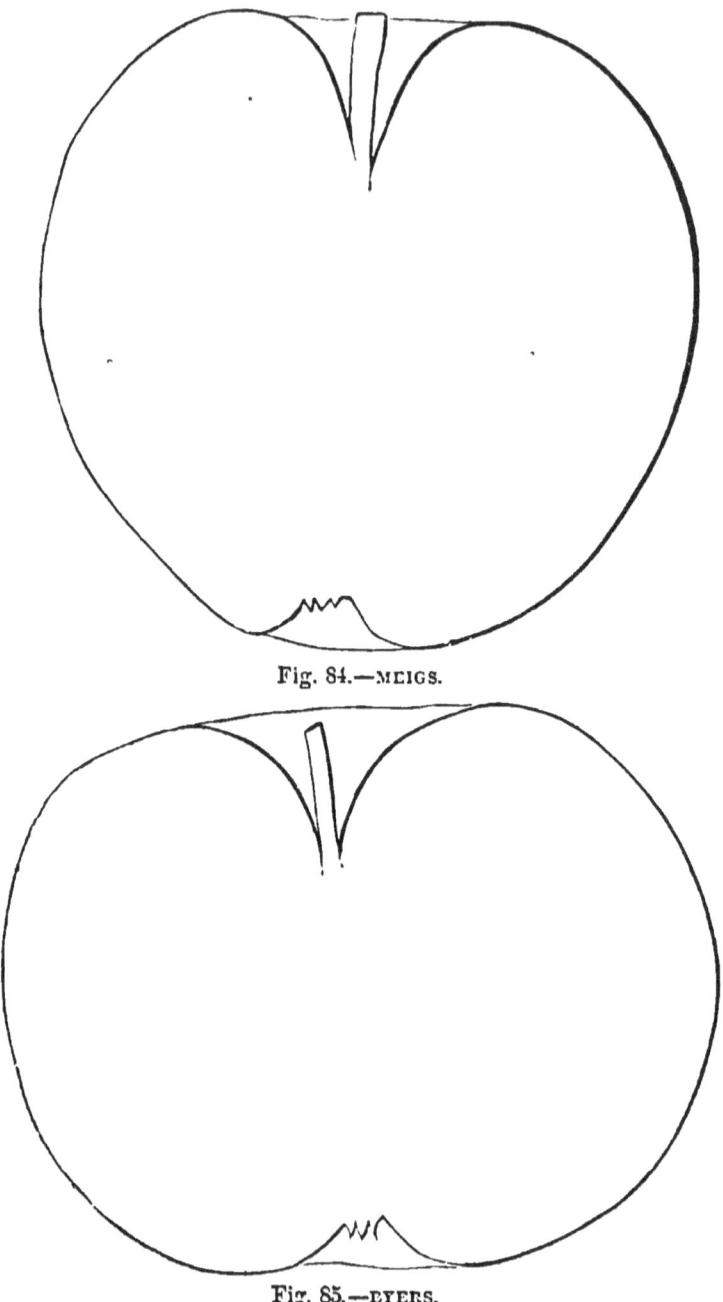

Fig. 84.—MEIGS.

Fig. 85.—DYERS.

covered with a marbling of red, and sprinkled with prominent yellow dots; calyx small, closed, and set in a narrow basin; stalk very short, thick, in a deep, narrow cavity; flesh yellowish-white, tender, juicy, with a rich, slightly sub-acid flavor. A fine native variety. Tree thrifty, and less infested with woolly aphis than many others. Ripens in September.

Byers, Buckingham, Batchelor.—This very popular apple is known by fifteen or twenty names. Fruit large to very large; a little oblate in form, narrowing toward the eye; skin rich yellow, nearly covered with bright red, dark crimson on the side exposed to the sun, sprinkled with white specks; calyx small, open, in a rather deep basin; stalk very short and fleshy, inserted in a moderate sized cavity, which is russeted; flesh white, tender, fine grained, juicy and rich, of a sub-acid flavor. Ripens in October. A splendid fruit.

WINTER VARIETIES.

Walker's Yellow.—Large, oblong or oval; skin yellow, with a slight blush to the sun; stem short, and set in a deep cavity; calyx large, open, in a small basin; flesh white, of firm texture, and acid flavor. Raised by George Walker, Esq., of Pulaski Co., Georgia, where it ripens in October, and keeps until February. A fine Southern variety.

Cullasaga.—Large, regular, and a little conical; skin yellow, and nearly covered with crimson; calyx small, in a moderate basin; stem short and fleshy; flesh yellow, tender and juicy, of a fine aromatic flavor. Ripens in October. A first rate variety, a seedling from the Horse Apple, by Miss Ann Bryson, of N. C.

Summerour, or Nickajack.—Fruit large to very large, of an oblate form; color a yellow ground, striped with dark red, sprinkled with russet specks; calyx large and open, set in a broad, shallow basin; stem short, in a regular cavity; flesh juicy, tender and rich, mild acid. Ripens late, and keeps well until April. Originated by John Summerour, of Burke Co., North Carolina.

Red Warrior.—Fruit very large, nearly globular, but a little rhombic; color yellow, striped and marbled with light and dark red stripes, with russet specks and spots;

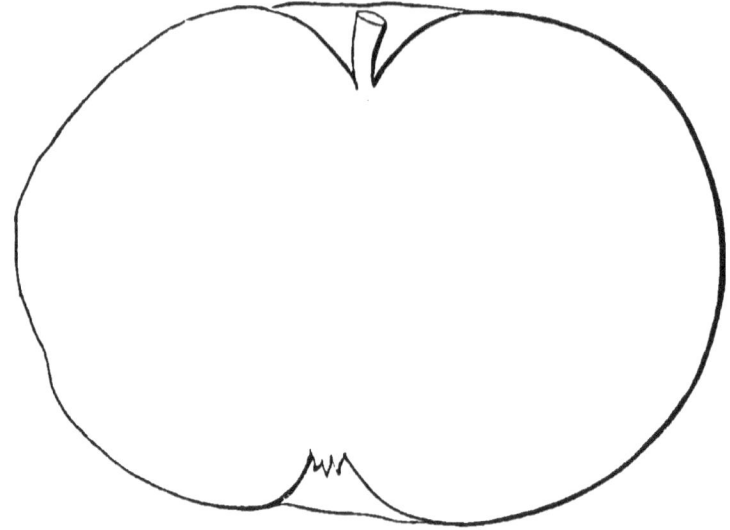

Fig. 86.—NICKAJACK.

stem medium size, three-fourths of an inch long; cavity medium; calyx closed, in an even, deep basin; flesh white, moderately acid, with abundant juice. From Montgomery, Alabama. Keeps until March. A very fine winter apple.

Cedar Falls.—Size medium to large; a little oblate in form; deep yellow, nearly covered with purplish-red, with a large patch of russet around the stem; flesh yellow, and of a firm texture; flavor exquisitely aromatic, sub-acid. Ripens November 1st, and keeps to February without shrivelling. A native of Forsyth Co., N. C. A No. 1 apple.

Oconee Greening.—Medium size, and resembles the

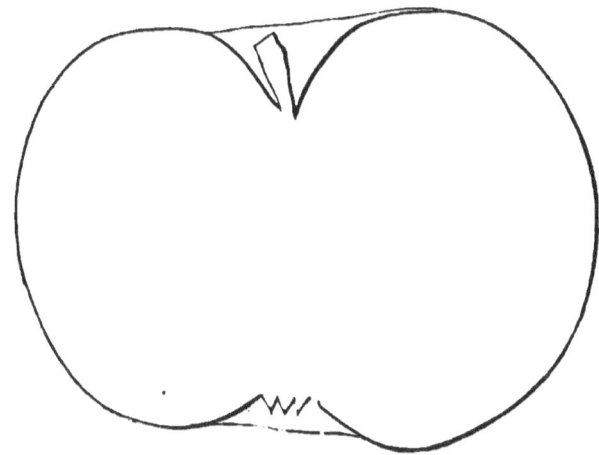

Fig. 87.—OCONEE GREENING.

Disharoon a good deal in external appearance, but keeps well much longer, and is of a more acid flavor.

Great Unknown.—Size large; regular in form; color a waxen yellow, beautifully shaded and marbled with carmine; stem slender, of medium length; calyx open, in a smooth basin; flesh yellowish, very tender, juicy, and delicious. An early winter fruit, and every way worthy of general cultivation. Origin unknown; found in the orchard of S. McDowell, Esq., in Macon Co., N. C.

Webb's Winter.—Size medium; form globular; color, greenish-yellow, shaded with dull red, with specks of russet; flesh yellow, juicy and tender, brisk, pleasant acid flavor; stalk long and slender, in an acute cavity; calyx small, in a regular, smooth, small basin. Ripens in November, and keeps well and good until February. The tree has slender, drooping branches. From Mississippi.

Chestoa, or Rabbit's Head.—Size medium; conical in form; color dark crimson on a greenish ground; stem short, slender, in a moderate cavity; fruit somewhat dis-

Fig. 88.—CHESTOA, OR RABBIT'S HEAD.

torted about the calyx, so as to resemble the nose of a rabbit; a patch of russet about the stem. Ripens in November, and keeps until March.

Elarkee.—Size medium; form conical; color dark red on a yellow ground; flesh yellowish, hard, and with sufficient juice; acid when first gathered, but becomes of pleasant flavor in March and April. Tree thrifty and very hardy. Origin, Macon Co., N. C.

Chestatee.—Medium to large; slightly conical; calyx in a hollow basin; stem short and slender, in a deep cav-

FRUITS.—VARIETIES AND CULTURE. 353

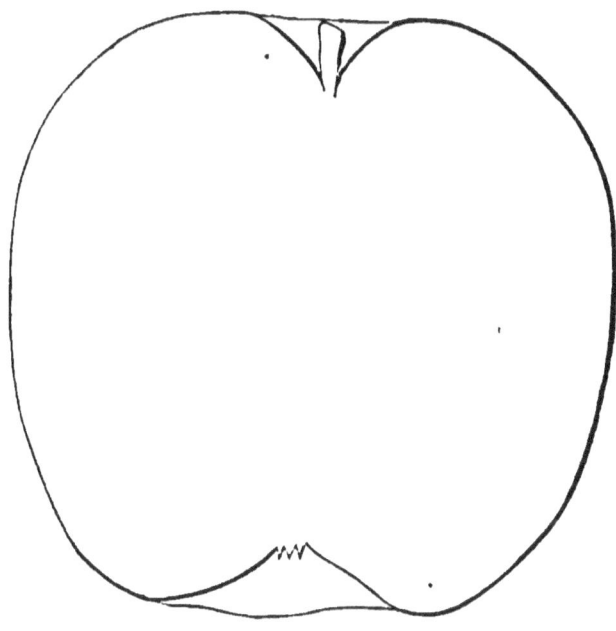

Fig. 89.—ELARKEE.

Fig. 90.—CHESTATEE.

ity, with spots and small specks of black; flesh white and juicy, rather too acid for a dessert fruit, but good for cooking. Ripens in September, and keeps until December.

Cattoogaja.—Large to very large; irregular and considerably ribbed, broadest at the base; yellow, mottled with black specks, and sprinkled with flecks of green; stalk of medium length, slender; cavity very deep; calyx in an open, deep basin; flesh yellowish, with a mild, subacid flavor. October to January.

Camak's Sweet.—Fruit medium to large; nearly round; dull whitish-green, mottled with green russet, the patches

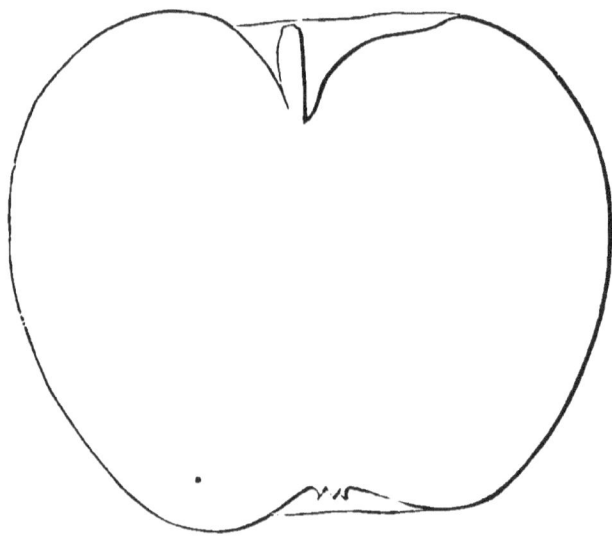

Fig. 91.—CAMAK'S SWEET.

of which are made up with small dots, with a dull blush cheek toward the sun; stem short and slender; cavity and basin broad; calyx closed; flesh firm and tender; scarcely sweet; juicy and fine flavored; best. Keeps until February.

Mangum.—Size small to medium; regular, slightly conical; stalk small, in a narrow cavity; color green,

FRUITS.—VARIETIES AND CULTURE.

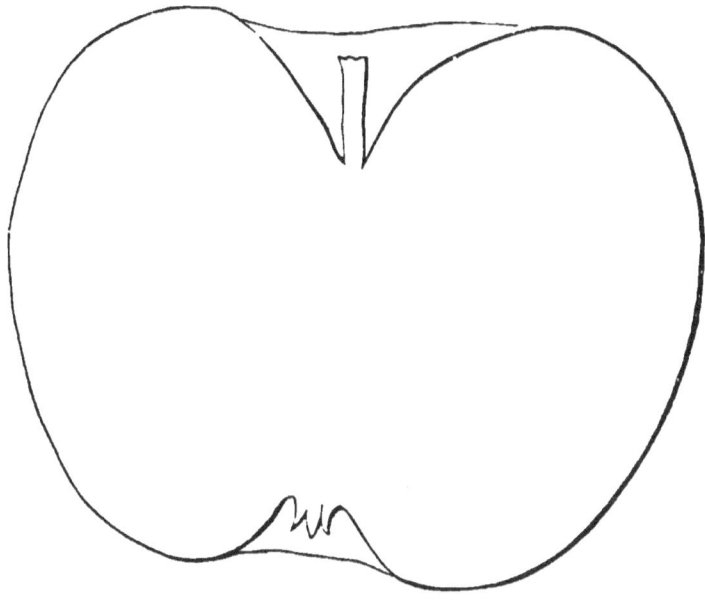

Fig. 92.—MANGUM.

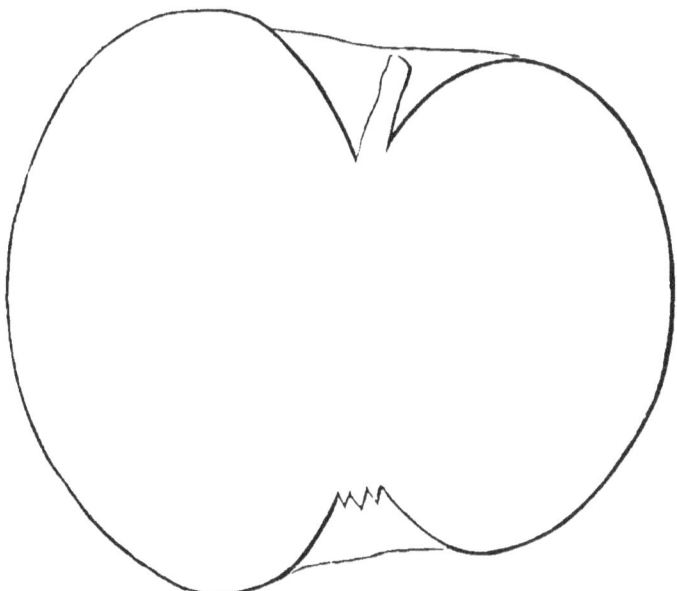

Fig. 93.—MOUNTAIN BELLE.

nearly covered with dark red stripes; flesh yellow and firm; of excellent quality, and keeps until March.

Mountain Belle.—Size medium to large; oblate and conical; color, an orange ground, shaded and striped with red; stem short, in a wide, deep cavity; calyx in a moderate sized, smooth basin; flesh white, hard, and juicy, a little tough in texture, and of a fair, sub-acid flavor. Ripens November to May. Second quality, but a famous keeper. A native of Habersham County, Ga., found in an old Indian field by J. Van Buren.

Van Buren.—Size medium to large; globular, and a little conical in form; color, yellow ground, shaded with dark red; with specks and patches of russet; stem short and fleshy, in a narrow, medium sized cavity; calyx small, and closed in a shallow basin; flesh yellow, juicy, and quite tender for a good keeper. Ripens in October, and keeps until April. A new and first rate winter apple, found and named by Elijah Sutton, Esq., Habersham Co., Ga.

Yahoola.—Fruit medium size; oblate in form; color, dull green, speckled and streaked with russet; stem long and slender; calyx medium size, in a moderate sized basin; flesh greenish-white, juicy, and of fair quality. Ripens in September, and keeps until January 1st. Tree with slender, wiry limbs. Origin, Lumpkin Co., Ga.

List of varieties recommended for cultivation in the Southern States:

SUMMER VARIETIES.	AUTUMN VARIETIES.
Early Harvest.	Buckingham.
Red June.	Disharoon.
Julien.	Myers' Nonpareil.
Aromatic Carolina.	Autumn Wine.
Sweet Bough.	Rome Beauty.
Red Astrachan.	Meigs.
Toccoa.	Chestatee.

WINTER VARIETIES.

Summerour.
Van Buren.
Mangum.
Cedar Falls.
Elarkee.

Camak's Sweet.
Great Unknown.
Webb's Winter.
Mountain Belle.
Gladney's Red.

APRICOT.—(*Prunus Armeniaca.*)

The apricot is a fruit somewhat resembling both the plum and the peach. The tree is ornamental as well as useful; larger than the plum, with glossy, heart-shaped, large leaves and white blossoms, which appear so early that they are usually killed by spring frosts. But, as with the nectarine, the great obstacle to its culture is the curculio, which may be treated as in the case of that fruit. In favorable seasons, the apricot is very productive. The apricot is a native of Armenia and other parts of Central Asia. In quality it is second only to the peach, but, coming earlier, it is very acceptable.

For jellies, tarts, and preserving in brandy or sugar, it is much esteemed, and is excellent when dried as directed for the peach. The apricot is generally budded on the plum stock; it is sometimes propagated on its own root, and also upon the peach. The plum is the hardier stock, and makes the better tree. It may be root-grafted on the Chickasaw plum. Those propagated by seed are usually very hardy and productive. On the peach stock, the tree is liable to be destroyed by the borer, and the fruit is inferior.

Apricots are apt to bloom so early in the spring that it is best to plant them in a northern exposure, where they will be retarded in blooming; by the side of a building, there is less danger of frost. It is just as necessary to shorten in the young branches of the apricot as those of the peach.

The best soil is a deep loam; cultivate and manure the same as the peach. The hardiest apricots are the Dubois, Orange, and Breda. The best varieties are Dubois and Early.

Dubois.—Fruit small, roundish oval, pale orange color, moderately juicy, sweet, and good; very productive and hardy. Ripens June 10th.

Large Early.—Fruit medium size, oblong and compressed; suture deep; skin slightly downy, pale orange in the shade, ruddy in the sun; flesh yellow, and separates from the stone, rich and juicy; kernel bitter. Ripens June 10th.

Orange.—Fruit medium, roundish, with suture hollowed at the stalk; skin orange, with a ruddy tinge; flesh dark orange, rather dry, and somewhat adhesive to the stone, which is small and roundish; kernel sweet; not first rate, but good for pies and tarts, preserving or drying; a good bearer. Ripens June 10th.

Peach Apricot.—Fruit very large, roundish, sides compressed, and with a distinct suture; skin yellow, but deep orange, mottled with brown, in the sun; flesh deep yellow, rich and delicious; the best variety in cultivation; stone rough. Ripens last of June.

Breda.—Small, roundish; color deep yellow, darker in the sun; flesh deep orange, high flavored, rich, and juicy, separating from the stone; kernel sweet; a native of Africa; hardy, productive, and fine for the dessert or preserves. Ripens middle of June.

Moorpark.—Large, roundish oval; skin orange, with a ruddy cheek; flesh bright orange, free from the stone, juicy, and of rich, luscious flavor; stone perforated;

hardly differs from the peach apricot, not quite so large, and a little later. Ripens July 20th. Very productive.

Hemskirke.—Fruit large, roundish, but considerably compressed on its sides; skin orange, with a red cheek; flesh bright orange, tender, rather more juicy than the Moorpark, with a rich, luscious flavor; stone small, and kernel bitter. Ripens July 1st.

Royal.—Fruit round, large, slightly compressed; skin dull yellow, with a darker cheek, faintly tinged with red; with a slightly marked suture; flesh pale orange, firm and juicy, with a rich, vinous flavor. Ripens July 1st.

THE BLACKBERRY.—(*Rubus villosus, etc.*)

We do not consider it necessary for us to give any description of this fruit, as it is well known by everybody, and is one of the greatest pests the planter and farmer have to contend with, springing up everywhere along the fences, in the field, the vegetable and flower garden. To us of the South it is amusing to see the excitement gotten up by Northern horticulturists about it. Their New Rochelle, Doolittle, Kittatinny, etc., etc., are thrown far in the background by the wagon loads that can be gathered from almost any of our old fields.

The Blackberry is a tolerable dessert fruit, continues a long time in bearing, and is also used for drying, for tarts, pies, puddings, jams, and preserves. A very good wine is made from the juice, which more nearly resembles Madeira than any made from our native grapes. There is a white variety, which differs from the black only in color, and is occasionally found growing wild amongst the black.

The Dewberry, (comprising both *Rubus Canadensis* and *trivialis*,) is also very common at the South; is running or trailing, and ripens its fruit some two weeks in advance of the high bush varieties, and the fruit is sweeter.

CHERRY.—(*Prunus vulgaris.*)

The Cherry, it is said, was brought from Asia by Lucullus, the Roman General; and from Rome its culture spread over Europe. In cooler latitudes some of the varieties are quite ornamental on account of their fine foliage and early white blossoms, but it stops growing and drops its leaves too early in our climate to be esteemed for this purpose. By the older authors the Plum and Cherry were placed in different genera, but the best botanists of the present time consider them both as species of *Prunus*, and the old name *Cerasus*, as applied to the Cherry, is dropped.

In the Southern States but few varieties succeed well, except the common Morello or Pie-Cherry. The trees of the finer varieties grow very well for some three or four years, and then commence splitting and dying on the south-west side of the trunk; we have seen a few that grew and bore fine crops for a few years when planted on the top of poor, rocky hills; the splitting of the bark appears to be caused by a too luxuriant growth. The trees should be planted in poor ground, and have but little or no manuring. Train the trees with low heads, so as to shade the trunks and protect them from the sun. Cherries are generally grafted or budded on the Mazzard or wild European stock, though the Mahaleb or Perfumed-cherry stock is preferable, as it dwarfs the tree, and is less liable to split and sun-burn.

It is not probable that the finer varieties of the Cherry

will ever be very successfully cultivated at the South until we raise seedlings suited to the climate.

Of the varieties described below, the Elton, May Duke, Sweet Montmorency, and common Morello, are the only ones that have ever produced good crops with us.

May Duke.—Fruit roundish, medium size, and in clusters; skin lively red at first, dark red when ripe; flesh reddish, tender, melting, very juicy; rich and excellent when fully ripe. Ripens early in May.

Doctor.—A heart Cherry, small, roundish heart-shaped, distinct suture; bright yellow and red, which are blended and mottled; flesh white, tender and juicy, with a sweet, delicious flavor. Tree cracks at the South.

Rockport Bigarreau.—Very large, heart-shaped; skin deep red on amber ground; flesh pale yellow, fine, juicy, with a sweet, rich flavor. Splits at the South.

Elton.—Very large, heart-shaped; skin pale yellow, with a mottled red cheek; stalk long and slender; flesh firm at first, becoming tender, juicy, with a rich, luscious flavor. Tree grows slowly, and is not disposed to split. Ripens May 20th to June 1st.

Kentish.—Fruit small to medium, round, a little flattened, grows in pairs; skin bright red, growing dark when ripe; stalk one and a fourth inch long, stout, and set in a pretty deep hollow; flesh melting, juicy, and of a rich, sprightly flavor. A hardy variety, and excellent for cooking.

Late Kentish.—Resembles the above, but is two weeks later, a little larger, and excellent for cooking, preserving, and drying.

Kirtland's Mary.—Very large, roundish heart-shaped; color light and dark red, mottled on a yellow ground; stalk of moderate size; flesh light yellow, half tender, rich, juicy, with a sweet flavor.

Black Heart.—Large, heart-shaped; skin glossy, dark purple, changing to black when ripe; stalk one inch and a half long, in a moderate cavity; flesh half tender, juicy, and of a rich, sweet flavor. A large, hardy tree, but disposed to split.

Downer's Late.—Fruit medium, borne in clusters, roundish heart-shaped, inclining to oval; skin smooth, of a soft, lively red color, mottled with amber in the shade; flesh tender, melting, with a sweet, luscious flavor.

Reine Hortense.—Fruit large, bright red, tender, juicy, nearly sweet, and delicious. Tree grows vigorously, bears well, and if planted on poor ground is not inclined to split. An excellent fruit.

Belle Magnifique.—A large red cherry; rather acid, tender, juicy, and rich; fine for cooking, and for dessert when fully ripe. Tree of slow growth, but bears profusely.

English Morello.—Tolerably large, roundish, nearly black; flesh reddish-purple, tender, juicy, of a pleasant sub-acid flavor. The common Morello of this country is smaller and inferior to the above. Ripens May 20th.

Plumstone Morello.—Large, dark red, rich and fine flavor; the best of all Morellos. Tree slow grower, and has small, wiry shoots.

Sweet Montmorency.—Fruit of medium size, round, and a little flattened; skin, pale amber in the shade, light red, slightly mottled in the sun; stalks long and slender, inserted in a small, even depression; flesh yellowish, tender, sweet, and excellent. One of the best at the South.

CURRANT.—(*Ribes rubrum.*)

The currant is a low shrub, a native of Great Britain and the northern parts of Europe and America; with smooth branches, doubly-serrate, pubescent leaves, and yellowish flowers, which ripen early in the spring. The fruit ripens with the later strawberries and raspberries. It succeeds and thrives admirably in our mountain sections, and will live and bear tolerably well here in a cool northern exposure, but would probably die the first season near the sea-coast.

The fruit is of an agreeable acid taste; when ripe it is used with sugar at the dessert, and also alone, or mixed with raspberries, for jams, jellies, and wine. It is used both green or ripe for stewing, tarts and pies. In cool climates it is the most easily cultivated and useful of small fruits.

The Currant is propagated from cuttings, which should be planted in the fall in a shaded place, but not under trees; the north side of a plank fence is an excellent situation, provided it is open to the morning sun.

The Currant requires a moist, rich soil, and should be trained as a bush. All the pruning it requires is to cut out the superabundant old wood, and to shorten that of the last season's growth.

The varieties we have cultivated are:

Red Dutch.—Fruit of large size, oblate, borne in clusters, and less acid than the common red; color, fine transparent red.

White Dutch.—Large, yellowish-white, less acid than the red varieties.

We could describe several other varieties, but not having had any success with them, we only give those with which we have succeeded.

THE FIG.—(*Ficus Carica.*)

The fig is a large shrub, or a low, spreading tree, according to the manner in which it is trained. Some varieties grow to the height of twenty or thirty feet, in favorable localities, but it generally does not reach above half that height. The leaves are large, cordate, and deeply sinuate, with three to five lobes, thick and pubescent on the under surface. The blossoms are not apparent, but concealed in the inside of the fleshy receptacle that becomes the fruit, which consists of a pulp, containing numerous pericarps enclosed in a rind, which becomes variously colored in the different varieties. Though the fruit is too sweet and luscious for those unaccustomed to it, it with use soon becomes a great favorite, and is perhaps the most wholesome and nutritious of fruits. The fig is a native of Asia and Africa, and has been cultivated from the earliest times. It is perfectly at home in all the low country and middle portions of the Southern States, and as universally cultivated below the mountain section as the peach. Large quantities of dried figs are imported into the United States, and are even sold in our midst. These, at very little expense, could be put up at home and even exported at a profit.

A good way to dry figs is to gather them when perfectly ripe; boil them in a preserving kettle in a syrup of nice sugar about five minutes. Take them out, dry them in a warm oven, or a kiln made for drying fruits; when dry they can be packed in drums or boxes.

Imported figs are dipped in a hot lye made of fig wood ashes, and dried on frames in the sun; when dried here they are apt to be infested with minute insects. The fig is readily propagated by shoots, or cuttings from the roots, planted in the fall or spring. Cuttings should be eight or ten inches long, and include a small portion of old wood at the base of each; if planted in a hot bed in January, they will make handsome plants the same season. Figs should be planted twelve to fifteen feet apart in good, rich earth. The Celestial Fig is best trained as a low tree. The best soil for the fig is a mellow loam of a calcareous nature.

Ashes, marl, or composts prepared with mild lime form the best manure. If the soil is too moist the fig continues its growth too late in the fall, when the new wood is killed by the frost; while young, it is best to protect the tree during winter with branches of evergreens. I have found that young trees will mature their fruit and wood much more perfectly, and better endure the winter, if the young shoots are broken off at the ends, and if all fruit forming after that is removed, and no more growth is permitted after the middle of September.

As a general rule, however, with the fig, the more it is pruned the less is the crop. This, however, does not apply to root pruning.

If from too rank growth of wood the tree drops its fruit, cut off all the roots that project more than half the length of the branches at any time during winter.

The nomenclature of figs is still very uncertain, as few are described with minuteness and accuracy. The names of several of our common varieties do not appear in the books, or they are so imperfectly described, that we do not recognize them.

DARK-COLORED VARIETIES.

Brunswick.—Fruit very large, long, pyriform, with an oblique apex; eye depressed; stalk short and thick; skin, pale green, tinged with yellow in the shade, dull brownish-red in the sun, and sprinkled with pale brown specks; flesh reddish-brown, pinkish at the centre, semi-transparent, rich, sweet, and high flavored. If I have the true variety the leaves are deeply cut, and generally seven-lobed. Wood of strong growth, and very hardy.

Brown Turkey.—Fruit large, oblong or pyriform; skin dark brown, covered with thick blue bloom; flesh red and delicious. Said to be very hardy and prolific. It may be our common blue variety.

Brown Ischia.—Fruit medium to large, roundish obovate; skin chestnut brown; flesh purple, sweet, and excellent; leaves broad and five-lobed.

Small Brown Ischia.—Fruit small, pyriform, with a short stalk; skin light brown; flesh inclining to purple, high flavored; leaves less sinuate than in the other sorts. This and the Brown Turkey are generally considered the hardiest varieties.

Black Genoa.—Leaflets narrow, and the leaf seven-lobed; fruit large, long, obovate, tapering to the stalk, which is slender; skin almost black, glossy, covered with purple bloom; flesh bright red, of excellent flavor. This continued to bear fruit abundantly until frost, and like the Brunswick is indispensable.

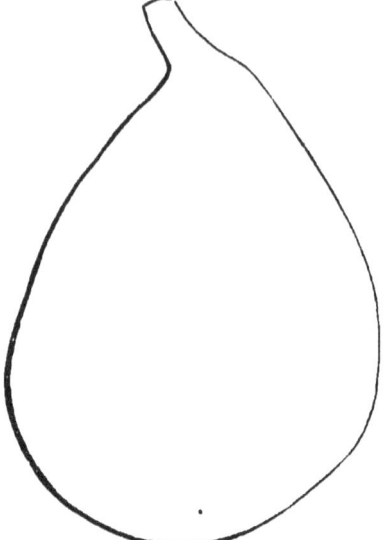

Fig. 94.—BROWN ISCHIA.

Celestial.—Fruit quite small, pyriform; stalk slender; skin very thin, dark colored, and covered with purple bloom; flesh light red, and of delicious flavor.

In dry weather the fruit hangs on the tree until it shrivels, improving in sweetness and flavor. Trees grow quite large, and are very productive, yielding constantly from July to October. Leaves five-lobed. May prove to be the Malta of Downing, and others. Very hardy.

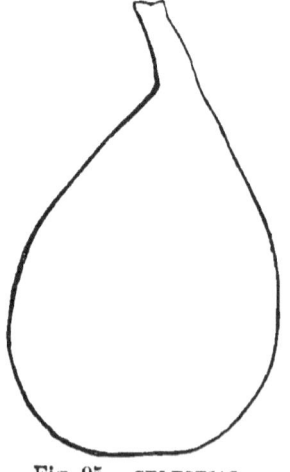

Fig. 95.—CELESTIAL.

The Common Blue.—This is rather inferior in flavor to the foregoing; but is very hardy and productive. Fruit large, oblong, bluish-purple; early, and produces two crops.

Pregussatta.—Fruit medium, roundish, flattened; skin purplish-brown in the shade, dark brown in the sun; flesh deep red, high flavored, and luscious. This is usually placed among the light-colored figs, but properly belongs here.

WHITE, YELLOW, AND GREEN VARIETIES.

Lemon White, or Common White.—Fruit turbinate, flattened; stalk short; skin pale yellowish-green; flesh white and sweet, not high flavored. Ripens quite early, and is a good bearer. Its color renders it a favorite for preserving.

White Genoa.—Fruit large, globular, a little lengthened to the stalk; skin thin, yellowish when ripe; flesh light red, and of sweet, delicious flavor. If protected, the fruit is the first to ripen. A good bearer. Indispensable.

Nerii.—Fruit small, roundish obovate; skin light greenish-yellow; flesh red, slightly acid, delicate and rich. Has borne here some years, and is a very nice little fig.

Alicante.—A very large and delicious purple fig, bearing abundantly early in the season, until frost, in the low country, but not suited to this latitude, as it is more tender than those described.

Black Ischia and White Ischia are said to be good. The above list we know are. The White Marseilles, Gentile, and Yellow Ischia are worthless. The Matanzas is said to be a very desirable variety, but as we have never seen the fruit, we cannot give a description of it.

GOOSEBERRY.—(*Ribes Grossularia.*)

The Gooseberry, like the Currant, is a native of Europe. Green, it is used for pies, tarts, and puddings; ripe, it is a very agreeable dessert fruit. It is more impatient of heat than the currant, and cannot be expected to thrive except among the mountains. It is, like the currant, propagated from cuttings, likes the same soil and treatment generally, even in the Northern States, and in our mountain region the fruit is liable to mildew, the foreign varieties being much more subject to it than the native varieties.

Houghton's Seedling and Downing's Seedling are the best native varieties we have seen. Woods earth, or leaf mould, and ashes, are the best manures for both the currant and gooseberry that we have tried.

THE GRAPE.—(*Vitis.*)

The vine was one of the first plants brought into cultivation. The foreign grapes are all varieties of *Vitis vinifera*, and came originally from Asia. Of native grapes, we have *Vitis Labrusca*, of which Isabella, Catawba, Concord, Diana, and Hartford Prolific, and many others, are varieties; *Vitis cordifolia* and *V. œstivalis* include the wild Summer, the Frost Grape, and of the cultivated varieties, the Ohio, Warren, or Herbemont, Lenoir, Taylor's Bullit, and a host of new ones of the same class; *Vitis rotundifolia* includes the wild Muscadine, or Bullace, of the South, and the Scuppernong, and, we are almost inclined to add, the Mustang.

Our American grapes are seedlings from the wild varieties, removed some one, two, and three generations from the original type. Foreign grapes do not succeed in our climate in open air or out-door cultivation. All the foreign varieties do well both North and South, in cold graperies, under glass.

The grape is a cooling and refreshing fruit, of the highest excellence; green, it is used for pies and tarts; when ripe, it is a nutritious and most delicious dessert fruit, and is also used for preserving and jellies. The dried fruit, or raisins, are employed extensively for the dessert, and in many preparations of cookery. The leaves are an elegant garnish to other table fruits, but the chief product of the grape is wine, which is superior to that made of any other fruit.

Large quantities of wine are now made in the United States, more especially in California, where most of the foreign varieties succeed. In the Southern States, vineyard culture has proved a failure with all derived from the Labrusca and Æstivalis species. After one or two fair crops, the vines become stunted and unfruitful, or if stimulated by extra culture and manuring, both vines and fruit mildew and rot. There are but very few varieties which can be depended upon with anything approaching to certainty, and we shall only recommend such, as we have thoroughly tested most of the celebrated varieties cultivated in the Northern States for the past six to ten years.

We here insert the mode of culture of a vineyard of the Catawba grape, together with the several methods of training the vine, as laid down in the first edition of this work, by Mr. White, but our subsequent experience compels us to say that we have been much disappointed in the results:

"For vineyard culture of the Catawba grape, the ground should be subsoiled with a plow, or deeply trenched. A declivity should be worked into terraces, with a slight inclination to the hill, that the water may be collected there to be carried thence to the main drains. The Catawba grape is planted by the vine-growers on level ground, in rows seven feet apart, and four feet in the row, but on hill-sides, three by five feet apart. The vineyard is laid off with a line, and a stake put down where each vine is to grow; then a broad hole, a foot deep, is dug, in which are placed two cuttings, six or eight inches apart at the bottom, in a slanting position, but with the top eyes only about an inch apart, and even with the surface; throw in a shovelful of well-decayed leaf mould, that the cuttings may strike freely. Cover with an inch of charcoal dust, or light mould, when the cuttings are planted. The cuttings should be short-jointed and well ripened, each cutting having about four eyes, or buds. Cut them off close to the lower joint, and about an inch above the upper. The earth should be pressed closely about the cuttings. The best time for putting them out is the last of November or December. The finest vines are raised from cuttings planted where they are to remain. Being undisturbed by removal, they are more thrifty and long-lived. Remove all the cuttings but one, if more than one succeeds, and use them to replace where others have failed. During the summer, keep the ground clean and light, by repeated hoeings, and pull off superfluous shoots, leaving but one or two to grow at first, and one eventually. Next spring cut the vine down to two buds, one of which remove when the vine shoots; drive a stake seven feet long to each plant. Chestnut, charred at the end, is very good, but locust and cedar are the most durable; tie the young vines to the stake, remove all suckers, and allow but one cane to grow. Keep free from weeds, and cultivate as before. The next spring, cut down to three buds, and the year after, to five, and this year, train two canes instead of one. The pruning should take place from November to the last of February. The third or fourth year, according to the strength of the vine, cut down the weakest cane to a spur of two or three eyes, and select the best shoot of the preceding year, cut it down to six or eight joints, bend it over in the form of a hoop, and tie to the stake, or fasten it to the adjoining stake, in a horizontal position.

"The bow form, figure 96, is the best. Training the vine in this form checks the flow of sap, and causes the buds to break more evenly, retarding growth and increasing productiveness.

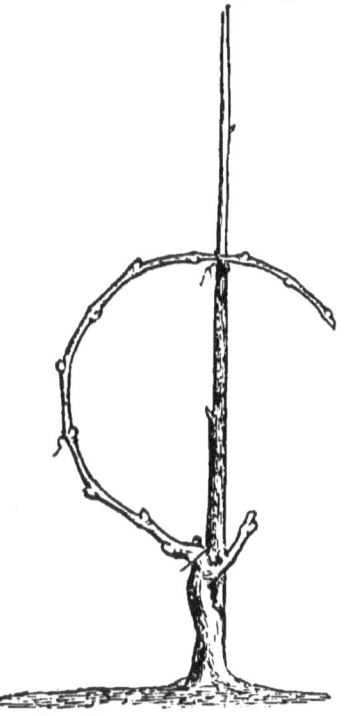

Fig. 96.—BOW TRAINING.

"From this bow the fruit is to be produced the current year, and the bearing wood of the next year from the spur left for this purpose. The next winter, this bow is to be cut away, and the bow for the next crop is formed from the best branch of the new wood of last year. Keep the old stalk within eighteen inches of the ground. Tie the vines carefully, without breaking them, in damp weather, when the buds are swelling, the last of February or early in March. In the summer remove the suckers, and pinch off lateral shoots, leaving but two for the next year.

"The object is to throw the strength of the vine into the fruit and the next year's bearing branches. The vineyard should be heavily manured once in two or three years. Wood ashes and gypsum are good applications, and are thought to prevent the rot. The trimmings of the vines, dug in, are found to be beneficial; but leaf mould, well rotted, with the addition of lime and ashes, is the best application. Vines highly manured and allowed to grow rampant, covering a large space, will produce a weak and worthless vine, and continue in bearing but two or three seasons." We have only copied the foregoing remarks for the purpose of giving a system for the benefit of amateurs and those desirous of experimenting, and not as our own views, as we tried all methods with the Northern varieties, and found all to fail, in the prevention of rot and mildew.

If vines are protected by a coping of boards, so as to protect them from the rain and dew, a few varieties succeed very well for two or three years. Vines planted by the side of a building, so as to be partially protected by the projecting roof, ripen perfectly for a few years, while those exposed decay.

Wine.—There is no more art or mystery in making wine than in making cider. The grapes are crushed between wooden rollers, which run sufficiently near each other to crush the grapes, but not the seeds.

To make red wine, the crushed grapes should stand about twenty-four hours, before pressing, so as to extract a portion of the coloring matter from the skins, when they may be pressed by means of an ordinary screw press. To each gallon of juice, one and a half pound of good clarified sugar must be added; if made from the pure juice of the grape, the wine will be thin, weak, poor, acid, and astringent stuff, not better than hard cider. All the best foreign wines have a large portion of brandy added; such as the Madeira and Sherry have near twenty per cent. In February or March following, the wine should be racked off into clean casks, if intended for still wine, or bottled, if for foaming wine; at the time of bottling, a tablespoonful of No. 1 clarified sugar must be put into each bottle, which should be well corked. Some recommend rock candy to be added. We have found nothing better than good clarified sugar.

VARIETIES.

Catawba.—Clusters, of medium size, shouldered, somewhat loose; berries, large, round; skin, rather thick, pale red in the shade, but deep red in the sun, with lilac bloom; flesh, slightly pulpy, juicy, sweet, with an aromatic, rich, musky flavor. Ripens last of August.

Concord.—One of the best of the Northern varieties, but the juice is too weak and thin to make a good wine. Clusters, large, loose, and well shouldered; berries, very large, juicy, sweet, with but little aroma; a fair dessert grape; color, black, with a heavy bloom. Vine very vigorous, and the fruit is less liable to rot and mildew than any other Northern variety.

Perkins.—Does very well at the South, and is next to the Concord in exemption from disease; berries, large, and slightly oval; color, a pale, dingy pink; flesh, hard, but not pulpy, sweet and good, but destitute of aroma; is a very good dessert fruit. Vine vigorous and productive.

Clinton, which succeeds well here, is but one remove from our wild Summer-grape; clusters, medium size, shouldered, compact, similar to its parent; berries, round, below medium size, black, covered with bloom, juicy, with large seeds, and some acidity, and tough pulp. Ripens a little later than Isabella, but improves by hanging upon the vine.

Warren, or Herbemont's Madeira.—When this grape does perfect a crop, and the fruit is thoroughly ripened, it is the most delicious of all the American grapes. Unless protected by some kind of covering, it rarely produces a crop of fruit, being very liable to the rot. This grape becomes eatable the middle of August, but should not be picked before the 1st of October, if to be eaten by a connoisseur. Few persons have ever seen it when perfectly ripe, and fewer still have ever tasted it.

The Scuppernong.—We consider this very peculiar grape one of the greatest boons to the South. It has

Fig. 97.—THE SCUPPERNONG.

very little resemblance to any of the grapes of the other sorts. It is a rampant grower, and requires little, if any, care or culture; grows well in any soil south of the Potomac River; has none of the shaggy bark peculiar to other vines, and bears only from the old, and not from the current shoots, as do other grapes. The leaves are cordate, or heart-shaped, coarsely serrate, smooth on both upper and under surfaces. It blooms from the 15th to the last of June, and ripens its fruit the last of September and beginning of October. It has no diseases, in wood, leaf, or fruit, and rarely, if ever, fails to produce a heavy crop. We have never known it to fail.

It will produce a greater weight of fruit than any other variety in the world. The clusters vary in size from two to twenty berries, and the berries in size from three-fourths of an inch to one inch and a quarter in diameter.

Vines, six years transplanted, have this year given us an average of three bushels to each vine, and we shall be disappointed if they do not double every year for many years in the future. It is the sweetest and most luscious of any grape we have ever seen or tasted; makes a fine, heavy, high-flavored, fruity wine, and is peculiarly adapted to making foaming wines. The vine should be trained on an arbor or scaffold, and should have ample room to spread; for, if it becomes matted, it dies in the interior, and fails to produce fruit; give it room to spread itself, and it will do so, both in vine and fruit. The directions before given for making wine apply also to this; it requires one and a half pound of clarified sugar to one gallon of juice.

We are credibly informed that a vine of this variety is growing near Mobile which has produced two hundred and fifty bushels of grapes in a year, and we know that vines ten years old have given and will give thirty bushels per vine. A bushel of this grape will give from three to three and a half gallons of juice, according to ripeness.

The aroma given off by this grape, when ripening, is of honied sweetness, and very fragrant and delicious; it can be detected for some considerable distance. Neither insects or birds ever attack the fruit; 'possums and coons are fond of these grapes, as they fall from the vine.

We do not hesitate to recommend this variety to our friends at the South, and pledge our reputation, as a pomologist, that he who plants it will never regret having done so.

MULBERRY.—(*Morus.*)

This genus includes two species worthy of cultivation, both hardy, deciduous trees, ripening their fruits in May with the later strawberries. The fruit is of very agreeable flavor, and of abundant sub-acid juice. An agreeable wine may be made of the juice. All the species of Mulberry are of the easiest culture, and are generally propagated by cuttings of the branches or roots. The former should be shoots of the last season, having one joint of old wood; they may be three feet long, and buried half their length in the soil. The tree requires little or no pruning.

The soil should be a rich, deep, sandy loam. The fruit falls when ripe; hence, when the tree commences bearing, the surface below should be kept in short turf, that the fruit may be picked from the clean grass.

Black Mulberry, (*Morus nigra,*) is a native of Persia, and is a slow-growing, low-branched tree, with large, tough leaves, often five-lobed, producing large and delicious fruit, frequently an inch and a half long, and an inch across; black, and fine flavored. Tree a very poor grower.

Red Mulberry, (*Morus rubra,*) is a native of our woods; leaves large, rough, and generally heart-shaped; fruit an inch long, sweet and pleasant, but inferior to the black. The vigorous growth and fine spreading head of this variety makes it worthy of culture as an ornamental tree. It is the most tenacious of life of any tree we have ever met with; twenty-seven years since we dug one up in our garden, and annually up to the present time shoots put up from fragments left in the ground, and thus far we have been unable to exterminate it. If the cherry is planted near the house, and the Mulberry a little more distant, the latter will often attract the birds from it.

Downing's Everbearing was originated by Charles Downing, of Newburgh, N. Y., from the seed of *Morus multicaulis*. Tree very vigorous and productive; an estimable variety, and surpassed by none except the black English, and possessing the same rich, sub-acid flavor. It continues in bearing a long time. Fruit one and a quarter inch long, and nearly a half inch in diameter. Color maroon, or intense blue-black at full maturity; flesh juicy, rich, and sugary, with a sprightly vinous flavor.

NECTARINE.—(*Amygdalus Persica, var. lævis.*)

The Nectarine is merely a peach with a smooth skin; it is impossible to distinguish the tree from the peach by its leaf and flowers.

Nectarines usually produce nectarines from the seed; but the Boston Nectarine originated from a peach stone.

The tree is cultivated and pruned like the peach, and is propagated by grafting or budding on peach stocks. The great difficulty in raising Nectarines (and the same is true of the apricot and plum), is the curculio. The smooth skin of these fruits offers an inviting place for this insect to deposit its eggs. The injured fruit may be known by being marked with a small, semicircular scar, as if cut by a baby's nail.

It is useless to plant either the Nectarine, Apricot, or

Plum, especially in sandy soils, unless the trees are daily jarred, and the insects collected on sheets as they fall, and immediately destroyed. A limb may be sawed off a tree, and the stump hit a few smart blows with a mallet; if gently shaken, the insect will not let go its hold. Or another plan is to plant the trees by themselves, and admit poultry and hogs to eat the fallen fruit, which will, if other fruit gardens are not near, protect the crop. The borer infests the Nectarine as well as the Peach. Aside from the curculio, the nectarine is as hardy and easily raised as the peach, though scarcely equal to the best peaches in flavor. It requires the same soil and treatment as the peach. The best varieties are:

Hunt's Tawny.—Leaves serrate; flowers small; fruit medium size, roundish oval, with a swollen point; skin pale orange, dark red in the sun, mottled with russet specks; flesh orange, juicy, melting, and rich; a good bearer. Ripens July 10th. *Free.*

Violet Hative, or Early Violet.—Glands reniform; flowers small, fruit large, roundish, pale yellowish-green, with a purplish-red cheek, mottled with brown; flesh whitish-red at the stone, melting, juicy, and delicious. Ripens July 20th.

Elruge.—Glands reniform; flowers small, fruit medium, roundish oval; suture slight; skin pale green, with deep violet or blood red cheek, and minute brown specks; flesh pale green, pale red at the stone; melting, juicy, and rich; stone oval, rough, and pale colored. Ripens July 25th.

Downton.—Glands reniform; fruit large, roundish oval; skin pale green, flesh-red at the stone; melting and delicious. Ripens July 25th.

Boston.—Glands globose; flowers small; fruit large, roundish oval; skin bright yellow, with a deep red cheek;

flesh yellow, not rich, but sweet and pleasant. Ripens last of July. *Cling.*

New White. — Glands reniform; flowers large; fruit large, nearly round; skin white, with slight tinge of red in the sun; flesh white, tender, juicy, vinous, and rich; stone small. Ripens August 1st.

Stanwick.—A European variety; skin pale greenish-white, shaded into deep violet in the sun; flesh white, tender, juicy, and rich, sweet, and without the slightest prussic acid flavor. Ripens August 1st. *Free.*

The best clingstone nectarine is the Early Newington, and the best of all nectarines is said to be the Stanwick. Temple's is said also to be a fine variety.

NUTS.

There are several kinds of Nuts worthy of cultivation by every planter, many of which are ornamental shade trees, besides being valuable for the fruit they yield. For convenience, we class them under one head.

Chestnut, (*Castanea vesca*).—The Chestnut is a very large forest tree, and common to both continents. The Spanish Chestnut or Marron, produces a very large, sweet nut, and is propagated by grafting on our common chestnut. There are several varieties of this, of which "Marron de Lyon" is the best. It will bear the second year from the graft. Chestnuts are difficult to transplant when taken from the woods. The improved varieties are much superior to the wild sorts. The chestnut as a shade tree is very effective in landscape gardening.

Shell-bark Hickory, (*Carya alba*).—This tree is found in fertile soils all over the United States, producing the common thin-shelled, white hickory nut. The tree is very regular and beautiful for ornamental purposes. There is considerable difference in the size and flavor of the nuts of different varieties. It is generally cultivated by planting the nuts in the fall; these should be slightly covered with leaf mould.

Filberts, (*Corylus Avellana,*) are generally raised from layers. They should not be allowed to sucker; but trained to form low heads near the ground, which should be kept tolerably open by thinning out the small spray, and shortening back the young shoots every spring. Of the varieties,

Cosford is a large, oblong nut, with a thin shell, and of fine flavor. Prolific.

Frizzled.—Known by the frizzled husk; nut medium size, oval, compressed; husk hairy; shell thick; kernel sweet and good. Productive.

White Filbert.—Like the last, but with a light yellow or white skin; husk long and tubular; nuts ovate.

Madeira Nut, (*Juglaus Regia,*) is a fine, lofty tree, with a handsome, open head, producing the well-known nuts of the shops. It is produced from the seed, or by grafting. Likes a rich, moist soil. *Juglaus Præparturiens* is similar to the above, but bears fruit when three years old, and is valuable on this account for the garden.

Black Walnut, (*Juglaus nigra,*) should have a place in the grounds of the amateur, as it is not only a fine shade tree, but is valuable for its fruit and timber.

Pistachio Nut, (*Pistacia vera,*) an ornamental tree, producing agreeable flavored nuts, is much cultivated in Southern Europe.

The tree is diœcious, so that to produce fruit the male and female trees must be planted together. The nuts are oval, the size of the Olive, slightly furrowed, with a mild-flavored, oily nut. The tree grows to the height of fifteen or twenty feet. Nuts of this variety have been distributed in various parts of the Union by the Patent Office. The tree will probably succeed in the low country.

OLIVE.—(*Olea Europea.*)

The Olive is a low-branching, evergreen tree, rising to the height of twenty or thirty feet, with stiff, narrow, bluish-green leaves. The fruit is a drupe, of oblong, spheroidal form; hard, thick flesh of a yellowish-green color, turning black when ripe. The tree is a native of Greece and the sea-coast ridges of Asia and Africa; it has been cultivated from time immemorial for the oil expressed from its ripe fruit. Where cultivated it answers all the purposes of cream and butter, and enters into every kind of cooking. Unripe olives are much used as pickles, which, though distasteful at first to most persons, become by custom exceedingly grateful, promoting digestion, and increasing appetite. The ripe Olive is crushed to a paste, when the oil is expressed through coarse hempen bags into hot water, from which the pure oil is skimmed off. If the stone is crushed the oil is inferior. Lime and potash should be applied as fertilizers, should the soil be deficient in these substances.

Propagation and Culture.—Olive plantations are generally formed from the suckers which grow abundantly from the roots of old trees.

It grows readily from cuttings and seeds. Knots and tumors form on the bark of the trunk, which are removed with a knife, or planted like bulbs an inch or two deep, when they take root and form new trees.

The cultivated Olive may perhaps also be grafted on our *Olea Americana, or Devil Wood,* which abounds on our sea-coast. The best trees are from seeds which commence bearing in five or six years, but are not remunerative until ten or twelve years old. The trees produce fifteen to twenty pounds of oil per year, and their longevity is greater than that of any other fruit tree. The dry limestone soils of Florida would probably become exceedingly valuable if planted with the Olive.

It should be tried wherever the Orange will survive the winter. In planting, the trees are set from thirty to forty feet apart. The European varieties are many, but we enumerate only a few.

Olea angulosa is a hardy variety, with scanty foliage; fruit reddish, with long stem; it is preserved in some places.

"Oil of medium quality," says Gonan, but very good according to others.

Olea amygdalina is the variety most commonly cultivated; fruit almond shaped; is often pickled. Oil very sweet.

Olea Cranimorpha, or Weeping Olive, is a large and fine tree, with drooping branches; fruit small, crooked, pointed, very black.

Olea spherica has fruit more round than any other variety. Oil delicate.

Olea oblonga yields fruit best for pickling; oil fine and sweet. Produces abundantly. Tree hardy.

THE ORANGE, LEMON, ETC.

The Orange, (*Citrus Aurantium,*) is a native of Asia. The rich golden fruit displayed among its dark, glossy, evergreen foliage renders it the most beautiful of fruit trees. The tree grows to the height of twenty to thirty feet, with a round, symmetrical head; the bark of the trunk is of an ashy-gray, while that of the twigs is green. The leaves are of a fine, healthy, shining green; its blossoms are delicately fragrant, and as the tree is in all stages of bearing at the same time, in flower and ripe golden fruit, nothing can surpass an Orange grove in attractiveness. The wild, bitter-sweet orange is found in various parts of Florida as far north as 29°; its occurrence is said to be indicative of a good soil. It may have originated from the Seville orange introduced by the Spaniards. The orange at this time is extensively cultivated in Florida, and somewhat on the coast of Georgia and Carolina.

Lime is essential to the healthy growth of the tree; the best soil is a deep fertile loam on the banks of rivers.

The wild orange taken from the woods is generally used as a stock to graft the most desirable varieties upon.

The scale insect, *Coccus Hisperidum*, and others, prove annoying to those who attempt to cultivate the orange in green-houses, but can be destroyed by washing the leaves and wood with a strong decoction of tobacco heated nearly to boiling heat; the warm liquid irritates the insect, so that it looses its hold, permitting the liquid to enter between it and the wood or leaf.

There are about forty varieties of oranges cultivated, of two principal classes, viz.: The Sweet or China Orange, and the *Bitter Seville* or *Wild Orange*. The latter class is much the more hardy, but of no value as a dessert fruit. They are used in cooking, preserving, wine making, and for flavoring. Of the sweet oranges, the Maltese has a thick and spongy rind, red and delicious pulp, but sometimes with a trace of bitterness. The glands which secrete the oil are prominent.

St. Michaels.—Small, with thin, smooth rind, and small glands; pulp light colored, and of a luscious, sugary taste; often seedless. The most delicious of all oranges.

Mandarin.—Is a small, flattened fruit, with a thin rind, parting freely from the pulp, frequently separating itself; pulp dark orange, juicy, and rich.

Havana, or Common Sweet Orange, is a well-known variety of good size and rough rind; pulp yellow, and well filled with delicious juice.

Bergamot.—Has small flowers and pear-shaped fruit. The leaves, fruit, and flowers are all very fragrant, and much used by perfumers.

Otaheitan Orange.—Is a very small variety, and makes a beautiful bush in the green-house; fruit small and round; color pale orange; flesh rather dry, but sweet and palatable; has winged leaves same as the common orange.

The Lemon, (*Citrus Limonium,*) is cultivated like the orange, but has longer, lighter colored leaves, with naked petioles or footstalks; flowers tinged with red externally; fruit oblong, with a swollen point; pale yellow color, with an acid pulp. Used mostly for flavoring, and lemonade and other cooling drinks. The trees are usually very productive.

The Lime, (*Citrus Limetta*).—Has smaller flowers than the lemon, which are white; fruit small, round, and pale yellow color, with a slight protuberance at the end; very acid. Used for the same purposes as the lemon. The green fruit makes a delicious preserve.

Citron, (*Citrus Medica*).—Has large, oblong, wingless leaves; flowers tinged with red or purple; the fruit is very large and lemon shaped, with warts and furrows. Rind thick and fragrant, pulp sub-acid. Used for preserves.

Shaddock, (*Citrus Decumana*).—Has leaves winged like the orange; flowers white; fruit globular, and very large, weighing often six to eight pounds; rind very thick; pulp dry, sweetish, or sub-acid, but not very desirable, except for its showy appearance.

PEACH.—(*Amygdalus Persica.*)

The Peach is a native of Persia, whence its cultivation has proceeded westward; but it has nowhere found a soil or climate more congenial to it than in these Southern States. Indeed, the peach is the favorite, and in many instances the only, fruit tree cultivated by our planters. It requires a soil of but moderate fertility; its enemies and diseases are but few, and the return so speedy that there is no excuse for being without good peaches. We entirely escape the yellows and the curled leaf, I believe, except in the case of Northern imported trees, which generally recover, though checked for a season. The peach borer is very abundant, but from the luxuriant growth of the trees it seldom causes their death. The worm in the fruit is very annoying, especially in the white-fleshed varieties; it is best prevented by permitting pigs and fowls to consume all the fallen fruit of the orchard as it drops.

The Peach-Tree Borer.—(*Trochilium exitiosum.*)—The moth comes abroad from midsummer until October. Its body is of steel-blue color, with an orange band around the middle of the abdomen of the female. Her wings are blue, while those of the male are clear and glossy. The eggs are deposited the latter part of summer, at the base of the trunk, on the soft bark; when hatched they bore their way under the bark, sometimes proceeding upwards along the trunk, at other times downward into the root. Its presence is made known in spring by the effusion of gum; as it does not penetrate the wood, it is easily traced by its holes under the bark. The worm is soft, white, with a tawny, yellowish-red head, and sixteen feet, growing to over half an inch in length. It forms a tough, pod-like cocoon on the side of the root, jutting just above the surface. Remedies are various. Haul the earth from the collar of the tree, clean away the gum, and cut out the grub with a knife and kill it; or pour scalding water into his haunts from the spout of a tea-kettle, which will kill the grub and benefit the tree; leave the basin about the root of the tree open, and reëxamine a few days later, as some of the worms may have escaped. Where the mercury does not usually sink below 8° during the winter, it is best to leave the collar of the tree uncovered and exposed to the action of frost during winter. In spring, a small mound of ashes, or slaked lime, or even earth, should be placed about the base of the trunk, which will render the borer less likely to attack the tree. These should be spread over the surface in autumn. The trees should be closely examined in autumn and spring.

A somewhat serious difficulty in peach culture is the result of bad pruning. It is the tendency to overbear and break down the limbs from the excess of the crop. More peach trees are destroyed or badly injured from this cause than any other. Peach trees should always be pruned by cutting off the extremities of the branches, so as to leave about one-half of the last year's growth. The fruit is produced on these small branches; and by reducing the top in this manner, overbearing is prevented, the fruit is effectually thinned, and is larger, finer flavored, and nearly as much fruit can be taken from each tree without danger of breaking. The tree is also kept low and close, and more trees and larger crops can be grown to the acre.

This method of pruning is called *shortening in*, or heading in, and is expeditiously done with pruning shears. Old trees that have got out of shape can be pruned and brought into a symmetrical form by sawing off limbs of two or three years' growth at or near the forks; by this method old trees can be renewed in vigor as well as in form. Pruning can be performed at any time when the leaves are off. If it is wished to make young trees produce early, they may be shortened in the last of July, the year they are transplanted. Care should be taken that the branches do not divide into forks, as they are exceedingly apt to split when bearing a crop of fruit. The peach, like all other fruit trees, should branch low, say within two feet of the ground, and be kept in a pyramidal or round form, as nearly as can be done.

The loss of the fruit by decay as it approaches maturity is more annoying than anything else in peach culture.

If the season is warm and wet, very few kinds ripen well if on moist or rich earth or soil. There is a very common opinion that peaches propagated from the stones of unripe fruit are more liable to rot than those from stones or pits of fully ripened fruit; some also think decay is caused by planting the trees too deep. It is, however, certain, that some varieties are much more subject to decay than others placed in the same position.

The most suitable soils to ripen sound and high flavored fruit are dry, but moderately fertile; hills and hill sides generally are the best locations for the peach; thinning the fruit so that no two peaches touch each other is very necessary in order to prevent decay. The peach is mostly used in its fresh state for the dessert, and is generally considered the most delicious fruit of temperate climates. When allowed to ripen on the tree, it is the most wholesome of fruits, and as an article of food is considerably nutritious. Peaches are also used for pies, are preserved in brandy and sugar, and are excellent when dried for winter use. For culinary purposes, the Clings are most preferred. Peaches and cream form a delicious dessert dish.

For drying take those of the best quality, just as they are ripe enough to eat; halve them, remove the stones, and sprinkle over them a little nice sugar, and dry them in a brick oven, moderately warm. Thus prepared the aroma and flavor are preserved, and they are free from insects. If the peaches were fully ripe, no cooking will be required, but when used they are simply soaked in cold or warm water. Sufficient sugar, varying with the acidity of the fruit, is added before drying. The firm, yellow fleshed are the best for drying. Peaches thus prepared are only inferior to the fresh fruit, as they retain much of the flavor. Dried in the usual way from unripe fruit, exposed to the sun, much of the flavor is dissipated. Peaches are excellent preserved in self-sealing cans, which now can be purchased at reasonable prices.

Lime, potash, and the phosphates, are the chief elements the peach requires in the soil. Bone-dust and wood ashes are valuable applications, much more suitable than common animal manures. They may be dressed with compost of woods' earth, or swamp muck, if the soil is very poor.

When the trees are planted, the holes may be made large, and enriched with well-decayed manure, to give a good growth of wood. For this purpose guano is an excellent application; but it is fatal to the tree if it comes in contact with the roots. I have applied it with success to all kinds of fruit trees. After the holes are dug, a little guano is sprinkled in them; this is then covered with about two inches of good mould, on which the tree is planted. When the tree is planted, another sprinkling of guano may be added, and covered with a little more earth; two or three tablespoonfuls are sufficient for a tree, and but a small quantity is required for a large orchard. For this purpose, as well as for manuring most shrubs, rose bushes, etc., few applications are so cheap and satisfactory. After the tree begins to fruit, applications of lime, ashes, or leaf mould are much better than those which excite growth, as they do not impair the flavor of the fruit or induce decay.

The peach is best propagated by budding and grafting upon seedling peach stocks. There are, however, many varieties of the clings, particularly, that reproduce themselves from the seed, especially if the tree from which the stone is taken stands apart from other varieties. It is believed that the stone of a seedling is more apt to reproduce its kind, than if taken from a budded tree. Seedlings often escape frosts that are fatal to the finer varieties, but the highest flavored varieties of seedlings are often quite as susceptible of injury as those budded or grafted; those varieties bearing large flowers are much less liable to be injured by frost than those having small ones.

Plum stocks are recommended by foreign writers; but they are of little use in this climate, for the graft soon outgrows the stock, and breaks off. Peach stocks are raised by planting the stones two or three inches deep, in the autumn or winter. If the stones are cracked, they are more sure to grow. Abundance of stocks can often be procured, by taking the volunteers that spring up under the trees in early spring, when about an inch high, and transplanting in rows three feet apart, and one foot in the row. Plant them in good soil where they will grow rapidly; if the season is good they will be of sufficient size to bud in August. When the inserted buds start in the following spring, the stocks may be cut down to within two inches of the bud, and then keep rubbing off the shoots or robbers for at least two months; otherwise the inserted buds will be overpowered by them, and die, or make but feeble growth.

The buds had best be inserted in the north side of the stock to screen them from the sun. Peach trees raised, or varieties originating in the Northern States are not at all unfitted for our climate, yet there is some risk of importing trees from the North on account of diseases peculiar to that section from which Southern raised trees are exempt.

Some varieties of European fruits are found to succeed better here than where they originated, but as a general rule, all fruits succeed best in their native locality.

Peach trees in transplanting are set twenty feet apart

each way, which gives one hundred and eight trees to the acre. They may, if shortened in yearly, be set fifteen feet apart, which will give one hundred and ninety-three trees to an acre; in gardens fifteen feet is generally the best distance.

Peaches are so much alike in general character—the difference in outline, color, flavor, and texture being less than with other plants,—that it is necessary in order to determine the name of a variety to resort to other methods of distinction.

The two most obvious distinctions or divisions are into freestones and clingstones; or, as we call them, soft, and plum peaches; the flesh of the former parting freely from the stone, and being of a melting consistency; and that of the latter named sorts adhering to the stone, and being of a firmer texture. The English give to these divisions the names of "melters" and "pavies."

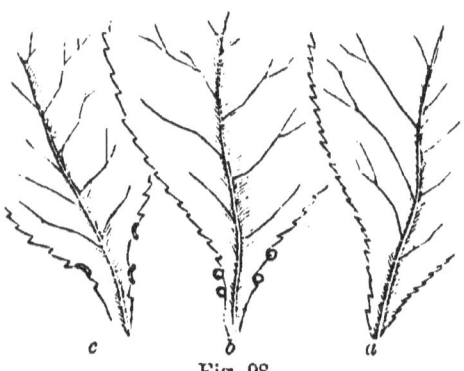

Fig. 98.

Both these grand divisions are subdivided into classes according to the color of the flesh, viz.: those with light colored, and those with deep yellow flesh. These classes are again divided into three sections. At the base of the leaf of some varieties will be found small glands, which are either round and regular, or oblong and irregular, or kidney shaped; while others have no glands, but are more deeply cut or serrated like the teeth of a saw.

Hence the three sections, viz.: 1. Leaves serrated, without glands, *a*, fig. 98; 2. Leaves with small, round, or globose glands, *b*, fig. 98; 3. Leaves with large, irregular, reniform or kidney-shaped glands, *c*, fig. 98.

From the blossom another characteristic is derived, giving us two subsections: the first embracing large flowers, red in the centre, and pale at the margin; the second, small flowers, tinged with dark red at the margin. Most native peaches in this vicinity have large flowers, but the great mass of the finer varieties have small flowers.

Varieties.—The following varieties have been tried in this vicinity, and are found among the most desirable. They are classed pretty much in the order of ripening. A full list of good clingstones, in succession, from the begining to the end of the peach season, is yet to be obtained. All named are good bearers.

Columbus June.—Glands reniform; flowers small; fruit medium to large, flattened, or slightly hollowed at the apex; suture shallow; skin pale yellowish-white, with a rich red cheek; flesh slightly red at the stone, melting, juicy, and high flavored; excellent. Ripens here June 20th. *Free.*

Hale's Early.—Glands globose; fruit medium, nearly round; skin mottled red, cheek dark red; flesh white, melting, juicy, and high flavored; flowers large. Tree vigorous, healthy, and an abundant bearer, ripening ten days or two weeks before any other good variety. *Free.* (*Thomas.*)

Early Tillottson.—Leaves deeply serrated, without glands; fruit medium, round; skin nearly covered with red ground; color pale yellowish-white, dotted with red, the cheek being quite dark; flesh white, red at the stone, to which it adheres slightly, although a freestone; melting, rich, and juicy, with a high flavor. Ripens from the 15th to the 20th of June. *Free.*

Serrate Early York.—Leaves serrate, glandless; flowers large; fruit medium, roundish oval; suture slight; skin thickly dotted with pale red on a greenish-white ground, dark red in the sun; flesh greenish-white, tender, melting, full of rich, slightly acid juice. Ripens June 20th. *Free.*

Walter's Early.—Glands globose; flowers small; fruit above medium; color nearly white, with a fine, red cheek; flesh whitish, slightly red at the stone, melting, juicy, sweet, and fine flavored; not so easily injured by frost as some others; likes sandy soil; succeeds as far South as Mobile. Ripens July 1st. *Free.*

Early Newington Free.—Glands globose, flowers large; fruit medium to large, round; suture distinct; skin dull yellowish-white, dotted and streaked with red, cheek rich red; flesh white, red at the stone, to which it partially adheres; juicy, melting, and vinous. Ripens early in July.

George 4th.—Glands globose; flowers small; fruit large, round, with broad suture; skin white, dotted with red, cheek rich dark red; flesh pale, melting, very juicy, with rich, luscious flavor; stone small. Ripens July 10th. *Free.*

Gross Mignonne.—Glands globose; flowers large; fruit large, roundish, apex depressed; suture distinct; skin dull white, mottled with red, and with a purplish-red cheek; flesh red at the stone, melting, juicy, with a rich vinous flavor; stone small and very rough; perhaps the best freestone peach in cultivation. Ripens July 10th. *Free.*

Crawford's Early.—Glands globose; flowers small; fruit yellowish-white, with a fine red cheek; flesh yellow, melting, sweet, and excellent. Ripens middle of July. *Free.*

Belle de Beaucaire.—Glands globose; flowers small; fruit very large, roundish, with a protruding point; suture shallow, but distinctly marked; skin yellowish-green, with a red cheek; flesh pale greenish-yellow, red at the stone, a little coarse, but melting and delicious, full of rich, vinous juice; skin slips readily from the flesh without the use of a knife. Ripens last of July. *Free.*

Oldmixon Cling.—Glands globose; flowers small; fruit large, roundish oval; suture at the top; skin yellowish-white, dotted with red, cheek red; flesh light, melting, juicy, and rich, with a high, luscious flavor. Ripens last of July, and early in August.

Late Red Rareripe.—Glands globose; flowers small; fruit large, roundish oval; skin downy; color grayish-white, marbled with red in the sun; flesh pale, juicy, melting, and of a rich, luscious flavor. Ripens last of July.

Late Admirable.—Glands globose; flowers small; fruit large, roundish oval; suture distinct; apex swollen, acute; skin pale yellowish-green, with a pale red cheek, marbled with dark red; flesh pale, melting, and fine flavored. Ripens August 10th to 15th. *Free.* A superb peach.

Crawford's Late.—Glands globose; flowers small; very large, roundish; suture shallow, but distinct; skin yellow, with dark red cheek; flesh deep yellow, red at the stone, juicy, and melting, with rich, vinous flavor. Ripens early in August. *Free.*

Newington Cling.—Leaves serrate: flowers large; fruit large, roundish; suture slight; skin pale yellowish-white, with a fine red cheek; flesh pale yellowish-white, deep red at the stone; melting, juicy, and rich. Ripens August 10th.

Lemon Cling.—Glands reniform; flowers small; leaves long; fruit large, oblong, narrowed at the top, with a swollen, projecting point; skin dark yellow, reddened in the sun; flesh fine yellow, red at the stone, flavor rich and vinous. Ripens August 10th.

President.—Glands globose; large, roundish oval; suture shallow; skin downy, pale yellowish-green, with a dull red cheek; flesh pale, but deep red at the stone, very juicy, melting, and high flavored; stone very rough. Ripens August 15th. *Free.*

Blanton Cling.—Leaves large; glands reniform; fruit large, and shaped like Lemon Cling, with the same projecting point; color rich orange, with a slightly reddened cheek; flesh orange yellow, firm, but full of delicious vinous juice. Later and better than Lemon Cling. Reproduces itself from seed. Ripens August 10th.

Tippacanoe.—Glands reniform; flowers small; fruit very large, nearly round, with a point; skin yellow, with a fine red cheek; flesh yellow, juicy, with a fine vinous flavor. Ripens August 20th. *Cling.*

Van Buren's Golden Dwarf.—Glands reniform; flowers small; fruit large, nearly round, with a swollen point; suture deep; skin yellow, beautifully dotted and marbled with carmine; flesh yellow, firm, with plenty of juice, vinous; leaves large and close, dark rich green. Tree a dwarf, growing to the height of 2 or 3 feet. A fine fruit, and very distinct from the Italian dwarf, which is a white freestone, and of very poor quality. Ripens August 15th. A very ornamental variety. *Cling.*

Chinese Cling.—Leaves large and very dark green; fruit very large, sometimes weighing one pound; color creamy yellow, with a pale red cheek in the sun; flesh pale yellow, coarse, but of good vinous flavor, juicy enough, but has a little too much prussic acid flavor. Tree a very vigorous grower; flowers large. Ripens August 10th.

White English Cling.—Glands globose; flowers small; fruit very large, oval; suture slight, with a swollen point; skin clear, creamy white, with a slight hue of red in the sun; flesh white, free from red at the stone, to which it firmly adheres; very rich, juicy, and high flavored; as it is free from color, one of the best for preserving in brandy or sugar. Ripens August 20th.

Baugh.—Leaves with globose glands; fruit medium, roundish, terminated with a small point; suture slight; skin pale yellow, nearly white, with a slight blush toward the sun; flesh pale yellow, melting, and juicy, with a sweet, pleasant flavor. *Free.* Ripens October 1st.

Baldwin's Late.—Fruit large and round, with a swollen point; skin greenish-white, with a pale red cheek; flesh firm, juicy, and melting, and good flavored. Ripe October 20th, and will keep for several weeks in the house. *Free.*

Pride of Autumn.—Glands reniform; flowers large; fruit medium size, oval; skin white, with a red cheek; flesh white and firm; flavor vinous, juicy. A fair October. Cling.

Eaton's Golden Cling.—A premium peach from N. Carolina; flowers large; fruit large, and resembles Crawford's Late in appearance; color bright yellow, marbled with bright red, dark on the sunny side. The best late Cling we have yet seen. Ripens October 10th.

PEAR.—(*Pyrus communis.*)

The pear is often found growing wild in hedges in various parts of Europe, China, and Western Asia. It is a thorny tree, with upright branches, tending to the pyramidal form. The wild fruit is exceedingly harsh and astringent; but no fruit whatever is more delicious, sugary, and melting, than its best improved varieties. The pear was early brought into cultivation; there were thirty-two varieties in Pliny's time, yet they were "but a heavy fruit, unless boiled or baked," and it was not before the seventeenth century that it became really worthy of culture for the dessert. Indeed, the majority of the best varieties have originated within the last fifty years. The pear, under favorable circumstances, is a long-lived tree. The Endicott pear tree, still living in Danvers, Mass., was planted by Gov. Endicott, in 1628, or eight years after the landing of the Pilgrims.

M. Bosc mentions trees in Europe which are known to be 400 years old. Even in this State, trees that were in full bearing forty years ago are still healthy, vigorous, and productive. It will endure, in suitable soils, greater extremes of heat than the apple, succeeding well in latitudes too warm for the latter fruit to flourish. It is better adapted to southern climates than the apple, while in cold climates it succeeds as well.

The pear is the most delicious of fruits for the dessert; and, in this latitude, by choosing proper varieties, we are able to have them ten or eleven months of the year. The finer kinds often sell in the cities for one or two dollars per dozen. It is excellent for baking, preserves, and marmalade. It may be dried like the apple and peach, and, with or without sugar, will keep for years. Perry is made from the juice, as cider from the apple. The wood is fine-grained and compact, and, dyed black, is used in place of ebony.

Dessert pears should have a sugary, aromatic juice, and a soft, melting, subliquid texture. Some few of a crisp, firm, or breaking consistency, are very good. Pears for stewing or baking should be large, firm-fleshed, and moderately juicy. The harsh, austere kinds are thought best for perry.

Gathering and Preserving the Fruit.—Most varieties of the pear are much better if picked from the tree before fully ripe, and ripened in the house. Indeed, some few kinds, like the Heathcote, Bartlett, and Van Assche will ripen well if gathered at any time after they are half grown. When a few begin to turn yellow and ripen on the tree, then gather the whole crop.

Many of the most delicious varieties, if allowed to

ripen on the tree, become dry, insipid, and only second or third rate. They will also ripen more gradually, last longer, and be less liable to loss or injury, if ripened in the house. It is said, however, a few varieties do best to ripen on the tree. When gathered, some few kinds ripen more perfectly by exposing them to the light and air. Most of them do best, however, in kegs or small boxes, or on the shelves of a cool, dark fruit room, each one separately enveloped in paper or loose cotton. This is not necessary with the summer varieties. Pears, like apples, must be gathered by hand, with the same precaution to prevent bruises, or they will soon decay. Winter pears should hang as long as may be upon the tree. A week or two before their proper time to ripen, bring them from the fruit room into a warm apartment; this will much improve their flavor.

Propagation and Culture.—Pears are propagated by budding or grafting on seedling pear stocks or on certain varieties of the quince. Pear suckers should never be employed for this purpose, for they seldom have good roots, and the trees are short-lived; a great deal of prejudice exists against pear culture from this cause. Seedlings raised from the thrifty-growing kinds that are found about the country are much more healthy than those raised from the improved varieties.

Sow the seed thickly in autumn, in drills eighteen inches apart, or, better still, mix the seed with sifted sand in a box, and place it out doors during winter, and sow in the spring, when they begin to sprout, in good, rich earth; the latter mode saves the seed from being destroyed by ground mice.

Ashes are an excellent application to the seed bed; the soil should be moist, as much of the value of the stocks depends on vigorous and continued growth the first season. Take up the stocks in November or December, shorten the tap-root, and reset them in rows four feet apart, putting those together which are of about the same size. The best of them, if in a good, rich soil, will be fit to bud during the next summer, and nearly all the balance can be whip-grafted the ensuing spring.

Many kinds of pears grow well on the quince, and come some years earlier into bearing. We have found the common quince to be equally as good as the Angers, when worked side by side with them. The fruit produced from trees worked on the quince is usually larger and better flavored than on the pear, and the trees can be set much nearer together. They come into bearing in two or three years, but are not as long-lived as when worked on the pear stock. In planting the trees, on pear stocks, they should be set twenty feet apart; but as these will be several years before they come into bearing, the spaces should be filled up with dwarf trees, growing on the quince stock, so as to have them, when planted, ten feet apart. Thus a plantation of sixteen trees, set in a square, on the pear stock, would require thirty-three on the quince to fill the intervals—making a square of seven trees on a side. This will prevent the attacks of the quince borer, and add to the longevity of the tree.

The soil must be kept clean and well tilled; but it should not be deeply spaded within two feet of the trunks of the trees. No fruit tree will be healthy or bear well if the ground is deeply spaded near its stem. The pear likes a deep, strong loam, similar to that required by the apple. Iron is beneficial; hence the pear succeeds well in our red clay loam, if deeply dug and sufficiently manured. For pears on the quince stock, the soil should be deep and cool. From the analysis of the wood and bark of the pear tree, it is apparent that wood ashes and superphosphate of lime cannot but be very beneficial to the growth and fruitfulness of the pear.

In pruning the pear, the object is to make it throw out

branches within a foot of the ground, and to encourage its growth in its natural pyramidal shape.

Not much pruning is required the first year; but any shoot that, by over-growth, threatens to destroy the beauty of the tree should be pinched in at once. When the tree is transplanted, if it has been out of the ground for any length of time it must be severely shortened in. If the tree has good roots, the top will soon be renewed. Severe pruning at this time is the only way to make the tree branch out near the ground, so as to shade the trunk and give a fine pyramidal shape. To secure this, plant maiden trees, or those one year old from the bud. When they have grown one year, cut back the branches in the winter; pinch in any shoots, during the summer, that would mar the symmetry of the tree, or remove them entirely, if superfluous.

Head back the leader each year, to strengthen the side branches. The leader must be shortened more or less, according to its vigor. A little practice will enable any one of ordinary judgment to form his trees in the desired shape. Do not let the branches remain so close together that, when they come to bear, they will cause the fruit and foliage in the interior to suffer from want of air; keep the lower shoots the longest by pinching those above, when disposed to overgrow them. This makes a beautiful tree, ornamental even for a flower garden.

The great obstacle in pear culture is the blight, a disease whose virulence is almost peculiar to this fruit tree. The causes are not well known; some attribute it to insects, others to electrical causes, and others to atmospheric causes, and yet others to late and immature growth of wood, which is frozen the subsequent winter.

Yet, notwithstanding all these theories and proposed remedies, the blight goes on from year to year with unabated violence.

With us, the past three years have been particularly

disastrous, for, out of some two hundred and fifty trees, not more than twenty have escaped the pestilence. The frozen sap theory has been a very plausible and favorite one with Northern pomologists, but is not the correct one, for the reason that the sap never freezes here in our warm climate.

There is but one remedy for the disease that we have ever had any success with, and that is the free use of the saw and knife. Cut off the diseased limb, or trunk, a foot below the lowest affected spot, and you may sometimes save the life of the tree, but not always.

Whenever the leaves begin to wither, or the tree ceases growing, at once examine the trunk and larger limbs for the gangrened spot, which is sure to be on one or both; when you have once discovered the diseased spot, don't hesitate, but amputate it at once; it will result in the death of the tree if you let it go on, and it can do no more if you kill it by a surgical operation.

We have thus far found no difference in good, bad, and indifferent cultivation. In our vegetable garden, where the soil is rich and well cultivated, we have lost by blight, within the last three years, at least three-fourths of our trees, and in our orchard, in sod, and in moderate cultivation, about the same proportion. Dwarfs and standard trees have fared alike.

Query.—Have we not poisoned the whole race of pears by working it on the quince stock? For this tree is subject to the same disease, and when it attacks it, it usually dies. If so, how are we to get out of the scrape? Sowing seeds and raising new ones will not help us; for the seeds themselves are impregnated with the virus, which will, sooner or later, manifest itself. The only remedy will be to go back to such trees as the Endicott, Dix, and Seckel; sow the seeds from these, and get a new, pure, and unadulterated race to begin with, and keep them clear from the quince stock.

A greater number of varieties of the pear are in cultivation than of any other fruit. Of those that have fruited here, the following are the most desirable. The varieties do not always observe with us the order as laid down in the books:

Joannet.—The earliest pear with us, ripening in May; but it is small, and of indifferent quality, though it bears well, and is desirable to fill out the season.

Madeleine comes next in succession; fruit medium, obovate, tapering to the stem, which is long and slender, set on the side of a small swelling; skin smooth, yellowish-green; calyx small, in a shallow basin; flesh white, melting, juicy, sweet, and perfumed. Ripe from the 1st to the 15th of June.

Abercromby.—A seedling from Alabama; size medium to large; ovate in form; greenish-gray color, with a blush cheek; flesh white, juicy, and rich; stem short and fleshy; the best large early pear we have. Ripens June 10th. Tree a poor grower.

Doyenne d'Eté.—Fruit small, roundish, slightly turbinate; skin smooth, light yellow, shaded with bright red, sprinkled with small gray or russet dots; stalk rather short, thick, fleshy where inserted in the fruit, in a very slight depression; calyx small, partly closed in a shallow,

Fig. 90.—DOYENNE D'ETE.

slightly corrugated basin; flesh white, melting, juicy, and sweet. The best very early pear; ripens with, and supe-

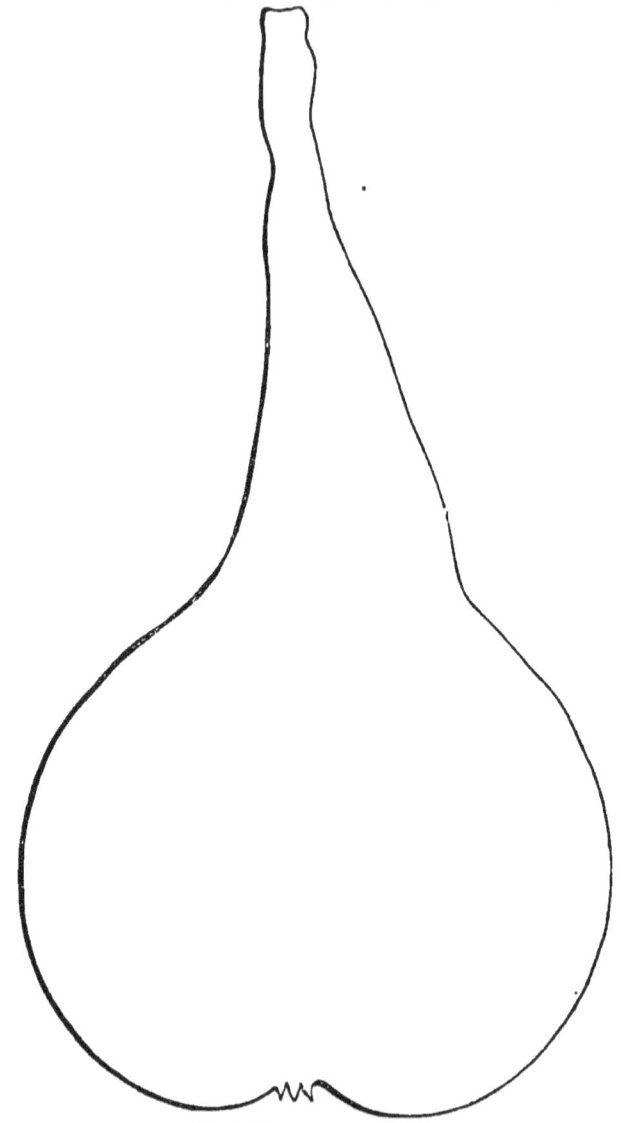

Fig. 100.—BEURRE BOSC.

rior to, the Madeleine; in Georgia early in June, in New York last of July. Tree vigorous; an early and profuse bearer; leaves long, oval, pointed, and dark green; seeds dark.

Beurre Bosc.—Fruit large, pyriform, somewhat uneven, tapering gradually to the stalk; skin smooth, dark yellow, nearly covered with rich cinnamon russet; stalk varies sometimes, being large and fleshy, as in the figure, or long, rather slender, and curved; flesh white, melting, buttery, abounding in rich, sugary, and delicious juice, slightly perfumed. Ripens, Georgia, in September and into October; New York, October and November. Tree healthy and productive.

Louise Bonne de Jersey.—Fruit large, oblong, pyriform; skin smooth, glossy, pale green in the shade, brownish-red in the sun, sprinkled thickly with minute dots; stalk about an inch long, obliquely inserted without depression or with a fleshy base; calyx small, open, with rather long segments, in a shallow, uneven basin; flesh greenish-white, very juicy and melting, and excellent. Ripens, Georgia, August 10th, and through the month; New York, September and October. The tree

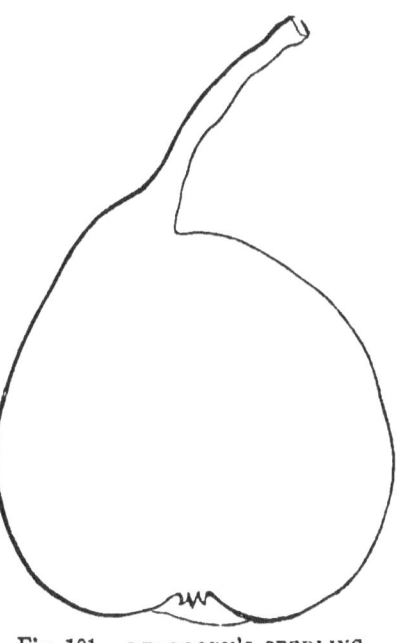

Fig. 101.—DEARBORN'S SEEDLING.

is an upright, vigorous grower, forming a fine pyramid. The fruit is much better on the quince than on the pear.

Dearborn's Seedling.—Tree vigorous, with long, dark brown shoots, fruitful and healthy; fruit small, turbinate, regular; skin very smooth, clear light yellow, sprinkled with minute dots; stalk an inch or more long, sometimes erect, inserted in a slight depression, but in my specimens generally as in the figure; calyx with spreading segments, in a shallow basin; flesh white, fine grained, juicy, and melting, sweet and sprightly, not rich. Ripens in Georgia, early in July; in New York, middle of August; valuable.

Bloodgood.—Fruit medium, turbinate, (at the South often oblate,) generally thickening abruptly to the stalk; skin yellow, considerably russeted in dots and net-work patches; calyx large, open, in a slight depression; stalk obliquely inserted, about an inch long, dark brown, fleshy at its base; flesh yellowish-white, buttery, with a rich musky aroma, melting and sweet; core small. Georgia, last of June; New York, last of July. Generally larger than in the figure.

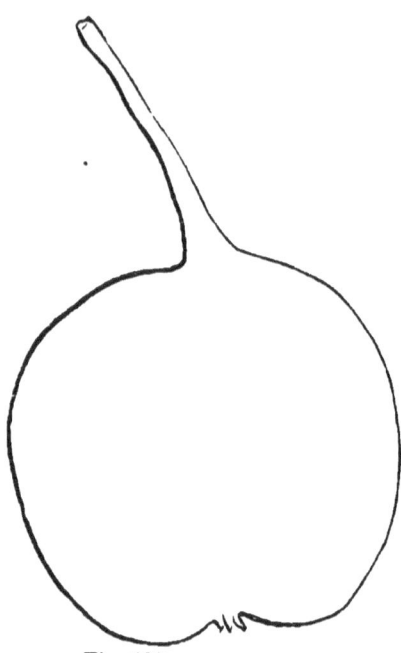

Fig. 102.—BLOODGOOD.

Manning's Elizabeth. —Growth of tree moderate; shoots reddish, dotted with brown; fruit rather small, regular oblate inclining to obovate, or Doyenne-shaped; skin smooth, bright yellow, dotted with russet, with a bright red cheek; stalk scarcely an inch long, often a little fleshy at its base, inserted in a shallow, regular cavity; calyx open, in a broad, shallow basin; flesh white, juicy, melting, with a sprightly saccharine flavor. Ripens, Georgia, July 10th; New York, middle and last of August. The best pear of its season; productive.

Bartlett.—Fruit large, irregular, knobby, obtuse-pyriform, often much more oblong than in the figure; skin very thin, smooth, clear light yellow, with a slight blush in the sun, sprinkled with minute russet dots and with

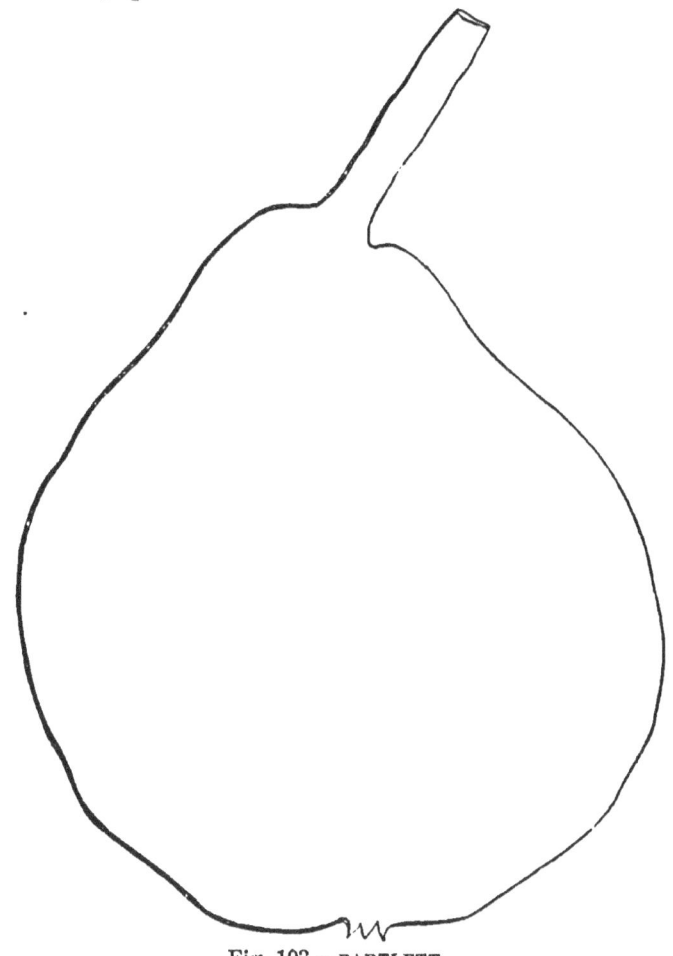

Fig. 103.—BARTLETT.

faint russet markings towards the stem; stalk about an inch long, stout, in a shallow cavity; calyx small, partly open, in a very shallow, slightly plaited basin; flesh white, exceedingly fine-grained, melting, full of agreeable, vinous juice. Ripens, Georgia, through August; New York,

September. Specimens that fall before they are fully grown, ripen nicely in the house. Sometimes too acid, but one of the most desirable sorts. Origin, England, 1770. Tree quite fruitful, and bears young.

Henry the Fourth.—Fruit varies from the size figured to small, roundish pyriform, irregular, skin pale greenish-

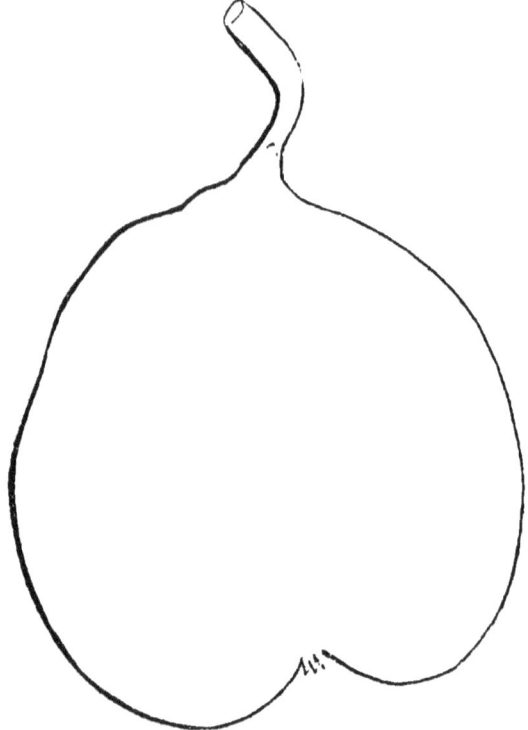

Fig. 104.—HENRY THE FOURTH.

yellow, clouded with darker green, and dotted with gray specks; stalk about an inch long, twisted obliquely, planted on an irregular prominence, or under a swollen lip; calyx small, closed; basin shallow and abrupt; flesh white, exceedingly juicy and melting, with a pleasant perfumed flavor; a dull fruit externally, but a nice dessert pear, bearing abundantly, and continues several weeks to ripen successively. Ripens, Georgia, from the 20th of July into September; New York, September.

Brandywine.—Fruit above medium, varying from oblate-depressed-pyriform to elongated pyriform; skin yellowish-green, dotted and sprinkled with russet, with a bright red cheek; stalk fleshy where it joins the fruit; calyx open; basin shallow; flesh white, juicy, melting, sugary, and somewhat aromatic. Georgia, ripe the middle of July; New York, the last of August. Growth vigorous and upright; leaves small, deep glossy green; productive.

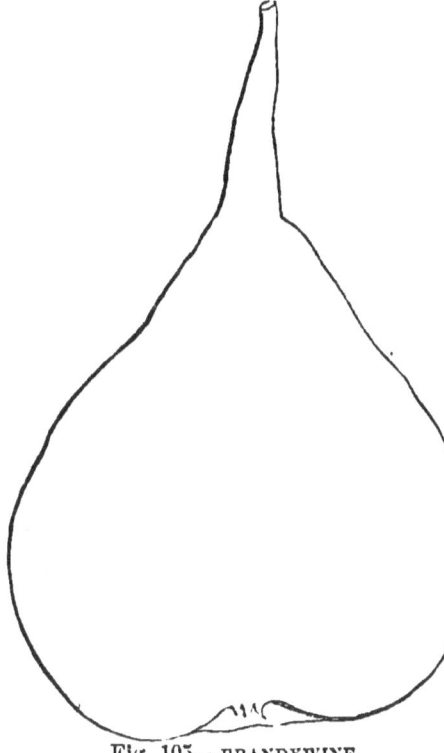

Fig. 105.—BRANDYWINE.

Doyenne, White.—The White Doyenne, or Virgalieu, is one of the most esteemed pears. Fruit medium to large size, generally larger than the figure, varying from obovate-pyriform to oblate; skin clear pale yellow, regularly sprinkled with small dots, with a fine red cheek; stalk from one-half an inch to over an inch long, generally a little curved, and planted in a small, round cavity; calyx small, closed, in a shallow, generally smooth basin; flesh white, fine-grained, buttery, melting, with a rich, delicious flavor. Ripens, Georgia in August; New York, September to December.

Selleck.—Fruit varies from obovate to obtuse-pyriform, somewhat ribbed; skin fine, rich yellow, thickly dotted and sprinkled with russet, full russet about the base of the stalk; stalk long and curved, fleshy at its insertion in a moderate cavity; calyx partly closed, in a small, uneven

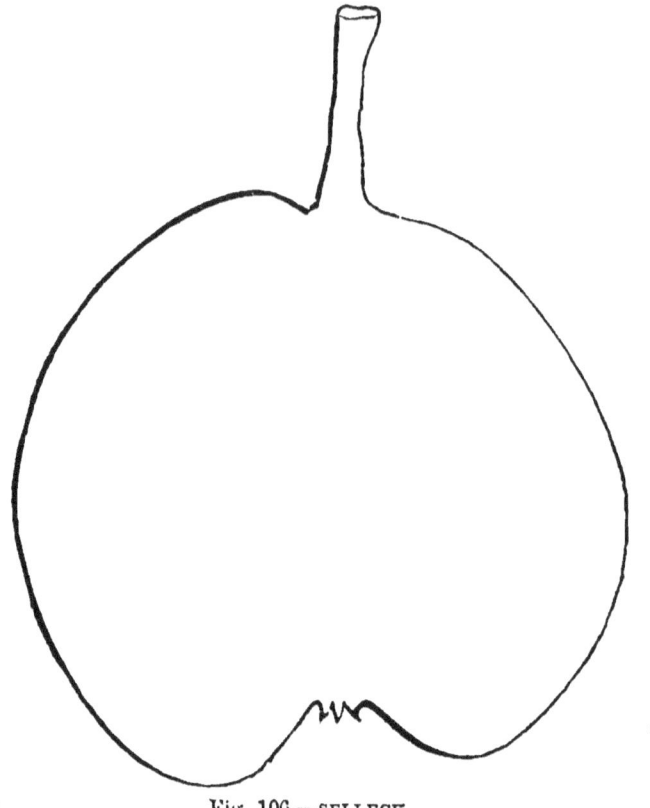

Fig. 106.—SELLECK.

basin; flesh white, firm, juicy and melting, sugary, with a rich, aromatic flavor; keeps well without decay at the core; a very valuable sort. Ripens, in Georgia, 20th of August; New York, in September.

Van Assche.—Tree vigorous and fruitful, with reddish-brown shoots and plump buds; fruit medium, or large, turbinate, inclining to conical, in very large specimens oblate; skin light yellow, with numerous russet and red dots, with a bright red cheek; stalk an inch long, rather stout, obliquely planted in a slight depression; calyx partly closed, in a broad, deep, and wrinkled basin; flesh white,

Fig. 107.—VAN ASSCHE.

fine-grained, juicy, with a delicate blending of sweet and acid, and a rich, excellent flavor. Ripens, August in Georgia; October, in New York; generally larger than the engraving.

Nabours.—Fruit medium to large, varying from oblate to obovate and obscure pyriform; skin greenish, rough, often with dull russet, and sprinkled with white dots; stalk slender, long, curved a little, fleshy at the base, and set in a slight depression; calyx small, partly closed, set in a deep, narrow basin: flesh whitish, melting, fine-grained, buttery, abounding in sugary juice. Where suffered to overbear, or hang too long upon the tree, it lacks flavor; otherwise good. From North Carolina. Tree healthy and vigorous, with stout shoots; very productive.

Duchesse d'Angoulême.—Fruit very large, obovate, varying from oblong to oblate, with a knobby, uneven surface; skin dull greenish-yellow, dotted and spotted with russet; stalk about an inch long, quite stout, set with an inclination in a rather deep cavity; calyx closed, set in a narrow, somewhat knobby basin; flesh white, buttery, very juicy, with a rich, sugary flavor. Excellent for so large a pear. Brings the very highest prices in market. Ripens, Georgia, the latter half of August into September; New York, in October. From France.

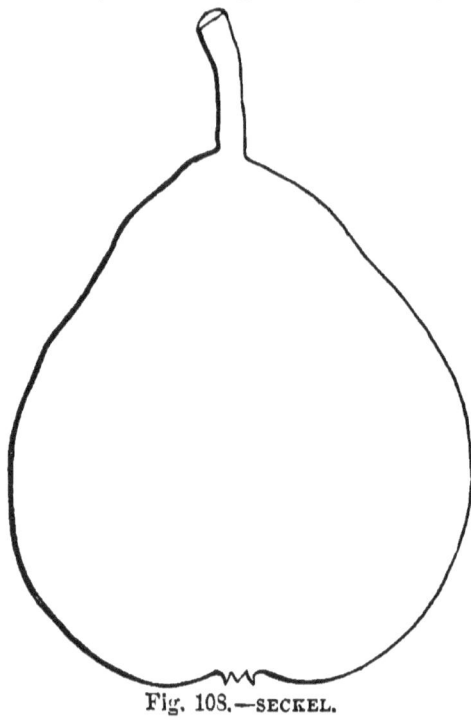

Fig. 108.—SECKEL.

Seckel.—Fruit small, generally obovate; skin at first brownish-green, at last becoming yellowish-brown, with a bright red, russet cheek; stalk half to three-fourths of an inch long, slightly curved, set in a slight depression; calyx small, open, in a very shallow basin; flesh whitish, buttery, very fine-grained and melting, filled with rich, sugary, aromatic juice. Ripens, Georgia, the last half of August and into September; New York, September and October,

Tree of slow growth, but remarkably healthy and productive. Origin, Philadelphia. This is by many considered, and perhaps justly, the very best variety of pear.

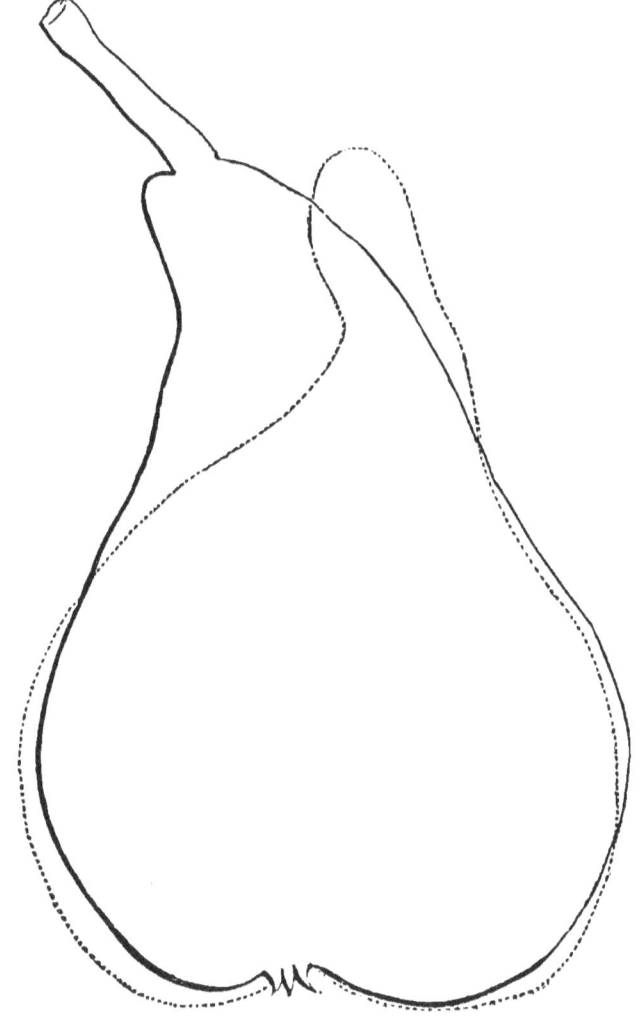

Fig. 100.—BEURRE CLAIRGEAU.

Beurre Clairgeau.—Fruit large, pyriform, with unequal sides; skin warm yellow, inclining to fawn, thickly sprinkled with large, yellow dots, with russet tracings and spots, shaded with orange and crimson; stalk short and stout, often fleshy, and inserted by a lip at an inclination, or in an uneven cavity; calyx open, with stiff segments; flesh yellowish, buttery, very melting and juicy, with a sugary, vinous flavor. Ripens, Georgia, September to October 10th; New York, October to January. A beautiful fruit, often so much larger and broader than the cut, that it could not be figured on this page. Tree vigorous, and an early and profuse bearer.

Compte de Flandre.—Fruit large, pyriform; skin yellowish, dotted and marked with russet, particularly about the stalk; stalk long, inclined in a shallow, plaited, russeted cavity; calyx open, set in a shallow basin; flesh whitish, buttery, juicy, a little coarse or granular, rich, but somewhat astringent near the skin. Ripens, Georgia, the middle of September and lasts into October; New York, November. This pear considerably resembles Passe Colmar, which it excels in size and flavor.

Belle Lucrative.—Fruit medium, obovate to obscure pyriform; skin pale yellowish-green, with dots and traces of russet; stem varying from short, stout, and fleshy, to more than an inch long, often obliquely inserted in a slight cavity; calyx open, in a medium basin; flesh fine-grained, melting, full of rich, sugary, and delicious juice. Ripens, Georgia, in August; New York, last of September. A Flemish variety. Tree of moderate growth, very fruitful, and bears young; one of the very best.

St. Michael Archangel.—Fruit above medium size, obovate-pyriform; skin smooth, shining, greenish-yellow, sprinkled with russet dots; stalk an inch long, inclined, fleshy at its insertion, and surrounded by russet; calyx small and closed; basin small and uneven; flesh yellowish-white, tender and melting, abundant in sugary juice, with an agreeable perfume; an excellent fruit. Tree healthy, vigorous, and fruitful. Ripe, Georgia, last of August; New York, October.

Catherine Gardette.—Fruit roundish-obovate, sometimes obscure pyriform; skin light yellow, with russet dots and markings, with carmine dots to the sun; stalk an inch long, curved, a little fleshy at its base, inserted in a slight, generally russeted, depression; calyx small, in a

Fig. 110.—STERLING.

narrow basin; flesh fine, buttery, melting, sweet, and with a delicate perfume. Ripens, Georgia, early in October.

Sterling.—Fruit medium, and varying from oblate to obovate, or obscure pyriform; skin yellow, with a few russet patches, and a mottled crimson cheek; stalk medium, inserted in a slightly plaited cavity; calyx small, open, in a medium basin; flesh somewhat coarse, juicy, melting, with a sugary, brisk flavor. Ripens, Georgia,

July 15th; New York, the last of August. Keeps a long time after gathering, and is an excellent fruit to send to a distant market. Very desirable. Tree vigorous and upright, with yellowish-brown wood. An early and productive bearer.

Beurre Richelieu.—Fruit large, pyriform, sometimes truncate; skin greenish, changing to yellow, with russet dots and markings; stalk short, fleshy at the base, inserted by a lip and inclined, in a broad depression; calyx small, closed, in a furrowed basin; flesh buttery, melting, juicy, with a fine, sweet, aromatic flavor. Georgia, October; New York, December. Tree vigorous and productive.

Passe Colmar.—Fruit large, varying from obovate to obtuse-pyriform; skin rather thick, yellowish-green, turning yellow when mature, a good deal russeted about the eye and at the base of the stalk; stalk rather long, often fleshy at its base, inserted in an uneven cavity; calyx open, in a slight, regular basin; flesh yellowish, fine, melting, and juicy, with a sweet, rich, aromatic flavor. A rapid grower and profuse bearer, but if the fruit is not well thinned, it will be small and astringent. Georgia, October and November; New York, December.

Glout Morceau.—Fruit large, varying in form from obovate to obtuse-pyriform, and often depressed somewhat; skin pale greenish-yellow, marked with small dots, russeted about the stem, with a brownish cheek on the more exposed fruits; stem long, slender, in a slight cavity; calyx mostly open, in a rather deep basin; flesh white, fine-grained, very melting, juicy, sugary, and perfumed. A fine, pyramidal, healthy grower, and quite fruitful. Georgia, October and November; New York, December.

Josephine de Malines.—Fruit medium, truncate, obconic; skin yellowish, somewhat russeted, especially about the base and crown, and sprinkled with russet dots; stalk long, stout, curved, inserted in a moderate, russet-lined cavity; calyx small, open, with caducous segments, in a slight basin; flesh greenish-white, buttery, very juicy, sugary, melting, and perfumed. An excellent keeper. Georgia, October to January, and has been kept until

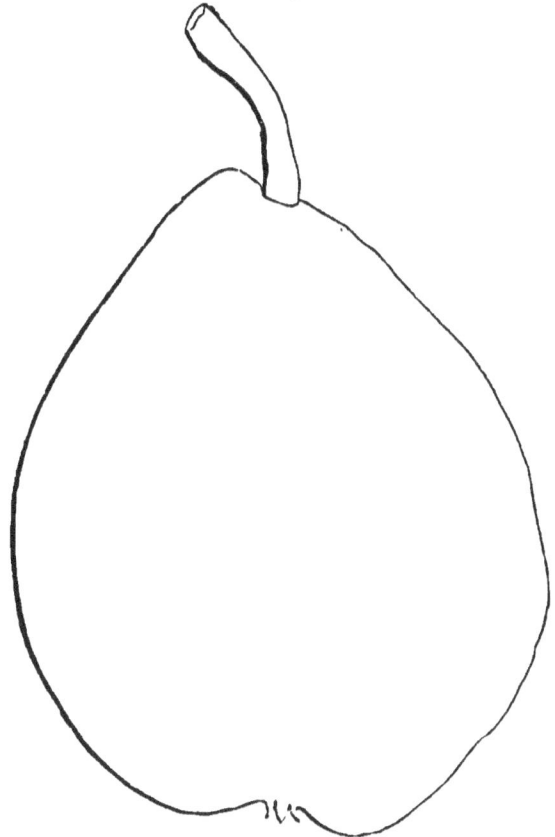

Fig. 111.—SOLDAT LABOUREUR.

March; New York, November, and through the winter. Tree productive and vigorous.

Soldat Laboureur.—Tree vigorous, with upright, chestnut-colored wood, and succeeds well on the quince. Fruit rather large, oblique-pyriform, largest toward the centre; skin smooth, pale yellow when ripe, shaded with thin greenish-russet; stalk rather stout, about an inch long, curved, inserted in a small, abrupt, russet-lined cavity; calyx open, scarcely sunk in a slight basin; flesh yellowish, a little granular, melting, juicy, sugary, rich, and perfumed. One of the very finest, ripening a little later than the Columbia. Georgia, the middle of September; New York, October and November.

Belle Epine Dumas.—Fruit medium or large, long-pyriform; skin green, becoming greenish-yellow as it ripens, with small brown dots, and at the South is generally somewhat marked with russet about the base and stem; stalk long, rather stout, curved a little, swollen at the base, inserted in a slight depression; calyx small, partly closed, in a shallow, regular basin; flesh white, fine, melting, juicy, rich, sugary, and perfumed; core medium, with large, long, pointed seeds. Georgia, October; New York, November and December.

Parsonage.—Fruit medium or large, obovate, inclining to obtuse-pyriform; skin warm yellow, rough, often shaded with dull crimson, netted and thickly dotted with russet; stalk short, stout, curved, fleshy at its insertion; calyx open, with short, stiff segments, in a russeted, shallow basin; flesh white, somewhat coarse, granular, sugary, and refreshing. In Georgia it has kept until November. Tree fruitful and healthy.

Beurré Gris d'Hiver Noveau.—Fruit medium to large, obovate-truncate, obscurely pyriform; skin pale yellow, mostly overspread with golden russet, with a crimson cheek; stalk stout, inclined and curved, inserted by a lip, or in a slight wrinkled depression; calyx open, in a moderate basin; flesh somewhat granular, buttery, melting, abundant in rich, sugary juice, with a peculiar aroma. Georgia, October; New York, November to February.

Doyenne d'Alençon.—Fruit medium, varying from roundish oval to obovate or pyriform; skin rough yellow, shaded with dull crimson, dotted thickly and sprinkled with russet; stalk rather short, stout, in a medium cavity; calyx small, mostly closed; flesh somewhat granular, buttery, juicy, sugary, rich, sprightly, and perfumed. Georgia, November to January; New York, December to March.

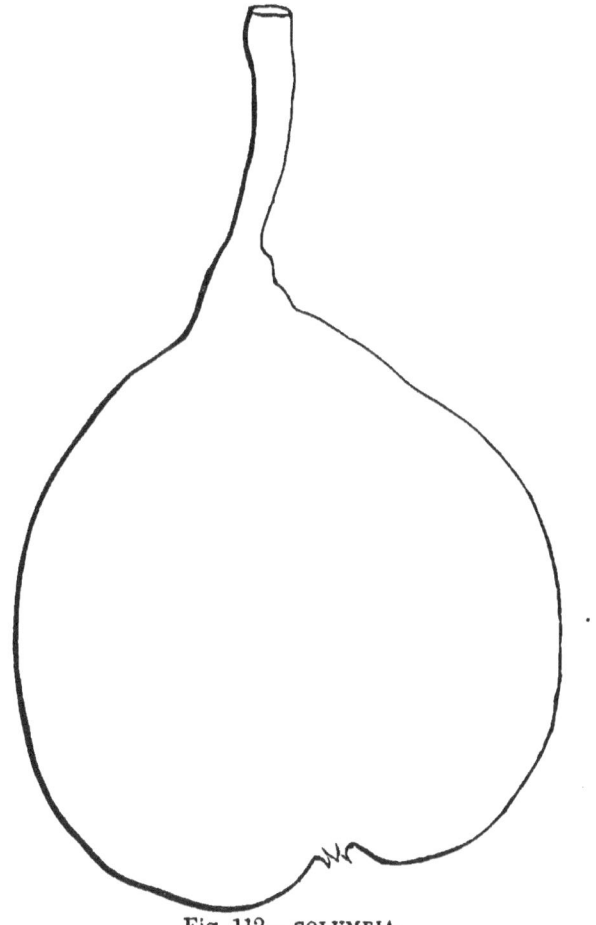

Fig. 112.—COLUMBIA.

Columbia.—Fruit large, oblong-obovate, or pyriform, often simply obovate, broadest in the middle; skin smooth, pale green, turning yellowish when ripe, with a soft brown check, dotted with russet, with a little russet also about the stalk and calyx; stalk about an inch long,

18*

rather stout, slightly curved; calyx small, partly closed, in a shallow basin; flesh white, fine-grained, melting, and abundant in rich, sugary juice. Ripens, in Georgia, from the 15th of August to the last of September, and is not

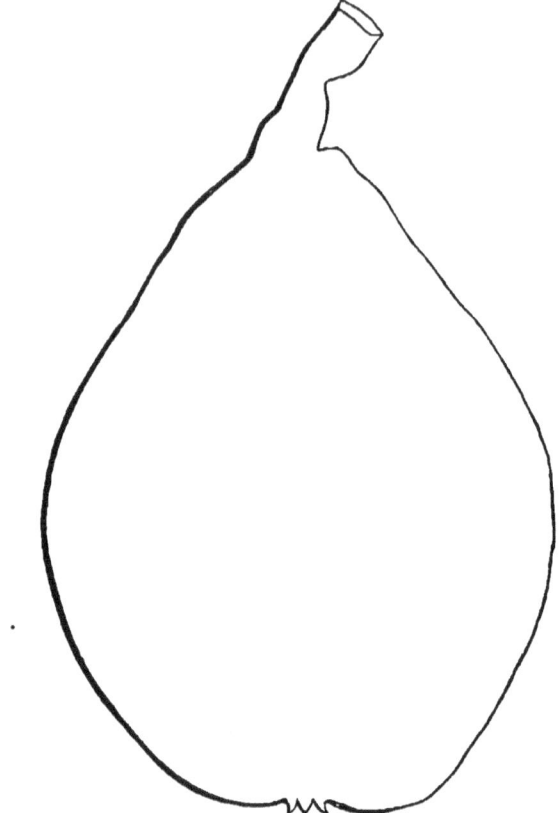

Fig. 113.—ST. GERMAIN.

excelled by any other pear; in New York, November, and is said to be variable there, but generally fine.

St. Germain.—Fruit large, irregular, oval-pyriform, tapering to the eye and stalk; skin yellowish-green, a good deal covered with russet, with a brown cheek; stem stout, swollen at its insertion, generally planted obliquely by the side of a small, fleshy swelling; calyx small, open, in a very shallow basin; flesh yellowish-white, a little gritty, melting, juicy, rich, and sugary. Georgia, October and November; New York, November and December. This is one of the most desirable pears grown at the South. Tree healthy and productive, and the smallest fruits always of excellent flavor.

Winter Nelis.—Fruit medium to small, varying from oblate to roundish obovate; skin yellowish-green, but generally a good deal covered with russet; stalk an inch long, curved, and planted in a narrow cavity; calyx open, in a shallow basin, with stiff, short segments; flesh pale yellowish-white, fine-grained, buttery and melting, abounding in rich, sugary, aromatic juice. Ripens, Georgia, in October; New York, Dec.

Fig. 114.—WINTER NELIS.

Lawrence.—Fruit large, obovate, obscurely pyriform; stalk rather short, inclined, inserted by a lip or in a slight, regular depression; cavity generally partly closed, in a broad shallow basin; skin fine lemon yellow, uneven, sprinkled thickly with small dots; flesh white, a little granular, buttery, with a very rich, sugary, aromatic flavor. Georgia, September 20th to October 20th; New York, November to January. Tree of moderate growth, very healthy; an early and abundant bearer. Far the most desirable pear of its season.

Easter Beurré.—Fruit large, obovate or obtuse-pyriform; skin yellowish-green, sprinkled with large russet dots, and marbled somewhat with greenish-russet; stalk rather stout, in abrupt cavity; calyx usually small, closed, in a plaited basin; flesh white, fine-grained, buttery, juicy,

Fig. 115.—EASTER BEURRE.

and sweet. Georgia, November to March; New York, January to May. Succeeds best on quince.

Jaminette.—Fruit large, varying in form from obovate, narrowing to the stalk, to oblate; skin green, turning to pale yellowish-green when ripe, dotted with brown, and marked with russet; stalk rather short, obliquely planted in a slight depression, (in obovate specimens without depression,) and surrounded with russet; calyx small, open, in a slight basin; flesh white, a little gritty at the core, juicy, buttery, and sweet. A good fruit, but must be eaten as it begins to soften, or will be found decayed at the core. Georgia, October.

PLUM.—(*Prunus Domestica.*)

The plum tree is probably a native of Asia, whence it was early introduced into European gardens. The tree grows from fifteen to twenty feet high, and is conspicuous early in spring for its white blossoms.

Loudon asserts that it is probable the natural color of the fruit is black; but the cultivated varieties are of various shades of green, yellow, red, and blue. It is a delicious dessert fruit, in its best varieties, and is very much esteemed for pies, tarts, and preserves.

It is also dried for winter use. The prune, or dried plum, enters considerably into commerce. When fully ripe, plums are, in moderate quantity, very nutritious and wholesome, but in an unripe state are more apt to disagree with the stomach than most other fruits.

Prunes are dried by artificial heat. They are laid singly, without touching each other, on plates, which are placed in ovens, after the bread is removed, or in kilns prepared for the purpose, and occasionally moved and turned. In order to have them fair and glossy, they must be suddenly cooled when taken from the oven. They should be dried carefully and gradually. They are excellent when dried with sugar, as directed for peaches. From the analysis of the stones, bark, leaves, and wood, it is evident that common salt is one of the most essential manures to apply to the soil in which the plum is cultivated. Burnt clay, swamp muck, common salt, and wood ashes, are among the best fertilizers.

Propagation and Culture.—The plum is generally budded or grafted upon stocks raised from the seed of some free-growing variety. The Chickasaw plum, however, makes a very good stock; it should be grafted at the collar, and transplanted so deep that the scions can throw out roots. This stock makes very pretty dwarf trees for the garden. By this mode, the tree can be propagated at any time during the winter months.

Stone fruits require to be grafted early in the season. In transplanting where they are to remain they should be twelve feet apart. The best soil for the plum is a heavy clay loam, moderately rich. The fruit is better in a clay soil than in a sandy one, and when planted in a sandy soil, clay should be added. There are three obstacles to be overcome in raising the plum successfully. The first and greatest is the curculio, which infests all the smooth-skinned stone fruits.

The Curculio, or Plum Weevil, (*Conotrachelus Nenuphar,*) is a short, thick, rough beetle, of a dark brown or blackish color, varied with spots of white and yellow; with a long snout hanging down in front like an elephant's trunk. It makes a small, crescent-like incision upon the side of the plum and cherry, just after they are set, in which it drops an egg. From this is hatched a small, white, footless worm, which bores into the fruit, causing it to drop prematurely from the tree. The worm enters the ground, and in three or four weeks comes out, and the successive broods attack the plum, apricot, cherry, nectarine, and peach, until the fruit ripens. Their incisions have been found in the limbs of the pear tree. The beetle, if discovered, feigns death, and can hardly be distinguished from the dried flower buds by careless observers. The instinct of the curculio leads it to avoid puncturing fruit that hangs over a beaten path, a hard, paved surface, a pond of water, or pigsty, where the larva would be unable to enter the soil or would be destroyed by enemies. It is not so destructive in clayey or hard soils. The remedy that has hitherto proved most successful is to pave the ground so that the grub cannot enter it to complete his transformation. Picking or sweeping up the fruit as fast as it drops, and boiling it for pigs, before the worm can enter the earth, has also been found beneficial; likewise jarring the tree (by striking sharply with a mallet on the stump of a limb removed for the purpose) as soon as the fruit is the size of a pea, and collecting the insects on a white sheet as they fall, and destroying them. As the insects are torpid in the morning, that is the best time for the operation, which should be kept up until the fruit be-

Fig. 116.—CURCULIO MAGNIFIED.

begins to ripen. Plant all stone fruits in an enclosure by themselves in which pigs and poultry are admitted; these will collect the fruit as fast as it falls, and tread the ground firmly together, so that it is not easy for the insects to enter it. None of these methods will be fully effectual if there are neglected trees near by from which the insect may emigrate. The most *reliable* of them is jarring the trees, and destroying the insects daily; the next is giving access to a large flock of ducks and chickens, which, destroying the perfect insect, are a much more efficient remedy than the pigs alone. It is, perhaps, fortunate to have the crop entirely cut off by frost, as often as every third year, in order to check, for a time, the rapid increase of this pest of the orchard.

Another serious difficulty is the rot; to prevent this, the varieties least subject should be selected and planted, with the roots not too deep, and the fruit thinned, if very abundant upon the tree.

The third obstacle to plum culture is, happily, not very prevalent in the South. It is a black knot, or excrescence, growing upon the bark and young wood. The bark swells and bursts, and finally assumes the appearance of a "large, irregular lump, with a hard, cracked, uneven surface." The flow of sap is obstructed by this tumor, and its poison is gradually disseminated over the whole tree. The dark-colored fruits are most infected. The disease also attacks the common Morello cherry. It appeared here, for the first time, in the year 1853, on a tree from the North. None have appeared since that time. The only remedy is to cut off every branch or twig that shows a tumor, and burn it at once. As the plum throws out long, straggling branches, which are unsightly and unproductive, this should be remedied by shortening in, as with the peach, so as to form a round, compact head. Most stone fruits require to be shortened in, more or less, or the growth becomes unsightly and the tree short-lived. It is an excellent plan, where practicable, to plant a tree or two near the door of the house and kitchen, where there is considerable passing and repassing and the ground becomes hard-trodden. Such trees are less infested by the great enemy to stone fruit—the curculio—which is quite a timid, as well as cunning, insect.

VARIETIES.

Chickasaw.—(*Prunus Chickasa.*)—A tree or two of both red and yellow varieties of this, our indigenous plum, should be admitted into the garden. The fruit is much improved, both in size and flavor, by cultivation. Some trees produce better fruit than others. Leaves lanceolate, and more like the peach than the plum; branches thorny; fruit small; skin either light red or yellow; flesh yellow, very juicy and sweet, but somewhat astringent about the stone, to which it adheres. Ripe here about the 20th of May; lasts a month. Doubtless many excellent varieties will be originated from this hardy native fruit. Some are now found nearly free from astringency. This plum appears to be free from curculio, and never fails to ripen a crop.

Sea, or Early Purple.—Ripens 8th of June, and is here the earliest of plums; fruit small, roundish; skin brownish-purple, with a slight bloom; flesh greenish-yellow, sweet, juicy, and parts from the stone; highly perfumed. This nice little plum was, I believe, first introduced here by some grafts received from Germany. It does not rot.

Prince's Yellow Gage.—Fruit medium size, broadest toward the stalk; suture slight; skin golden yellow, slightly clouded, and with copious white bloom; stalk an inch long, inserted in a small cavity; flesh deep yellow, sweet, juicy, and fine flavored; freestone; tree very productive; fruit lasts a long time; one of the best for a long time in this climate. Ripe June 10th.

Bingham.—Fruit large, oval; skin deep yellow, spotted with red toward the sun; stalk in a small cavity; flesh yellow, juicy, rich, and delicious; clingstone; tree a fine grower and good bearer. Ripens July 1st.

Columbia.—Very large, roundish; skin brownish-purple, with fawn-colored specks; bloom thick and blue; stalk an inch long, stout, in a narrow cavity; flesh orange, not very juicy, sugary, rich, and excellent; freestone. Ripe June 20th. A magnificent variety, of excellent quality. Tree hardy and productive.

Elfry.—Branches small; fruit less than medium size, oval; skin blue; flesh greenish, sweet, juicy, and excellent; freestone. In this climate, the Elfry is one of the most desirable of plums. It generally escapes the curculio and the rot, if properly thinned. Tree thrifty and hardy. An indispensable variety. Ripe July 1st.

Jefferson.—Fruit of the largest size, roundish oval; stalk an inch long, pretty stout; suture distinct; skin golden yellow, purplish-red on the sunny side, and thinly covered with white bloom; flesh deep orange, a little dry, good; not equal to the description in the books. As the tree bears abundantly, and the fruit ripens late, hangs long on the tree, and is entirely free from decay, it is indispensable. The handsomest of all plums. Ripens last of July and first of August.

Red Magnum Bonum, or Purple Egg.—Large and beautiful; egg-shaped; violet red, deeper in the sun, with small gray dots; flesh greenish, rather firm, juicy, and agreeably sub-acid; freestone. A fair plum for the table, and makes the best of preserves. Ripens July 10th. Not much subject to rot.

Washington.—Tree vigorous; leaves large, broad, glossy, and rumpled; wood light brown; fruit very large, roundish oval; suture shallow, except at the stalk; skin pale greenish-yellow, faintly marbled with green, changing at maturity to darker yellow, with a bright blush in the sun; stalk short, in a shallow, wide cavity; flesh yellow, firm, sweet, and luscious; stone pointed, and separates freely. Ripens, Georgia, early in July; New York, the latter half of August. This is one of the most attractive and desirable varieties in all sections.

Harvest Gage.—Fruit rather small, roundish oval, with a slight suture; skin pale yellowish-green, with a thin, white bloom; stalk short and slender, in a very slight cavity; flesh pale greenish-yellow, juicy, sweet, and excellent; adheres to the stone. Ripens early in July in Georgia, just before the Washington.

Rivers' Early Favorite.—Fruit medium, or a little below, roundish oval, with a shallow suture; stalk very short; skin deep blackish-purple, sprinkled with russet dots, and covered with a thin, blue bloom; flesh greenish-yellow, very juicy, sweet, of excellent flavor, separating freely from the small stone; shoots slender, slightly downy. Ripens, Georgia, June 15th to 30th; New York, August 1st. An excellent, early, dessert plum, following immediately the Jaune Hative. Productive.

Duane's Purple.—Branches downy; fruit very large, oblong, swollen on one side of the suture; skin reddish-purple in the sun, paler in the shade, dotted sparsely with yellow specks, and covered with lilac bloom; stalk slender, of medium length, in a narrow cavity; flesh amber-colored, juicy, sprightly, moderately sweet, adhering partially to the stone. Ripe, Georgia, July 10th; New York, August 10th, with the Washington.

Jaune Hative.—Fruit small, roundish obovate, with a suture, generally shallow on one side; stalk short and slender; skin pale yellow, with a thin, white bloom; flesh yellow, juicy, of sweet, agreeable flavor; freestone. The earliest plum to ripen, which it does from the 1st to the 20th of June; branches slender and downy. Tree resembles Howell's Early.

Blue Plum.—A native plum, generally raised from suckers; fruit medium size, roundish, scarcely oval; suture very obscure; skin dark blue, with a light bloom; stalk half an inch long, inserted in a shallow cavity; flesh yellowish-green, juicy, sweet, and refreshing; adheres to the stone; shoots smooth; leaves rather small. A very pleasant and agreeable plum, and the tree is a fine bearer. Does not rot.

QUINCE.—(*Cydonia vulgaris.*)

The quince is a small, hardy tree, seldom growing over twelve to fifteen feet in height; thickly branched; with ovate leaves, whitish underneath, on short petioles; the flowers are white or pale pink color, and the fruit appears on shoots of the same year's growth, varying in shape, but having a resemblance to that of the apple or pear. It is, when ripe, highly fragrant, and of a fine golden yellow color, making the tree quite ornamental. Quinces are seldom eaten raw, but for baking, stewing, preserving, marmalades, or pies, along with apples, they are much esteemed. They are also dried for winter use, giving an excellent flavor to dried apples and peaches.

For these purposes the quince has been long in cultivation, having been in great esteem among the Greeks and Romans. The mucilage from the seeds was formerly used in medicine instead of gum-water. The quince is propagated from seed, layers, slips or cuttings, and grows very readily from the latter. Cuttings, if planted about the time the buds commence swelling in the spring, rarely fail to grow. Quinces usually reproduce themselves from seed, but occasionally vary. Quince stocks are very much used for budding the pear upon, for which the Angers quince is preferred, although we have found the common or apple-shaped equally good in every respect. The quince likes a deep, moist soil and cool exposure, growing naturally upon the banks of streams. It, however, grows to admiration in any good, rich, friable soil, and no tree is more benefited by manuring, especially with vegetable manure. Salt is said to act beneficially if applied during winter. If applied occasionally in small doses at a distance from the trunk, the fruit will not drop; plant the trees ten feet apart.

The quince is subject to the blight, like the pear, and is

also attacked by the borer which infests the apple; the blighted portion must be cut off and burned, as with the pear. The borer must be dug out.

The best fruit is obtained from those trained in the form of a tree, but on account of the borer it is best to use the bush form with three or four main stems, so if one is destroyed there are others left to take its place. Thus trained, the bush should be moderately pruned, or the fruit will be inferior. If there is an over-crop, the fruit should be thinned. The quince begins to bear when three or four years transplanted. Varieties:

Apple or Orange-shaped.—This is the common variety, with large, roundish fruit, with a short neck; skin light golden yellow; flesh firm, but stews tender; leaves oval; shoots slender. If the core be cut out and the hole filled with sugar and baked, it forms a fine dessert dish.

Pear-shaped.—Fruit large, pyriform, oblong, tapering to the stalk; skin yellow; flesh of firmer texture than when preserved, and not quite as good in flavor and color as the former. Fruit ripens a fortnight later, and when picked, keeps much longer; leaves oblong-ovate. Tree of more vigorous growth, but does not bear so well.

Portugal.—Fruit still more oblong, of lighter color, milder flavored, and of better quality than the preceding kinds; leaf larger and broader; shoots stouter; ripens between the other two; a shy bearer, pretty good as a stock for the pear. Tree larger than the other varieties.

Angers.—A variety of the last, the strongest grower of all the quinces, and much used for pear stocks. The fruit is said to be larger and better than any other kind.

Chinese Quince, (*Cydonia Sinensis.*)—Leaves resemble those of the common quince in form, but have a glossy surface; the flowers are rose-colored, with a delicate fragrance, similar to that of the violet. The fruit is very large, oblong, and somewhat ribbed like a muskmelon;

skin golden yellow; flesh hard and acrid, but is said to make a desirable preserve. A very beautiful shrub when in fruit.

THE RASPBERRY.

The raspberry is a low, deciduous shrub, of which several species are common along the fences, both in Europe and America. The large-fruited varieties most esteemed in our gardens all originated from the long cultivated *Rubus Idæus*, or Mount Ida Bramble, which appears first to have been introduced into the gardens of the south of Europe, from Mount Ida. It is now quite naturalized in some parts of the country. Besides this we have growing wild the common black and white raspberry, or Thimbleberries, (*Rubus occidentalis*,) and the red raspberry, (*Rubus strigosus*,) with very good fruit.

Uses.—The raspberry is held in general estimation, not only as one of the most refreshing and agreeable fruits for the dessert, but it is employed generally for preserving, jams, ices, sauces, tarts and jellies; and on a larger scale by confectioners for making syrups, and by distillers for making brandy. Raspberry wine is made in the same way as currant wine, and is considered the most fragrant of all domestic wines.

Propagation.—The raspberry is propagated by suckers or by dividing the roots. The seeds are planted only when new varieties are desired.

Soil and Culture.—The best soil is a rich, deep loam, rather moist than dry, provided it is not too much exposed to our hot Southern sun. The raspberry succeeds best at the South when planted on the north side of a fence or building, but where it can have the morning sun; planted in the shade of trees it never does well. Give a good manuring every spring with well-rotted stable manure, and keep clear from grass and weeds with the hoe; prune out the old dead canes every spring. A fine late crop can readily be obtained by cutting over the whole stool, in the spring, to within a few inches of the ground. They will then shoot up fresh wood, which comes into bearing in August or September.

Varieties.—The finest raspberries in general cultivation for the dessert are the Red and White Antwerp, Fastolf, Orange, Cushing, French, Franconia, and Philadelphia.

The common American Red is most esteemed for flavoring liquors, or making brandy and cordials; and the American Black is preferred by most persons for cooking.

The ever-bearing varieties are esteemed for prolonging the season of this fruit.

Red Antwerp.—This variety is also known as Old Red Antwerp, Knevett's Antwerp, True Red Antwerp, Howland's Red Antwerp, Burley, etc. It is the common Red Antwerp of England and America, and is quite distinct from the North River variety, which is shorter in growth, and has conical-shaped fruit. Canes strong and tall; spines light red, rather numerous, and pretty strong; fruit large, nearly globular, color dark red, with large grains, and covered with a thick bloom; juicy, with a brisk vinous flavor.

Yellow Antwerp.—Large, nearly conical, pale yellow, sweet and excellent; canes strong and vigorous, light yellow, and spinous; bears a long time, and does moderately well at the South.

American Black, (*Rubus occidentalis*.)—Small, flattened, black or dark purple, with a whitish bloom; later and more acid than the preceding. This is the well-known Thimble-berry; succeeds well here. From its rich, acid flavor it is the best for cooking, as in tarts, pies, puddings, etc. It is much improved by pruning and cultivation; should be set at wider distances than the other varieties, as it grows more rampant. The Ohio Ever-bearing is a variety of this, but bears through the season.

American White.—Similar to the preceding in all respects, except the color of the fruit and canes, which are both of a pale yellow and covered with a white bloom. The White is a little sweeter than the Black, and ripens some ten days earlier. Both varieties are propagated by the tips of the canes, which droop upon the ground, and then take root and form new plants or stools; after these have taken root the old cane dies.

American Red.—A sort of mongrel between the Antwerp variety and the American Black. Fruit of medium size, light red; flavor not so acid as the American Black or White, and more juicy than either of those varieties. A vigorous grower, and succeeds well at the South; canes of a brownish-red color and with darker spines.

Fastolf.—One of the most vigorous of the foreign varieties, and does very well in Georgia. Fruit very large, roundish, conical, purplish-red; tender, rich, and high-flavored. Canes strong, erect, branching, with strong spines. The foregoing are all that we can recommend for Southern cultivation from personal experience. The variety cultivated in the Northern States is very large; many of them we have tested here with but poor success.

STRAWBERRY.—(*Fragaria.*)

The botanical name of the strawberry is derived from the delightful fragrance of the ripe fruit. Its common name has arisen from the ancient practice of laying straw between the plants, to keep the ground moist and the fruit clean. This fruit is fragrant, delicious, and universally esteemed. The first offering of the season, in the way of ripe fruit, nothing that comes after it can excel "a dish of ripe strawberries smothered in cream," or fresh from the plant. It is, indeed, the most popular and wholesome of all the small fruits; for, besides its grateful flavor, the sub-acid juice has a cooling quality peculiarly acceptable in summer. In addition to its excellence for the dessert, it is a favorite fruit for making jams, ices, jellies, and preserves.

The English wood strawberry was the first brought into cultivation. Says old Tusser, turning over its cultivation to the ladies, as beneath his attention:

> "Wife, unto the garden, and set me a plot
> With strawberry plants, the best to be got,
> Such growing abroad, amid trees in the wood,
> Well chosen and picked, prove excellent good."

Plants taken directly from the field into the garden yield at once a tolerable crop. This climate is well adapted to the culture of this fruit, since by giving the plants a due supply of moisture, fruit can be gathered the greater part of the summer and autumn.

In its natural state, the strawberry generally produces perfect or hermaphrodite flowers; the hermaphrodite are those which have both the stamens and pistils so well developed as to produce a tolerably fair crop of fruit. Cultivation has so affected the strawberry in this respect, that there are now three classes of varieties. First, those in which the male or staminate organs are always perfect; but the female, or pistillate organs, are so defective that they will very rarely bear perfect fruit. Those are called staminate. Second, those in which the female, or pistillate organs, are perfect; but in which the male organs are generally so defective that they cannot produce fruit at all, unless in the neighborhood of, and fertilized by, staminate or hermaphrodite plants. Impregnated by these, they bear enormous crops. Third, those which, like the native varieties, are true hermaphrodites, that is, perfect in stamens and more or less perfect in pistils, so that they generally produce a tolerable crop, and, in favorable seasons, the pistils being fully developed, they will produce a good one.

This is called the staminate class in some books. The first of these classes, the staminate, rarely producing fruit, and running exuberantly to vine, should be dug up wherever found, since the hermaphrodite are productive, and equally useful for fertilizing. It is to the pistillate varieties, fertilized by the hermaphrodite, that we must look for large crops of fruit.

In beds of each of these varieties, seedlings will spring up, differing from the parents; but runners from any variety will always produce flowers of the same class and similar in all respects to the parent plant. By the due admixture of hermaphrodite and pistillate plants, five thousand quarts have been picked from an acre at Cincinnati, where the strawberry season is usually less than a month.

Potash, soda, and phosphoric acid are the elements most likely to be wanting in the soil. Wood ashes and the carbonates of potash and soda prove very beneficial applications.

The good effects of applying the phosphates, or lime, have not been so apparent, perhaps, owing to there being enough already in the soil.

Propagation and Culture.—To raise the strawberry in perfection requires good varieties, a proper location, careful cultivation, vegetable manure, mulching the roots, and regular watering.

The strawberry bed should be in the lowest part of the garden, succeeding best on a bottom near some little stream of water, where the soil is moist and cool; no trees or plants should be allowed to overshadow it, to drink up the moisture of the soil. New land is the best, and the most easily kept free from weeds. The soil should be dug or plowed deep.

It is not required to be very rich, unless with decayed vegetable matter, as animal manures produce only a growth of vine. Plant good, vigorous runners from old stocks, three feet apart each way; three rows of pistillates, and then one row of good hermaphrodites, and so on, until the bed or plot is filled; cultivate precisely as you would corn, and as often. As the runners appear, cut them off, and keep the plants in hills; this is a much better plan than to permit them to run together and occupy the entire surface of the ground; after the beds have done fruiting, still keep them clear from grass and weeds, and when the leaves fall from the trees in the fall, give a good coat of these as a winter protection.

There is no fruit which has been so greatly improved within the last ten years as has the strawberry, in size, productiveness, and flavor; it is now as generally cultivated as the apple or any of our standard vegetables. Most of the then esteemed varieties are now superseded by new and improved ones, amongst which stand pre-eminent Wilson's Albany, Jucunda, Agriculturist, Dr. Nicaise, Downer's Prolific, McAvoy's Superior, and some others.

VARIETIES.

Wilson's Albany.—This is the most popular strawberry now under cultivation in the United States, although not of first quality in flavor, being rather too acid, but as it is a very hardy variety, vigorous grower, and very productive, it will long be a favorite fruit for domestic cultivation. Fruit large, very dark red, conical in form, trusses short and stout; leaves large, dark green, with short petioles. An enormous bearer, and continues for a long time. One of the most desirable varieties. A standard sort.

Hovey's Seedling.—When we consider the size, flavor of its fruit, and its habit of long-continued bearing, this is one of the finest of strawberries. Like all the pistillate berries, it needs a fertilizer. It is an old variety, and still remains one of the best, and is excelled in flavor by few of the new kinds. Leaves large, bright green, with long petioles, which stand erect; fruit very large, conical, bright scarlet; seeds slightly imbedded; flesh firm, with a rich, luscious flavor. Should be in every garden.

McAvoy's Superior.—This won a prize of $100 at Cincinnati, as the best pistillate variety, for size, flavor, and fruitfulness. Leaves dark green, serrate; footstalk long, trusses of fruit full; berry large, of rich dark color, irregular, roundish conical; seeds large, slightly sunk; flesh crimson and white, tender, and juicy; core of rather open, coarse texture; too soft for a market fruit.

Triomphe de Gand.—A foreign variety, but one that succeeds well at the South. Leaves large, bright green, on long petioles, or footstalks; fruit large, and in high trusses, bright scarlet, and of excellent flavor; fruit resembles Hovey's Seedling in appearance.

Jucunda, or "Our 700."—A fruit of great merit, distributed by J. Knox, of Pittsburg, Pa. Fruit very large, of a conical form, occasionally cockscombed; color bright scarlet; of firm flesh, yet tender and juicy, sweet, and delicious. Probably the most popular variety now grown, if we except Wilson's Albany. We do not hesitate to recommend it for general cultivation.

Agriculturist.—A seedling by Seth Boyden, of Newark, N. J., which, from the encomiums bestowed upon it, must occupy a very prominent place in the great list of new and desirable varieties; as we have never seen the fruit, we can only speak upon the opinions of those competent to decide upon its merits.

Dr. Nicaise.—Judging from the plates we have seen of this new European variety, which is as large as a good-sized apple, and the transports of praise bestowed upon it, it must meet with a ready sale, if nothing more. How it will prove, on further trial, remains to be seen. We shall neither recommend nor condemn it, as we have never seen it.

Downer's Prolific.—A seedling from Kentucky; with us it has no remarkable traits about it, and we have cultivated it for several years. In some places it proves to be very prolific and a very desirable variety, some even considering it as one of the very best of the new varieties.

We could add many others of prominent claims to the foregoing list, but think we have described and recommended a sufficient number to satisfy any amateur or market gardener.

INDEX.

Almond........................334
    Bitter.........................335
    Common......................334
    Ladies' Thin-shelled........335
    Long Hard-shelled..........335
Angelica........................322
Anise...........................323
Apple...........................335
    Aromatic Carolina..........345
    Bachelor......................349
    Bough.........................344
    Buckingham..................349
    Buff............................346
    Byers..........................349
    Camak's Sweet..............354
    Cane Creek Sweet...........344
    Cattoogaja...................354
    Cedar Falls..................350
    Chestatee....................352
    Cheston......................352
    Cullasaga....................349
    Disharoon....................346
    Early Harvest...............342
    Early May,....................341
    Elarkee.......................353
    Fall Pippin...................345
    Great Unknown.............351
    Habersham Pearmain.......347
    Horse.........................346
    Julien.........................343
    Maiden's Blush.............343
    Mangum.....................354
    Meigs.........................347
    Mountain Belle.............356
    Nickajack....................349
    Oconee Greening...........351
    Rabbit's Head...............352
    Red June.....................342
    Red Warrior.................350
    Summerour..................349
    Toccoa.......................345
    Van Buren...................356
    Walker's Yellow............349
    Webb's Winter..............351
    Yahoola......................356
    Yellow June.................344
Apricot.........................357
    Breda.........................358
    Dubois.......................358
    Hemskirke...................359
    Large Early..................358
    Moorpark....................358

Apricot—Orange...............358
    Peach.........................358
    Royal.........................359
Artichoke......................161
    Jerusalem....................165
Asparagus......................166
Balm............................323
Basil............................172
Bean, Kidney..................175
    Algiers.......................176
    Black Speckled.............176
    Butter........................177
    Carolina.....................177
    Dark Prolific................176
    Dutch Case-knife..........176
    Early Mohawk..............175
    Early Valentine.............170
    Late Valentine..............175
    London Horticultural.....176
    Newington Wonder........175
    Royal Kidney...............175
    Wax..........................176
    White Prolific..............176
    English Broad..............173
    Dwarf Early................174
    Dwarf Windsor............174
    Long-pod...................173
    Mazagan....................173
    Lima..........................176
Beet............................180
    Bassano.....................180
    Early Long Blood..........181
    Early Turnip-rooted......180
    Extra Early Turnip........180
    Long Blood.................181
    Nutting's Selected Dwarf..181
    Sea-Kale.....................184
    Short's Pineapple..........181
    White........................184
Bene............................323
Blackberry.....................359
Black Walnut..................380
Bones............................54
Boneset........................324
Borage..........................325
Borecole.......................186
Broccoli.......................187
Brussels Sprouts..............187
Budding........................112
Bulbs............................98
Burnet..........................188
Burnt Clay.....................44

INDEX. 439

Cabbage 189
   Bergen........... 190
   Curled Savoy......... 191
   Drumhead Savoy...............191
   Early Battersea 190
   Early Dutch....................190
   Early Winningstadt........... 190
   Early York... 190
   Flat Dutch........ 190
   Green Glazed.................190
   Red Dutch......................191
   Savoy..........................191
Capsicum.... 274
Caraway...........................325
Cardoon...........................197
Carrot.............................203
   Altringham 203
   Early French Short Horn.......203
   Early Horn.................... 203
   Long Orange..................203
Cauliflower 199
Celeriac............................212
Celery.............................205
   Curled White..................205
   Early Dwarf Solid White.......205
   Red Solid................... ..205
   Seymour's White................205
   White Solid....................205
Chamomile.........................326
Charcoal........................... 45
   Burning........................ 46
Cherokee Rose. 18
Cherry.............................360
   Belle Magnifique...............362
   Blackheart.....................362
   Doctor........................361
   Downer's Late.................362
   Elton... 361
   English Morello................362
   Kentish.... ... .361
   Kirtland's Mary................361
   Late Kentish...................361
   May Duke......................361
   Plumstone Morello............ 362
   Reine Hortense 362
   Rockport Bigarreau........... 361
   Sweet Montmorency.... 362
Chervil.............................215
Chestnut...........................379
Chick-Pea......................... 214
Chinese Yam.......................226
Chives.............................214
Chlorine........................... 33

Ciboule............................259
Citron......... 384
Cives........ 214
Clary..............................326
Colza.............. 290
Cold Frames....................... 71
Composts......................58–88
Coriander......................... 326
Corn...............................216
   Dent...........................216
   Eight-rowed Sugar.............216
   Extra Early................... 216
   Stowell's Evergreen............216
Corn Salad........................220
Cow-Pea...........................220
Cress, American 221
   Garden........................221
   Winter... ... .221
Crossing and hybridizing 95
Cucumber..........................222
   Early Cluster..................223
   Early Frame....................223
   Early Short White Prickly......223
   Long Green Prickly............223
   White Spined................. 223
Currant............................362
   Red Dutch.....................363
   White Dutch...................363
Cuttings 104
Dewberry..........................360
Dill................................326
Edgings........................... 16
Egg Plant..........................228
   Large Prickly-stemmed Purple..228
   Long Purple...................228
   Striped Guadaloupe...........228
Elecampane....................... 327
Eschallot......................... 301
Endive...................... ...230
   Broad-leaved Batavian.........230
   Large Green Curled...........230
   White-flowered Batavian.......230
Evergreen Thorn................... 16
Fencing............................ 16
Fennel.............................327
Fetticus...........................220
Fig.................................363
   Alicante..... 367
   Black Ischia 367
   Black Genoa 366
   Brown Ischia 366
   Brown Turkey..................365
   Brunswick......................365

Fig—Celestial.................366
   Common Blue..................367
   Common White.............. 367
   Lemon White..................367
   Nerii..........................367
   Pergussatta...................367
   White Genoa......... 367
   White Ischia..................367
Filberts............................380
   Cosford 380
   Frizzled......................380
   White.........................380
Forwarding of Early Crops......... 66
Frames 67
French Turnip.....................291
Frost, Protection from.............152
Garbanza 214
Garden, Aspect and Inclination.... 12
   Form of....................... 15
   Laying out.................... 15
   Situation of.................. 11
   Size of....................... 14
Garlic.............................233
Gherkin............................223
Gooseberry.........................368
Grafting, 116—Cleft, 119—Mode and Time of, 117—Root, 119—Splice, 118—Whip........................118
Grafting Wax.......................117
Grape. 368
   Catawba.......................373
   Clinton 373
   Concord.......................373
   Herbemont's Madeira...........373
   Perkins.......................373
   Scuppernong...................374
   Warren....................... 373
Ground-Nut........................234
Ground-Pea........................234
Guano............................. 53
Guinea Squash.....................228
Gypsum............................ 44
Holly, American................... 19
Hop...............................237
Horehound.........................328
Horseradish.......................235
Hot-beds.......................... 67
Humus............................. 23
Hybridizing....................... 95
Hyssop............................328
Implements........................ 73
   Bell-glass 85
   Bow-saw....................... 80

Implements—Budding Knife... ... 81
   Bush-hook..................... 82
   Crowbar....................... 76
   Cultivator.. 74
   Dibble........................ 78
   Drill Rakes................... 78
   Folding Ladder................ 83
   Garden Engines................ 84
   Garden Roller................. 74
   Grafting Tool................. 82
   Grass-edger................... 82
   Hand Glass.................... 85
   Hand Syringes.... 85
   Hedge Shears.................. 81
   Hoes......................... 76
   Lawn Scythe................... 82
   Level 79
   Line and Reel. 79
   Manure Forks.................. 76
   Marker........................ 78
   Orchardists' Hook............. 84
   One-horse Turning Plow........ 73
   Pick.......................... 75
   Plant Protectors.............. 86
   Pole Pruning Shears........... 80
   Potato Hook................... 77
   Pruning Saw................... 80
   Pruning Knives................ 81
   Pruning Scissors.............. 81
   Pruning Shears................ 80
   Rake.......................... 77
   Screens 79
   Scuffle Hoe................... 77
   Shovels....................... 76
   Spade Fork.................... 76
   Spades........................ 75
   Standing Ladder............... 84
   Subsoil Plow.................. 73
   Tallies....................... 83
   Transplanter.................. 78
   Trowel........................ 78
   Turf Beetle................... 74
   Vine Scissors................. 81
   Vine Shields.................. 85
   Watering Pots................. 84
   Wheelbarrow 74
Inarching.........................121
Indian Cress......................256
Insects...........................156
   Apple Bark-louse..............337
   Apple Bupestris...............338
   Apple-root Blight.............336
   Apple-tree Borer..............338

INDEX.

Insects—Apple-tree Caterpillar.....339
    Apple-worm...................310
    Bill-bug........................219
    Codling Moth..................316
    Corn-borer.....................219
    Corn-worm....................218
    Curculio......................422
    Handmaid Moth...............339
    Onion-fly......................262
    Palmer Worm.................310
    Peach-tree Borer..............385
    Plum Weevil..................422
    Squash-bug...................308
    Squash-vine Borer............309
    Tent Caterpillar..............339
    Thick-legged Apple Borer.....338
    Turnip Flea-beetle............318
    Woolly Aphis.................337
Japan-Pea........................238
Japan Quince..................... 19
Jerusalem Artichoke..............165
Kale, Buda.......................186
    Turner's Cottager's...........186
Kohlrabi.........................238
Lactuca sativa...................242
Lambs' Lettuce..................220
Lavender........................329
Layering.........................101
Leaf Mould...................... 48
Leek.............................239
Lemon...........................384
Lentil............................211
Lettuce..........................242
    Brown Dutch.................242
    Butter.........................242
    Curled India..................243
    Early Cabbage................242
    Hammersmith................242
    Hardy Green.................242
    Neapolitan....................243
    Paris Green Cos..............243
    Philadelphia Cabbage.........243
    Royal Cabbage...............243
    Victoria Cabbage.............243
    White Paris Cos..............243
Lime.........................32-43-384
Lime and Salt Mixture............ 47
Lime-rubbish.................... 43
Liquid Manure................... 56
Liquorice........................329
Loamy Sand..................... 22
Macartney Rose.................. 16
Madeira Nut.....................380

Manures......................... 30
Manures, Animal................. 51
    Bird.......................... 53
    Green......................... 50
    Indirect action of............. 40
    Management of............... 52
    Organic....................... 45
    Saline and Earthy............. 43
    Sources and Preparation...... 43
Marigold.........................246
Marjorum........................246
    Pot............................246
    Sweet..........................246
Marl............................. 44
Medicinal Herbs..................322
Melon............................247
Melon, Beechwood...............247
    Christiana....................248
    Citron........................247
    Hoosainee....................248
    Netted Cantaloupe............248
    Skillman's Fine Netted........248
Mice.............................160
Mint.............................330
Mulching........................140
Mulberry........................376
    Black.........................376
    Downing's Everbearing.......377
    Red...........................376
Mushroom.......................250
Muskmelon......................247
Mustard.........................254
    Black.........................254
    White.........................254
Nasturtium......................256
Nectarine........................377
    Boston........................378
    Downton......................378
    Early Violet...................378
    Elruge.........................378
    Hunt's Tawny.................378
    New White....................379
    Stanwick......................379
    Violet Hative..................378
Night Soil........................ 56
Nitrate of Potash................. 44
Nitrate of Soda................... 44
Nuts.............................379
Okra.............................257
Olive.............................381
Onion............................258
    Large Red....................258
    Potato........................258

Onion—Silver-skinned..............258
    Top........................258
    Tree 259
    Welsh......................259
    Yellow Strasburgh..........258
    Yellow Danvers.............258
Orach..............................264
Orange.............................382
    Bergamot...................384
    Havana.....................384
    Mandarin...................384
    Otaheitan..................384
    St. Michaels...............383
Osage Orange....................... 16
Parsley............................265
Parsnip............................267
Pea................................269
    Bishop's New Long-pod......270
    Black-eyed Marrowfat.......271
    Cedo Nulli.................269
    Daniel O'Rourke............269
    Dwarf Blue Imperial........270
    Early Charlton.............270
    Early Emperor..............269
    Early Frame................269
    Early Kent.................269
    Early Tom Thumb............270
    Extra Early................269
    Fairbanks' Champion........270
    Huir's Dwarf Mammoth.......271
    Knight's Tall Marrow.......271
    Large White Marrowfat......270
    Napoleon 270
    Prince Albert..............269
    Victoria...................270
Peas, Sugar........................271
Pea-nut............................234
Peach..............................385
    Baldwin's Late.............395
    Bangh......................395
    Belle de Beaucaire.........392
    Blanton Cling..............394
    Chinese Cling..............394
    Columbus June..............391
    Crawford's Early...........392
    Crawford's Late............393
    Early Newington Free.......392
    Early Tillotson............391
    Eaton's Golden Cling.......395
    George IV..................393
    Grosse Mignonne............392
    Hale's Early...............391
    Late Admirable.............393

Peach—Late Red Rareripe............393
    Lemon Cling................393
    Newington Cling............393
    Oldmixon Cling.............393
    President..................393
    Pride of Autumn............395
    Serrate Early York.........391
    Tippecanoe.................394
    Van Buren's Golden Dwarf...394
    Walter's Early.............392
    White English Cling........394
Pear...............................395
    Abercromby.................401
    Bartlett...................405
    Belle Epine Dumas..........416
    Belle Lucrative............412
    Beurré Bosc................403
    Beurré Clairgeau...........411
    Beurré Gris d'Hiver Noveau.416
    Beurré Richelieu...........414
    Bloodgood..................404
    Brandywine.................407
    Catharine Gardette.........413
    Columbia 417
    Compte de Flandre..........412
    Dearborn's Seedling........403
    Doyenne d'Alençon..........416
    Doyenne, White.............407
    Duchesse d'Angoulême.......410
    Easter Beurré..............420
    Glout Morceau..............414
    Henry the Fourth...........406
    Jaminette..................420
    Joannet....................401
    Josephine de Malines.......414
    Louise Bonne de Jersey.....403
    Madeleine..................401
    Manning's Elizabeth........404
    Nabours....................409
    Parsonage..................416
    Passe Colmar...............414
    St. Germain................418
    St. Michael Archangel......412
    Seckel.....................410
    Selleck....................408
    Soldat Laboureur...........415
    Sterling...................413
    Van Assche.................408
    Winter Nelis...............419
Pennyroyal.........................330
Pepper.............................274
    Cayenne....................275
    Large Sweet Spanish........275

INDEX.

Pepper—Long................275
   Tomato..................275
Peppermint..................330
Peruvian Guano..............53
Phosphates..................35
Phosphoric Acid.............35
Pindar.....................234
Pipings....................111
Pistacio Nut...............380
Pits........................72
Plum.......................421
   Bingham..................425
   Blue.....................427
   Chickasaw................424
   Columbia.................425
   Duane's Purple...........427
   Early Purple.............425
   Elfry....................426
   Harvest Gage.............426
   Jaune Hative.............427
   Jefferson................426
   Prince's Yellow Gage.....425
   Purple Egg...............426
   Red Magnum Bonum.........426
   Rivers' Early Favorite...427
   Sea......................425
   Washington...............426
Potash......................33
Potato, Irish..............276
   Ash-leaved Kidney........277
   Fox Seedling.............277
   Mercer...................277
   Prince Albert............277
Potato, Sweet..............281
   Brimstone................281
   Common Yam...............281
   Hayti Yam................282
   Nansemond................281
   Red Bermuda..............281
   Small Spanish............281
Pot Marigold...............216
Profits of Gardening........65
Propagation of Plants, 87—By Cuttings, 104—By Division, 98—By Layers, 101—By Roots, 101—By Seed........................87
Pruning, 122—General principles of, 126—Implements for, 125—To improve form, 127—Mode of operating, 126—To reduce Fruitfulness, 129—To renew growth, 128—Summer, 124—Time for, 123—At Transplanting, 129—Winter........123

Pumpkin....................286
   Cashaw...................286
Pyracanth...................16
Quince.....................428
   Angers...................429
   Apple-shaped.............429
   Chinese..................429
   Orange-shaped............429
   Pear-shaped..............429
   Portugal.................429
Radish.....................287
   Black Spanish............288
   Black Winter.............288
   Chinese Rose-colored Winter...288
   Early Scarlet Short-Top..287
   Oval Rose-colored........287
   Purple Turnip-rooted.....287
   Scarlet Turnip-rooted....287
   White Chinese............288
   White Turnip-rooted......287
   Yellow Summer............288
Rampion....................290
Rape.......................290
   Edible-Rooted............291
Raspberry..................430
   American Black...........431
   American Red.............432
   American White...........432
   Fastolf..................432
   Red Antwerp..............431
   Yellow Antwerp...........431
Rhubarb....................291
Rocambole..................293
Root Cuttings..............111
Roquette...................294
Rosemary...................331
Rotation of Crops...........60
Rue........................331
Runners.....................99
Ruta-baga..................316
Sage.......................332
Salsify....................294
Salt........................43
Sandy Loam..................22
Savory, Summer.............296
   Winter...................296
Savoy Cabbages.............191
Scaroles...................230
Scions.....................116
Scorzonera.................296
Scurvy Grass...............297
Sea Kale...................297
Seeds, Maturity and Soundness of,

88—Preservation of, 95—Sowing of, 91—Time required to germinate, 93—Time of sowing, 90—Vitality of.................... 89
Shaddock........................... 384
Shading............................ 141
Shallot............................. 301
Shell-bark Hickory................. 379
Skirret............................. 302
Slips............................... 101
Soda................................. 34
Soils, 20—Argillaceous, 20—Calcareous, 23—Depth of, 24-28—Improvement of, 25—Organic, 23—Sandy, 21—Texture of............ 25
Soot................................. 44
Sorrel.............................. 303
Southernwood....................... 333
Spearmint........................... 330
Spinach............................. 304
   Flanders......................... 304
   Lettuce-leaved................... 304
   New Zealand...................... 306
   Prickly-seeded................... 304
   Round-leaved..................... 304
   Winter........................... 304
Squash.............................. 307
   Bergen........................... 307
   Cocoanut......................... 307
   Early Bush Scollop............... 307
   Summer........................... 307
   Valparaiso....................... 307
   Winter........................... 307
Strawberry.......................... 433
   Agriculturist.................... 436
   Dr. Nicaise...................... 437
   Downer's Prolific................ 437
   Jucunda.......................... 436
   Hovey's Seedling................. 436
   McAvoy's Superior................ 436
   " Our 700 "...................... 436
   Triomphe de Gand................. 436
   Wilson's Albany.................. 435
Subsoil plowing...................... 30
Suckers............................. 100
Sulphur.............................. 37
Superphosphate of Lime............... 54
Swamp Muck........................... 47
Sweet Potato....................... 281
Swiss Chard........................ 124
Tansy.............................. 333
Tan-bark............................. 49

Tanyah............................. 309
Tarragon........................... 310
Teltow............................. 291
Terraces............................ 12
Thoroughwort....................... 324
Thyme, Common...................... 311
   Lemon............................ 311
Tomato............................. 312
   Cherry........................... 313
   Early Red........................ 313
   Fejee Island..................... 313
   Gallagher's Mammoth.............. 313
   Large Red........................ 312
   Large Smooth Red................. 313
   Large Yellow..................... 313
   Pear-shaped...................... 313
Training........................... 133
Transplanting...................... 134
   Preparation of Trees for......... 138
   Herbaceous Plants................ 139
Tree Box............................ 19
Trenching........................... 28
Tubers.............................. 99
Turnip............................. 315
   Cabbage.......................... 316
   Early Red-top Dutch.............. 315
   Early White Dutch................ 315
   French........................... 291
   Purple-topped Swede.............. 316
   Ruta-Baga........................ 316
   Skirving's Improved Swede........ 316
   Swedes........................... 316
   Sweet German..................... 316
   White Globe...................... 315
   White Norfolk.................... 316
   Yellow Aberdeen.................. 316
   Yellow Dutch..................... 316
Vegetable Marrow................... 308
Vegetable Oyster................... 294
Watering........................... 142
Water Cress........................ 319
Watermelon......................... 320
   Clarendon........................ 321
   Ice Cream........................ 320
   Imperial......................... 320
   Mountain Sweet................... 320
   Ravenscroft...................... 321
   Souter........................... 321
   Spanish.......................... 320
Wine............................... 372
Wormwood........................... 333
   Roman............................ 333

www.ingramcontent.com/pod-product-compliance
Lightning Source LLC
Chambersburg PA
CBHW032137010526
44111CB00035B/601